Daniel Pidgeon

An engineer's holiday

Notes of a round trip from long. 0 to 0

Daniel Pidgeon

An engineer's holiday
Notes of a round trip from long. 0 to 0

ISBN/EAN: 9783337141219

Printed in Europe, USA, Canada, Australia, Japan

Cover: Foto ©Andreas Hilbeck / pixelio.de

More available books at **www.hansebooks.com**

AN ENGINEER'S HOLIDAY

OR NOTES OF A

ROUND TRIP FROM LONG. 0° TO 0°

BY

DANIEL PIDGEON, F.R.S., Assoc. Inst. C.E.

IN TWO PARTS

PART I.—WEST.   PART II.—EAST

SECOND EDITION

LONDON:
KEGAN PAUL, TRENCH, & CO., 1, PATERNOSTER SQUARE
1883

PREFACE.

A TOUR of the World makes many radical changes in those ideas about foreign countries which are insensibly gathered in the course of time from the reading of books and newspapers.

I landed in America, a prospective admirer of its people and institutions, and left it, after five months' stay, charmed with the courteous kindness of its private citizens, astonished at the breadth and boldness of the national mind, and convinced that, so far as power and prosperity are concerned, the great republic is on its way to become the foremost nation of the modern world. But I looked for political enthusiasm, intellectual aspiration, and republican simplicity of life among the people of the United States. I found politics a close profession, material well-being the goal of ambition, and luxury rampant among the rich.

I believed that the Japanese were, next to the white races, the most advanced people in the world, whose intelligent appreciation of a civilization higher than their own had led to the overthrow of a remotely ancient social and political system, too rigid for Western ideas of progress. I found them cultured, courteous, and charming; but insincere and reactionary in policy, un-business-like and untrustworthy in affairs.

I thought that the Chinese were a stationary people, prejudiced, dishonest if not vicious, and the slaves of a degrading form of self-indulgence. I found them cold and ungenial, it is true, but acute and enterprising men of business; industrious, orderly, and reliable workers; economical and abstemious in their habits; a real benefit to the foreign countries where they settle; but impoverished and hampered in their otherwise certain development at home by the tyranny of a corrupt and alien rule.

I imagined that India was a rich extension of the British Empire, with more to give, whether of wealth or strength, to England than to gain from her. I found her the poorest country in the world, which, strain our strength as the task may, we are in honour bound to dower with security, peace, justice, and culture; all the blessings, in fact, of civilized rule.

These are my excuses for having thrown some private notes of travel over trodden ground into the form of a published book. I shall be glad if my readers find in the volumes themselves any other justification for their appearance.

LONDON, *April* 1882.

CONTENTS.

PART I.—WEST.

CHAPTER I.

THE ATLANTIC—NEW YORK.

The Atlantic passage—Arrival in New York—Henry Hudson's third voyage—Aspect of the city—Business men—Up Town and Down Town—American luxury—Democracy in America and Europe—The churches of New York—The river ferries—High prices 1

CHAPTER II.

ON THE RAILROAD.

The national system of travelling—The long car—Railway companies as advertisers—Speeds—Locomotive engines—Pullman cars—Sale of tickets—Yankee advertisers 10

CHAPTER III.

WASHINGTON.

"The City of Magnificent Distances"—North and South—The negro question—The Capitol—The House of Representatives—Debating—Politics and politicians—The Treasury—National banking—Forgeries—Patent laws and Patent Museums—Why American workmen are inventors—The Smithsonian Institution—Neglect of natural science in America—The department of Agriculture—The Potomac—Shad-fishing 15

CHAPTER IV.

PHILADELPHIA.

Charles II. and William Penn—Independence Hall—The Declaration of Independence—The science of numbering streets and houses—American hotels—The Academy of Natural Sciences—The Academy of Arts—Science and Art in America—The old Philadelphia Hospital—American medical degrees—Chestnut Street—Philadelphians and New Yorkers 23

CHAPTER V.

THE COAL-FIELD OF PENNSYLVANIA.

The Alleghanies—Geological structure—The coal-field—Bituminous and anthracitic coals—Mauch-Chunk—First discovery of coal—The Lehigh river—Early difficulties of navigation—The Gravity Railroad—Present condition of coal trade—The Switzerland of America—Coal-mining—Iron-smelting 31

CHAPTER VI.

ACROSS THE ALLEGHANIES.

Pennsylvanian farms—The Juniata Valley—Rural Huntingdon—A noisy Arcadia—Village life in America—Altoona—Workshops of the Pennsylvania Railroad—A *conversazione* under difficulties—American gallantry—The passage of the Alleghanies—Cresson Springs—Agriculture on the watershed—The old "Portage Railway"—A great geological section 36

CHAPTER VII.

PITTSBURG.

The English and French in America in the eighteenth century—Fort Du Quesne—General Braddock's defeat—Pittsburg—The Monongahela and Alleghany rivers—"The Smoky City"—Iron and glass making—Manufacturing waste and economy—Bridge-building—Specialised manufacture—Blast furnaces—Protection—Municipal government—Bad roads—Coal for the South—A dirty night 41

CHAPTER VIII.

THE OIL REGIONS OF PENNSYLVANIA.

Mineral oil and the early settlers—First use of petroleum for illumination —Oil "struck" for the first time—The rush to the oil regions—The valley of the Alleghany river—The Alleghany Valley Railroad—Queer company—Odd names—Derricks—Oil wells—Well-sinking—"Spouters"—Discharging depôts—Tank cars—Pipes—Natural gas —Fires—Oil City—Refining petroleum—Value of oil claims—Wells running dry—Storage tanks—Explosions—An industrial battle-field   49

CHAPTER IX.

ODD PHASES OF FAITH AND FEELING.

Lake Chautauqua—A deserted village—A sacred grove—In the Holy Land—The Sunday School Assembly—Instruction and amusement—A model of Palestine—The ark and Horeb—Life among the Methodists — Pickerel fishing — Decoration Day — Jamestown — A little "brag," but no "bosh"   55

CHAPTER X.

NIAGARA.

The Falls of Niagara—The Niagara river—Queenstown Heights—How the Falls recede—Proof of their recession—Rate of recession—Behind the scenes—A swim in the rapids—Allen's canal—Utilization of Niagara Falls—Man *versus* the Falls—Glacial drift—Agassiz's continental ice-sheet—The retreat of the ice—Ice-marks—Erratics—Farming and fruit-growing—A Canadian vineyard—Drummondsville —An Indian reservation—Refinement among the redskins—An ethnological error   61

CHAPTER XI.

ON THE GREAT LAKES.

From the Falls to Buffalo—American lake steamers—The transport of grain from the north-west—Erie Canal—Welland Canal—Montreal *versus* New York—The war of 1812—A naval engagement on Erie—Lake Huron—Lumbering   70

CONTENTS.

CHAPTER XII.
MACKINAW.

England and France in the north-west—Jesuit missions—Père Marquette Dâblon—Allouez—The discovery of the Mississippi—Joliet—Death of Marquette—Mackinaw—Indian half-breeds—The Chippeways—A backwoods practitioner—Mackinaw Fort—The massacre—" The British Landing "—Mr. Astor and the fur trade—The Mission House —Catholics at Mackinaw—Religious tolerance—Our yawl on the lake—Huron scenery 78

CHAPTER XIII.
CHICAGO.

Some American traits of character—The first settlement of Chicago—Its growth—The fire of 1871—Present aspect—The Middle States— Chicago their natural capital—The seamy side of the city—Hogs, grain, and lumber—The stockyards—The packing-houses—Pig-killing extraordinary — " Rendering " — Dr. Wolff— The abatement of a nuisance—A grain elevator—A party of Sioux—Base-ball—A great book store—Western impudence—Fire alarm and fire extinction— Teutonic Chicago—The plutocratic quarter—Raising the city— Moving houses 85

CHAPTER XIV.
EN ROUTE FOR THE ROCKY MOUNTAINS.

From Chicago to Cheyenne—Life in a Pullman car—International copyright—The Prairies—American agriculture—The homestead law— Peasant proprietors—No labourers—American agricultural competition—Land laws—The Missouri—Nebraska—Cattle-raising—The Plains—Prairie dogs—Sage brush—No game—The Railroad—Old emigrants' road—Prairie sunset—Thunderstorm—Mirage—" Eating stations "—Cheyenne—The Rocky Mountains in sight—Irrigation— Longmont—The " Colorado zephyr " 99

CHAPTER XV.
IN THE ROCKY MOUNTAINS—ESTES PARK.

Physical sketch of the United States—The Cordilleras—The parks of Colorado—Staging in the mountains—Cañons—Flumes—Structure of the Rocky Mountains—Weathered granite—Estes Park—Society

in a solitude—The scenery—The climate—Electric sparks—The
Black Cañon—Long's Peak—"Good society"—Equality in the
West—The dignity of labour—The earl's cottage—Our host's home
—Hank Farrar, the hunter—English and American sportsmen—
Stage-driving—Mountain roads—Sea or plain? 110

CHAPTER XVI.

DENVER.

The plains and the range—Transparent air—Coal-pits in the desert—
The Colorado Central Railway—Armed passengers—A flood in the
Platte—Rain in Denver—The *raison d'etre* of Denver—Its first settle-
ment—Present aspect—No women—" Transients "—The Chinese—
Public order—Highway robbery—A " social hop "—Flies—The
English in Colorado—Senator Hill's smelting works 121

CHAPTER XVII.

THE MINING CAMPS OF THE ROCKY MOUNTAINS.

A mountain railroad—Clear Creek—Black Hawk—Central City; a
high town—The Cornish in Central—Discovery of silver in Colorado
—Silver *versus* gold—Nature as a gold-digger—A gulch mine—
Fissure vein mining—The gospel of gold—An electrical discharge—
Idaho Springs—The " Beebee House "—A " Health-resort "—Vale-
tudinarians—Washed out—The " Great Ice Age "—Georgetown—
Big boulders—The Ice Age again—Green Lake—A glorious view—
Dinner at Denver—The balloon repaired 129

CHAPTER XVIII.

MANITOU—PIKE'S PEAK.

Another Health-resort—American ladies—Ascent of Pike's Peak—
" Wouldn't take twenty dollars to walk it "—A half-way house—An
invalid—The summit and meteorological station—The view—The
" Fontaine qui bouille "—The process of cutting a cañon—The
" Garden of the Gods "—Monument Park—Strange wind-worn
rocks 139

CHAPTER XIX.

THE GRAND CAÑON OF THE ARKANSAS—LEADVILLE.

The Arkansas river—The " Mesas "—Cañon City—The Grand Cañon
—The upper Arkansas Valley—Leadville—The Arkansas Valley

Railroad—Mountain railroading—The discovery of silver-bearing carbonate of lead in the upper Arkansas valleys—The birth of Leadville—Its rapid growth—A "hard" mining camp—Life in Leadville—On the Denver and South Park Railroad—Kenosha Summit—The highest railroad in North America—The Platte Cañon 147

CHAPTER XX.

SALT LAKE CITY.

Crossing the summit of the Rocky Mountains—The Laramie Plains—Cattle and game—Echo and Weber Cañons—The Wahsatch range—The "Devil's Gate"—An old lake-bed—The City of the Saints—Fort Douglas—A powerful argument—Joe Smith and Mormonism—The Mormon exodus to the west under Brigham Young—The halt in Salt Lake Valley—The rise and progress of Young's community—What have the Mormons done?—At the tabernacle—The Mormon theocracy—Polygamy—The future of Mormonism—Great Salt Lake 157

CHAPTER XXI.

LAKE TAHOE—VIRGINIA CITY.

The Great American Desert—Old lake-beds—The American Indians—The ascent of the Sierra Nevada—Carson City—The Washoe range—Timber Flumes—Hank Monk—Lake Tahoe—"Yank's Landing"—Campers—A ball at "Yank's"—Life at "Yank's"—Ascent of Tellac—Mount Davidson—Virginia City—A mountain railroad—Discovery of the Comstock Lode—The Bonanza mines—Excellent organization—A "Pan Mill"—The "Bonanza kings" 169

CHAPTER XXII.

SAN FRANCISCO.

The Truckee River—Summit of the Sierra Nevada—Snow-sheds—Physical aspects of the Sierra Nevada—The central plain of California—A great wheat-field—Californian farms—Mexican titles—A big ferry-boat—San Francisco—Fog—Cool weather—Buena Yerba—The native Californians—The first finding of gold—Marshall's saw-mill—The rush to the diggings—Growth of San Francisco—Vigilance Committee—The aspect of the city—The Coast Range—

Californian wine and fruit growing—Fruit-canning—The Cliff House
—The Seal Rocks—The Pacific coast—Spiritualism in San Francisco
—The Chinese—The Californians of to-day 181

CHAPTER XXIII.

The Chinese in America—Chinatown.

The Chinese in the United States—Chinatown, San Francisco—A pawnbroker's shop — Opium-smoking — Sam-Li's restaurant — A Chinese lodging-house—Prostitution—Joss-houses—The theatre—Character of the Chinese—The Chinese persecution—Mob violence and State injustice—Ostensible reasons for the persecution—"We are ruined by Chinese cheap labour"—The Burlinghame Treaty—Justice for the Chinese 197

CHAPTER XXIV.

The "Big Trees"—Yosemite Valley.

Dowd's discovery of the big trees—*En route* to the Calaveras Grove—The pine belt of the Sierra Nevada—The big trees—On the way to the Yosemite Valley—Washed out—Hydraulic mining—Deserted mining camps—Last sight of the big trees—The Yosemite Valley—Mountaineering in the High Sierra—The Sierra Nevada—Staging to Madera—San Francisco again—On board the Pacific mail-steamer —At sea 210

PART II.—East.

CHAPTER I.

The Pacific.

A Pacific mail-steamer—A typhoon—Chinese sailors—Chinese passengers—Chinese students abroad—Feudal China—"The Inconsistencies of the American People"—The *Gulf of Tokio*—"An intercepted letter"—Gulls—"I have lost a day"—"Japan is in sight!" 229

CONTENTS.

CHAPTER II.

YOKOHAMA—FIRST IMPRESSIONS.

PAGE

"The Land of the Rising Sun"—The settlement of Yokohama—The town—"The Bund"—"The Bluffs"—Jinrickishas—Our hosts—The native town—Street Scenes—Mississippi Bay—Cultivation—Rice-harvest—A lovely view—A native fair—"The Scotch of the East"—The Chinese question again—The Jap *versus* the Chinaman—Stagnant trade 238

CHAPTER III.

A JAPANESE "AT HOME."

Mr. Okowa—A Japanese railway—The wayside scenery—Our fellow-passengers—Intoning—The great clothes question—Jinrickisha-men—Mr. Okowa's paper-mill—A Japanese interior—A native dinner—Japanese society—A Japanese day—The position of women—Marriage 248

CHAPTER IV.

ENOSHIMA—KAMAKURA—DAIBUTZ.

A carriage and pair—"Following the custom of the village"—Japanese houses—Japanese children—An accident—*Naturalia non sunt turpia*—A bad road—Men or children?—Are they in earnest?—Our first tea-house—Watering the horses—Katase—The route—The Island of Enoshima—Comfortable quarters—A fish dinner—Dressing under difficulties—The origin of Enoshima—Benten, the dragon-tamer—Old friends—How did we come here?—Divers—Kamakura—The cockpit of Japan—The temple of Hachiman—Yoritomo's sword—Daibutz—A great casting—Shinto and Bhuddhism—Religion in Japan—"Miya" and "tera"—My kingdom for a chair 255

CHAPTER V.

TOKIO (JEDDO).

The city of Tokio—The castle of the Shogun—The streets—Street scenes—Water *fêtes*—The Yoshiwara—Prostitution in Japan—"Gueshas"—Singing and dancing—The Insetz Kioku—A scientific welcome—A kite manufactory—Industrial reform in Japan—Tiffin at the German Legation—Art collecting—Shiba and Uyeno—The tombs of the Shoguns—Asakusa—A "matsuri"—Devotion—Wax-works—Shooting galleries—The "Ameya"—Is Tokio a city? ... 267

CHAPTER VI.

MYANOSHITA—HAKONE.

Fish or flesh?—The geology of Japan—The buggy again—From bad to worse roads—Japanese rivers—Floods—Take care of the planks, and let the piers take care of themselves—Odowara Bay—Tonosawa—Drawing lots for a job—A hill-side path—The tea-house at Myanoshita—Our handmaidens—"Not at all!"—The Otomi-tonga Pass—Fusiyama—The flanks of a volcano—Snow—Snakes—Land-crabs—Land-shells—A Japanese Buxton—Myanoshita village—Wood-turning—A modest retreat—A Japanese garden—A glorious view—Stone prayers—A Highland loch—Fusiyama again—The sulphur springs—Physical comfort—The new Joseph—Shampooing —A sorrowful "Saionara" 278

CHAPTER VII.

SETTLEMENT LIFE AND VIEWS.

American variety *versus* Japanese monotony—Yokohama races—The road—The course—The riders—Settlement life—A Japanese theatre—The stagnation of trade—Imports and exports—Smallness of native wants—Unbusiness-like character of the Japanese—Contrast with the Chinese—The opening of the country—What the foreigner asks for—What the Japanese reply—A dead-lock—*Il faut q'une porte soit ouverte ou fermee*—What will the end be?—Allies within the gates—Caste in Japan—The "samurai"—The farmers—The artisans—The traders—The coolies—Wanted: a public opinion—The Japanese Government—*Renaissance* or revolution?... 286

CHAPTER VIII.

A TRIP TO NIKKO.

The start—Kobé—The wayside scenery—Rice-harvesting—A hedge of camellias—Hoe *versus* plough—Agricultural animals and implements—Rice-stripping—Winnowing—The rice-pounder—Handicraft and pedicraft—The farmers of Japan—Tenure of land—Rents —Tenant right—The land-tax—*La petite culture*—Nakada—An avenue of cedars—Utsonomiya—An earthquake — Nikko—The volcanic range—The Nikko temples—A Japanese Pygmalion—Art in Japan—Architecture—Sculpture—Painting—A good run—The snowy range—A cheap ride 295

CHAPTER IX.

HIOGO—KIOTO—NAGASAKI.

Farewell, Yokohama!— Kobé—Hiogo — The settlement—The Hiogo Kioto Railway—A fine farming country—Ploughs—Bullock-carts— Careful cultivation—Kioto—The city—Art treasures—Silk-weaving —Theatres—Jugglers—A magic lantern—The Oigawa rapids—A wild towing path—The "Light of Asia"—The Peninsular and Oriental ship *Malacca*—The Inland Sea—The Straits of Shimonoseki—Nagasaki—A dead port—Desima—A chapter in the history of Japanese Christianity—Japanese coal—The East *versus* the West ... 305

CHAPTER X.

NEW JAPAN.

Old Japan—The Mikado—The Shogun—The dual government—Four centuries of feudalism—New Japan—The arrival of Commodore Perry—Makes a treaty with the Shogun—Treaties made with the European Powers—Anger of the clans—Coalition of the clans— Attack on foreigners—The southern clans—Action of Aidzu— Bombardment of Kagoshima and Shimonoseki—The civil war begins—Defeat and death of the Shogun—Re-establishment of the Mikadonal power—The end of the Shogunate—Yokohama during the civil war—The hatred of foreigners—The abolition of the feudal system—The new constitution—An oligarchy and its difficulties— Rule or anarchy?—The financial situation—A coming crisis— Three courses—Wanted: a public opinion—What will the end be? 313

CHAPTER XI.

HONGKONG—CANTON.

England's outpost — Hongkong Harbour—Victoria — Society—"The good old times"—Commercial discontent—A protecting flag—The

Pearl river—Approach to Canton—A great fire—The river population—A dangerous disembarkation—Shamien—Our hosts—Canton streets—Industries—Temples—The Bell of Canton—The Examination Hall—The water-clock—Tartar Canton—Chinese Canton—Chinese justice—The prisons—Men or beasts?—The execution-ground—Chinese character—Chinese art—Civilization in China—A corrupt Government 323

CHAPTER XII.

THE STRAITS SETTLEMENTS.

Singapore—"Have a dive?"—Tropical vegetation—A kind welcome—The Chinese in Singapore—The Tamils—The Malays—The markets—Athletics in the tropics—The botanical gardens—A dinner-party "Wallace's line"—Penang—The Rajah of Queda—Chinese coolies—Tobacco-planting—England's unconscious allies 332

CHAPTER XIII.

CEYLON.

Life on board the *Teheran*—Flying-fish—Salpæ—Galle Harbour—A motley crowd—Men or women?—Cinghalese costumes—Handsome boys—The Afghans—The Moorman—The Dutch East India Company—*En route* for Colombo—Wayside scenes—Cocoa-nut palms—Trotting bullocks—"That my present!"—Coral bricks—Cabook—Colombo—Nuwara-Eliya—The Kandy railroad—"Patenas"—Gampola—Rambodda—A European flora—Nuwara-Eliya—Ascent of Pederotallagalla—Tropical Forest—Elephants—Jungle life—Coffee cultivation—*Hemileia vastatrix*—Worn out—Cinchona—Liberian coffee—Peradeniya—Kandy—The Temple of Buddha's Tooth—Colombo—A pleasant dinner—Ceylon—The Portuguese—The Dutch—The English—British Rule—A colonial crisis 340

CHAPTER XIV.

MADRAS—CALCUTTA.

Christmas in the tropics—English Settlements in the East—Madras—The surf-boat—A dilapidated town—the native town—Return tickets not available for this trip—The Southern Cross—Indian civil

Servants—The pilot—The Hooghly navigation—"Pull baker, pull
devil!"—The King of Oudh's palace—Calcutta—The Strand—The
Meidan—The Citadel—The Mahratta Ditch—The Black Hole of
Calcutta—The Hyde Park of Calcutta—The native town—The foun-
dations of Manchester—Native merchants—John Chinaman again
— The "mild Hindoo"— Servants and masters — Native dress—
Calcutta races—A *fête* at the Zoo—A brilliant crowd—Crows—Dinner
in a "chummery" 354

CHAPTER XV.

IN THE HIMALAYAS.

En route for Darjeeling—Crossing the holy river—A narrow-gauge
line—"Snaky" work—A "sleeping-carriage"—The battle of the
gauges—The Terai—First view of the Himalayas—The hill tramroad—The jungle—Climbers—Orchids—Tree-ferns—A temperate
flora—Kursiong—A "tonga"—Darjeeling—Sikkim—Drs. Campbell
and Hooker—Hill races—In Mangolia—Buddhism in *profundis*—
praying-wheels—The Bhotea porter—Native houses—A primitive
spinning-wheel — The bazaar at Darjeeling—In the clouds — The
snowy range — Kinchinjanga — Tea-planting — Cinchona-growing—
Dear labour—Coolie immigration—China *versus* India as a tea-
grower 364

CHAPTER XVI.

BENARES.

Indian servants—East Indian Railway—The Ganges Valley—"The
Holy City"— Vedism — Old Buddhism — Buddhism — Puranism—
Phallic worship— The bathing ghats — Temples — Idolatry—The
streets — Brass-work — Merchants—Indian conjurers—The burning
ghat—A funeral—Piety in high places—View of Benares 375

CHAPTER XVII.

LUCKNOW—CAWNPORE.

The province of Oudh—"The City of Stucco Nightmares"—The
Mutiny—Sir Henry Lawrence—Defence of the Residency—Cawn-
pore—Wheeler's entrenchment—Nana Sahib—Colonel Havelock—
The Well—The relief of Lucknow—The siege of Delhi—End of the
Mutiny—The bazaar at Cawnpore—Indian manufactures 384

CHAPTER XVIII.

AGRA.

The Moguls—Akbar—Shah Juhan—Aurungzebe—End of the Mogul rule—Agra Fort—Sikandra—The Palace of Akbar—The Moti Musjid—The Jehangir Mahal—The Taj Mahal—*Pietra dura* work—View from the Taj—Indo-Saracenic architecture—The Pathan periods—The Mogul School—Futtehpore-Sikri—The decadence—Contemporary Hindoo art 395

CHAPTER XIX.

DELHI.

Shah Juhan—Juhanabad—Old Delhi—Fort Lalkot—Rajah Pithora—Afghan incursions — Mahomet Ghori's invasion of India — The Moguls—Sacking of Delhi—Modern Delhi—Vicissitudes—The Fort—The Palace—The Pearl Mosque—The "peacock throne"—The Jumma Musjid—Relics of the Prophet—The Chadni Chowk—The Cashmere Gate—A marriage procession—Street scenes—A Mahometan service—Old Delhi—Khootub's Column and Mosque—Pathan and Hindoo art — Timour the Tartar—Asoka's lat—A Buddhist monarch 408

CHAPTER XX.

JEYPORE—BOMBAY.

The Rajpootana State Railway—Jeypore—The Palace—Street scenes—The "Light of Asia"—Indian art—The city of Amber—The Indian desert—Indian bridge-building—Camels—An Eastern Nevada—Monkeys on the line—Arrival at Bombay—The city and harbour—The Parsees—The Towers of Silence—The Caves of Elephanta—The Apollo Bunder 418

CHAPTER XXI.

ENGLAND AND INDIA.

What has British rule done for India?— Physical changes — Commercial development—Moral improvement—Poverty of India—The land question in Bengal—Checks on population—The pressure of population on the soil—Rise of rents—The Rent Act of 1859—The land question in Madras—Over-population—The remedies—A land law for Bengal—Indian finance—European government and Asiatic revenue—Cheap civilized rule—Representation—A great experiment 427

CHAPTER XXII.

HOMEWARD-BOUND.

The Peninsular and Oriental steam-ship *Sumatra*—The Milky Sea—Aden—" Have a dive !"—Volcanic Hills—Artificial water—The Red Sea—Suez—From Suez to Cairo—The Nile inundation—Fertile Egypt—Cairo—Street scenes—The bazaars—Dogs—Tombs of the Mamelukes—Mosque of Sultan Hasan—Cairo University—Dancing dervishes—The Palace of Gezireh—"Improvement" in Egypt—The Fellahin—Agriculture—Stationary Egypt—The Pyramids of Ghizeh—" Hard work !"—The Sphinx—The Temple of the Sphinx—Egyptian chronology—Boulak Museum—Ancient art—Ancient theology—Marriette Bey—Memphis—The Apis Tombs—The Tomb of Ti—A desert view—The Isthmus of Suez—Ancient canals—M. Lesseps' canal—Passage of the canal—Port Said—The Mediterranean—Malta—Gibraltar—The Holiday is over 436

PART I

WEST

AN ENGINEER'S HOLIDAY,

OR NOTES OF A

ROUND TRIP FROM LONG. 0° TO 0°.

CHAPTER I.

THE ATLANTIC—NEW YORK.

April 17—May 4, 1880.

THE Atlantic was crowded with icebergs during the spring and early summer of 1880, but the prudent captain of our steamer the *Algeria* took us too far south to see them. We thus missed a spectacle which the steamship *Belgenland* enjoyed a month later, when in latitude 43° N., she passed two fleets of bergs—one on either side of the Newfoundland Banks—numbering together not less than a hundred, the largest of which was a mile long, and towered two hundred feet above the water.

Any one who doubts the theory that climate is dependent on ocean currents should sail the North Atlantic. It is a witches' caldron where two immense streams of hot and cold water meet but do not mingle, though they are so closely apposed that a ship may pass in her own length through temperatures differing by twenty degrees. When the prevalent westerly wind shifts a few points to the south, it coincides with the Gulf Stream, and saturated with its warm vapours, prostrates the ship's passengers with the atmosphere of a hot-house. When, on the other hand, it veers a little north, it brings the cold of the polar current over the starboard bow and sends every one hurrying below for ulsters. There is no equilibrium and consequently no peace in such a sea where a flat calm at breakfast, a gale at noon, and a halcyon sunset may all be expected. Thus a shift of the wind from south-west to north-west brought us on one occasion a succession of fog, warm sunshine, tropical rain, and heavy snow, within a few hours, while, to complete the meteorological variety, night dressed our yards and masts with St. Elmo's fire. The shining trail which streams from our screw is singularly sensitive to these changes: when the wind is warm the wake is brilliant with phosphorescent animals; when cold there is hardly a sparkle.

Although the *Algeria* is a slow ship we make three hundred miles a day in favourable weather, but this is reduced to less than two hundred whenever there is much head wind. It does not pay to drive a vessel of this kind too hard; you may burn the coal, but without getting a corresponding speed out of her. On the other hand, crack steamers like the *Britannic* can be advantageously forced in the teeth of a gale, and this is why the "tubs" are not badly beaten in fine passages, though they may be four or five days longer than the clippers in crossing when the wind is adverse.

The captain's cabin is socially a very agreeable resort, and illustrates the age we live in. Darwin's "Origin of Species" and Spencer's "Sociology" are on the book-shelves, while a recent French novel lies on the chart-table. These books would surprise the captain of an East Indiaman of twenty-five years ago, who was usually learned in no arts but seamanship, and read in no other literature than the log.

The passage of the North Atlantic is much like other voyages until the seventh or eighth day, when the steamer crosses the polar current—that region of mists and bergs. Then very often the air thickens without warning to the consistency of a London fog; the whistle shrieks its warning from minute to minute; the captain keeps the bridge, and is not seen at meals; every one is chilly and apprehensive. If you go forward, braving the rimy air, there stand the watch like statues, every faculty of their being concentrated in their eyes.

When under these circumstances the thermometer suddenly drops, it is known that somewhere behind the veil of yellow mist ice is close at hand. But the speed is not slackened, way being kept on the ship in order that if the moment for action comes she may answer her helm quickly and easily. Thus, instinct with a painful watchfulness, the great steamer advances in the gloom to whatever may befall. If a berg is sighted while still half a mile off, all will be well, for there is time enough with a speed of twelve knots to alter the course, but one does not care to think of what would happen if the keen eyes on whose acuteness the safety of the ship depends should be baffled by the fog.

In the happy absence of such incidents the time of our passage passed quickly and pleasantly, and in view of the early break-up of some pleasant intimacies, we hailed the pilot with regret. He picked up the *Algeria* while she was still a hundred and ninety-five miles distant from New York, and such is the competition among these men that their handsome schooners are sometimes met three hundred miles away from shore.

It was midnight when we anchored in the harbour of New York, and were boarded for the mails by a characteristic American steam-tender. This vessel was a small steamer with big paddles and a great "walking beam" oscillating above a high maindeck. Over her masthead hovered a gigantic gilt eagle, whose outspread wings seemed to cover the ship from the waist to the bow. In the wheel-house, an elegant circular saloon enclosed with sliding plate-glass panels, sat the master, whether mariner or mechanic it would be hard to say, smoking, lounging, and steering. There was nothing in the skipper's manner to indicate which of these three occupations was the most important, and his superintendence of the mail transfer had the same casual, unofficial air. But the work was very quickly done, and already we began to discern that we had reached a country where officers can be smart without uniforms, and where no man's profession can be inferred either from his clothes or his manners.

Henry Hudson was seeking in a third voyage that passage to the Indies which was the dream of the seventeenth century, when he anchored, in 1609, near Sandy Hook. No white man had ever before sailed up the noble stream that bears his name, but beautiful as he thought the "Groot" (Great) River, he never saw it again, for the Dutch East India Company cared nothing about its exploration, since it did not lead to India.

Wise James I. had before this chartered two companies for the purpose of colonizing North America, but kept them a hundred miles apart in order to prevent their quarrelling, and into that vacant space Holland, after Hudson's discoveries, naturally slipped, founding the territory of New Netherlands. Next year (1614), Adrian Block, trading in skins, lost his ship by fire and wintered with his crew in log huts on Manhattan Island, which was bought from the Indians ten years later for £24 sterling by the Dutch.

New England and New Netherlands never agreed, while Block's town of New Amsterdam grew but slowly under an inelastic colonial system, so that in the course of time the New England emigrants surpassed the Dutch in numbers and wealth. At length, after many quarrels, the town fell to an English fleet in 1664, changing its name to New York in honour of the king's brother to whom Charles II. gave the province. The city long retained the Dutch language and many Dutch peculiarities. Dutch names are still common, while the Jour de l'An, Easter eggs, Santa Claus, and other Continental festivals have become incorporated into American life and manners.

One cannot step for the first time on American soil without some retrospection. History we know will soon be forgotten in the roaring streets of New York; but while our steamer threads her way through the crowded river to the quay, a first and last thought of Henry Hudson's voyage past these banks, then "pleasant with grass and flowers and goodly trees," where Indians came to meet him in canoes "made of single hollowed trees," scarcely three hundred years ago, is not out of place.

New York is unattractive at a first glance. It is English in its business-like air but with a Continental varnish. The houses are built in square blocks, usually of red brick, very high, and with windows shaded by green jalousies. Here and there are some fine buildings, as the Post-Office, the newspaper offices, and a few very large stores, but the city possesses no dominating architectural features. The "elevated railroads," carried through the streets on staging at the level of the first-floor windows, are convenient but extremely ugly. Neither does a Londoner easily accustom himself to the sight of innumerable telegraph wires stretched along rough posts throughout the city. The Americans themselves have not a word to say for their badly paved roads, or for the absence of a decent system of cabs. Street locomotion is carried on entirely by trams and omnibuses, the rails of the former being laid in such a manner as to make carriage traffic almost impossible, while the latter are excellent liver-shakers, but have no other merit. The bad roads are worse kept. Broadway itself is thickly littered with the *débris* swept from shops and warehouses, which it is apparently no one's business to remove. Boxes and casks, containing domestic refuse, stand out on the side-walks before every door in many of the good streets. The municipal cleanliness of Paris or London is quite unknown.

But no sooner does one pass from the street into the house than all is changed. Within the public and private offices, stores, and warehouses of the city, order, neatness, and comfort are supreme. While successful merchants and professional men in London often spend the business day in dark recesses of grimy old houses, their American brethren are lodged luxuriously and surrounded by the last appliances for the easy conduct of work, from a newly patented bill file to the telephone or telegraphic printer. "I guess we live the most of our lives here and expect to be comfortable," said a friend to whom I expressed my sense of the contrast.

The wish for comfort and luxury is a striking American trait. It shows itself in the adoption of everything that tends to reduce friction in daily life. It dictates the complex but convenient hotel system, the sale of railway tickets at offices on the street, the general use of the lift, the type-writer, the telegraphic printer, and the telephone. It is seen in the fitting and furnishing of a merchant's office, from the handsome decorations to the comprehensive bureau, the scientific safe, and the easy-chairs. If the street gives an impression of makeshift, and seems to partake of the camp rather than the city, the warehouse and store are palaces where nothing is too good for the entertainment of industry.

And one soon becomes aware that industry occupies very different positions in England and America. We worship other gods beside our occupation. To possess land and enjoy the influence it brings, is an ambition with most of our merchants and manufacturers. By our unwritten code of caste, the trader, as in the half-civilized East, stands below the soldier and the landed proprietor.

The American man of business, on the other hand, owns no divided allegiance, his own work interests him above all other things; and whether he runs a barber's shop or rules a great factory, he has but one aim—to be "top of the heap."

"Up Town" and "Down Town," Fifth Avenue and Wall Street, are the opposite poles of New York life and society, just as the City and West End are with us. Down Town life is much like our own, though more excited and feverish. The English visitor however has heard of the go-ahead Yankee, and being prepared for unusual commercial activity finds the merchant no more speculative than he expected. But the life which fills Fifth Avenue in the afternoon astonishes and perplexes him not a little. Magnificent carriages, rich liveries, costly horses, and splendid toilettes, crowd the fashionable quarter. An air of unbridled luxury pervades the scene and there is no public drive in Europe where gold flows in a deeper stream. Yet side by side with this pomp walks republican equality in a mechanic's suit—a figure which would seem out of place among such surroundings anywhere else in the world; while here, the man of the people eyes and enjoys the spectacle without envy or sense of inferiority, soberly hoping that one day all this may be his.

The case illustrates the essential difference between democracy in America and in Europe. The lives of the vast majority of European workers run in grooves which have been cut so deep by time and custom, that to "do their duty in that station of life in which it has pleased God to call them," is all that is practically within the power of the masses. Hence the democrat, feeling the hopelessness of rising, would drag others above him down. No such grooves exist in the States, where it has "pleased God" to place any station within the reach of every man, and where consequently every worker hopes to rise. Luxury and labour elbow each other good-humouredly enough on the brilliant side-walks of Fifth Avenue, and the new-comer finds both the love of the first, and its complacent tolerance by the last, a complete surprise.

The churches of New York are very numerous but generally without architectural merit, exception being made of the new Catholic Cathedral, a beautiful Gothic pile of pure white marble worthy of any country or age. The characteristic American Churches must be sought in Fifth Avenue, and if few of them are of striking design externally, they are beautifully decorated and luxuriously fitted within. "Religion is nothing in this country if it is not comfortable," said the minister of one of these chapels-of-ease; and certainly the hard seats of an Anglican church offer a strong contrast with the couches of a New York place of worship.

Mechanical ventilation, softly carpeted aisles, deep seats and thick cushions, warmth in winter, coolness in summer, good music, and popular preachers,—these are the things which make religion comfortable here. But fans strew the sittings; no one kneels to pray or stands to sing; and the service is heard, like an opera, from a luxurious stall. It is not only at the Madeleine one may see pretty, perfumed sinners, who give themselves up for a moment to holy thoughts, slipping a well-gloved hand under the bonnet for a hasty examination of the chignon, and slily surveying the neighbouring toilettes, only when the soul has satisfied its divine aspirations. The American spends freely, whether on self, wife, or church. Not only is a high rent paid for sittings, but the privilege of occupying these is annually sold at auction and large premiums are thus obtained. The money is spent in procuring the best available preaching talent and congregations pride themselves on possessing distinguished men; while under this quasi-competitive system, popular divines command large incomes and a high social position.

I found the Rev. Henry Ward Beecher's church at Brooklyn densely filled with a congregation of the wealthy "upper classes." Comfort as usual reigned in all the arrangements, the flock listening to both pastor and choir from luxurious fauteuils. Christianity and cushions have certainly "kissed one another" in New York. The pursuit of material success may be said to engage the whole attention of Americans at present. There are highly cultured circles in all the eastern cities, but they are out of harmony with the mass of well-to-do citizens, retiring in habit, and exclusive in manner. Plymouth Church is recruited not so much from this class as from the intelligent, active, ambitious, and wealthy commercial order, who yearn, like other men, for the higher life which material success cannot give. But while the rebound from the prose of existence is idealistic in character among cultured men, it is always spiritualistic in the case of a congregation such as I have endeavoured to depict. Hence, as might be expected, Mr. Beecher's sermon was an eloquent and passionate plea for doubling the life of the city with the ecstasy of the saint—the message of the camp meeting, enlarged, refined, and adorned as befitted his audience; satisfying while it stimulated the needs of emotion, but leaving the intellect starving.

The great river ferries are an important feature of New York. There are at present no bridges across the Hudson or East rivers, and communication between the city and Brooklyn and Jersey City, its extensions, is by steam ferry. The boats, or rather flats, are of gigantic dimensions, very comfortably fitted, and beautifully kept. There are spacious saloons for passengers, deck space for waggons, and a bar for refreshments. Bow and stern are alike, bluntly rounded and fitting accurately into corresponding recesses in the wharves, so that passengers and teams go on board as if on a continuous road. The transit is made quickly and quietly, and the service is so perfect that the inconvenience of an island situation is hardly felt by New Yorkers. A great suspension bridge will shortly connect New York and Brooklyn, but will hardly surpass the ferries in convenience. As the railway termini lie across the Hudson, each railroad company has its ferry, and once on board the boat one is practically already in the cars.

The visitor who lands in America believing that a dollar in New York equals a shilling in London, is nevertheless astonished not so much at high prices as at their capriciousness. While he can live like a prince for sixteen shillings, or like a gentleman for twelve shillings a day, he cannot buy the *Herald* for less than twopence-halfpenny, though the publishing price is three-halfpence. Shaving costs a shilling, and a drink the same sum. A shoe-black demands fivepence for his services, and a cabman is occasionally to be found who will jolt body and soul asunder over the wretched roads, at the rate of eight shillings an hour. Competition is not popular in America. Everybody wants large profits. From rival railroads to rival retailers, every one prefers combination to competition. Even the buyer is a consenting party. He likes paying a high price, and such artificial values as the above, which seem ridiculous to a new-comer, are cheerfully approved by Americans. Some people explain all this by saying that commerce in the States has been reared upon protection; but the Yankee, though a smart man of business on the surface, is a republican sentimentalist not far below, and gives a benevolent width to the proverb, "Live and let live," wherever the claims of labour are concerned.

CHAPTER II.

ON THE RAILROAD.

May 4.

I FOUND myself at the New York depôt of the Pennsylvania Railroad, bound for Washington, with no bones broken, after a cab ride from the Brevoort House to Desbrosses Street. In the baggage office a numbered brass plate was strapped to each of my pieces, and duplicate checks having been handed me, I strolled off free of all impediments, to buy a seat in the Pullman "parlour car." The transaction, which is rather like taking a stall for the opera, resulted in my pocketing a piece of paper with "Car No. 2; Seat No. 30," printed thereon, and this was my reserved seat for the journey. "Parlour cars," used for day travelling, are handsome rooms of gilded walnut-wood, furnished with numbered easy-chairs. A smoking-room and lavatory are attached to each carriage, and a servant is in attendance who, if politely asked, will lay a lunch, cool wine, or bring iced water from the reservoir.

Every American thinks the national system of travelling vastly superior to ours, but there is a good deal to be said on both sides of the question. Setting Pullmans on one side for the moment, the ordinary "cars" are long carriages holding about forty passengers disposed in rows two deep on either side of a central gangway. The space allotted to each person is very small. The seats are thinly cushioned and have pivoted iron backs which swing over to "face the horses," whichever way the train goes. There is no room to carry wraps or small baggage unless the neighbouring seat is unoccupied; the traveller himself is cramped during the day, and sleeping at night is impossible. On the other hand, he is free to wander from car to car, or divert himself on the platform outside; iced water is always at hand in summer, and the carriage is warmed in the winter. The newsboy keeps a comprehensive store-box in the corner, and is always peddling literature, candy, cigars, and pea-nuts in the gangway. The Pullman "parlour" and "sleeping cars" have each their good and bad points. In the former, upholstery has been considered before comfortable easy-chairs; while the latter, though giving an excellent bed, are too stuffy at night, and the day seats are singularly angular. All drawbacks notwithstanding, railroad travelling is not fatiguing in America, the freedom to move about affording so much change and rest.

Railway companies compete for custom by advertising comfort and safety, in a way of which we know nothing in England. Their time-tables, often pictorial and descriptive pamphlets, boast of "rock, road-beds, steel rails, the Miller platform and coupler, and the Westinghouse break;" or exhibit maps whose topography is seductively direct.

The speed of the Washington express does not exceed thirty-five miles an hour, but new locomotives with six-and-a-half-feet driving wheels are now in course of construction which will compass the distance from New York to Philadelphia, ninety miles, in as many minutes. Engines with small coupled driving wheels are in general use in the States, and they suit the rougher tracks and heavier grades of the railways very well. A really fast train between New York and the political capital is however much wanted, and the Pennsylvania Railway Company have lately made such improvements in their permanent way as will permit the use of speeds like our own over this section of their line. American locomotives are second to none in design and workmanship, though the cow-catcher, spark-arrester, big bell, and driver's "cab" look strange to unaccustomed eyes. All these things, however, have their *raisons d'être* in a country of unfenced lines, forest fires, street stations, and extreme temperatures. Automatic brakes are universally applied in the States, but the points and crossings, switches and signals, are far behind our own in merit.

The bridges along the line are all of one type; trussed iron girders, much lighter and more graceful in appearance than our own. The Susquehanna river is crossed by an exquisite structure of many spans, which looks like a spider's web in the distance.

The American love of comfort provides some welcome accommodation in the Pullman cars. Our train for example allowed no time for refreshment by the way, but an "agent" took orders for lunches as we approached Philadelphia, whence they were telegraphed on to Wilmington. On reaching this place half an hour later, a man came "aboard" with a pile of flat baskets, each of which opened across the knees into a white-napkined table, and enabled one to lunch as comfortably as in the dining-room of an hotel. Whenever the train stopped a boy passed quickly through carrying telegraph forms in his hand and crying, "Messages to all parts of the world!" which might be sent without rising from a luxurious seat. Finally the express agent inquires your destination and the name of your hotel, receives your checks, and gives you his own in exchange, stating that your baggage will be in your bedroom on your arrival. This is an independent service paid for at the uniform rate of twenty-five cents or a shilling per package, and the English traveller soon learns why Americans travel with only one trunk apiece, and if he is an economical man, at once despatches his hat-box and superfluous bags to await his return in New York. If there were decent roads and cabs in the country I should not give the preference to the express man, who is by no means so prompt as he represents himself to be, but he is a necessity in America.

Railroad tickets are sold at all sorts of prices, and the dearest place to buy them is at the booking office. The companies make contracts with agents, to whom they allow heavy discounts, and where there is much competition these men undersell one another. The rate per mile is less for long than for short journeys, and a smart man going west—to Omaha for example—will book through to San Francisco and sell the balance of his ticket on the train. The "conductor" again issues tickets in the train at "conductor's prices," the tariff of which may or may not be posted in the cars, and if changes in the traveller's plans should make it convenient to book in this way there is always an unknown loss on the transaction. The whole system is distasteful to the English tourist who has not learned how to bargain for his tickets, and never knows to what extent he has been "bled."

All the way from New York to Washington the road is flanked with advertisements, painted in gigantic letters upon every gable, shed, fence rail, or boulder which can be seen from the train. The state of New Jersey appears to be given over to a quack, who is never tired of repeating, "Try Schenck's Seaweed Tonic!" "Take Schenck's Mandrake Pills!" "Schenck against the world for mild aperients!" If the Yankee tradesman could reach the rainbow with a paint-brush, he would worry heaven to "Try Hop Bitters!" or chew "Gail and Ax's Navy Plug!"

CHAPTER III.

WASHINGTON.

May 5–9.

WASHINGTON has been aptly called "The City of Magnificent Distances." It is five miles long by three miles wide, but only a small portion of this area is built over. The site was chosen by Washington himself, who laid the corner-stone of the Capitol in 1793, and seven years later the seat of Government was shifted from Philadelphia to the city built for its reception.

The national metropolis was laid out on the same scale as the national hopes for its future; but man only proposes, and the population, which was planned for millions, had not reached 150,000 in 1875. Meanwhile the distances remain. Pennsylvania Avenue, the principal street, is a hundred and sixty feet wide. From the Capitol as a centre it is a mile and a half to the Treasury and White House; a mile to the Post-Office and Department of the Interior; and a mile in another direction to the Smithsonian Institution; while the United States Naval Observatory lies in latitude 38° 53' and longitude 77° 8', entirely out of reach in a cabless country. All this is magnificent, but it is not common sense. The stores and private houses "make believe very strong," and during the session of Congress almost persuade the visitor that he is in a first-class city. Washington at any rate has good roads and is well paved. At the time of the civil war its streets were bottomless bogs, now they are models for the rest of the Union.

The traveller's attention is first arrested, not by the fine public buildings of the city, but by the negroes. New York, without his knowledge, has already stood for the portrait of America, and the sight of black faces is a surprise, recalling the separate identity of the South, and suggesting questions, once more disquieting than they are now,—Will the South finally amalgamate with the dominant section of the nation? and, What will become of the negro? For my own part I believe that the amalgamation will take place. The great estates are breaking up; the contempt of trade is breaking down. Manufactories are rising. Northern capital is welcomed. The new generation begins to follow mercantile and mechanical pursuits. Men who despised business take an interest in the multiplication of factory chimneys. These are signs of the times which point to the ultimate adoption of Northern ideas of progress and development. The negro on the other hand is in course of absorption. From some unascertained cause, this race, so prolific in slavery, does not increase when free. Black blood tends by preference to mingle with white, and may do so since the abolition of the Southern marriage laws. Emigration is carrying large numbers of coloured men westward, where white marriages or death will thin their ranks. Thus the questions to which no reply was possible fifteen years ago may be answered hopefully to-day.

The State buildings of Washington are much more magnificent than we in England are apt to suppose. The Capitol is probably one of the finest public buildings in the world. The Treasury is a splendid classic pile of grey granite. The Post-Office and Department of the Interior are white marble palaces; while the Smithsonian Institution is a beautiful Romanesque building of warm red sandstone. It is worthy of note that the dome of the Capitol is built entirely of iron, though there are no external indications of this, the material being used with great architectural skill.

The gallery of the House of Representatives is open to all the world, and I entered it with very mixed views about the American Parliament. On the one hand I was prepared for a perfunctory discussion in a noisy House, whose members were engaged with their own rather than with public affairs. On the other I had some expectation of hearing hard names, if not pistol-shots, exchanged across the floor. But we are taught to expect too much by our newspaper writers, and I was a little disappointed with the proceedings.

A Bill for extending the Congressional Library was under consideration. The speeches were excellent and attentively listened to. Republican freedom certainly dispensed with ceremony to a remarkable degree in the customs of the House, but I saw nothing that impaired the dignity of a legislative assembly.

One soon learns that "politics" and "politicians" are opprobrious names in the States. The former is a disreputable profession; the latter are "scallowags." Americans are never tired of denouncing both, and almost always attribute their degradation to universal suffrage. In this I think they are wrong. It is quite true that a political machinery exists which is operated for the benefit of professional politicians, but these men, unscrupulous as they are, are really controlled by a healthy public opinion. There are doubtless persons who would sacrifice even national honour and good faith for their own advantage, but if masters of the political situation, they are nevertheless servants of the people, whose soundness is proved by the limits which they unconsciously impose on those who manipulate the popular vote. If the masses were really unfit for the franchise, "politicians" might easily become dangerous enemies of the common weal, instead of the mere self-seekers they are. The degradation of political and municipal functions in America is in truth due to neglect of their public duties on the part of citizens who are too much engrossed in their own affairs; and all that is required for the purification of politics is that the natural leaders of the people should reassume responsibilities which in the early days of the republic were sought, not shirked, by the best men in the country. The professional politician will die hard no doubt; but dissatisfaction with the present state of things is so general, and the Americans are so capable, as the Tweed affair proved, of "straightening out" admitted difficulties, that the proper remedy will be applied before long, and we shall hear no more about the evil results of universal suffrage.

The Treasury is one of the finest public buildings in Washington, second only to the Capitol in architectural excellence. The national paper currency is manufactured here, and in its great safes are kept the deposits of all the national banks in the country. The banking system of America was legislatively remodelled shortly after the war, and private banks were everywhere replaced by national banks, established under conditions requiring a certain relation between capital and population, the deposit with the Treasury of national bonds equal to one-third of such capital, and State supervision of the accounts. Any banking corporation having complied with these conditions is entitled to receive and issue Treasury notes amounting to ninety per cent. of its deposit in the Government safes. The security of the public under this system is very great, and "greenbacks" are current everywhere at their full value, an advantage which will be appreciated by every one who has tried to change local notes in England, or the paper of the Bank of Bengal, a State institution, in any other Indian Presidency. Treasury notes practically supersede metallic money in the States, the clumsy silver dollar is hardly ever seen, and the small change carried in the pocket consists of "quarters," ten-cent pieces, and "nickels." The first is like our shilling in size and value, the second like our sixpence, and the last is a plated coin value twopence halfpenny. There are copper cents in America, but as nothing costs less than a nickel, they are of no value to the traveller.

The Treasury deposits amount to such vast sums, that special safes, secured by "time locks," are used for their reception. The latter consist of an ingenious combination of chronometer and lock, whose bolts cannot be shot except at nine o'clock every morning and for ten minutes after that time. Three officials, each provided with a combination of letters only known to himself, must all be present in order to unlock the safe. If the door is not opened during the ten minutes in question, the clock secures it as before until the same hour on the following morning.

Some clever forgeries are shown in the Redemption Office, a department for receiving and exchanging worn-out or mutilated greenbacks. In one case fifty 500-dollar notes were each cut across into fifty narrow strips. One strip was then taken from each note in regular succession, and the fifty abstractions pasted side by side on a piece of paper, making a new 500-dollar bill. Each of the original notes, consisting now of forty-nine strips only, was similarly backed, the absence of one narrow strip being easily overlooked. When the trick was detected it was found that the process, which no one had anticipated, was not illegal, and the ingenious operator consequently escaped punishment.

The acknowledged pre-eminence of Americans in the mechanical arts is largely due to their patent laws, and the Patent Office at Washington is a department specially interesting to Englishmen. It costs £30 to protect an invention for six months in England, and nearly £200 to secure it for the full term of fourteen years. Our patents are issued to all applicants, without any official examination into the novelty of the process sought to be protected, and an inventor must therefore ascertain by a laborious search through the records, whether his or any similar scheme has been previously patented. All this puts patents entirely out of the reach of our working men, who as a matter of fact do not invent.

The cost of a patent in the United States, protecting the inventor for seventeen years, is only £7. Examiners determine whether an invention is novel, thus saving the cost of a search. Classified models of every patented invention are displayed in the Patent Museum, making it easy to ascertain what has been previously done by others. It is not difficult for an operative to examine models, while the reading of voluminous specifications might be a hopeless task.

Patentees in the States are very frequently working men, and there is no doubt that this is due to the character of the American patent laws. In England on the other hand, working men cannot afford to take out patents if they would. This is a national disadvantage in the growing competition between the two countries, but there are other reasons why workmen invent on the other side of the Atlantic and do not here. The traditions of the workshop in England are not favourable to improvements. Our artizan objects to cheapening work, and resists rather than promotes the adoption of labour-saving appliances. He fears "making work scarce," and thinks the more a job costs and the longer it lasts the better for him. He has never been encouraged by the hope of reward to scheme new means for expediting work, and it is equally against the principles of his order and the rules of his Trade Union to do so.

Shop traditions in America are of a totally different kind. The workman sees that cheap production means increased demand, and does not treat every job of work as if there were no other to follow it. Any improvement he may suggest in tools or processes is considered by the employer, and if adopted paid for. Trades Union rules are not restrictive, and it is the custom of his class to be perpetually scheming. The patent laws as we have seen, are conceived in his interest, and he takes advantage of them whenever he hits upon anything that seems worth securing.

At the present moment we are divided between admiration and

alarm at the mechanical skill of the States, and deplore the growing insecurity of our position as American competition makes itself felt in one branch of manufacture after another. Our fears indeed exaggerate the inventive powers of our Transatlantic cousins, who are certainly not superior to ourselves in originality, though being greater users, they are greater improvers of all mechanical appliances. Unless we can not only cheapen the cost of patents, but change the traditions of our workshops, it is to be feared that America may in future oust us out of one industry after another, for we are badly handicapped in the race. Patent law amendment has been talked of for years in England, but will not be accomplished until the public are alarmed on the subject. Neither will the artizan become, as he might do, an ally in our competitive battle with the States, until the employer recognises the value of his co-operation, and encourages invention in the workshop by every means in his power.

I searched the booksellers' shops in New York without success for a compendious geological handbook of America, a *vade mecum* such as Ramsay has given us for England, Geikie for Scotland, and Hull for Ireland. The publishers said that nothing of the kind existed or was demanded by the public, and referred me to the voluminous reports of the United States Geological Survey, which though excellent, did not meet my case.

The absence of such a book is only one among many indications of the neglect with which science is generally treated in America. There are many able scientists and original workers in the States, as the names of Agassiz, Dana, Draper, Marsh, Cook, Whitney, and King sufficiently prove, and science is taught in the universities, colleges, and schools of America; but there is little popular appreciation of natural knowledge for its own sake. Nowhere are men readier to apply scientific knowledge to practical and profitable uses, but the interest seems to cease with the application, and so far as pure science is concerned, the great majority of Americans are Gallios.

The Smithsonian Institution at Washington, endowed by James Smithson, an Englishman, "for the increase and diffusion of knowledge among men," is to some extent a case in point. It has an excellent reputation in Europe for the liberal and enlightened way in which it endeavours to carry out its founder's cosmopolitan intentions by printing and distributing scientific works. Yet, saving a valuable and excellently arranged ethnographic collection, deposited there *en bloc* by the United States Geological Survey, its museum is neither valuable nor well-arranged, being indeed little better than an old curiosity shop, rarely visited except by travellers like ourselves, or by negroes at holiday times.

A different state of things prevails in the neighbouring "Department of Agriculture," whose scientific activity however does not disprove what has been said above. Agriculture is usually conducted by the rule of thumb; yet the growth of plants and animals depends on biological laws requiring the nicest research for their elucidation. The systematic experiments of Messrs. Gilbert and Lawes are perhaps the only important efforts which have yet been made in England towards applying the methods of science to agricultural questions. In Germany on the other hand obscure and difficult problems of biology are being vigorously attacked on behalf of agriculture, and America, it a Gallio in science, has a single eye for everything that fosters business. Farming is one of her chief industries, and on its behalf Congress has taken the unusual course of subsidizing a department for the examination of all agricultural questions of national importance. A research on the growth of "sorghum," the Chinese sugar-cane, is now in progress at Washington, whose results promise to be of immense importance in states where the climate is too cold for the cultivation of the ordinary sugar-cane; and a laborious analytical examination into the relative feeding values of all the grasses of America is also in hand. The Department of Agriculture is an institution we should do well to copy. It is directing inquiry into the fundamental principles of growth both in plants and animals, and laying down new lines, much needed in England just now, for the guidance of the farmer.

The Potomac is a wide shallow stream, with low well-wooded banks of drift, and abundantly stocked with shad, an excellent fish which is taken on a very large scale a few miles below Washington. A trip to see the nets hauled, with a fish dinner to follow, is one of the amusements of the city, and a "shad bake," or "plank shad excursion," was always a favourite form of picnic in old Southern days. It was a stifling morning when we left the city with a party of perhaps a hundred people, in a large river steamer. The Potomac was gay with shipping of all kinds, from brigs in cargo for Washington, to fishing crafts and pleasure yachts. The latter are more like saucers than boats. Each carries a single mast, stepped near the bow, and one great mainsail, with a boom nearly twice the length of the yacht. They are exquisitely built, and sail like the wind. The river near Washington is full of shallows, covered with miles of stake nets, in which great quantities of Potomac herrings are taken at every tide. Fifteen miles below the city is Mount Vernon, the burial-place of George Washington, on passing which the steamer's bell tolled solemnly, and shortly afterwards we reached the fishery.

Shad are taken in seines not less than three miles long, which are hauled twice in every twenty-four hours by a steam-engine and windlass fixed on shore, the tackle being quite unmanageable by hand. When the net reaches shallow water it is surrounded by a semicircle of black fellows who, standing close together and waist-deep in the water, keep up a constant stamping to frighten the fish and prevent their escaping. Meanwhile large "scows," or flat-bottomed boats, are brought alongside the seine and filled with shad by means of wooden scoops. When loaded, these are taken in tow by a steam-tug, and the fish are landed in Washington market within an hour or two of being caught. The seines are shot from a large boat propelled by forty rowers, or in the case of some companies, by a steamer. These long nets cost

£1000 each, and the whole plant of a shad fishery is worth nearly £2000.

When the scows had been loaded we landed by a rickety stage and found dinner awaiting us in a big wooden shanty on the bank. This primitive hotel stood among maples and hemlocks growing thickly around, but hardly shading it from the sun, which beat fiercely down although it was yet early in May. Within, everything was clean, but rough, the tables made of sawn boards, no tablecloths, and chairs of the simplest structure. Negro waiters ran to and fro with plates of baked shad and great jugs of coffee. No one drank any intoxicating liquor, although the shanty seemed red-hot, and we, dripping like sponges, were quite ready for a cool "cocktail." Outside the shed, a wood fire about a foot in width and nearly twenty feet long was blazing. This was bordered on either side by a wide plank set edgewise in the ground with its face to the fire. The freshly caught fish were nailed to the planks and after ten minutes' roasting served, only a little hotter, judging from appearances, than the black cooks who tended them. Shad, shad roe, and coffee, all hot, brought us rapidly near the fusing point, and having satisfied hunger, we beat a quick retreat from the wooden oven to the deck of the steamer, seeking air. But the morning breeze had died away, and sweltering under the pitiless sun we began to understand what summer in the sunny South must be like.

Washington looks imposing when approached from the river. Its granite and marble buildings glitter in the brilliant sunshine, while an atmosphere clear as that of Italy makes distance seem of no account. The dome of the Capitol—a more striking object than the cupola of St. Peter's itself—towers above all the other piles, and when sunset tinges with rose the pure whites and greys of marble and granite, it must be admitted that there are few fairer cities than that of the " magnificent distances."

CHAPTER IV.

PHILADELPHIA.

May 10-15.

WHEN Charles II., richer in American land than English gold, gave a promise to William Penn in liquidation of a claim for money lent by his father to the king; he set up a rival monarch, the "Quaker King," as his settlers liked to call him, in whose capital a century later kingly power received a deadlier blow than that which struck the "Martyr" on the scaffold in Whitehall.

"My province" said Penn on landing, "is a free colony for all mankind, and its people shall be governed by laws of their own making." These were strange words in an English mouth at the end of the seventeenth century, as they would be in some European countries to-day, but they were pregnant with freedom.

Penn's forest capital was a hamlet of three or four cottages scattered in clearings among the pines in 1681; it is a city of nearly a million inhabitants to-day. He called it "Brotherly Love" (Philadelphia) and by the "divine right" of love and justice alone did the Quaker king rule the settler and the savage. Expelled from the University of Oxford for attending meetings of Quakers, exiled by a king too divine to pay his debts, Penn left this country to found a city where the principles of government which he proclaimed to an obscure group of colonists were afterwards to be affirmed in the Declaration of American Independence, and adopted as the basis of national life by what is now the freest, if not the greatest people in the world. If kings possessed divine insight, and learned bodies had saving knowledge, Charles II. would never have let William Penn, the Christian statesman, loose on the world. Better for king and priest to have kept him pining moneyless in gaol; but happy for mankind that he had the courage to accept the distant patch of primitive forest, and faith in the power of liberty to reclaim and govern it.

The most interesting object in all the United States is "Independence Hall," the old "State House" of Philadelphia. It is the cradle of American liberty; the first meeting-place of the "Continental Congress;" the spot where Adams, Jefferson, Franklin, Sherman, and Livingston, a committee of the Congress, drew up the Declaration of Independence, and whence the "bell of liberty" proclaimed the birth of free America.

This modest building, which reminds the English visitor of an old-fashioned town hall, was built in 1735 as a permanent place of meeting for the assembly of Pennsylvania which had hitherto managed the affairs of the colony from all sorts of temporary abodes. Here the newly formed Congress met for the first time in 1775, removing as we know to Washington in 1800. The hall is now used as a court-house and for municipal purposes, but it is also a national museum, containing a collection of historical relics both of the colonial and revolutionary periods. Among the former are Penn's original charter of the city of Philadelphia and a painting of himself negotiating with the Indians. The later time is illustrated by a copy of the Declaration of Independence,* and portraits both of its signers, and the soldiers who distinguished themselves in the war. These were painted by an Englishman named Sharples, and are excellent works of art. The English type of face prevails in them to a remarkable extent, the characteristic American features of the present day having evidently not yet arisen. The pictures hang round a chamber called the "Congress Hall," preserved in exactly the same state as when the Declaration was signed within its walls; and in a corner of the room is the old "liberty bell"—cracked, and replaced in the belfry by a fac-simile —whose tongue first told that America was free. It bears an inscription very characteristic of the fine old colonists who hung it in their State House tower: "Proclaim liberty throughout the land to all the inhabitants thereof."

* The original is carefully preserved at Washington, and it is much to be regretted that lapse of time is destroying the ink with which it was written.

It is an impressive sight, this modest but dignified chamber, with its familiar eighteenth-century furniture and its intensely old-fashioned English air. The faces which look out from the walls are like those of our grandfathers, and belong without exception to earnest and capable men who are fully conscious of their responsibility and the importance of the matter in hand. Dr. Franklin's portrait shines with his cheerful wit. It is easy to believe that he looked thus when prudent John Hancock, who headed the members of Congress coming up to sign, said, pen in hand, "We must be unanimous, gentlemen; there must be no pulling different ways. We must all hang together." "Yes," said Franklin, "we must all hang together, or else we shall all hang separately." They laughed at the sally; but there were anxious hearts among those who laughed. It is pleasant to see with what enthusiasm Americans regard these germs of their national life, while, far removed as we are from the policy of that day, it is also pleasant for English visitors to be reminded that the brave men who planned and bled for American freedom were so conspicuously Englishmen.

Philadelphia is larger than any other city in the Union, and its paved streets measure three hundred and fifty miles. It is second to New York in population, but first in manufactures, surpassing the capital in the amount of money invested and number of hands employed in its factories.

American cities are laid out in square blocks like a chess-board, but happy irregularities sometimes occur, as in the case of Broadway which cuts diagonally across New York; and at Washington, whose streets are partly radial, partly rectangular—"the city of Philadelphia griddled across the city of Versailles." The town of Brotherly Love on the other hand is quite "on the square," as might be expected in a Quaker city, and it consequently illustrates perfectly the American science of numbering houses. The city lies like a great chequer-board between the Delaware and Schulkill rivers, whose courses are roughly parallel at this point. The divisions between the chequers coincide with the cardinal points of the compass, and all the streets running north and south are numbered consecutively from 1 to 30, beginning at the Delaware. These are crossed at right angles by named streets, the houses of which are numbered from east to west, all between First and Second Streets being between 100 and 200, and all between Second and Third Streets between 200 and 300, and so on; so that the number of each house indicates the number of the street in which it is situated as well. Thus, if the number of a house is 836, Eighth Street is east and Ninth Street west of it. In like manner streets running north and south are allowed 100 numbers for every square they are distant from the central, or Market Street, either north or South. In going about the city therefore, whenever one can see a number he can calculate his exact distance from Market Street or the Delaware. This is scientific but prosaic. An Englishman would not like to have such an address as " No. 1710, Eighteenth Street ;" while to be identifiable by a number has something of the convict about it.

The "Continental" at Philadelphia may stand for a portrait of American hotels generally, in describing which it is necessary to make comparisons more or less "odorous." An English hotel is a place to eat, drink, sleep, and be cheated ; where the maximum of electro-plate is combined with the minimum of mutton cutlets ; where wine, ice, and baths are ruinous luxuries ; where bed-rooms are cleaned before the arrival of guests, but not during their stay ; where the waiters, to say the best, think more of their tips than your comfort ;—a place which the traveller enters leaving hope behind, and leaves, but for his bill, with pleasure. The guest of an American hotel, on the other hand, pays a fixed tariff of from twelve to sixteen shillings a day, and there are no extras. He is lodged in a bed-room, often with a sitting-room, and always with bath and retiring rooms attached, which are kept scrupulously clean. Four meals almost overlapping each other in time are served daily, and one may therefore feed at any hour. I have counted eighty-two dishes on a dinner *menu*, any or all of which may be ordered at discretion. Ice is a drug both at table and in the bed-rooms; no one drinks wine, so there is no temptation to order anything simply "for the good of the house." Practical lifts, which *really* abolish the staircases, are running all day, and can be called from any floor by an electric bell. The waiters are independent in their manners, but attentive to orders and require no "tips." The bar dispenses Olympian nectars. The hall is an exchange, telegraph, and telephone office, railway booking office, and mart, where every want from a suit of clothes to a cigar may be bought. The hotel "clerk" is an official having no equivalent in England. He is an equal with whom, if you are wise, you will shake hands on arrival and leaving. There is no local information which he cannot give you, and he furnishes it with a frank pleasure in being of use that is delightful. Some of these great houses can accommodate more than a thousand guests, and cost as much as three-quarters of a million sterling to build and equip. Yet, in spite of their size and complication, they are "run" with the smoothness of a private house. The order and cleanliness is perfect, the service far better than ours, and every *employé* is kept up to the mark by vigilant heads of departments who are felt but not seen.

The janitor of the Academy of Natural Sciences looked quite surprised to see a visitor, and I paced the spacious galleries of this home of knowledge quite alone. Natural science is not more popular in Philadelphia than at Washington, though here, as there, it receives the homage of fine buildings. Material success is confessedly the leading pursuit in America, but it is followed with so much intelligence that it is difficult to believe the Americans are not an intellectual nation. Gradually, however, one learns that the breadth of view and readiness to entertain new ideas so delightful to a new-comer are strictly confined to business, to which if science does not minister it is neglected.

In a less degree the same thing is true of art. Philadelphia possesses a fine Academy of Arts, with charming picture galleries, consisting of a group of large central halls having side rooms opening into them, so that there is a general view of the saloons from every point, giving the visitor a delightful sense of lightness and freedom. The schools too are excellently designed, but the amount of art work going forward within these walls is surprisingly small for so great a city. I counted from thirty to forty students where I expected to find hundreds.

No one who looks critically at the toilettes of Fifth Avenue, or at Tiffany's exquisite silversmith's work and jewellery, can deny that the Americans have excellent taste; and probably no European capital contains finer private galleries of modern pictures than New York. But it cannot be said that the cultivation of art any more than of science is characteristic of the American people. This is probably only a transition state of things. Americans who have resided, been educated, or had frequent communication with Europe, cultivate the Muses assiduously; and from this union of Old World culture with New World freedom there has arisen a charming social life in many of the Atlantic cities. But these coteries are the leaven, and we are talking of the lump.

The old Pennsylvania Hospital, built in 1750, is another relic of the colonial age which is extremely English in character. The building is worth a visit on this account, but it also furnishes a capital example of the application of scientific principles to practical wants. Warming and ventilation were not much considered in the construction of eighteenth-century buildings; but the American medical man characteristically likes to use the best appliances for his work and has no notion of making a bad job for want of good tools. In accordance with modern ideas he has consequently introduced a system for supplying the wards of the old hospital with fresh air in any required volume and at any required temperature. A large fan, driven by steam-power, draws atmospheric air from a pure source and drives it through a chamber furnished with coils of hot-water pipes whose temperature is regulable at will. The pure air thus dried and warmed is introduced into the wards at the floor level, whence it flows through gratings in the ceiling into tall chimney shafts. There are no fires, no open windows, and no draughts, and pyæmia, the curse of ill-ventilated hospitals, is unknown.

In view of the advanced character of such arrangements it seems paradoxical that medical education in the States is so perfunctory, and that medical degrees should be obtainable with almost scandalous ease. A medical student in England cannot obtain his M.D. in less than seven or eight years, during a large portion of which time he is employed on clinical work. In America, on the other hand, a student can take his degree within at most three years, during which time his attention has been wholly given to book-work; so that it is actually possible for a medical man to commence practising before he has felt a pulse or taken a temperature. I do not say this occurs, but only that it can happen.

Each state has its own degree-giving bodies, often constituted, especially in sparsely peopled states, by not very enlightened legislatures; and in certain parts of the Union degrees may consequently be obtained by men without any real knowledge, and in almost any school, whether of medicine or quackery. The public sentiment of America is so jealous of any interference with freedom of opinion that it resolutely objects to selecting any one system of medicine in which to grant degrees. The title of "Dr." consequently gives no guarantee that the holder is an educated man; and a crowd of unscrupulous quacks, many of them indisputable doctors, infest the States to an extent which is unknown in any other country. As the properly qualified members of the profession advertise their names and official addresses—every doctor in the States has an *office*—the quack cannot be distinguished from the educated practitioner by the use of so general a custom, and he flourishes in proportion to his skill as an advertiser. Quack advertising is a gigantic institution in America, and the quantity of patented medicines manufactured is almost incredible. Some of these remedies are produced in great factories, and fabulous fortunes are made by their proprietors. It may be said that the demand for nostrums creates the supply; but American quackery is fostered to such an extraordinary degree by the promiscuous granting of medical degrees that it is more than time some centralized system should be established which, favouring no school of medicine, should at least require a competent knowledge of the structure and functions of the human body from every American M.D.

Chestnut Street is the fashionable promenade and contains all the best hotels, offices, and shops. Here may be seen two more fragments of Old England : " Penn's Cottage," the first brick house built in Pennsylvania for William Penn ; and the old "London Coffee-House," now a tobacco shop, another brick house, built in 1702, and frequented by the city magnates in the colonial days. The residential streets of Philadelphia are embellished with handsome houses of brown stone and white marble, but there are few gardens. Roads and pavements, as usual elsewhere, are disgraceful, thanks to the absence of municipal public spirit, but nothing can exceed the order and cleanliness of the homes of the well-to-do classes. Housekeeping in the Atlantic cities is carried on with the thoroughness of business, and not in the sloppy way too common at home. Whatever may be the faults of American "helps," they are not visible to foreigners, and are more than compensated for by good management on the part of mistresses. A good many laborious and dirty operations are certainly saved in American houses by the use of mechanical arrangements, especially in regard to warming and the disposal of waste water, but the credit of excellently well-kept houses belongs to the housekeeper nevertheless.

The Philadelphians differ essentially in character from the New Yorkers. The latter are cosmopolitan, speculative, and easy of approach. The former are provincial, prudent, and exclusive. The two cities are great rivals; and while New York boasts its larger population, its greater commercial activity, and its social splendour, Philadelphia prides herself on her more important industries, her commercial solidity, and social propriety. New York thinks itself brilliant, and Philadelphia slow. Philadelphia on the other hand considers herself safe, and New York speculative. Perhaps an Englishman's training disposes him to lean to the Quaker rather than the cosmopolitan view.

CHAPTER V.

THE COAL-FIELD OF PENNSYLVANIA.

Mauch-Chunk, May 16–19.

ALL the eastern cities are built on the "Atlantic slope," which is a low plain bordering the Atlantic coast and having a width of from fifty to a hundred miles. Beyond this rise the Alleghanies, which are not so much a chain of mountains as a plateau crested by several chains, separated from each other by elevated valleys. East of the Hudson river the hills form irregular groups, but in Pennsylvania they become long, parallel ridges, varying from two thousand five hundred to four thousand feet in height, with a total breadth of a hundred miles.

The subterranean floor of the Alleghanies is composed of Primary rocks which, in a much earlier stage of the world's history, formed a great range of mountains probably higher than the Andes. Under the influence of rain and frost the *débris* of these easily weathered felspathic rocks accumulated in the neighbouring ocean, where they formed the Palæozoic strata constituting the present Alleghany chain. While the old mountain range was thus being slowly destroyed, the sea which received its *débris* was gradually deepening, and so continued through periods of such vast duration that the sedimentary beds derived from the ruins of the Primary rocks were piled up to a thickness of nearly seven miles. At length the ocean ceased to deepen, and the period of deposition closed with the Coal-measures, which constitute a subordinate system in the vast and varied Palæozoic succession.

These stratified rocks were next subjected to enormous lateral pressure, produced probably by the falling inward of the earth's crust, which must have repeatedly occurred as the internal mass shrank on cooling; and resulting in the formation of great folds, or crumples, such as are made by laterally squeezing the leaves of a book. The greater part of the ridges thus produced have since been planed down by denudation, but their original height is indicated by the curves which remain, while the depth of the corresponding troughs is similarly inferred. The present plateau of the Alleghanies is only a small fragment of these great convolutions, and the greater part of the once continuous Coal-measures have been swept away, only those escaping which lie in the deep troughs, or "synclinals."

The Pennsylvania coal-field consists of three such synclinals, lying in three narrow parallel glens, known as the Schulkill, the Mahoning, and the Wyoming valleys, stretching westward right across the state. The original area of the Pennsylvania coal-field cannot be defined, so much of it having been destroyed by erosion, but it probably extended to the Catskills and Southern New York, and might have been continuous with the coal of Rhode Island, New Brunswick, and even Nova Scotia; while it certainly spread westward in an unbroken sheet across the state of Ohio and joined the fields of Indiana and Illinois.

West of the Alleghanies the coal is bituminous, while east of them it is anthracitic in character. There is a regular progression in this respect from west to east, the coal passing by almost insensible degrees from its most gaseous to its dryest condition, and this change coincides with the more or less disturbed state of the Coal-measures themselves. Among the crumpled ridges of the mountain range the beds are upturned at high angles, covered by disturbed strata, and exhibit frequent outcrops; while westward of the hills they are almost flat and the overlying rocks are undisturbed. The position in the former case is favourable to the gradual escape of the hydrogen once contained in the coal, while in the latter instance the gas has been retained. To this circumstance the Atlantic cities owe their freedom from smoke. New York and Philadelphia have the bright atmosphere of Paris, but manufacturing towns west of the Alleghanies are as dingy as any in England.

The little town of Mauch-Chunk, built on the river Lehigh, an affluent of the Delaware, lies in the very heart of the Pennsylvania coal region, and possesses a special interest as the cradle of the American coal trade, while the Lehigh Valley itself is called the Switzerland of America. About the middle of the eighteenth century a hunter trapping over its wilds built his camp fire on "Summit" Hill upon half a dozen big stones, which to his great astonishment took fire and burnt like logs. In the course of time the story reached Philadelphia and excited the attention of some of the enterprising citizens, who ultimately chartered the Lehigh Coal-Mining Company in 1792, and commenced to work this strangely discovered coal-field. Companies were modest bodies in those days, and this one began by authorizing an expenditure of £5 for making a road from the outcrop on Summit Hill to the foot of Mauch-Chunk, or Bear Mountain, the nearest point on the Lehigh. This river is a shallow stream with a number of rocky ridges extending almost across the stream and giving rise to many rapids. Nothing could look less promising for navigation than the Lehigh in dry weather, but the Quakers were sturdy men, and fuel was already a want in Philadelphia. The coal was carted to the river by mules and shipped in great flat-bottomed scows of very light draught, and these, when there was water enough, ran the gauntlet of rocks and rapids for forty miles at which point the Lehigh joins the navigable Delaware. In the course of a short time the bed of the river was paved with the wrecks of the scows, but very little coal reached Philadelphia, and after much labour and disaster the attempt was abandoned as useless and the enterprise slept for nearly thirty years.

In 1818 a new survey was made of the Lehigh, and it was improved for navigation. Two years later another company, called "The Lehigh Navigation Company," was formed, and the two corporations having amalgamated, the first cargo of coal reached Philadelphia in 1820. It was three hundred and sixty tons in weight and stocked the market for a year! Five years later the prospects of the trade had improved so much that a canal from Mauch-Chunk to White Haven on the Delaware was projected and opened in 1829. After being many times nearly destroyed by floods, this work was almost ruined in 1862, when the Lehigh Valley Railway was built to replace it and the canal abandoned. Simultaneously with the cutting of the canal, a railroad, the first in Pennsylvania and second in the States, was constructed from Summit Hill to Mauch-Chunk. In the beginning this was simply a grade some nine miles long, falling gently from Summit around the hillsides to the level of the river; but the outcrop, which alone had hitherto been worked, became inadequate to supply the increased demand, and the seam was accordingly followed into the valley on the other side of the hill where fresh pits were opened. The Gravity Road was improved and extended to the new workings, powerful winding engines were substituted for the mules which had hitherto hauled the empty trucks up from the wharves to Summit, and the whole system brought into a condition of efficiency which reflects the utmost credit on the men who carried out the work at a time when the principles of railway construction were little understood. It is said that one of the chief mechanics employed was sent to England on one occasion for the purpose of learning some trifling details of rail-laying. He returned with only part of the required information, having omitted to make any notes, and his memory failing him in one important particular. Notwithstanding the length of the voyage he was sent back again for the missing link, and the incident proves the earnestness with which a new and difficult enterprise was attacked.

The Lehigh Valley Railway has long since superseded the Gravity Road, and Summit Hill has been pierced by a great tunnel, through which the coal from all the numerous pits finds its way to the rails; but the old route remains intact and is used every summer as a pleasure road by tourists. From the top of its highest inclines magnificent views are obtained of a country very much like the Jura, while the descent by gentle grades to Mauch-Chunk along hillsides densely clothed with primitive forest of chestnut and oak, with an undergrowth of rhododendron and azalea, forms not the least charming part of the trip.

We have seen that sixty years ago a shipment of three hundred and sixty tons of coal glutted the Philadelphia market. Ten years later two other coal-fields besides that of Lehigh had been opened in the Schulkill and Wyoming valleys respectively, and the production had advanced to 170,000 tons. Within another ten years the Shamokin coal measures were tapped, and 800,000 tons marketed; while ten years ago, the coal raised in Pennsylvania amounted to nearly 24,000,000 tons—about one-fourth of the whole output of England, and the industry gave employment to thirty thousand people. A second railway—the Central of New Jersey—now runs through the Lehigh Valley, which is hardly wide enough to contain the street, the river, the canal, and the rails. The Mauch-Chunk hotel flanks the railroad closely, and the visitor is soon made aware that the Switzerland of America is no quiet solitude. From the "Mansion House" he either sees or hears trains of a hundred and fifty cars each following within sight of one another in a continuous stream all day and night. The engines toll a huge bell as they pass through the village and their whistles emit a thrilling bass note, while the automatic brakes are operated by a steam aspirator whose penetrating hiss is worse than the whistle. Such are the accompaniments of romantic scenery in the Switzerland of America.

Coal-mining is conducted quite differently in England and in the Alleghanies. The seams with us are rarely more than a few feet in thickness, and, though often much disturbed, are not far from horizontal. The anthracites of Pennsylvania, on the other hand, are fifty and sometimes even eighty feet thick, and lie in highly inclined beds. The bituminous coals west of the Alleghanies are thinner and nearly level. The latter are consequently worked by shafts, as with us, but the steep and thick seams of the former district are usually reached by horizontal tunnels pierced in the hillsides, and the coal is quarried rather than mined. The chief ironworks of the States are collected in the Lehigh and neighbouring valleys, and the first furnace ever erected in the States for smelting iron with anthracite coal was built at Mauch-Chunk itself, that "happy father of twins"—the coal and iron trades of America.

CHAPTER VI.

ACROSS THE ALLEGHANIES.

Huntingdon and Altoona, May 20-24.

THE traveller designing to go west from the Pennsylvania coal-field by the Pennsylvania Railway, returns from his short excursion into the eastern valleys of the Alleghanies to the Atlantic slope, and turning his face south, skirts the feet of the mountains until he reaches the Susquehanna at Harrisburg.

The country between Mauch-Chunk and Harrisburg is some of the oldest settled land in Pennsylvania, and looks like a smiling agricultural district in England. The farms, cultivated by their owners, are seldom more and sometimes much less than a hundred and sixty acres in extent. Near market towns they are worth as much as £50, but in the country they sell for £10 an acre. Numerous villages, pretty farmhouses, cleared fields, small enclosures, good fences, and capital crops, chiefly of artificial grasses, remind the tourist of Europe rather than America. The first contact with such small farms is a surprise to Englishmen, who usually but erroneously suppose that farming is always conducted on a very large scale in the States.

After crossing the Susquehanna on a long bridge, light as a cobweb in appearance, the train follows the valley of the Juniata for more than fifty miles into the heart of the Alleghanies. The hills are generally not more than a thousand feet in height; they are wooded to their summits, and intersected by numerous valleys carrying unimportant streams. The banks of the Juniata are thickly clothed with sumach and acacia, the latter filling the air with a delightful fragrance.

If, warned by the din of the American Switzerland, and mindful that his next resting-place is the home of the great workshops of the Pennsylvania Railway, the traveller elects to woo sleep in some quiet retreat on the way, he is not unlikely to spend a night in the agricultural village of Huntingdon. In that case, he finds himself on stepping out of the cars in the main street of the place, there being no platform, and the "depôt" only a neighbouring shop for the sale of tickets; while the railway, one of the greatest arteries of commerce in America, is flanked on either hand by the hotels, shops, and dwelling-houses of the village. A constant stream of traffic pours along the line, passenger and emigrant trains during the day, corn and coal trains both night and day. The big bell and deep toned whistle are seldom silent, but the villagers seem to like it. They loaf into the bar in the morning, a mixture of master mechanic and labourer in appearance, and read the paper, or take their "whisky straight." At night they sit in groups on the side-walks bordering the rails, with heels up, chatting, chewing, and spitting. At the corner near the depôt is a telegraph office, the main street is lined with wires, half a dozen of which enter each of the two village "hotels," and the click of the sounder can be heard whenever the trains are silent. The side streets, laid out as usual on the square, and planted with acacias, are a mass of ruts and holes as to the roadway, while the side-walks consist of planks, badly fastened, and often with loose ends. The "cottages" are boarded houses, roofed with shingles; there are no gardens, and the women spend the hot evenings seeking air on their door-steps, nicely dressed, with their hair carefully, not to say fashionably, arranged. Sometimes from an open window the notes of an American organ float out into the warm still air, heavy with the scent of acacia blooms. Here and there an ugly chapel breaks the monotony of the street, or a square brick church with an open-work cast-iron spire, accentuates the surrounding prose. From a picturesque point of view pastoral Huntingdon is a failure, but these sincerely unromantic people cannot see it. They are serenely sure that it is all right, and would think it superior to the prettiest English village.

Such places as Huntingdon, even more than New York City or Philadelphia, illustrate the fundamental differences between national character in America and England. The rural life of the two countries is as far as the poles asunder, both in outward semblance and inward spirit. The English hall and squire, the old church and parson, the village green, the thatched cottages, the patient people, and simple costumes, form a strange contrast to the hotel, the wooden chapel, the railway and telegraph, the board houses and "high-toned," well-clad people of Huntingdon; but this is nothing to the gulf which separates the mind of the English rustic, with an ambition too often bounded by parish relief, from that of the American "hired man," who alternates between working for others at high wages during the busier agricultural seasons and tilling his own acres in the intervals.

Altoona lies at the very foot of the highest and most westerly ridge of the Alleghanies. It is a city of fifteen thousand inhabitants, built since 1850, when the site, then primitive forest, was chosen for the erection of the vast machine-shops of the Pennsylvania Railroad. These works are the only interesting feature of Altoona, which is another Huntingdon in appearance. They are well situated for supplies of coal and iron, laid out on an enormous scale, and fitted with everything that engineering science can suggest for improving and expediting work. Hence the locomotives and rolling stock of the Pennsylvania Railway Company, all of which are built within these walls, are unsurpassed in excellence of workmanship.

The hotel at Altoona abuts on the railway, whose four lines of way are constantly roaring with traffic. The Medical Association

of Pennsylvania was holding its annual meeting here on the day
of our visit, and a kind of open-air *conversazione* took place in the
evening after the reading of papers was over. The scene, though
interesting, was not a little incongruous to English eyes. A large
number of ladies and gentlemen, all *en grande tenue*, lounged, sat,
or strolled, chatted with old friends or made new, on the verandah
of the hotel, which occupied exactly the same position in regard
to the railroad as the platform of a station does with us. Meanwhile travellers embarked and disembarked, great walls of trunks
were made and unmade in the midst of the conversationalists,
great trains of coal, corn, and emigrants roared through the
echoing depôt, bells tolling and whistles blowing. Across the
way the clanking workshops added to the din, while to crown all,
a terrific thunderstorm burst over this Pandemonium. But society
was not stirred in the least. It made polite speeches, smiled, and
flirted happily, and seemed entirely unaware of any incongruity
in its surroundings.

This little *réunion* of ladies and gentlemen, few of whom were
intimates, offered us many opportunities of observing that gallantry towards women for which America is famous. Women in
the States are surrounded with privileges unknown in the Old
World. They can appear alone anywhere and at any time. They
may travel from the Atlantic to the Pacific coast without an escort.
They may claim as a right attentions which are only accorded as
a favour in Europe. With a touch of her fan or parasol, a lady
may indicate to a perfect stranger that she desires his seat in
a concert-room or an omnibus. When this is yielded she may
take it without thanks. Or she may load her male companion
with trifles without paying for his service with a smile. All this
might be called chivalrous but for the curiously common place air
which it assumes. The charm of small cares lies in their being
rendered as much to please the giver as the receiver. But a
pretty girl in America sends a young man on her errands in so
business-like a manner, that she looks selfish and he a little silly.

The ascent of the Alleghanies begins just beyond Altoona. The grades are not severe, and two magnificent locomotives carry the train easily and quickly up to the summit, a distance of eleven miles. Here, at three thousand feet of elevation, the astonished traveller finds iron furnaces in blast and extensive coke hearths blazing. A few miles further on all traces of coal and iron industries disappear, and a comfortable hotel presents itself at Cresson Springs, where it is extremely refreshing to spend twenty-four hours in the cool bracing air of the summit, before descending into the heat and smoke of Pittsburg. The watershed of the Alleghanies is a wide plateau, densely covered with forests of oak, maple, pine, and hemlock, diversified with numerous cleared farms and land in the course of clearing. The crops grown at this elevation are chiefly oats and artificial grasses, but wheat will ripen. Uncleared land is worth from five to ten dollars an acre, and clearing costs about ten dollars an acre more. The trees are felled at about two feet from the ground, and the stumps allowed to rot—an operation which takes five years with hemlock, fifteen years with oak, and as much as fifty years with pine. Descending the western slope of the range, the railway follows the valley of the Conemaugh, falling by gentle slopes through a lovely country of densely wooded hills, furrowed by numerous side ravines. The remains of another railroad are constantly seen from the cars, sometimes above and sometimes below the track followed by the trains. This is the old "Portage Railway," which in pre-locomotive days carried loaded canal boats in sections over the hills by a series of inclined planes. On reaching the eastern base of the mountains, the sections were once more united, and the complete barge relaunched. The whole thickness of the Palæozoic strata of the Alleghanies is exposed in the railroad cutting, the beds lying in a great trough, or synclinal basin, so that they are first passed in reverse order and afterwards in the proper order of superposition. As the train traverses mile after mile of this magnificent section, the mind loses itself in a vain endeavour to realise the lapse of time during which the vast pile of sediments was built up. Equally in vain it tries to picture the forces which subsequently crumpled the mass, seven miles in thickness, into gigantic folds; and lastly, but still vainly, it asks how long since rain and frost began to pare down the Andean ridges to the small fraction of their original mass which constitutes the present Alleghany chain.

CHAPTER VII.

PITTSBURG.

May 25-27.

THE English colonies of America in the middle of the eighteenth century were confined to a strip of land lying along the Atlantic coast. The French who had explored the great lakes, the Illinois, Ohio, and Mississippi rivers, establishing trading posts, forts, and missions on their way, claimed all the interior regions from the St. Lawrence to the Gulf of Mexico, and were quite as anxious as the aborigines with whom they traded to keep the English out of all that region. Our colonists indeed began to feel so hemmed in that the Governor of New York wrote to England saying that if the French were allowed to hold all they had discovered, England would not have a hundred miles from the sea anywhere. It was under these circumstances that George Washington was sent, in 1753, to remonstrate with the French officers who objected to the English making a survey of the Ohio Valley. The mission came to nothing, but Washington on his way home selected a spot at the confluence of the Alleghany and Monongahela rivers for the erection of an English fort. The Virginian Government approved of his project and sent an expedition to carry it out, whereupon the builders were attacked and driven away by the French, who finished the work themselves and called it Fort Du Quesne. In the summer of 1755, General Braddock with a veteran English army tried to retake the post, but his ignorance of Indian warfare caused him to suffer a crushing and bloody defeat. This repulse gave rise to the greatest excitement throughout the colonies and in England, while it left the French in possession of all the country west of the Alleghany Mountains. Three years later however Fort Du Quesne surrendered to Washington, and its capture was one of the most important incidents in the French and Indian war of 1755-63,which ending unfavourably for France and her savage allies, determined the question whether the French or the English should control the continent of America. It is worthy of remark that the same question was answered with regard to India in the same year, and in the same way; for with the disgrace of the great Dupleix, in 1754, began the fall of French power, and with the recall of his almost equally great lieutenant Bussy, in 1758, passed away the last chance of French supremacy in India.

On the site of Fort Du Quesne now stands the manufacturing town of Pittsburg, looking down upon whose busy streets we cannot but wonder what would have been the effect on America if a different result had attended the international colonial struggles of the eighteenth century. The Monongahela and Alleghany rivers, flowing one north and the other south, drain the western slopes of the Alleghanies for a distance of three hundred miles and finally unite to form the Ohio. At their point of junction they have thrown up a delta upon which Pittsburg is built; and as both rivers run through steep bluffs of carboniferous strata, the town is hemmed in by rocky walls. The city has out-grown the delta and thrown one offshoot called Alleghany City across the river of that name, and another called Birmingham across the Monongahela. All the flat land is covered, and still there is not room enough for the private residences of merchants and manufacturers, which have been obliged to spread over the top of the neighbouring bluff, whose steep sides are scaled by several steam inclines. The view of Pittsburg from above on a still day is like "hell with the lid off," the whole city being covered with an opaque pall of black smoke, lurid here and there with the flames that issue from the chimneys of rolling-mills. Iron and glass-making are the chief industries, but a large amount of miscellaneous engineering work is also carried on. The Alleghany and Mononghela flow through inexhaustible coal and iron fields, while the Ohio, which is navigable to its junction with the Mississippi at St. Louis, forms an open road to the Gulf. Pittsburg accordingly supplied the Southern states with coal, iron, and manufactures in their palmy days, before water carriage was supplemented by railroads; and since these were introduced the city has become the centre of a new and extensive trade with the growing Western states.

"The stranger," says the guide-book, "will have missed the city's most characteristic sights if he fails to visit some of its great manufacturing establishments;" which is perfectly true in more than one sense of the words. America is at once the most economical and lavish of nations—lavish of her natural resources, but economical to the last degree of labour. Even in the Eastern states, where manufacture is much older than in the West, and conducted more upon European lines, waste of material occurs such as would make all the difference between profit and loss in the Old World, where competition has brought prices down to their lowest point, but which passes unnoticed in the States, where a high price is ensured by the protective tariff.

Eastern extravagance however is economy compared with western waste. The very smoke of Pittsburg tells the traveller beforehand what to look for within the walls of the great rolling mills, where, instead of a scientific use of fuel, he finds the slovenliness of Staffordshire. The American Iron Works cover seventeen acres of ground, and employ three thousand hands, but are interesting rather on account of their extent than for their management, the quality of economic production which we associate with American industries being conspicuous by its absence. The same thing may be said of the glass-houses, which are also generally inferior to similar establishments in Germany and England, while the window glass they produce is poor in colour, and the table-ware lacks both design and finish.

But if the rolling-mills and glass-houses are open to criticism,

Pittsburg offers examples of other industries, such as bridge-building for example, where labour is economized in a manner of which we know nothing in England. Indeed, we have no establishments at all similar to those in which the beautiful trussed girders of American railroads are made. The bridges for a railway line in England are designed by the civil engineer, who issues drawings and specifications to contractors for tenders, usually accepting the lowest estimate. It is seldom that a type of bridge is selected to which the various structures on the line are as far as possible conformed, and as every engineer has his own views on the subject of bridges, no two of them ever adopt similar designs. The contractor, on the other hand, is not a bridge-builder by trade; his chief business may be that of a founder, a boiler-maker, or an iron-ship builder, and he only works to the engineer's drawings and specifications. Under these circumstances, establishments fitted with a special bridge-making plant cannot arise, for every new contract requires new preparations. Excellent work is no doubt done in this way by our civil engineers, but with a commensurate expenditure of time and money, the system excluding the use of labour-saving machinery.

In America, on the other hand, bridge-building is a specialized business, like the manufacture of watches or sewing-machines, and a visit to one of the Pittsburg bridge factories is a delightful surprise to an English engineer. An excellent building, planned for the purpose, contains all the plant and tools. Girders of many sizes are made, but all conforming to a given type of construction, and drawings, specifications, and prices of bridges of any span on this type are furnished upon application to the railway engineer, who works them into his plans, and finally orders them as he would rails or sleepers. These bridges are made almost entirely by machinery, and the pieces being accurate and interchangeable are never even put together in the workshop, but assembled at the site of the structure. I was not surprised to hear that girders thus built can be supplied practically on receipt of order, or that large spans can be fixed in a few days.

Speciality in manufacture is an extremely characteristic American peculiarity, and next to the national habit of inventing and improving is the means by which the States have become our competitors in many mechanical industries. With us the artificer has been and still is too much a Jack-of-all-trades, a thing which, as in the case of bridge-building, forbids the extended use of labour-saving machinery, and involves too much handwork. Not only is this system costly, but its products are inferior in finish and uneven in quality, while it tends to increase the number of trifling and unnecessary variations in the goods produced. The American on the other hand gives his whole attention to the manufacture of a single article, trusting, even when this is a thing in small demand, to make a market by cheapening its production. With this view, he "gets up"—to use his own phrase—a machine or a series of machines, which in regard to any given manufacture perform automatically, and therefore cheaply and accurately, all the processes which the Jack-of-all-trades does by hand, turning out a better, cheaper, and more even article than his competitor, and beating him in his own market, in spite of the high prices of wages and materials in the States.

Pittsburg is a centre of the iron trade, and is surrounded by blast furnaces which, though good, are not in advance of our own. I visited the Lucy furnaces, belonging to the Messrs. Carnegie—favourable examples, as I was informed, of a modern plant—and found that their yield of iron per ton of fuel is less than with us. If ever America adopts a free-trade policy, one of its first results will be an improvement in American iron-making, for the profits of this industry are so great under the protective system, that iron-masters are not stimulated to do their utmost in cheapening production. Nowhere is pig-iron made under more favourable circumstances than at Pittsburg, where the coal and iron are both extremely accessible, and lie side by side upon the banks of a great navigable stream, while labour is not much dearer in Pennsylvania than in Yorkshire, skilled men at the Lucy furnaces earning seven shillings, and labourers five shillings a day.

Granting then for the sake of argument the favourite protectionist position of Americans—that a tariff is a premium willingly paid by the nation for the purpose of fostering its budding industries, one fails to see that the iron-master of Western Pennsylvania needs any further nursing. His natural advantages, mechanical skill, and the present price of labour put him on a practically equal footing with his English competitors. The man who gets very rich in America is the manufacturer; the man who pays is the American consumer. I saw a small blast furnace plant near Pittsburg, whose owners, starting with borrowed capital twenty-five years ago, are now millionaires. They did not make this money by their brains, for their furnaces are not so scientific or so productive as many at Middlesborough; and they would probably have done very well for themselves if their customers had been allowed to keep the greater part if not the whole of the import duty on pig-iron in their own pockets.

A bird of passage can only peck at great questions like this one of free trade, but it is clear, and will be admitted by the Americans themselves, that no manufacturer who can profitably sell his goods in European markets requires further nursing at the expense of American consumers. Yet it is a fact that within the last ten years a number of clever American merchants have settled in London, for the purpose of introducing their native manufactures, many of which are sold in England at lower prices than in the States themselves. The raw materials of these goods are often imported from England, and pay a heavy duty on the other side, notwithstanding which, thanks in a great measure to the system of specialization already referred to, the finished articles are re-exported, to compete with all the world in open markets, by gentlemen who claim protection from foreign competition at home. Englishmen need not be anxious for Americans to become free traders. The prospect of an enlarged market in the States for our manufactures is seductive, but the impulse which the abolition of the tariff will give to American skill and enterprise will end, though the people do not see it themselves at present, in their importing fewer and exporting more manufactures than either nation anticipates.

Municipal government is a very weak point in Pittsburg. The town is wretchedly paved, with water-rolled pebbles, the pavements and roads are filthy, and the drainage very defective. I was told by a merchant residing in one of the principal business thoroughfares, that the tradesmen subscribe for the purpose of cleansing and watering this street themselves, in addition to paying their rates. The tram rails are so badly laid that driving a buggy is dangerous, and in some of the busiest parts of the town the locomotive is constantly shunting cars. Yet just outside the city there are miles of excellent roads which appear to lead nowhere and have only a house or two flanking them here and there. These have been made in many cases by means of municipal corruption. There is a great deal of suburban property on one side of Pittsburg which is convertible from farm value into "town lots" by making roads. The owners of this land do not spend money on the work, because they can find members of the city council who, for a consideration, will vote for "the improvement," and when a sufficient number of councillors have been bought the thing is done. "But why don't you get the representation out of such hands?" says the English visitor, conscious of municipal purity at home. "I guess we are too busy making money," is the reply of the frank man, or "It's the fault of universal suffrage," says the gentleman who can spare no time from private for public business. This abnegation of duty on the part of the natural leaders of the city leads to other results. I found no such thing as a mechanics' institute or any similar organization in Pittsburg, but there are plenty of saloons and beer-gardens, where the great mining population of the district too often get "full" on Saturday nights, like other similar populations nearer home.

The condition of the farmers at the back of the industrial town forms a strong contrast to this state of things among the dwellers in the city. This part of Pennsylvania was very early settled, and chiefly by Germans, who are old-fashioned, never moving from their homesteads, and still speaking English with a strong accent. Their farms are small as usual, being seldom more than two hundred and fifty acres, and often half that size; but they are a prosperous class of people, who bring up their children well and give them an excellent education.

The Alleghany river, upon whose banks the famous oil regions are situated, is distinguished by floating patches of petroleum. The Monongahela on the other hand is a shallow stream, which taps the chief coal-fields of the district, and being naturally unnavigable, is crossed by numerous dams usually full of loaded coal barges. The wharves of Pittsburg itself are crowded with huge stern wheeler steam-boats, waiting at the present moment for water in the Ohio to take the great fleets of coal barges in tow for St. Louis and the Southern states. Our hotel overlooks the Monongahela, but though it is night, no breath of cool air moves along its valley. The sluggish smoke hangs its opaque curtain between the near and opposite banks of the river, and lurid patches appear at intervals upon, and fade from this murky screen. The piazza is lined with the chairs of guests, gasping for air, or talking slowly and with low voices, of patents, contracts, and stock companies. If I speak to a neighbour, he says, "How?" politely, and shows himself ready to discuss the wear of rails on steep gradients, or the character of all the neighbouring railroad tracks; but aside from such subjects he prefers silence. *Ne sutor ultra crepidam* is a golden rule in the States; men seldom talk except about things which they understand, and this makes them seem taciturn, especially when they are with ladies. All the sweet cleanliness of Washington and Philadelphia is gone. My bedroom, whose windows, the temperature being 84°, are necessarily open, acquires a measurable film of "blacks" during the night, and I rise on the last morning of my stay in Pittsburg with a feeling of relief at the prospect of leaving this hot, industrious city, with its dirty and depressing atmosphere, for the fresher air and purer skies of the Alleghany river, whose course we are about to follow to the oil regions of Pennsylvania.

CHAPTER VIII.

THE OIL REGIONS OF PENNSYLVANIA.

Oil City, May 27.

THE early settlers of New York and Pennsylvania States were aware that mineral oil existed in the head waters of the Alleghany river and its affluents, to one of which they gave the name of Oil Creek. The Indians also collected crude petroleum from the surface of Seneca Lake, whence the name of "Seneca oil," and used it, like the settlers, as medicine. Petroleum was first applied to a practical purpose in 1845, by the Hope Cotton Company, who mixed it with sperm oil for the lubrication of their spindles. Five years later it was burned for the first time in lamps, and when its value for illumination was established, the search for a sufficient supply commenced in earnest.

The Pennsylvania Rock Oil Company was formed in 1858, and on August 26 in the following year they "struck oil" at a depth of seventy feet from the surface, in a well sunk about a mile south of the now flourishing town of Titusville. The rush to the oil region which followed upon this success can only be compared to the Californian gold rushes of 1849-50. Within sixteen months, or by the end of 1860, upwards of two thousand wells had been sunk, and the production became so enormous that oil was a drug, and sold for a shilling a barrel. At the present time there are four thousand oil wells in Pennsylvania, representing a capital of five millions sterling, and yielding annually four hundred and twenty million gallons of oil, having a value of seven millions and a quarter sterling.

The Alleghany Valley Railroad, on leaving the "smoky city," runs for some miles through suburbs of factories, iron works, and oil refineries, whence it emerges on the river which it follows for a hundred and thirty miles to Oil City. The river-banks are at first low and cultivated, but soon rise into high wooded hills, the western bases of the Alleghany range, around whose feet the river sweeps in bold and changing curves. The scenery, though on a larger scale, is remarkably like that of the famous Sharpham Woods on the Dart, and retains the same features all the way to Oleopolis. For more than three-fourths of this distance the route lies through the lower coal measures and villages, either rural or mining, occur at every few miles. These are collections of wooden houses closely skirting the railway track, which really forms the main street of the village. The hotel, as usual, is practically a part of the depôt, and the best stores and houses are built on the line. Here and there a neater little dwelling than common displays the name of the doctor or attorney, conspicuously painted on a big sign-board. With a little more of the picturesque about their construction, these wooden dwellings might recall the homes of Switzerland, but there is nothing out of America to which an American village can truly be likened. The male inhabitants, who loaf about the depôt in some numbers on the arrival of a train, appear to have plenty of leisure, and are dressed in shirt-sleeves, wide straw hats, and wellington boots drawn over their canvas "pants," a costume which, like that of American artisans generally, wears an air of compromise between the claims of labour and society.

When once the great cities are left behind, the traveller soon discovers that there are no conventional "ladies and gentlemen" in America, the national machine being run for and by working men. Our car was occupied by a party of boiler-makers, most of whom being already "full," were of course anxious for another drink of "old Bourbon" at every stoppage, and the journey was consequently enlivened by a fight, an exhibition of fine art in oaths, and an accident to one of the gentlemen boiler-makers, who having delayed too long at a particularly seductive "bar," jumped for the train, already in motion, and landed face downwards on the track. Sympathizing friends administered whisky externally and internally to the wounded man during the remainder of the trip, and when we left the cars at Oil City, the interesting invalid was as well as could be expected under the circumstances.

Incongruity, naive as Mrs. Malaprop herself, is one of the characteristics of America. One meets with it everywhere, from the public bar, the luxury of whose furniture and decoration is little in keeping with the very mixed society frequenting it, to the palatial buildings which spring from the unkempt streets of the great cities. But nowhere is this quality more oddly exemplified than in the names of the stations on the Alleghany Valley Railway. Not long after leaving Pittsburg, we found ourselves at Verona, and hardly had we equilibrated our boiler-makers with this classic name, than we arrived at Kittanaing, running thence in rapid succession through Cowanshaock, Parnassus, Catfish, Tarentum, and Scrubgrass.

Shortly after leaving Scrubgrass, the train enters the oil region. The scenery still consists of wide river sweeps, flanked by high wooded hills sloping steeply to the water; but this primitive simplicity is suddenly broken by a forest of derricks, which line the river on both sides, or show their heads among the trees on the hillside, and even crown the hill-tops. A derrick is like the tall wooden framework called a pile-driver, with which every one is acquainted, but more strongly braced together, and about seventy feet high. Below it is the oil well, a hole of some few inches diameter, sunk, it may be a hundred, it may be a thousand feet into the ground. It is bored by means of an iron bar, armed at its lower extremity with steel, or, in the case of very hard rock, diamond cutters, and attached to the "walking" (or oscillating) beam of a small steam-engine. While the borer delivers a succession of blows, it is slowly rotated by hand, forming in fact a "jumper," exactly like those used by quarrymen in drilling for blasts, and as the hole deepens, length after length is added to the borer by screwed unions. A pulley fixed in the head of the derrick, together with a wire rope and windlass driven by the engine, furnish the means for withdrawing the boring rods from the well, in order to clear it of *débris*. A clever instrument called the "sand pump" is used for this purpose. It consists of a sheet-iron cylinder with a butterfly valve at the bottom, which on the removal of the rods is lowered by means of the rope and pulley into the hole. Water being either present or supplied, the sand pump sinks into the soft mud left by the borer, and the valves closing on its withdrawal, it comes to the surface loaded with *débris*. With these simple tools the well-sinkers of Petrolia pierce the hardest rocks and bore to enormous depths, dealing with difficulties caused by the irruption of water or breakage of rods with the utmost ingenuity.

The well when bored may, if productive, be a "spouter" or require pumping. The most remarkable example of a flowing well is the Lady Hunter, near Petrolia City, where oil was struck on October 9, 1874, and the fact proclaimed by a tremendous rush of gas, followed by a jet of petroleum, which shot upwards in a column more than a hundred feet high. Three thousand barrels were ejected on the first day, and nearly one hundred and sixty thousand barrels within the following six months, at the end of which time the well was still flowing at the rate of one hundred and fifty barrels a day. The wells on the Alleghany river have long ceased to flow, and the oil is pumped up by the engine, which forces it through pipes into great storage tanks, whence it flows as required to discharging depôts situated on the railway; light wooden scaffolds fitted with a number of delivery pipes, nozzles, and cocks, by means of which a train of tank cars is rapidly filled. The tank cars are cylindrical vessels, like boilers mounted on railway wheels and axles, holding eighty barrels each, and about four thousand of them are always about on the lines, or lying at the discharging depôts of the district. Three thousand miles of pipes have been laid for the transport of oil from its various sources to the storage tanks and railways, accomplishing silently and cheaply work which, if carried by road, would need more than a thousand waggon teams.

Gas usually rises from oil wells for some time before the flow of oil is established, and in some cases continues to do so permanently. There are iron works in Western Pennsylvania fired with natural gas, which is sometimes carried as far as forty miles from its source to the factory.

The blackened ruins of derricks and engine-houses beside the track tell of the frequent occurrence of fires in the Alleghany valley, and discharging stations are occasionally passed where a ghastly skeleton of iron pipes supports itself above the ashes of its wooden scaffold, one knows not how. The strip of forest between the rails and the river is cumbered with charred trees sometimes still smouldering, while clouds of smoke rolling up from the woods tell us that, even as we pass, a great forest fire, whose flames we cannot see in the daylight, is raging on the opposite hillside.

In the centre of this strange district lies Oil City, built on a small delta formed at the junction of the Alleghany river and Oil Creek, and hemmed in by high bluffs, up whose steep sides the town tries to clamber. This place is no longer the headquarters of the oil-trade, which, so far as production is concerned, has, since the discovery of flowing wells in another Pennsylvanian county, gone to Bradford; but the oil exchange is still held here, and the town is the centre of all large buying and selling operations.

The process of refining crude petroleum is one of distillation. Volatile bodies such as benzine come over from the stills at a very low heat, and as the temperature is gradually raised, a variety of other products appear, terminating in paraffin, which distils at about 1000° Fahr. The oil, deprived of its volatizable constituents, is treated with sulphuric acid to remove carbonaceous impurities, neutralised with caustic potash, washed, and finally barrelled for exportation. A residuary product resembling coke is burnt under the refinery stills.

Oil claims, a hundred feet long by fifty feet wide, used to sell for £400 in the palmy days of Petrolia, but since the comparative exhaustion of the district, similar properties are not worth £50. So many wells have been sunk that none are now flowing; some are not worth pumping, and others, which used to yield from fifteen hundred to two thousand gallons a day, give no more than twenty-five gallons. Still the aggregate production is large, and the Alleghany district furnishes a considerable proportion of the whole American export of petroleum. The crude oil is stored in large circular iron tanks, covered in from the rain. These are usually painted bright red, and being much like gas-holders in appearance, have a strange effect, peeping out from isolated spots among the trees of the primitive forest. Though protected by conductors, tanks are sometimes fired by lightning, and flowing wells, especially of gas, have frequently been accidentally ignited. In the former case the vessel is usually broached, by cannon if need be, and the fiery stream allowed to flow through the forest to the river. Explosions of gas, or oil spouters, on the other hand, occasionally offer phenomena not much inferior in splendour to those of a volcanic eruption.

Though peaceful now, the very appearance of this oil region, more like a field of battle than a field of industry, awakens reflections which only slumber even in the settled cities of America. Life in the New World is visibly a battle. Civilization and Nature are at open war; and man, the soldier of civilization, must conquer or die. To clear the virgin forest and transform it into cultivable land; to bring the grassy plains of the vast prairies under the plough; to make railroads across a scarcely known continent, and join cities parted by immense deserts; to fertilize these rainless wastes by means of the mountain snows; to control the Red Indian from frontier forts, or to prospect the lonely cañons of the sierras;—to be, in fact, the pioneers of coming generations: this is the task imposed upon the American people of to-day.

The struggle is not for mere subsistence, as with the masses of Europe. In the New World man is rather a gladiator than a labourer. Thrown into an arena where enormous gains may reward victory, he would not, if he could, avoid the combat; and be he backwoodsman, prospecter, oil-seeker, or frontiersman, nay even an engineer or a geologist, he leads the feverish life of a military chief whose aim is conquest and whose home a camp.

CHAPTER IX.

ODD PHASES OF FAITH AND FEELING.

Lake Chautauqua, Jamestown, May 28—*June* 4.

AFTER a month spent in the industrial cities, with the thermometer well up among the nineties, the traveller is glad of a few days alone with Nature, and we found her in one of her most peaceful aspects at Lake Chautauqua, where we halted for a rest on our way from the oil-fields to Buffalo. This little sheet of water, only a few miles distant from the eastern shore of Lake Erie, lies among low, softly rounded hills, in the middle of the finest dairy district in the state of New York. Its banks are park-like, and the surrounding scenery that of a cultivated and undulating English county, while its elevation of thirteen hundred feet allowed us to read with equanimity of New York City prostrated by a temperature of ninety-eight degrees. These sufferings of others, indeed, as in the days of Horace, seemed to enhance the pleasure of our daily cruise and dip, and give zest to the capture of every pickerel and catfish.

Thus lotophagously sailing, we landed one morning on a beautifully wooded point in search of a shady place for lunch; and, pushing our way through the thick maples, found ourselves in the streets of an apparently deserted village. It was a large, irregular group of pretty wooden cottages, built among, and completely embowered by virgin forest. Not a soul was to be seen, and we strolled through a labyrinth of leafy avenues, stumbling at length on a vast open-air auditorium, capable of seating several thousand people, but roofed only by graceful maples. We passed from this into a grove, where the young trees were labelled with white tablets bearing reverend names, which were repeated in the streets and avenues. The Rev. S. Strong, Professor Vail, and the Rev. Lewis Miller were among the chief sylvan deities; but the largest maple of all was consecrated to Mr. P. P. Bliss, the gifted composer of Moody and Sankey's music, in immortal verse as follows :—

> "The finest tree in the lot, I ween,
> Spreading so tall, so broad, so green;
> Beautiful, beautiful, beautiful tree,
> How very much you are like to me!"

Much impressed but not enlightened by the inscriptions in the sacred grove, we continued our search for information, and found ourselves successively before a building called the "Jewish Tabernacle," a model of Cheops' pyramid, and, finally, in the "Park of Palestine," evidently a relief map on a large scale of the Holy Land. Everything was labelled, but the more labels we read, the more puzzled we got. At length we struck a big regulation Yankee hotel, where we found a waiter smoking a cigar stub and wearing a week's beard, but who proved in other respects a worthy man. Although the establishment was evidently not "running," our friend "guessed he could fix us," and not only gave us a better lunch than our boat could furnish, but became our guide, philosopher, and friend for the rest of the day.

The Chautauqua Lake Sunday School Assembly is a vast educational, religious, and recreative institution, to which tens of thousands of people resort every season. This organization sprang out of the old camp meetings, and still retains some of their characteristic features, while it occupies an old camp meeting ground. It is the creation of the Methodist body, and was only established in 1874, but is being rapidly imitated by other religious communities, notably by the Baptists, who are building a similar, but more ambitious holy village on the opposite shore of the lake.

The assembly meets early in August, and opens its session by a tremendous dinner at the hotel. We had the privilege of seeing the printed *menu* of last year's feast, containing eighty-six dishes, which were honestly partaken of, dish by dish, by many excellent Methodists, if the statement of the waiter may be believed. The association comprises all the Methodist school teachers in America, most of the Methodist preachers, and a great number of Methodist families and children. The houses belong to the members, and are built on land purchased from the association under certain conditions. No intoxicating liquors are allowed; lights must be out at ten o'clock; sabbath-breaking is strictly prohibited; and subjection to the rules and officers of the assembly enforced. More than six thousand people live here during the session, which lasts three weeks, and there are often as many daily visitors as residents. A newspaper, printed on the ground, publishes a programme of proceedings for each day, every hour being apportioned either to meetings of societies, religious services, the teaching of children, or amusements of some kind. The Chautauqua Assembly is a kind of cross between Exeter Hall, the Sunday school, and the "Hall by the Sea" at Margate.

The meetings embrace those of the National Educational Association, the Chautauqua Teachers' Retreat, the School of Languages, the Foreign Mission Institute, the Musical College, Literary and Scientific Circle, together with lectures, concerts, class drills, stereopticon experiments, fireworks, the Brush electric light, and illuminated fountains. Certainly a remarkable *pot-pourri* of instruction and amusement. In the grounds are models, already referred to, of Palestine, Jerusalem, Mount Ararat, and the ark, the Jewish tabernacle, the pyramids, etc. Lake Chautauqua itself represents the Mediterranean Sea, and the ground to the eastward of it is fashioned into a great relief map of Palestine on a scale of a foot to the mile. The river Jordan, admitted through a tap, flows from its head waters at Dan through the Lake of Merom, the Sea of Tiberias, and the Dead Sea successively. Perched on the high land west of the Jordan stands a plaster model of

Jerusalem; a little south of it is Bethlehem; while salient points in Scripture history, such as Pisgah, the Mount of Olives, Ramoth-Gilead, Nazareth, Capernaum, Bethsaida, and others are duly located, and Sinai, rather out of place, dominates the whole. Once a day a teacher, dressed in Oriental costume, addresses an audience seated around the model, on the history and topography of the Holy Land. Thence the class proceeds, it may be, to Ararat, to see a dove let fly from the window of the ark, or to the wilderness, where the miracle of Horeb is repeated, by means of a cleverly hidden tap and the teacher's wand.

But amusement also plays a great part in the proceedings of the assembly. There are hourly excursions of steamers; rowing and sailing boats are laid up by the score under the maples; bathing houses line the lake where, dressed in becoming costumes, Methodists of both sexes join in the refreshing dip. Bazaars, ice-cream saloons, and bars for effervescing drinks are scattered here and there among the trees, which are threaded in all directions by secluded and romantic forest paths. At night there are lectures, entertainments, concerts, recitations, magic lanterns, and fireworks, while the woods glimmer with the scattered lights of Japanese lanterns. The curfew rings at ten o'clock, and at the same moment the electric lights are extinguished, and the candles of the Japanese lanterns expire. But the moonlight silvers the maple leaves; the fireflies hang their golden lace around the lake shore; the air grows balmier, and the forest paths more mysteriously romantic as the cool delicious night descends. It is difficult to believe that an unwritten programme of entertainments commences with the curfew? or must we suppose that emotion has been exhausted by the religious exercises of the day?

The stubbly waiter was only a Philistine sojourning in this Judæa, but such were not his views. He had been very kind to us, showing us everything, and explaining the Holy Land, the ark, and the miracles, with an evident wish that we might enjoy the whole thing as much as he did. "Many a time," said this Amalekite, "I hev sot on Sinai with a 'tony' gal, and watched the old patriarch work Horeb. Ef you'll come hyur and see the machine running in August mister, I guess I'll fix you in the best room on Ararat; thet ark is kep' for high-toned company, and you'll hev a good time, you bet. Why there's just a thousand gals flirting at you as soon 's your nose is inside thet amphitheàtre."

Lake Chautauqua is full of bass and pickerel, the latter a handsomely coloured fish like a pike in shape, as its name implies. It is taken by spinning and spearing, and is excellent eating. The fishing begins on June 1, when the lake is visited by many parties of ladies and gentlemen, who make a little festival of the opening day. On this evening there befell the most beautiful sunset which we had yet seen in America. We sat in the verandah of the hotel, watching the play of orange and crimson lights between the sky and the calm water till night fell, and the fireflies were darting to and fro among the trees. Presently a glowing point, like a larger firefly, slid out over the now dusky water from a wooded bay. It was the distant light of a pickerel spearer, and was soon succeeded by others, some nearer, some farther, until the whole surface of the lake was strewn with slowly moving meteors. Each boat carries two men, and a petroleum torch is fixed in the bow. Behind this stands the fisherman, his eyes protected from the glare by a screen. The second man rows the boat slowly along, and as the fish are attracted by the blaze the spearer delivers his weapon. It was a beautiful picture. A light mist lying on the surface of the water, concealed the boats themselves, while the trees were hung with the fireflies' nets of golden thread, through whose quivering meshes we saw the gliding torches cross and recross each other, as in the slow decorous figures of a dance. This silent but moving scene was canopied by a violet-black sky, sprinkled with brightening stars, while a line of pure yellow in the west reminded us of the faded sunset, as a strain from the overture sometimes lingers in the opera's sweetest air.

May 31 is Decoration Day, and a general holiday in America, when a procession is formed in every town for the purpose of visiting and decorating the last resting-places of soldiers who fell in the civil war. We went to Jamestown, at the extremity of Lake Chautauqua, for the purpose of witnessing this national ceremony. The procession was headed by a poor and noisy band, followed by a score of veterans carrying their old regimental colours. Only one of these men wore a uniform, which was shabby and ragged; the rest were dressed like, and probably were, mechanics. Behind them came a "fire company" in brilliant uniforms, their engine and life-saving apparatus shining with plating and paint. A second fire company followed in still finer cream-coloured clothes, white ties, and white kid gloves, and then the *hoi polloi*.

We marched with the last two miles in a blazing sun, the band playing dirges; and upon arrival at the cemetery, wound our way among the maples shading the graves to a stage already occupied by several ministers of religion, the orators of the day, and a choir. Proceedings commenced by decorating the graves with flags and flowers, after which every one gathered in a grassy amphitheatre around the platform. Prayers, choral singing, and addresses followed. The first were of the usual type, and the vocal music was good; but the speeches were the most notable features of the day, and that chiefly from their evident effort to do justice to the memory of brave men without wounding the susceptibilities of old foes, who are also fellow-countrymen. Civil war is the last misfortune of nations. Victor and vanquished are after all brothers, and the memories of the fallen on both sides would perhaps be better kept green by the silent strewing of laurels. Apparently the speakers felt this, for while fully expressing their reverence for the dead, a general sensibility for others gave that feeling a much more general expression than would have been the case if the soldier had fallen in conflict with a foreign foe. Hence the nation rather than the national heroes was exalted, and it is excusable if this circumstance lent some extravagance to the words of men striving to honour brave sons by praises of their mother country.

"We stand to-day," said one of the speakers, "the foremost

nation in history. The rulers of Europe are viewing with astonishment our rapid advancement, boundless resources, and the contentment, happiness, and prosperity of our people; while they witness with fear the discontent, turbulence, and unhappiness of their own. Pointing to her network of railways and telegraphs, her cities and villages, her two million farms, her boundless prairies, her vast tracts of forest, her fields of coal, her mines of iron and gold, her rattling looms, and the deep bass of her million spindles; to the smoke of ten thousand furnaces; to her homestead law, giving a farm in fee simple to whoever will work; to her schools and churches, her fifty millions of contented people, sheltered by the o'erhanging branches of the tree of liberty;—she proudly says to the world, 'These are the fruits of a hundred years in a nation conceived in liberty and dedicated to the proposition that all men are created equal.' Meanwhile in Europe, Nihilism and Socialism, seeking revenge in open revolution or cowardly assassination, are the legitimate growth of misgovernment, and of the natural desire on the part of the people to escape the burden of vast armies raised to support a power which they hate, and to escape from a pernicious land system which robs the labourer of the fruit of his industry."

Two candid Englishmen, sailing back in the cool evening to their hotel on Lake Chautauqua, found it necessary after much discussion to agree that if there were some "brag," there was little "bosh" in the oratory of Decoration Day at Jamestown.

CHAPTER X.

NIAGARA.

June 5–12.

EVERY tourist must visit Niagara but need not redescribe at length the great Falls, about whose beauty and sublimity enough has perhaps been said. The Niagara river is the overflow of the four great lakes, and its course between Erie and Ontario is made famous by the drop of a hundred and sixty feet over which the waste waters of these great inland seas take a sudden plunge. There is none of the usual prettiness of a cascade about this fall, whose enormous mass constitutes its chief claim to the admiration of the world. The river splits on Goat Island, but the bulk tumbles over the Canadian, or Horse-shoe Falls, beside which the American falls look like a weir. And the eye soon selects the crown of the horse-shoe as the central point of the picture. There, a translucent curve of green water bends slowly from the horizontal to the vertical, and plunges with apparent deliberation over the precipice, to lose itself almost immediately in froth and mist, while out of the hell-broth below rise clouds of the finest spray. These children of the air give the chief beauty to Niagara, for the smooth, repeated liquid curves and restless foam soon pall on the eye. The mist on the other hand, changes from beauty to beauty with every alteration of atmospheric conditions. Sometimes it sways hither and thither, like gauze in the shifting winds; at others it rises in unbroken columns whose capitals float away in billowy cumuli to join their shining companions in the blue. When the air is moist and the wind blowing gently from the falls, the valley becomes filled with luminous fog. On rarely bright still days, a shaft of vapour rises to more than a thousand feet in height, forming a stationary pillar of cloud, white as snow above where it is lost by absorption, and iridescent below where its base is wreathed in rainbows.

The country between Lakes Erie and Ontario consists of a nearly level plateau, terminating suddenly twenty-two miles north of Lake Erie in the bold precipitous cliffs nearly three hundred and fifty feet high, called Queenstown Heights. At their feet lie the towns of Lewiston and Queenstown, one on either side of the river Niagara, and thence the ground slopes gently and regularly to Lake Ontario. The cliffs are evidently an old shore-line, and the flat country was once a sea-bottom. The Niagara river issues from Erie in a wide tranquil stream, and flows over the surface of the plateau for about fifteen miles, when rapids occur, and then the cataract, the stream falling suddenly into a narrow gorge. This is best described as a trench three hundred feet deep and varying in width from two hundred to four hundred yards, which winds for seven miles like an artificial excavation through the plateau to Queenstown Heights, where the river debouches into the flat country, and flows in an almost level course to Lake Ontario.

The strata, on either side of the gorge, being nearly horizontal and formerly continuous, early suggested the idea that the falls once poured over Queenstown Heights, and have cut their way back to their present position. The existing lip of the cataract is a bed of hard limestone about eighty feet thick, supported by a similar thickness of friable shale. The falling water gives rise to extremely violent blasts of wind in the space between itself and the rock, which is consequently lashed with a perpetual storm of heavy spray. As the soft shales gradually yield before this attack, the limestone capping becomes undermined and drops from time to time, causing the falls to recede. The process is of course extremely slow, but there is some evidence of a slight change of position within half a century, while a description of Niagara, written in 1678 by the Franciscan missionary Père Hennequin, leaves no doubt that considerable alterations have taken place during the last hundred and fifty years. As however Hennequin was the first European to see the Falls, and that only a century and a half ago, the historical proofs of their recession are very slight; but fragments of an old river bed, containing shells of existing species, were found by Lyell on the banks of the present stream, and level with the plateau, at several points in its course between the falls and the escarpment at Queenstown. This fact leaves no reasonable doubt that the Niagara once flowed from Lake Erie across the whole width of the plateau to the edge of Queenstown Cliffs, whence the cataract has cut its way slowly back to its present position.

It would be extremely interesting if a regular rate of recession could be established, for this would enable the geologist to measure the minimum lapse of time which separates us from the glacial period, after whose occurrence the gorge in question was commenced. But the strata already cut through are of very various degrees of hardness, while in consequence of a slight inclination in the bedding, the hard rock forming the present lip will be at the bottom of the Falls when they have progressed two miles further southward. Wind and spray will make little impression on this compact limestone compared with what they now effect in the soft shales, and the cataract will probably remain almost stationary for ages, as has doubtless already been the case more than once in the past. Hence no reliable estimate can possibly be made of the lapse of time required for the digging of the trench. All that can certainly be known is that enormous periods have passed since the Niagara began to drain the upper lakes, yet the mollusca living in its waters to-day have undergone no change during all that time, as the shells found in the old river-bed testify. If then, living forms have remained unmodified at least as long as, and it may be much longer than, the time occupied in cutting the gorge in question, what must be the chronology of the whole geological succession to which the age of the phenomena in question bears an absolutely inappreciable proportion?

Excursions can be made to the back of both the Canadian and American falls, but that behind the latter is the more extensive and interesting. We dressed for the trip in waterproofs and list shoes furnished by the guide, whom we followed through the spray down a rough wooden stairway and path at the side of the Falls, until we reached the bottom, and then crept carefully along the face of the rock. Gusts of wind loaded with heavy spray made us shut our eyes and catch our breath at first, but once wet through, we advanced without further discomfort through a constantly increasing storm of wind and water. Here and there we found spots where local calms—due no doubt to the configuration of the rocks—prevailed, and in such places it was possible to keep our eyes open, though there was absolutely nothing to be seen except the heavy spray. On leaving the last of these shelters, the blasts became so violent as to suggest the propriety of holding on to something, and we thought that erosion of the shaly beds must be proceeding rapidly in such a hurricane. After traversing a hundred and thirty five feet, our guide stopped, declaring that it was impossible to go further; so we returned to daylight, not a little disenchanted after all the extravagant accounts we had heard of this trip. There is no real interest in penetrating behind the cataract, and a heavy thunderstorm in the absence of an umbrella is certainly more emotional. The guide showed us a spot below the falls where a safe backwater tempted us to a dip. We wanted no more tubbing than we had already had in the "Cave of the Winds," but only to say that we had swum in the rapids of Niagara.

About twenty-five years ago a Mr. Allen made a serious attempt to utilize some of the wasted water power of Niagara. With this view he dug a large canal from a point on the river above the falls to a plateau well adapted for building, about two miles below them. Here he proposed to erect a number of large turbines and let out power to factories which it was expected would be attracted to the neighbourhood. But the early works exhausted his resources. He became ill, and was forced to connect himself with others, who asked too high a price for their water privileges, and so the scheme failed. Allen's canal has now become the property of a wealthy and enterprising man, who has erected upon it a magnificent grist-mill driven by wheels of a thousand horse-power, together with a paper-pulping mill, a manufacture which requires a large supply of both power and water. The question of how best to utilize the forces of nature is much discussed in these days. Electricians declare that the mountain, hitherto considered immovable, is to be brought to Mahomet; and meanwhile the potential group of factories at Niagara and the actual collections of workshops at Belle Garde in Switzerland, and at the Falls of Schaffhausen on the Rhine, demonstrate the possibility of utilizing waterfalls. Coal itself is only a reservoir of energy, which we can tap when and where we please, but it is difficult of access, while the Falls are a great natural force, which is freely at the disposal of man.

While at Niagara we witnessed an obscure but spirited single-handed struggle between man and the natural force under review. In the spring of the year a great scow, coming out of Chippewa Creek, broke loose from the tug and entered the rapids. She stranded on a shallow a few miles above the Falls, in a position threatening the destruction of one of the small suspension bridges connecting the left bank of the river with a group of islands. The current at this point runs at a speed of twenty miles an hour, and the scow lay about a hundred yards from shore. Some rough trestles having been prepared, a man took one of them on his shoulders, and waded out into the stream with it for a distance of about ten feet. Here he pitched the trestle, and his mate pushed a plank out from the bank till its end landed on the frail pier. By the pathway thus constructed the wader returned to the mainland, and shouldering a second trestle again crept cautiously out into the current. The second was pitched like the first, and twenty feet out of three hundred were bridged. Within a few hours some fifty yards of staging was finished, when the wader reported, "Thar is three foot of water in a derned hole ahead, and we'll hev to pitch the next two trestles with a rig." We had no time to wait till the rig was made, and do not know whether this hero succeeded in reaching the scow; but if he was drowned there is one brave man the less in the world. The speed of the current was fearful, the bottom was of course concealed from view by the broken water, and the sound of the Falls was loud in our ears. A false step was certain death, for once fallen, recovery was impossible in such a stream. Yet, feeling his way with a pole, and loaded with the heavy trestle, without whose weight he could not have kept his feet, the man crept carefully but confidently out from shore, apparently as thoughtless of danger as a bricklayer's labourer on a ladder.

From the Arctic regions to the latitude of New York, the whole breadth of North America is covered with glacial drift, which varies from six hundred to two hundred feet in thickness in the middle and north-western states, while southward it becomes thinner and more evenly spread over the country. The drift consists of a vast accumulation of sand, pebbles, and boulders, always belonging to rocks lying north or north-west of their position, with beds of clay also evidently brought from the north by causes quite different to any of those now at work. Nearly every recently uncovered rock in the drift-covered region is grooved, scratched, or polished, and these marks point generally north-west, north, or north-east. Throughout these areas, erratics, or travelled blocks of stone, are found, which can only have been transported to their present sites by ice. It was for a long time a question whether land or sea ice had been the carrier of these various deposits, but it is now admitted that Agassiz's theory of an ice-sheet, continuous from the Arctic regions to the latitude of New York, is the only way of accounting for all the facts of American glaciation. Professor Dana has estimated that this sheet was not less than twelve thousand feet in thickness on the watershed of the St. Lawrence and Hudson's Bay, diminishing to four thousand feet on the east coast. Midway across the continent the vast *mer de glace* coalesced with a similar sheet issuing from the Rocky Mountains, whose summits were not covered, although the higher valleys were filled with enormous glaciers which fed the general mass below. In the course of time the rigorous climate of the glacial period changed. The ice retreated successively from the lowlands, the highlands, and the mountains, leaving Central America drowned in an inland sea derived from the melting ice. In the still waters of these internal oceans the alluvial soils of the Mississippi and Missouri valleys were laid down, and finally the inland seas themselves dried up under the influence of an arid climate, and the present land surfaces appeared. Unless mountainous, the country north of the fortieth parallel is almost uniformly drift or alluvium, through which the underlying rocks rarely protrude, and the traveller going north or west after leaving the flanks of the Alleghanies, finds the surface everywhere composed of beds of gravel, sand, or alluvium.

The surface of the plateau about Niagara is thinly covered with glacial drift, stripped of which the limestone is seen to be scored all over by ice. The marks are beautifully preserved and all point to the north. Travelled blocks of various primitive rocks, some of them many tons in weight, lie scattered in all directions. These are evidently derived from the gneisses of the watershed north of the great lakes and the St. Lawrence, and but for the forests which clothe the country about Niagara the whole district might seem to have just emerged from the ice-sheet of the glacial period.

The Niagara limestones weather into a soil carrying excellent crops of artificial grasses, while the shaly beds yield clays which form capital wheat and grass land. But the best farms are found on the warm sandy soils of the drift. A particular strip of this, bordering the river, and comprising only a few square miles, is especially suited to fruit-growing. Its apple orchards are very productive, and the trees exceedingly fine. Peaches, strawberries, and raspberries are extensively grown, and come in very early. Vines are being rapidly introduced around Niagara in the hope of replacing the peaches, which have suffered from a leaf disease during the last few years. The farms are small, fifty acres being the average size, while a hundred acres is rarely exceeded. Good land changes hands at from £20 to £30 per acre, and sometimes yields more than its cost in a single year's fruit crop. I saw one vineyard of three acres which last season produced eleven tons of grapes, worth £12 per ton. A Canadian vineyard, like other American industries, is rough and ready. Essentials are cared for, but finish is disregarded. The ground having been prepared by the plough, receives rows of wooden posts, driven about thirty feet apart, along which are strained three lines of old telegraph wire. Two vines are planted in each thirty-feet space, and six or eight shoots are trained vertically to the wires with cotton twine. The birds carry off the strings for nest-building, and it is a common thing to find nests among the vines constructed entirely of cotton thread; whenever a vine falls it is sure to be because the birds have untied it from the wires.

Farming only pays here when a man goes thoroughly into it himself, becoming his own bailiff and his own hind; labour is so dear that every operation must be skilfully economized, and a gentleman farmer would be bankrupt in a very short time. Still the village of Drummondsville, which is a centre of the rural industries round Niagara, is a flourishing place, and the farmers' wooden houses, if simple, are very comfortable. The farmers themselves are shrewd, active, and evidently prosperous, with the manners of business men rather than those of our agriculturists, though that pleasant rusticity which seems inseparable from the cultivation of the soil is not entirely wanting.

There is an Indian reservation near Niagara, where a tribe of Tuscaroras were settled by treaty nearly a hundred years ago. It is six square miles in extent, and occupied by four hundred families, each owning a house and land. No model village in England is more inviting in appearance. The fields are clean and well farmed; the crops, whether of grain, grass, or fruit, are magnificent; the fences are in good repair; the stock consists of handsome and healthy Durhams; the houses are well built, clean, and neat; and the whole reservation is superior in finish to American farms in general, challenging comparison in this respect with Lincolnshire or the Lothians. A heavy thunderstorm occurring during our visit, caused us to seek shelter at the house of Mr. Mount Pleasant, the chief of the tribe, by whom we were hospitably welcomed. The chief is a fine old Indian, who though nearly eighty years old, is as upright and active as a young man; and his wife, who belongs to the Senecas, is a quiet, shrewd woman. The house is a very pretty wooden building, excellently furnished, and provided with an abundance of good books, pictures, photographs, a piano and harmonium; in fact, a home of refinement. There was a daughter, educated in one of the eastern cities, who sang and played beautifully, and was very agreeable and intelligent. A Boston lady, interested in ethnology, was a guest in the house, collecting Indian folk-lore, and we were soon engaged in conversation with her about primitive man and the local geology. A strange position under the roof of a redskin. Yet some of us are bold enough to prophecy that peasant proprietorship will effect no change in Irish character, which seems almost equivalent to saying that the red man is more civilizable than the Celt. Our fair investigator had made one unfortunate expedition during her stay at the reservation. The chief assured her that skulls had been found in the neighbourhood, belonging to a race of men of whom the Tuscaroras had no traditions, and that these skulls were brachycephalic (Mr. Mount Pleasant used other words) to an extraordinary degree. She at once persuaded two young men to dig at the indicated spot, and at night, in order not to arouse the prejudices of the Indians. Skulls were found, but they did not differ from existing types, and by-and-by it was discovered that the forefathers of half the tribe were being disinterred.

CHAPTER XI.

ON THE GREAT LAKES.

June 12-15.

WE determined to travel by way of the great lakes to Chicago, making a short stay at the Straits of Mackinaw, between Lakes Huron and Michigan, for the purpose of seeing the timber or "lumbering" industry. From the Falls to Buffalo is twenty miles, the railroad skirting the Niagara river, and traversing a level country rich in apple and peach orchards. Buffalo lies half on Lake Erie, and half on the Niagara, and its position at the foot of the great chain of lakes gives the town considerable commercial importance. Here we found the steamer *Oneida*, one of the strange-looking lake-boats, having sides strengthened by deep "bowstring" girders running almost from stem to' stern, and making the vessel look like a Noah's ark carrying a railway bridge as deck freight.

American steamers combine the sea-going and shore-going elements very curiously. The British shipbuilder gives such a nautical character to every feature and fitting of a vessel that a landsman always feels his lubberhood keenly when on board ship. He is naturally crushed by a sense of ignorance on deck, but it is little better in the saloon whose approaches, seats, lighting, and accommodation differ from anything he has ever seen on shore; while his berth, with its port-hole, narrow bunks, and borrowed lamplight, is not a bed-room, but the roost of a tar, off watch. The traveller on board such a ship is never allowed to forget that he is only a passenger, or to lose sight of the humiliating nature of his position. In the States on the other hand, ships are made for passengers, not passengers for ships; and a landsman loses none of his accustomed dignity on taking up his quarters in the hotel-afloat which American shipbuilders have created. The deck itself has a less professional air, the saloon has a staircase, lights, tables, chairs, even doors, hinges, and handles, like those to which he has been accustomed; his cabin contains a real bed, and being on deck, is lighted by sliding sash windows, shaded with blinds, as in his own house. There is nothing of the "old salt" about the captain or crew, who may, and probably have, followed many occupations before becoming sailors. All this is pleasanter than sailing in more nautical craft under scornful nautical eyes.

The low pine-clad shores of Erie were lost sight of soon after leaving Buffalo, and there was nothing to relieve the monotony of the ocean-like scene except occasional meetings with grain ships. The agricultural states of Western America may be practically regarded as anxious to send all their surplus food stuffs to Liverpool, and Chicago is the centre where the grain collects. From this point there are three routes to the eastern seaboard:

first, by rail direct from Chicago to New York, Philadelphia, or Baltimore; second, by way of the lakes to Buffalo, and thence by the Erie Canal and river Hudson to New York; third, by the lakes to Buffalo, and thence through the Welland Canal to Montreal. The railway is of course the quickest of all these routes, but competition with shipping freights has greatly reduced the profits of the carrying companies, who wear out their rails and rolling stock to little advantage. Still the bulk of the grain traffic between Chicago and the Atlantic goes by rail, a great deal of stuff being picked up in Indiana and Ohio, states which lie east of Chicago and off the water routes. Grain shipped by the lakes and Erie Canal is carried in sailing vessels, or steamers, or towed in very large barges to Buffalo, where it is transhipped by means of "elevators" into the boats of the Erie Canal and, arrived at New York, is again transferred into Atlantic vessels. Cargoes were formerly shipped on the lakes exclusively in sailing vessels, but these have competed of late years with steamers of fifteen hundred to two thousand tons burden which are more profitable to the shipowner because of the greater number of trips they can make in the same time. Recently a new system has arisen. The large steamers, which carry passengers as well as cargo, are expensive both in first cost and maintenance, and are consequently being replaced by enormous barges, two or three of which are towed by a powerful tug. A tug is costly only in respect of its engines, the rest of the ship being cheaply built, while it only needs a crew of four men, instead of the twelve or twenty required by a great lake steamer. The barges are rigged with masts and sails, and are cast loose from the tug on bad weather arising, when they either fend for themselves, or shelter behind a point until the storm abates, after which they are again taken in tow. Each barge carries from thirty to forty thousand bushels of grain, the tug holding another fifteen thousand bushels, and the system beats both steam and sailing vessels for economy.

With the arrival of grain at Buffalo there begins a competition between the United States and Canada for the transport trade of the north-west, and it is still an open question whether Montreal or New York will ultimately control the grain traffic of America. The Erie Canal, which connects Lake Ontario with New York, is a great national work begun under difficulties in 1809, delayed by the war of 1812, finished in 1825, and enlarged in 1862. It is three hundred and fifty miles long, but no more than seven feet deep, and only admits barges of two hundred and twenty tons burden. From its commencement to its completion the Canadians watched the progress of the Erie Canal with keen interest, and finally, one of the clearest-headed men in the colony, William Hamilton Merritt, devoting years of enthusiastic labour to the construction of a rival route, caused the Welland Canal to be built, which, connecting Lakes Erie and Ontario by a channel twenty-seven miles long, cheats the Niagara Falls, and gives a clear water-way from the upper lakes to the head-waters of the St. Lawrence. This river is itself obstructed by rapids near Montreal, which were avoided by cutting a second canal, eight miles and a half in length, past the Lachine rapids, the two works together affording access from Lake Superior to the Atlantic. The Welland Canal was originally ten feet and a quarter, and the Lachine nine feet deep, accommodating vessels of six hundred, and four hundred tons respectively, while the Erie still remains only seven feet deep, its further enlargement, though often discussed, being difficult on account of its great length. But now a new factor in the problem of water transportation has appeared. The old freight boats have been succeeded by grain vessels of a thousand tons burden, and those ships cannot pass through the Canadian any more than the American canals. A further and uniform enlargement of the Welland and St. Lawrence Canals to a hundred feet in width and fifteen feet in depth, admitting vessels of fifteen hundred to two thousand tons, was therefore agreed to as part of the Canadian Confederation Scheme of 1867, and has already been completed so far as the Lachine Canal is concerned. The works on the Welland will probably be finished in two years from the present time, and it will then remain to be seen whether the efforts by which the Canadians hope to divert the carrying trade of the north-west, not only from Buffalo but from New York as well, will be successful. The St. Lawrence route is open for only half the year, and the process of enlarging the capacity of grain ships is still going on, there being already vessels on the lakes above Buffalo which could not enter even the new Welland Canal; but whether Canada gets the whole or only a part of the gigantic trade she is bidding for, there can be no question that with the completion of a clear water-way for vessels of two thousand tons from Lake Superior to the Atlantic, Montreal must become a serious rival to New York in regard to the transportation of grain. The five great Atlantic outlets are Montreal, New York, Boston, Philadelphia, and Baltimore, and of these New York at present receives rather more than half the grain coming from the north-west, while Montreal only handles ten per cent. of it, the remaining forty per cent. being pretty equally distributed between the three other ports. The New York traffic is partly rail and partly water-borne, that of Montreal is all water-borne, while Boston, Philadelphia, and Baltimore are connected with the west by rails only. When the Canadian Pacific Railway is completed there will be six great taps draining the north-west, a state of things which, while it warns the colony not to expect too much from its enterprising movements in the canal system, offers a bright prospect of further cheapening the transportation of bread stuffs between America and Europe.

Lake Erie is one of the few seas which have witnessed the surrender of an entire squadron of British ships. The efforts of Napoleon in the early part of the century to exclude English exports from the Continent were foiled by the rise of a vast system of contraband trade, and by the development of the carrying trade in neutral bottoms. Anxious to prevent the transfer of one of her important industries to other nations, England endeavoured to compel all vessels on their way to blockaded ports to touch first at British harbours; and claimed the right to search vessels for British sailors, a high-handed proceeding which led to a serious quarrel with America, terminating in the war of 1812. In this contest the States were as unfortunate ashore as they were victorious afloat. The defeat of the British frigate *Guerrire* by the *Constitution* was balanced by the capture of the American frigate *Chesapeake* by the *Shannon* in Boston harbour; but the loss of this ship and the death of her brave commander Lawrence, who fell exclaiming, "Don't give up the ship," was more than avenged on Erie. There, on September 10, 1813, a naval battle took place between a British squadron of six ships and nine American vessels, under the command of Lieutenant Perry, who sailed from the little town of Erie in the flag ship *Lawrence*, so named after the captain of the *Chesapeake*. This ship was disabled in the fight, and Perry transferred his flag to another vessel, but in the result the British squadron surrendered, and the American lieutenant returned with his prizes to Erie. Three years later the war was ended by the Treaty of Ghent, when the English claim to a right of search was silently abandoned, thanks to the exploits of the American navy.

Lake Erie opens into the small but pretty St. Clair Lake by the Detroit river, whose banks, generally covered with primitive forest, are cleared and settled all along the water's edge, and beautiful with fruit orchards, where excellent apples may be bought during the season for a shilling a bushel. The stream at the entrance of Lake Huron is almost a rapid, against which steamers crawl slowly upwards. The shores of Huron are very low and composed entirely of ice-borne drift. They are clothed with dark pine woods whose seemingly boundless extent impresses the mind with an overpowering sense of loneliness, and whose monotony is scarcely broken by "lumbering" villages, which hide among the pines, their presence betrayed only by clouds of yellow smoke hanging like a pall over the forest and adding to the melancholy of the scene.

"Lumbering" is the sole industry of these vast solitudes, and is conducted in the rough-and-ready way so characteristic of American enterprise. A company having been formed, a site on the lake shore is selected for the mills, and some square miles of timber lands, bordering on rivers or creeks debouching into the lake, are purchased from the Government. Pioneer gangs visit these "pine lands" in autumn, and establish permanent camps in favourable positions near the most important lake affluents; erecting stabling for twenty or thirty teams, and log huts for forty or fifty men. All being thus prepared, the camp is occupied as soon as the first snows fall, and felling is commenced in earnest. The fallen trees are cut into lengths, sledded over the snow to the river, and tumbled in; the mouth of the stream having first been closed by a strong boom which prevents the egress of timber into the lake. When four or five thousand pieces have accumulated behind the boom, they are formed into a raft in the following manner:—Thirty large logs, each sixty feet long, are chained together end to end, forming a string; a second similar string is then constructed, and the two are secured together by thirty cross-pieces, each sixty feet long, and sixty feet apart. The finished structure forms a floating and jointed framework, having thirty bays, each of which holds about a hundred and sixty logs; so that a raft contains nearly five thousand pieces of timber, and has a length of six hundred, and a width of twenty yards. When one is completed the boom is removed from the mouth of the river, and a steam-tug takes the raft in tow, then the boom is replaced and the river again filled with timber.

Before following one of these great floats to the mills, situated it may be many miles away, the camp deserves a moment's notice. The lumberers are chiefly Canadians, men of magnificent physique, but not of refined habits. The hard labour, remoteness, and severe winter climate all disincline the men from cleanliness, and while in camp they never wash, and hardly ever take off their clothing. They doff their "pants" and the heavy woollen "jumper" at night, but that is all. They earn about sixteen dollars a month, all rations being found, and receive no money payments while in camp. Though strict abstainers while at work, they loaf about the village saloon all summer, and having spent their last dollars go in debt at the "store" in order to keep going until the next season's work begins. None but the strongest frames can withstand the hardships of a winter camp in these latitudes, where the snows are deep and the temperature almost Arctic in severity; but the transport of heavy logs is so much more difficult on wheels than by sleds that the business of lumbering must always remain a monopoly in the hands of a class whose physique is superior even to that of an English navvy.

Lumber-towing on the wide and stormy waters of the lakes is not free from excitement and danger, as we learned later from the narratives of our Michigan boatman, John McCarty, who was for many years in charge of a tug. This man was once caught in a sudden gale, on a lee shore, with his raft to windward of the steamer. Fearing the loss of the vessel which was rapidly drifting ashore, he determined to "jump the raft" and at the risk of entangling the screw and smashing the engines, turned the tug, and drove her directly at the logs. These were submerged by the weight of the boat, and the propeller sent the sticks flying in all directions, but McCarty ultimately cleared the raft with all the machinery sound, and only his rudder damaged. Next day he picked up the raft which, though stranded, had not gone to pieces, and towed it safely to its destination. The lake is always dotted with floating timber and the shores are lined with the wreckage of years. Sometimes a storm breaks up a raft, sometimes destroys a "boom," when hundreds or it may be thousands of logs escape. These cumber the beaches, and add to the desolation which is so marked a feature of Lake Huron scenery.

The site chosen for the erection of saw-mills is always a sheltered bay, where a kind of floating dock, made of logs chained together and secured to piles, rides on the water for the reception of the rafts. Here the tug discharges its burden and then returns to camp, towing the empty framework back, to be refilled. The docks accommodate sufficient timber for the supply of the mill at all seasons, and present a really astonishing sight when full. Piers, constructed of waste wood, on a commensurate scale with the docks, are run out from the shore into deep water, forming wharves for the stacking and shipment of cut boards. The mill is erected by the lake side, and an inclined slide-way ascends from the water to its first floor, where the saws are placed, the ground floor of the building being occupied by the motive power and driving gear. The slide-way is fitted with an endless chain, which is fed by a man wearing high boots, with corked soles, and armed with a long boat-hook. This clever acrobat walks about over the floating logs with a skill that is only acquired after repeated duckings, and punts them one by one to the foot of the slide, where they are laid hold of by hooks attached to the endless chain, and carried to the saw-benches. These machines and others which handle the great tree trunks mechanically, are excellent examples of the survival of the fittest, being entirely different from and far superior to any similar tools in this country. The work is extremely heavy, yet the logs are rapidly adjusted, almost entirely without hand labour, on the saw-benches, from each of which a stream of cut boards issues at the rate of nearly a hundred feet a minute, or a mile an hour. A mill with two saw-frames turns out twenty million cubic feet of lumber per annum, worth £40,000 in Chicago; and lumbering, the distinctive industry of the great lakes, is a profitable enterprise.

CHAPTER XII.

MACKINAW.

June 16–20.

THE rivalry between France and England in the seventeenth century was worldwide in its extension. The two countries were neighbours in the West Indies, the East Indies, and in Africa; while in America, as we have already seen, Louis XIV. claimed sovereignty over all the known regions west of the Alleghany Mountains. French colonies had been planted in America years before the *Mayflower* anchored within Cape Cod; but France and England, rivals in the Old World, could not be partners in the New. Neither ambition nor commercial enterprise however carried the power of France into the western wilds, but the religious enthusiasm of the Church of Rome. A similar motive-power urged the pilgrims to colonize New England, and the two peoples in America were, in the first instance, parted more by religious differences than national jealousy. But a struggle, which terminated as we have seen in favour of England, was unavoidable between powers, divided by so many animosities, when lust of territory and desire for commercial supremacy had taken the place of the apostolic zeal which animated the Jesuit missionaries through whom Rome, as much as France, attempted the spiritual conquest of America.

Hardly was the Society of Jesus established than it gave to the world an army of devoted Christian soldiers, who raised the cross, not only among the old civilizations of India, China, and Japan, but even on the high lands of Abyssinia, the plains of Paraguay, and the slopes of the Sierra Nevada. The shores of the upper lakes were all first explored by Jesuit missionaries, who early penetrated into the heart of the Huron wilderness, disregarding toil, hardship, torture, and death, in obedience to their vows, and at the bidding of their superiors. If these men were superstitious ascetics, at least they were Christian heroes, often Christian martyrs, and always, although incidentally, explorers. Every town of importance in French America originated from their labours, and "not a cape was turned or a river entered, but a Jesuit led the way."

We left the steamship *Oneida* at Mackinaw, an island of many interesting memories, whence Père Marquette, one of the most distinguished yet unaspiring of these remarkable men, was long employed in extending Christianity, and confirming the influence of France in the vast regions between Lake Michigan and the head of Lake Superior, and where, spent after only thirty-eight years of toil, his body reposes. In the spring of 1668, Marquette was sent to take charge of the Ottawa Mission, as that around Lake Superior was then called, and he planted himself at Sault St. Mary, on the American side of the rapids which connect the upper lakes with Huron. Here he was joined in the following year by Père Dâblon, and the log church and cabins built by these two formed the first permanent settlement made in Michigan. In the same year, leaving Dâblon in charge of his Huron converts, Marquette travelled westward by Lake Superior, and having established a mission among the Chippeways on its southern shore, he pushed on to its western extremity, where he found several Indian villages, one of which was inhabited by Hurons who had lived several years before on Mackinaw Island.

Four years previously Allouez, another Jesuit missionary, had raised the Chapel of the Holy Spirit in these distant regions; and such was the power of his teaching that the scattered tribes roaming the deserts north of Lake Superior, the Potawatomies from Lake Michigan, and even the Illinois from the as yet unknown Mississippi Valley, pitched their tents around his cabin, and listened to the gospel message. These last spoke of their country, describing the noble river on which they dwelt, and the vast treeless prairies where buffalo and deer abounded. "Their country," wrote Allouez to his superior, "is the best field for the gospel;" and these letters first made the pale faces acquainted with the existence of the great stream, which Allouez in his correspondence called the "Messipi." The missions of Marquette and Dâblon were created by this great enthusiast, who, returning from the wilderness to Quebec for a few days in 1667, pleaded so fervently with governor and bishop for the establishment of more stations, that Sault and Lapointe were occupied in the two following years, and a third still more important mission established by Marquette at Mackinaw, in 1670.

While at Lapointe, Marquette, like Allouez, heard from native lips of the magnificent open country of the Mississippi Valley;

and in the autumn of 1669 he resolved on attempting its exploration, in order to carry the message of the Cross still further among the heathen. Nearly four years however elapsed before it was possible for the father to carry out his plans; but at length, in June, 1673, he started with Joliet, another Jesuit missionary, on the expedition. Leaving Lake Superior by the Fox river, they followed this stream to its head-waters, and carrying their boats across the narrow watershed separating these from the sources of the Wisconsin river, the two poor Jesuit missionaries reached the basin of the Mississippi. Launching their canoes upon the Wisconsin, the discoverers entered the great river after seven days, and floated thankfully southward nearly to the Gulf, over the vast and then unknown stream which within two centuries has become one of the chief highways of the world. Neither pride nor ambition swelled the bosoms of these explorers, whose absorbing piety purged every earthly feeling from their thanksgivings that God had thus widened the field for the spread of His Word. Of Joliet nothing is known except in connection with this expedition. He carried the news to Quebec, and then probably returned to the obscure toils, perhaps suffered the painful death of many another labourer in this section of God's vineyard; while Marquette halted on the spot where Chicago now stands, and preached the gospel to the Miamis for another two years. Then, worn out with the hardships of life in the wilderness, he set out in the spring of 1675 to return to his home at Mackinaw; but as he coasted along the shores of the lake, his strength gradually failed. His devoted Indian companions, feeling that the end was near, entered a little creek where they built a bark cabin, kindled a fire, and laid him down beside it. After shriving his companions and commending them to God, he professed his faith aloud upon the crucifix, and thanking God for permitting him to die a Jesuit missionary and alone, he passed away with the name of Jesus on his lips. Two years later, acting under Marquette's instructions given at Lapointe, the Indians reverently transferred his body to Point St. Ignace at Mackinaw, where it lies under the solemn pines, beneath the roof of the church which he himself had raised.

The village of Mackinaw, containing five hundred souls, is redolent of the backwoods. Indian half-breeds are numerous in its streets and are not bad-looking people, the women especially having fine faces and figures, while the shops are gay with Indian handicraft. Not many years ago the Chippeways assembled here once a year to receive their annual allowance from Government at the hands of the Indian agents—a class of men who unfortunately for the relations between the red skin and the white, have often been badly chosen for the discharge of duties demanding the strictest justice. The Chippeway claims have been extinguished for some years, and a characteristic spectacle is now lost to visitors. In the old days the tribes camped along the beach, and gave themselves up for a week or more to feasting and Indian merriment. The shops of Mackinaw are tiny general warehouses, where almost everything can be bought, but the store-keeper is a very different person from the huckster of an English village. The stock though miscellaneous, is well selected, and arranged in the most orderly manner on clean white shelves which surround the shop. The proprietor is an intelligent man of some importance, living on terms of friendly equality with every one about the place. The drug store, for example, is "run" by our good friend Dr. Baily, a properly qualified M.D., a wide traveller, a good doctor, and an excellent companion; who will either prescribe for patients or retail them quack medicines as they may desire; and who sells you an ounce of tobacco, a pound of soap, or a packet of fish-hooks, without loss of his professional dignity. His shop is a picture gallery of advertisements, and becomes a kind of club at night, where we refresh with "old rye," and discuss American politics and local history with the doctor himself and such neighbours as may happen to drop in.

The little town is dominated by a fort, which affords us the rare sight of American soldiers, whose appearance is smart and whose rifle practice is excellent. This fort was once a French post, and many an English adventurer, pushing up from the lower lakes to the upper waters in search of the furs of the north-west, left his scalp hereabouts in the hands of the savage subjects of France, to whom Jesuit zeal was trying to teach the law of love. After the question between France and England was finally settled on the Heights of Abraham, Mackinaw, together with all the French posts around the lakes, passed into the hands of the British, whose scattered soldiers, lost in the boundless woods, held these isolated spots at the imminent risk of massacre by the Indians, recently the allies of France. Such a massacre occurred at Mackinaw Fort two years after the British took possession of it, the Indians, presumably friends, having entered by stratagem, and a solitary trader alone escaping from the butchery which followed. The fort was again the scene of strife in the war of 1812, of whose naval aspects some mention has already been made, and the spot where our troops were disembarked is still called "The British Landing."

The island became very prosperous shortly after the war, having been chosen by Mr. Astor as the base of his widespread operations in the fur trade. His company, controlling an immense capital, had outposts scattered throughout the whole west and north-west, for which Mackinaw was the central mart and depôt. Here the trappers' supplies were collected from the company's store-houses in New York, Quebec, and Montreal; and hence they were distributed to the outposts. The furs on the other hand were brought annually to the island, whence they found their way to the eastern states and to Europe. At this time Mackinaw held nearly two thousand souls, mostly Indians; but the trade declined on Mr. Astor's retirement from the enterprise, to pass at length into the hands of the Hudson's Bay Company.

We quartered at a hotel called the Mission House—in memory, not of the seventeenth century apostles, but of the Christian work of Dr. Morse, father of Professor Morse the inventor of modern telegraphy, who visited the island in 1820 and preached the first Protestant sermon ever delivered in the north-west. Acting upon his report on the condition of the natives and traders, the United

Foreign Missions Society of New York established a church and school here in 1822, but the work of religious instruction and education slackened with the dwindling population, and upon the Indians altogether ceasing to resort to the place for purposes of trade, the enterprise was abandoned.

Once more the Romish Church is in the ascendant at Mackinaw. The Protestants are too few to support a clergyman, and we found their church dilapidated and unused, except for the entertainments of the "Caramel Minstrels," whose latest programme of comic songs was chalked on the canvas wings of a rough stage occupying the site of the displaced pulpit. The Catholic church on the other hand, built of wood, in the severest style of carpenter's Gothic, is in good repair, and evidently well attended. Our friend Dr. Baily was the only Protestant member of the village school board, yet, as we learnt with astonishment, the Catholic majority supports a conscience clause, and allows of no religious teaching in the Mackinaw schools repugnant to the feelings of parents. Thus do free institutions modify religious prejudices, and take the sting even from religious intolerance.

While at Mackinaw we hired a small yawl, whose skipper, John McCarty, as already related, saved his steam-tug from destruction on Lake Huron by "jumping" the timber raft which threatened to drive him on a lee shore. With him we sailed round the island, and explored the neighbouring shores, visited some of the great lumbering establishments, and touched at Point St. Ignace to see Marquette's grave. The fishing was excellent, and a dip, diversified with balancing feats on the floating logs, was our daily luxury. Nothing can seem more perfectly desolate than the low, silent, pine-clad shores of the lake, with their narrow white beaches, sprinkled with erratic pebbles of granite and gneiss, and cumbered with derelict logs of timber. But once landed, the forest is not without its attractions, at least in summer. There are clear spaces among the trees where the columbine displays its symmetrical scarlet blossoms, and the smooth brown stems of the wild cherry contrast with the silver bark of the birch; but even after our most enjoyable rambles among the pines, we thought that restraint had been exchanged for freedom when the forest was left behind us, and our yawl danced again on the sunlit waves of Mackinaw Strait.

CHAPTER XIII.

CHICAGO.

June 20-27.

THE navigation of the great lakes becomes monotonous after a time, and we stepped on board the *St. Louis* steamboat at Mackinaw, bound for Chicago, disposed rather for the observation of our fellow-creatures than of nature. The general want of interest shown by Americans in Europe and European concern had already struck and surprised me so much that I determined to test the question of its existence on the voyage. Strolling about the Treasury on the evening of our arrival in Washington, we fell into talk with a caretaker, who answered our inquiries about the building very intelligently, and appeared in other respects a well-informed man. Having satisfied our curiosity he said, "I guess you are tourists, gentlemen," to which we replied that we were from England, rather hoping that the man, who had answered so many of our questions, would ask us something about the "tight little island," if only for the sake of repaying him for his politeness. He paused for a few moments, and then with the air of a person who feels bound to make a civil speech, said, "And *haow's* England?" If the "tight little island" had been our sick relation and a perfect stranger to him, our friend could not have spoken with more polite indifference. The tone, impossible of reproduction, pricked such a big hole in the balloon of our national vanity that we collapsed on the spot. Nothing has since occurred to reinflate us; on the contrary we have, figuratively speaking, heard so many compassionate inquiries of "Haow's England?" that we are not anxious to air our nationality.

The Americans are great European tourists, and every steamer that leaves New York is crowded with innocents going abroad, but they are for the most part tarred with the same brush. Some of them, on their return, will own to having passed over rising ground in the Bernese Oberland; while others may naively complain, as happened once in my hearing, that the Highland hotels are inferior to those of Paris, and this city therefore to be preferred before the land of flood and fell. Once in an Oxford hotel I was asked, "Do you think I might shunt York Minster on my way to the north? I have seen everything here, and the English antiques are so much alike that I will lump them, and save a day, if you so advise." Willing to believe that these were exceptional cases, I began my search for a fellow-passenger with a genuine interest in the Old World, but found none. For Americans generally England is the country of Shakespeare and of some interesting "antiques." Paris, the Yankee heaven, is the beatified home of Worth and the birthplace of beautiful jewellery; while the balance of Europe is either a great *bric-à-brac* shop or a playground. The night of the Middle Ages, the morning of the Renaissance, the strife of peoples with priests and kings, the birth of free institutions, and the growth of nationalities, are naught in the ordinary American's valuation of Europe. Only the history of states, where men are born free and equal, is of any real human interest; the rest is sound and fury, signifying nothing. I do not think I overstate the case, and there is something to be said for this view. Human energies have necessarily been, as they still are, recklessly squandered on stupid issues in the European struggle for liberty. It is heart-breaking to sum the waste of courage and genius which has accompanied the evolution of humanity in the Old World. But while we crown with bay the heroes of freedom's battles, America is placed where the valour that we rightly honour, and its needlessness are both equally conspicuous. Whatever the reason, there is very little interest felt in the New World for the Old; but there is a great deal of confidence in the superiority of America to Europe in all respects.

There is less small-talk among the Americans than with us, and conversation is commonplace, solid, and argumentative. Men rarely speak about subjects with which they have not considerable acquaintance, but they are fond of discussion, which is conducted fairly and without heat. While making use of extravagant hyperbole to illustrate a position, they avoid all injurious expressions, and try to establish their points without appeals to prejudice, and without personality. They state a case slowly, listen to the other side patiently, and attach much weight to conclusions arrived at by the reasoning process. Prejudice, tradition, and custom are powerful dictators of opinion in Europe, and too often colour our convictions; while the deadly character of competition in a crowded country lends bitterness to every conflict which touches vital interests. In the States on the other hand, the competitive struggle is not *à outrance*, and the freedom of the career, developing individual character to an extraordinary degree, strikes off many fetters which bind thought in Europe.

The first white man to visit Chicago was Marquette, who preached the gospel there to the Miamis on his return from the discovery of the Mississippi in 1673. No settlement took place until 1804, when the United States Government built a fort; but this was abandoned in the war of 1812, and finally demolished. The first house was built in 1832, when Chicago numbered only a hundred souls. The first vessel entered the harbour two years later, and the first official census, taken in 1837, showed a population of four thousand inhabitants.

Forty years ago the site of Chicago was rolling prairie, covered with tall grasses, wild marigolds, and sunflowers, the haunt of the buffalo, and the home of the Indian. Thirty years later a busy city of three hundred thousand inhabitants stood on the same spot, but was suddenly swept out of existence by a great fire in 1871. While we in England feared that Chicago had received a mortal wound, the young athlete had but tripped for a moment in that arena where, though the struggle for existence never ends, the survival of the fittest is assured; and in the result the spot has proved to be the natural centre of the American grain trade, while now, only ten years after its practical annihilation, the city contains more than half a million inhabitants. The wooden shanties of 1871 have given place to warehouses and stores which remind the English visitor of Cannon Street or Queen Victoria Street. Great industries connected with the food supply of the whole world have arisen, and ministering to the wants which these create, a multitude of manufactures have clustered around the central interests. Stately public buildings serve the municipal wants of the city. Bold engineering works bring a splendid water supply through several miles of tunnel, from the purer depths of Lake Michigan. The private houses of wealthy merchants and manufacturers—palaces such as the American architect delights to rear—adorn the environs. Lincoln and South Parks, rivalling anything of the kind in Europe, lie one on either side of the city, which will soon be girdled by thirty miles of leafy boulevards.

The middle states of America, now no longer appropriately called the West, were almost untapped in 1850, and the heart of the continent, containing millions of square miles of fertile soil, was waiting for the plough. An immense commerce, for the control of which older cities were reaching out their hands, was about to flow from these hitherto unoccupied lands. Where should it find its centre? The situation of Chicago destined it for this position. Standing at the head of Lake Michigan, it commands the inland navigation, and its early citizens soon supplemented their natural advantages by the construction of railways in all directions. Thus placed, with the agricultural states of Ohio, Illinois, Iowa, Indiana, and Wisconsin at her back, with an uninterrupted water-way and direct railways connecting her with the seaboard, Chicago forms at once the natural focus for the productions of the Middle States, and the point whence grain, cattle, and hogs are distributed to the populous Eastern states and the markets of Europe. It also receives from the pine forests of Huron vast quantities of timber, which find their way either to the Southern cities and plantations, or to the ever-spreading emigrants of the treeless western prairies. The Chicago river is lined for seven miles with lumber yards, witnessing even more powerfully than the grain trade itself, to the energy of the city. For the corn which Chicago distributes is grown almost at her gates, but the forests of South Carolina are nearer the Southern markets than the pines of Huron; yet the business men of Chicago have created facilities for the distribution of timber which neutralize the natural advantages in favour of their Southern competitors. Within another thirty years Chicago may rival New York. There is room on the American continent for many capitals, and the Atlantic cities do not perhaps derive more importance from their manufacturing enterprise and command of European markets, than the Queen of the Middle States will shortly acquire from the rapidly increasing wants of the vast internal territory over which she rules.

Naturally enough, the city bears traces of its rapid growth. The great piles of handsome buildings are hustled by wretched little wooden houses. The side-walks are for the most part of planks, laid in a series of ups and downs, and so badly constructed that the loose boards often tip under the weight of the passer-by. The roads are dirt-beds, not yet filled up to the level of the side-walks—sloughs in winter and full of holes in summer. Open spaces, full of rubbish, and detached shanties are common in the best parts of the town, while the side streets are built almost entirely of wood, and are full of beer saloons. Altogether, Chicago is a city of contrasts, and the traveller's estimate of it will vary enormously according to his point of view.

The prosperity of the Queen of the Middle States rests on her trade in hogs, grain, and lumber, and so characteristic are the two former industries that no one can be said to have seen Chicago who has not visited one of the packing houses and a grain elevator. Of the former there are thirty-five, with a capacity for killing and curing which varies from a hundred hogs a day in the smallest concerns, to ten thousand a day in the largest. The total number of hogs killed in a year is upwards of five millions, and the average weight of each pig being two hundredweight, about fifteen hundred tons of pork a day, or half a million tons per annum, issue from the united doors of the Chicago packing houses.

In the agricultural states of the West, Indian corn is the staple crop. It is grown in vast quantities, and not being a breadstuff, is most profitably exported as pork. From a group of states therefore covering an area larger than England, streams of corn-fed hogs flow steadily to Chicago. Here they debouch into the "Stockyards," immense enclosures for the reception of all kinds of live stock, occupying an area of nearly three hundred and fifty acres, with a capacity for holding two hundred thousand animals of all kinds. Around these spacious reservoirs of human food the packing houses have arisen. Externally they are like great factories, but each is connected with the stockyards by an inclined roadway by which the hogs enter the building on the first floor. The incline leads to a pen within the packing house, where, among some hundreds of snuffing pigs, stand two men, almost naked, their bodies covered with filth from contact with the great unwashed. Over their heads is a simple railway, composed of a single bar of iron set edgwise, and provided with rollers which act the part of carriages. The rail is continuous throughout the whole length of the building, falling by gentle inclines from one end of it to the other, and serving to carry the carcases throughout their journey from pig to pork. Above the pen and railway there is a steam hoist controlled by an attendant, who in the first instance lowers a chain to the men below. They in the meantime have secured a victim from the crowd of pigs, and one of his hind legs is fastened by a spring clip to the dangling end of the chain. In a moment the hog is lifted into the air, screaming and kicking violently, and in another he hangs head down from one of the roller carriages, while the chain falls back into the hands of the penmen. Loudly protesting, the hog rolls smoothly down the descent of Avernus until he reaches the executioner, who awaits him standing alone in the middle of a pen much like the one above. This man also is nearly naked, befouled with mud and bristle like his fellows, and in his right hand gleams a short curved knife sharp as a razor. With a swift and apparently effortless turn of the wrist, he cuts the throat of the helpless screamer, who then continues on his way, silenced but still kicking, until he reaches the lower side of this chamber of horrors, which is closed by a sliding door. When a dozen carcases have accumulated, the door is opened, and the group roll forward until they hang over a large tank of boiling water, when the clips are tripped, and the hogs plump down into the hot bath, rolling about like porpoises, with their round backs only above the surface. After scalding they are lifted out on to a long, narrow, sloping bench, the upper end of which is occupied by an ingenious shaving machine, consisting of four drums, armed with revolving spring razors, so arranged that a pig passing through the system is shaved on four sides of a square, into which sectional figure the soft body is approximately squeezed during the process. A large portion of the hair is thus removed, and the rest is taken off by hand. Below the shaving machine the bench is occupied by ten men, five on either side, standing a few feet apart who, as the hog passes rapidly from one to another, remove more and more bristle, until he finally reaches station number five perfectly white and clean. Here the head is severed from the body, and thrown on one side as refuse. The trunk is once more hitched up to a carriage, and rolls forward to the dis-embowelling room, whose arcana are perhaps better left undescribed, and thence it presently issues, a spotless and attractive object, like that to which our own butcher complacently draws attention as " prime country-fed pork."

The hog now makes a long excursion to a distant room, far removed from the gory surroundings in which we have hitherto seen him, and here while still hanging, he is split in two with an axe, and the halves, as they accumulate from the fast-flowing stream of carcases, are rolled away in batches to the ice-house. All the animals slaughtered on one day remain in the cold chamber until the next, when the stiffened halves are brought out and severed by swift and accurate blows of a heavy axe into hind quarters, fore quarters, and sides. These are then taken to the trimmers, who artistically shape hams and shoulders, cut out ribs and spare ribs from the flanks, leaving flat sides of bacon. The trimmers' waste slips through shoots into a room below, where it is at once manufactured into brawn and Bologna sausages. The joints meanwhile descend by other shoots to the pickling department, where the shoulders and spare ribs are packed at once in barrels, which are afterwards injected with fluid pickle at a high pressure; while the hams and bacon are first allowed to lie for some days in dry pickle in a cold room, and then packed, the former in canvas bags, the latter in strong wooden cases, for the market. Such are the operations of a packing house, one of the largest of which occupies fourteen acres of land, contains sixty-four acres of floors, kills ten thousand hogs daily at certain seasons of the year, and employs more than two thousand hands!

The putrescible refuse produced in the packing and slaughtering houses of Chicago amounts to more than two hundred tons daily. This is converted into artificial manure by cooking and drying; and the business of "rendering" the offal into fertilizer was carried on, until the last few years, in so careless and unscientific a manner that Chicago was nearly poisoned by the noxious gases generated in the process. Early in 1877 however Dr. Oscar Wolff, a man of great energy, was appointed Health Commissioner, and backed both by municipal authority and public opinion, he determined on a thorough reform in the conduct of this industry. Means for abating the nuisance having first been devised, he tried to procure their adoption, but the offenders, wealthy and powerful corporations, were obstinate in their resistance to reform, and it was only after many failures and in face of great difficulties that Dr. Wolff succeeded in establishing the legal claim of the municipality to control the operations of the packers. A test case, which was vigorously fought right up to the supreme court by a determined combination of capitalists, was finally won by the Commissioner, and notice was given to the houses that unless the nuisance was forthwith abated, the Board of Health would seize and close every one of them. Once defeated, the packers showed the true American spirit, setting themselves heartily to work to apply and improve upon the suggested remedy, with the result that a system of rendering has been introduced which, working under strict municipal supervision, has completely cured the evil, with advantage to all parties.

Originally the offal was cooked in iron tanks by steam, at a pressure of forty pounds to the square inch, and the fetid gases generated during this process were allowed to pass directly into the open air. After eight or ten hours the tank was opened and the material drawn into wooden vats, where the fat was skimmed, the water drained away, and the solid remainder then transferred to the dryer. This consisted of a revolving cylinder, thirty feet long and three feet diameter, furnished with stirrers attached to the axle, and heated by a current of hot air passing through the chamber. Large volumes of noxious gases were generated in this process also, and when Dr. Wolff took the matter in hand, the atmosphere of Chicago had become almost unbearable.

Now, both cooking and drying take place in closed vessels, and the gases evolved, having first been drained of their watery vapour by condensation, are carried in pipes to a tank partially filled with gasoline, whence, charged with highly inflammable hydro-carbon vapour, they flow over the coal-beds of the furnaces, and supply additional heat to the steam boilers. In some cases a portion of the carburized gas is made use of to light the factory as well.

Chicago's facilities for the grain trade are probably unequalled in the world. There are nineteen grain elevators in the city, having a total warehousing capacity of sixteen million bushels, and handling yearly nearly one hundred and fifty million bushels. These buildings may be considered as great collections of corn-bins, provided with apparatus for receiving, unloading, and re-loading ships and railway cars. We visited one of the largest, and found a very ugly wooden structure, about three hundred feet square and a hundred and thirty feet high. Two receiving and one discharging lines of railway run through the house, the former in the centre, the latter on one side of it. Ten cars, each containing five hundred bushels of grain, can be unloaded at the same time, an operation which occupies six minutes. The trucks are cleared by mechanical scoops, operated by a quick-running windlass, and the grain falls from the truck into a pit, whence it is lifted by revolving buckets to the top of the house and discharged into a weigh-bin. As each car is emptied, the scoopmen telegraph the fact to the men above; the weight of the grain is ascertained and registered, together with the number and invoiced load of the car, and the contents of the weigh-bin are then spouted into a suitable store-bin. In discharging, the grain runs down wooden spouts, either into railroad cars or into vessels berthed in the basin adjoining the building. It takes twenty-five minutes to weigh and load five thousand bushels of wheat into trucks, but in the case of shipments a cargo is weighed and made ready beforehand, and half a dozen spouts fill up a vessel of ordinary capacity with some sixty thousand bushels in two hours and a half. The elevator we saw, though not the largest in Chicago, could receive a hundred and thirty thousand bushels and discharge a hundred thousand bushels a day. The mercantile operations of the grain trade are much facilitated by a system of State inspection and "grading." A certain number designates a certain quality of any given cereal, and the Liverpool merchant, who, for example, buys "No. 3" winter wheat, or "No. 2" barley, knows exactly what will be the character of the cargo forwarded to fill his orders.

The dining-room of the Grand Pacific Hotel was tenanted during one evening of our stay by a large party of Sioux Indians, returning to the Dakota reservation with their children, who had been educated in the schools of the east. They were clean, good-looking men, well dressed, for the most part in European clothes, and the young fellows who were going back to the wigwam were very pleasant bright youths, glad to be once more among their own people. None of the seniors could speak English, but the Indian agent who had charge of the party translated some of their names, which always refer to some incident in the life of each man. Among them were the following:—Jumping-Thunder, Poor-Wolf, Son-of-the-Star, He-Bear, Runs-after-the-Moon, Cloud-Bull, White-Cow, Passes-the-Evening, Red-Dog, Spotted-Tail, White-Thunder, Black-Crow, Iron-Wing, Two-Bear, Big-Head, Thunder-Hawk, Bull-Eagle, Brother-to-All, Medicine-Bull. There were several squaws with the party, who were not handsome, and some of the men had such feminine faces that we should not have suspected their sex but for their costume.

Base-ball is an American's cricket, and being anxious to see how it is played, I attended a match between the Troy and Chicago Clubs, each represented by a crack team. The game is something like rounders, and not so scientific as cricket, but a very manly form of athletics nevertheless. I was much struck with the contrast between the spectators present, and those to be seen at a good cricket match in England. There were few ladies; and the following notice, which I copied from a placard conspicuously displayed on the walls, will perhaps illustrate the difference to which I have alluded more perfectly than I could describe it:—"The umpire is not to be hissed, insulted, or have any indignity offered him by the spectators. GENTLEMEN will, and others must, be guided by the above hints." This would read oddly at Lord's; but there were a good many "others" among the gentlemen on this occasion, and no doubt the Chicago Base-Ball Club knows its business.

There is a book store at Chicago which must, I think, be the largest retail booksellers' shop in the world. Certainly there is nothing like it in London, whether for the amount or variety of its stock of high-class literature both native and foreign. Its existence literally speaks volumes for the intelligence of Chicago, as do the several excellent literary journals published in the city; and I learnt from Mr. Jansen, the cultivated proprietor of the store in question, that there is immense literary activity existing here alongside of the earnest pursuit of wealth. While I was talking to this gentleman one day, an incident occurred which illustrates Western freedom, or as we should call it, Western impudence. The newsboys peddle papers unchallenged in the halls and corridors of hotels, and even inside the shops, of America, and a very dirty street arab came into Mr. Jansen's store pressing his wares obtrusively on customer after customer, perambulating the large and handsome hall as if it were his own. Mr. Jansen stood it for some time, and at last in the gentlest manner ordered the boy out, whereupon the young ruffian turned on him like a tiger, showed fight, and in violent language refused pointblank to stir. I came very near boxing the impudent young rascal's ears; but Mr. Jansen only followed the custom of his country in treating the trespasser with what seemed to me absurd forbearance.

The American system of fire alarm is interesting and has been brought to great perfection in Chicago. The city is divided into districts, each of which is provided with one or more fire stations, or as we should call them, fire-engine houses, while alarm boxes to the number of five hundred are distributed throughout the city, being usually attached to lamp-posts and conspicuously painted. Each box presents a crank-handle to the public, upon turning which a bell rings, and the number of the box from which the alarm proceeds is recorded on a Morse printing instrument at a central station. On receiving such a warning, the central station calls all the fire stations, whether one or many, situated in the threatened district, giving the number of the box from which the alarm proceeds. If the fire gains ground and additional help is needed, the central office is notified from the nearest box, and the engines of a second or even third district are called in the same way as the first. The fire-engine, team, and firemen are always ready to start. From the ceiling of every station a complete set of harness hangs, provided with hinged collars, which close with a snap, the whole being tilted up on one side so as to admit the horse to his place. The same electric current which sounds the gong unlatches the doors of the stalls, and the horses trot instantly to their proper positions; the swivel harness is tilted over their backs, the collars clasped and they are ready to go. Meanwhile the driver climbs to his seat, and on his pulling a cord hanging from above, the street doors fly open, while the act of starting opens a gas-tap and sends a rush of flame into the fire-box, lighting a fire already laid; the same action shuts the taps of a circulating system which keeps the boiler full of hot water while standing; and the first pull on the reins releases the harness from its ceiling supports. In the next moment the engine is sailing away at a gallop, getting under way in twenty seconds in the day-time, or thirty seconds at night.

At one salvage station in Chicago where there is only a waggon, the men get out in five seconds, night or day; indeed they can do it quicker at night. In this case not only are the horses released by the alarm current, but the same agency pulls the coverlets off the firemen's beds, opens trap-doors in the bedroom floor, and lets fall slides, through which the men slip direct from their beds into the waggon. There are two drivers, and the man who is first on the box, takes up the reins, while the second draws on his "pants" and boots, lying ready one inside the other on the seat. This done, he takes the lines from No. 1, who pulls on his boots and "pants," so that half a block is sometimes covered before the second man has dressed.

By the kindness of "Fire-Marshall" Sweeny we saw the system in operation, and verified with our own eyes and watches the surprising times given above. At one moment the whole building was wrapped in apparent repose. The waggon-room was silent and deserted, the horses were shut in their stalls, while upstairs, eight active fellows feigned sleep under the bed-clothes. Suddenly a gong gave one loud stroke, and as if by magic, the team appeared in place duly harnessed, the coverlets flew to the ceiling of the bedroom, whose floor yawned and swallowed the men as they rolled from their beds into the shoots. Before the Morse instrument had finished printing the number of the box from which the alarm proceeded, before the last reverberation of the gong had died away, the waggon was tearing along the street at a furious gallop, the whole thing having occupied less than five seconds.

America is a great solvent of nationalities. Even the stiff-necked Englishman becomes Americanized in time, while the adaptive German is soon absorbed. Chicago is full of Germans. There are whole streets where the names over the shops are without exception German, and the city is crowded with lager beer saloons, kept by Germans, and displaying German signs. Yet, saving his love for the beer-garden, the Teuton loses all trace of his origin within a few generations in the States, becoming thoroughly American not only in speech and manner, but even in appearance; and it is striking to feel oneself, as happens in many parts of Chicago, in a German town, and yet hear nothing but English spoken.

The banks of Lake Michigan are low and flat, and the surroundings of Chicago have a melancholy air. Michigan Avenue, the plutocratic quarter, lies partly on the lake, and contains some magnificent houses, among which is a palace of Mr. Pullman's; but while the architecture of these wealthy homes, sometimes classic, sometimes Gothic, sometimes Romanesque, has a certain charm, an Englishman always feels surprised at the smallness of the grounds surrounding great houses in the States. Gardening certainly is not a national taste in America.

Chicago was originally built on a swamp, and had no proper drainage either into the lake, or the canal which connects the Chicago river by way of the Illinois with the Mississippi. When the question of sewerage became urgent it was proposed to raise the whole city twelve feet above its original level, and this bold proposition was actually carried out. Great stores, warehouses, hotels, and private dwellings were jacked up and removed, sometimes long distances from their first sites, business being carried on as usual during the operation. Even now it is not uncommon to see a house travelling slowly along one of the less crowded streets, with chimneys smoking, and perhaps even the piano going. We met two such phenomena during our stay; and nothing that we saw in Chicago so forcibly reminded us at once of the energy of its early citizens, and the marvellously short career of a city which was an ash-heap ten years ago, and is the rival of New York to-day.

CHAPTER XIV.

En route FOR THE ROCKY MOUNTAINS.

June 28–30.

THE traveller going west from Chicago may choose between three railroads, which run in parallel courses from the capital of the central states as far as the Missouri river. Each of them "touts" vigorously for custom; their rival time-tables are illustrated works of fiction, and they all advertise the addition of a comfortable dining-car to the usual Pullman "sleeper"—a novelty which on these long journeys is very agreeable, not only from a hungry man's point of view, but because it furnishes a means of whiling away time that might otherwise hang heavily.

The trip from Chicago to Cheyenne, where we made our first halt, occupied two days and two nights, but we certainly were not dull on the road. When tired of our books and easy-chairs, we lounged on the platform, smoking, chatting, and viewing the country, or strolled through the train and amused ourselves with the varied groups of passengers. Here was a knot of Chinamen going west, or a coupled of blanketed redskins; there a flaxen-haired family of Scandinavian emigrants, or a party of Irish exiles. When tired of talking to one or another of these groups we had a rubber; or if night were falling, watched the clouds aflame with the fiery colours of a prairie sunset; while a good bed and the dining-car supplied us with ample material comforts. Nor were our mental wants neglected by the newsboy, who not only peddled papers, pea-nuts, candy, and cigars, but plied us with copious cheap literature both heavy and light.

The American reprints of our best contemporary authors are very tempting ware. Not only can all the best and worst novels, from George Eliot to Ouida, be bought for from fivepence to tenpence apiece, well printed, on excellent paper; but such books as the "Memoirs of Madame de Rémusat," Justin McCarthy's "History of our own Times," and Matthew Arnold's "Wordsworth," are offered at similar prices in the "Franklin Square Library," published by Harper Brothers. The question of international copyright is a delicate one to discuss with Americans, as indeed would be the proprietorship of your own handkerchief with a pickpocket; but the subject is capable of original treatment, and was recently placed in quite a new light by the *New York Herald*. "We believe," says Mr. Bennett's paper, "that the absence of an international copyright is more widely regretted in this country than in England, though for a different reason. People lament that this system makes cheap such trash as Wilkie Collins,* and makes dear those good books which can only be purchased in an English edition; while it well-nigh arrests the literary activity of this country. The land is flooded with foreign thought, and consequently dwarfed in all that part of its intellectual activity which would choose to manifest itself in literature. If American literature were protected by a copyright law which would compel proper remuneration to foreign writers, this would be otherwise."

Although the *Herald*, being furious against Mr. Wilkie Collins, is more anxious to say something offensive about his works than

---

* It is only fair to Mr. Collins to say that the article from which I quote was written in reply to some excellent if severe remarks of his on the question of international copyright.

to elucidate the question of international copyright, this remarkable utterance is worthy of a moment's consideration. It certainly is not complimentary to the literary activity of America to say that it is arrested by the widespread publication of low-priced English "trash;" yet this is the writer's position, for he tells us that good or thoughtful books are not cheaply reproduced, but must be bought in dear English editions; while in the same breath he declares that native ideas are swamped in a flood of foreign thought. The *Herald*, being angry, forgot that some of the best contemporary English literature is reproduced in a cheap form side by side with the "trash"; witness the examples I have already given: but thoughtful books like these, sown broadcast throughout the States, ought surely to stimulate rather than drown the literary activity of the country. It is not disgraceful for America to admit, what the catalogues of her publishers silently proclaim, that she has not yet become a literary nation, but it would be more dignified if she paid for the "foreign thought" she now steals, instead of accusing it of dwarfing her literary energies. The Americans are not only greedy readers, but great buyers of books. The circulating library which fosters the production of "trash" in England, is happily unknown in the States, and its place is taken by the issue of large low-priced editions. Book-buyers are critical readers, and the American system encourages a habit of judicious selection; while the circulating library lowers literary taste and checks the formation of private collections of books.

Leaving Chicago, the train enters at once on the prairies, which, though they appear level, are low, rolling hills of drift. These were formerly covered with buffalo grass and flowers, but the first has been almost entirely replaced by cultivation, while the sunflowers and marigolds fringing the sides of the track, are all that remain of the last. On either side of the railway a wide, well-farmed, undulating country, and far reaching views, remind the traveller of the Lothians; while the fields are green with oats, and the lush foliage of Indian corn. Here and there stretches of prairie grass occur, which, diversified as they are with groups of oaks, give a park-like appearance to the scenery; but the prairie becomes quite treeless about fifty miles beyond Chicago.

The prairies form probably the most important natural feature of America, for in them is centred her great agricultural wealth. They are vast natural meadows, sometimes hundreds of miles in extent, having a deep soil of great fertility, with scarcely any exposures of the underlying rocks. The whole of America between the Alleghanies and the Rocky Mountains is a flat depression, occupied as far south as lat. 40° by the glacial drift which remained after the ice age had passed away. This drift covers the feet of the Rocky Mountains, and forms great shoulders on their flanks, whence it slopes gently to the valley of the Mississippi; while a similar slope extends from the western side of the Alleghanies to the "Father of Waters" which occupies the middle of the continent, and carries the drainage of its central depression to the Gulf. The drift of the Mississippi valley is overlaid by the "bluff" formation—a thick widespread deposit of fine adhesive yellow loam, or loess, obscurely stratified, and derived from the muds of the shallow inland seas which covered Central America after the close of the glacial period. This material is easily dug by the spade, but resists atmospheric influences so perfectly that walls of wells and railroad cuttings stand like masonry. Where the loess has been excavated by rivers, the banks have cliff-like sides, sometimes more than two hundred feet in height, which rise so steeply from the water that a man cannot climb them, although they have no rocky framework and are destitute even of pebbles. These thick beds of finely comminuted soil cover vast areas, sometimes hundreds of miles across; they form the arable land of the great corn and wheat growing states, and constitute the finest farming region in America; the heart of what is at present the granary of the world.

Good land and plenty of it—not manufacturing skill or supremacy—is the true secret of America's prosperity. Four-fifths of her total exports consist of raw materials and food stuffs, and nearly one-half of them are food stuffs alone. If we as free traders are right in believing that her methods of fostering manufacture are mistaken, it is fortunate for the States that such a policy affects only one-fifth of her whole turn-over. There is still more than twice as much unimproved as improved land in America; and her land legislation is in strong contrast with her industrial policy, being wise and liberal instead of short-sighted and reactionary. Under the free homestead law, every naturalized citizen of the United States can have a farm of a hundred and sixty acres without charge, solely upon condition that he puts a specified amount of work into the land within a given time; and after the law has been complied with in this respect, he may if he pleases "pre-empt" a second hundred and sixty acres at an almost nominal price per acre. Favoured by such an Act, men with little capital, and even very poor men, can become proprietors by hiring themselves out during the busier agricultural seasons at the high wages prevailing in a country of few labourers, and working on their own homesteads in the remaining months of the year. There are two and a half millions of farms in the States, many of which have been acquired in this manner; and the effect of the homestead law is to turn industrious emigrants into proprietors, instead of allowing them to remain labourers, to the disadvantage of State and individual alike. In the four great farming states of Illinois, Indiana, Iowa, and Ohio, there is only one labourer to every four farmers—a state of things which stimulates personal energy and develops character in a remarkable manner, and a consummation devoutly to be wished in the British Islands. For this question of tenant *versus* proprietor is becoming the *crux* of English agriculture in face of the ever-increasing American competition. We alone of all nations retain a modified feudal system, with the result that the condition of the English agricultural labourer is a disgrace not only to our Christianity but to our commercial insight. During the year 1880, just half a million pairs of hands poured into the United States, and the greater part of them found their way to the land. If American law did not encourage proprietorship and discourage tenancy, these emigrants would remain only labourers in exile; but instead of this they become land-owners, and in the act of extending the cultivation of cheap land, strike blow after blow at the prosperity of English agriculture. There is no surplus land in England, but that is no reason why law and custom should both try to diminish the number of English land-owners. We cannot give our labourers homesteads, but we can free the land, and leave the rest to the action of time and natural laws.

The trains of all the three competing lines arrived at Council Bluffs, the terminus of the Chicago and Rock Island Railway, within a few moments of each other, after a run of nearly five hundred miles. We gave ourselves an excellent farewell dinner in the travelling restaurant, and toasted the sentiment heading its *menu* in a bottle of Perrier-Jouet—

> "Whizzing past the station, rattling o'er the vale,
> Really this is pleasant, dining on the rail."

The Missouri is a wide, turbid stream of yellow water, flowing between high bluffs of loess, far removed from its existing bed. It is crossed by a beautiful iron cobweb, rather than bridge, and on the farther side of the river the Union Pacific Railway receives the passengers for the transcontinental journey. This road follows the valley of the Platte, an affluent of the Missouri, for nearly three hundred miles, over level country skirted on either hand by rolling prairie. The Platte was probably a vast stream when America was emerging from the melting glaciers, and its old banks form remote bluffs on each side of the present river. After crossing the Missouri, the train enters the state of Nebraska, throughout whose eastern half cultivation steadily declines, and whose western moiety has all the appearance of a desert. The rainfall is very unequally distributed in North America, varying, in regard to the line of our route, from an ample supply in the eastern states, to zero in Colorado. The prevailing winds, blowing from the Pacific are westerly, but their moisture falls chiefly on the Sierra Nevada, only a little of it reaching the Rocky Mountains, and none passing further eastward. The Atlantic moisture on the other hand penetrates beyond the low barrier of the Alleghany range, and is strongly reinforced by evaporation from the great lakes, whose vapours supply rain to and beyond the middle states. The western half of Nebraska however, together with Wyoming and Colorado, has an almost rainless climate, and the soil can only be cultivated by the aid of irrigation. It is believed that the moisture belt has followed the railway, or rather the westward extension of cultivation to which the railway has given rise, and much is expected from the further planting of trees. Grants of land in the arid district are made both by the State and the Union Pacific Railway, on conditions of tree culture, but it seems very doubtful if any expedients short of irrigation, will avail for the successful prosecution of agriculture in so dry a region.

Western Nebraska and Wyoming are now, and will probably always remain, cattle-raising states. The soil, though so parched, produces nutritious dwarf grasses, formerly the food of the buffalo, who lived in vast herds among the natural meadows bordering the feeble prairie affluents of the Platte. The wasteful Indian and indiscriminate slaughter of these animals for the sake of their skins, have almost exterminated the buffaloes, but their place has been taken by tens of thousands of cattle, which graze summer and winter on the prairie grasses both on this and the further side of the range. The winter snows, though sometimes deep enough to be fatal to sheep, do little harm to cattle, which thrive and multiply without attention of any kind and without artificial shelter. "Wyoming," said a ranchman with whom I fell into conversation in the train, "is God's own footstool for cattle." Once a year there is a "round up," when the beasts are driven by mounted stockmen into great corrals, or enclosures; part of the stock is selected for sale, and the calves, running beside their mothers, are branded with the distinctive mark of each proprietor: after which the herds are again turned loose, animals which cannot be definitely claimed by any one being divided among the ranchmen. Cattle-raising is a profitable business, and is pursued by many Englishmen who like the sporting character of the life, and think it more befitting a gentleman than commerce or agriculture.

We were sleeping when the train passed from the cultivated into the uncultivated portion of Nebraska, and awoke to find ourselves surrounded by a yellow brown desert, stretching in all directions to the visible horizon. Here and there were villages of the marmot-like prairie dogs, who sat up on end and watched the passing train, or bolted into their holes at our approach. Scattered tufts of sage brush abounded, together with a dwarf pear-shaped cactus, with a large and beautiful yellow bloom. Game of all kinds was conspicuous by its absence; instead of herds of buffalo and deer, we only saw one antelope. But a strange spoor puzzled us for a long time. Every here and there, beaten tracks radiated from the telegraph posts, while a close inspection showed that many of the posts themselves were rubbed smooth up to a certain height from the ground. After many guesses we concluded that the cattle "bless the Duke of Argyll" on these rough masts, and even learnt that the beasts are dainty in their choice, for the smoothest tree stems were always selected, and those having projecting knots, however small, avoided.

I was not much impressed with this portion of the Union Pacific Railroad as an engineering work, and presume that the constructive wonders, of which we hear so much, will be found hereafter among the mountains. The line is straight and nearly dead level for hundreds of miles. The loess forms a good natural road-bed, upon which the sleepers are laid down without preparation of any kind, and the rails are simply secured with hooked spikes. There are very few bridges west of the Missouri river, the prairie affluents of the Platte being few, and usually small enough to be crossed by culverts. The line is unfenced after leaving the cultivated country, and the train clears the track of cattle by means of the whistle during daylight and the cow-catcher at night. The depôts are rough wooden houses, usually accompanied by a few tiny shanties, which from want of wood in this treeless region are often made entirely of old sleepers daubed with mud. These are the desolate homes of the well-tenters, or men in charge of the windmills and pumps which furnish water to the locomotives from wells bored through the drift down to the bed-rock. The road rises imperceptibly from the Missouri Valley to an elevation of five thousand feet at Sidney. Here the snow, of which little falls even at this elevation, drifts into depressions, crossing which the rails are protected by snow sheds; rough lean-tos of boards and posts, like the first stage of a child's house of cards. The old emigrants' road follows, like the railway, the level bed of the Platte, and is almost always in view from the train. We passed many waggon teams during the day, and saw many camp fires at night, never without thoughts of the early pioneers who were spent by the thousand toils and dangers of the desert, for the advantage of those who now follow them luxuriously in a Pullman sleeping car.

The air of the prairies is indescribably pure and exhilarating. The sun sets dressed in garments of scarlet and gold such as he never wears in Europe, and for a few minutes before his departure all heaven is aflame; but no sooner has he fallen below the horizon than the shadows of night descend, and the chill of winter succeeds to the heat of day. On the first night of the trip we were awakened by a prairie thunderstorm. No rain fell, but the lightning flashed so quickly that at no time could I count more than four or five between the discharges, which for the most part were quite continuous; while the thunder sounded as if the train were being smashed to atoms. Next morning, the sun being hot and the air clear, we saw a great deal of mirage. The high bluffs of the old river-bed seemed to become islands, lying in wide spaces of silver grey sea and receding to enormous distances: the last effect was a purely subjective one, for as the pseudo-islands returned to their true forms, their real distance became apparent.

How we lamented the late dining-car while travelling on the Union Pacific Railroad! Three times a day the train stops for meals at "eating stations"—a most fitting title for what are in no sense refreshment-rooms; and a medley crowd of human beings, clad for the most part in brown holland coats, or "dusters," rushes tumultuously into the tepid saloon, while the engine blows off steam with open throat, and gongs are clashed as the signal that food is ready. All the world is hungry and dirty, but there is no time to negotiate for a sprinkle from the hose with which the car reservoirs are filling, so we jostle, white, yellow, and red skins alike, in the ardent competition for good places and early service. Two or three dishes of tough meat—antelope is often served—and one or two sweets, eaten in haste and washed down by tea, coffee, or iced water, promote an indigestion which the best Havannah fails to allay; and we learned at length that a store of canned meats and fruits, which the coloured attendant kindly keeps and eats for us, together with a bottle of champagne, fresh from the ice of the water reservoir, is the best substitute for the travelling restaurant.

Arrived at Cheyenne, the Rocky Mountains were in full view, but we left the train at this point, and turning south by the Colorado Central Railway, skirted the range for about fifty miles to the little village of Longmont, whence we proposed to enter the mountains, our first objective being Estes Park, the property of Lord Dunraven. Cheyenne itself, now the centre of the cattle trade of Wyoming, was only settled in 1867, acquiring almost immediately a population of six thousand souls, thanks to the operations of the Transcontinental Railway, since the completion of which the town has slightly diminished in numbers. Like all the cities of America, called into sudden existence as camps for the armies of civilization in their rapid western march, Cheyenne was once a headquarters of rowdyism, where there was a "man for breakfast" every morning, while almost every house was a

EN ROUTE TO THE ROCKY MOUNTAINS.

gambling den or a brothel. But Cheyenne is orderly enough now. The mining towns of California taught America how to deal with turbulent populations, and as the number of steady citizens increased a vigilance committee was improvised, who promptly hanged some of the worst desperadoes, with the effect of encouraging the others either to mend their ways or depart.

The Colorado Central Railroad skirts the Rocky Mountains closely, traversing beds of coarse drift which lie upon the hillsides to heights of more than five thousand feet. Above these appear the higher slopes and summits of the hills, whose feet are deeply buried in the enormous masses of rubbish which have been excavated from the glens by the action of ice and shot around the base of the range, whence the plains stretch away like a boundless ocean, out of whose yellow and hazy levels rise blue hills, seamed with dark glens, rough with forests, and capped with scattered patches of gleaming snow. The route crosses some of the chief affluents of the Platte river, whose sources are the snows of the range. Such Pacific vapours as escape condensation by the Sierra Nevada, deposit their remaining moisture as snow on the Rockies, but no rain falls from them on the plains, the air sponge being completely wrung out by the mountains. The streams are used for irrigation, and the valleys of the Cache la Poudre, the Big Thompson, Little Thompson, and St. Vrain rivers, have been partially changed from deserts into gardens by this means. Large tracts however still remain unwatered, and there are spots in the fertile areas to which water cannot easily be carried; hence the train crosses now a wilderness, and now a wheat-field, which succeed each other like strips of cropping and ploughed land in an allotment ground. The soil, an easily worked sandy loam, lends itself admirably to the excavation of the ditches, which are cut out by a scoop-like plough, labour being too dear in America for the use of the spade. The work, though roughly done, is almost as effective as the elaborate grading of the Lombardian plains, which has cost centuries of patient labour.

Longmont is an irrigated oasis, surrounded on all sides by arid desert, and depending for its water supply on the snows of the Rocky Mountains. To-morrow we shall follow the stream that supplies its people, fertilizes its land, and waters its shade trees, into the heart of the range, whose peaks we can see clearly outlined on the evening sky across fifteen miles of intervening plain. The hills to the southward were capped with heavy thunder-clouds on our arrival, and the lightning was flashing brilliantly, while a cold air sighed as if a storm were coming. "It will surely rain to-night," we said to our host. "I guess not," was the answer; "the 'Colorado zephyr' blows up most nights and there's rain on the range every day in the two summer months, but it a'n't rained any in Longmont for thirteen months, and won't to-night." Which prophecy came true. The black cap remained firmly fixed on the brows of the hills, the breeze died out; only the high, silent lightning continued to flash incessantly long after two weary Englishmen had sought their hard but welcome couches.

CHAPTER XV.

IN THE ROCKY MOUNTAINS—ESTES PARK.

July 1-14.

THE United States present to the traveller crossing them from east to west three well-marked divisions which may be called the eastern, middle, and western regions. The first includes the Atlantic slope and Alleghany range, the latter a series of parallel ridges, nowhere more than seven thousand feet in elevation, densely wooded, and separated by fertile valleys, settled, and cultivated. The middle region comprises the great central depression of the continent, a vast basin of drift and alluvium more than a thousand miles wide, and rising gently on either hand from the valley of the Mississippi to the flanks of the Alleghanies on the east, and those of the Rocky Mountains on the west. The western division is a tangle of mountains extending from the edge of the plains to the Pacific. The eastern border of this vast assemblage of hills is usually called the Rocky Mountains, and its western edge the Sierra Nevada, but the space intervening between these two ranges is filled with rock masses which, though broken by immense stretches of plain, are never quite detached; and American geographers now proposed to designate the groups of mountains occupying Western North America as the Cordilleras, the old name of the Andes remaining applicable to the South American chains bordering on the Pacific. From the moment the traveller enters the Cordilleras from the east, he "threads his way," to use the words of Professor Whitney, the State geologist of California, " through narrow, intricate defiles, winds around or crosses over innumerable spurs and ridges, traverses narrow valleys, and occasional broad plains, the former sometimes green and attractive, the latter always arid and repulsive to the last degree. He never descends below four thousand feet above sea-level, and is never out of sight of mountains; these always environ him with thinly wooded flanks, and sterile and craggy summits, often glistening with great patches of snow, which gradually lessen as summer approaches. In the distance, these mountain ranges, behind their atmosphere of purple haze, seem massive and uniform in character; as he approaches each one, he finds it presenting some new charm of hidden valley or cañon deeply countersunk into the mountain side. As he rises still higher, he may quench his thirst at the refreshing spring of pure water fed by the melting snow above, while the grandeur of the rocky masses, the purity of the air, the solitariness and the almost infinite extent of the panorama opened before him, when he fairly reaches the summit, leave upon his mind an ineffaceable impression of the peculiar features of our western mountain scenery. It is through and over these mountain ranges that the Pacific Railway threads its way across the continent." That portion of the Rocky Mountains lying within the limits of the state of Colorado is distinguished by the occurrence of great natural parks. Of these North, Middle, and South Parks are the most considerable, and Estes Park is perhaps the most beautiful. All of them are elevated plains, sometimes more than two thousand square miles in extent, and from seven to ten thousand feet above the sea, surrounded by the peaks of the range and watered by the streams flowing from its snows.

We left Longmont in a four-horse stage, a coach with the body hung upon leather straps, springs being useless in mountain vehicles. Our route for the first ten miles lay over the plain, irrigated here, and arid there, a chequer-board of wilderness and vegetation. At the eleventh mile we entered the St. Vrain Cañon, where at a height of four thousand feet from sea-level, the mountains themselves began to appear above the vast beds of drift which cover their feet and slope from their shoulders to the Mississippi, six hundred miles away. The word "cañon," adopted from Spanish America, denotes a river valley with steep sides, such as is excavated by running water in rainless countries where streams originate in remote sources and have no lateral affluents. This state of things results in the cutting of deep notches instead of the open V-shaped valleys to which we are accustomed; and these notches, called cañons when large, and gulches when small, are peculiarly characteristic of the Cordillera scenery.

Our road—save the mark!—wound up, and sometimes through, the St. Vrain river, dominated on the right by high sandstone cliffs, and fringed on the left by a narrow strip of cultivated land and cottonwood trees, whose green leaves were a welcome sight after the treeless plains. "Flumes," or wooden spouts, tapped the stream here and there, and carried its fertilizing waters, by rough but often boldly conceived aqueducts, to the rainless fields of the arid desert below. Presently from beneath the sandstone cliffs the granite core of the mountains appeared and the structure of the range became apparent. Below the drift of the plains a level sheet of sedimentary rocks stretches right across the middle region of America and was once continuous to the Pacific·

IN THE ROCKY MOUNTAINS—ESTES PARK.

Through this floor the primitive rocks forming the mass of the Cordilleras have been thrust forcibly upwards, and the once horizontal strata now lie broken and tilted at high angles on the mountain sides. The sandstone cliffs in the St. Vrain Cañon are the edges of such uplifted strata, and though not so highly inclined as similar rocks flanking the range elsewhere, they plainly bespeak the intrusive character of the mountain masses. The granite has crystallized into huge irregular cubes, which weathering most at their bounding surfaces, produce the effect of cyclopean masonry, whose courses have been worn by time and disturbed by subsidence or convulsion. These seeming walls and towers are capped here and there by isolated blocks, poised as if by the hand of man, and threatening to fall with every gale. They, like the logan stones of Cornwall, are the result of weathering, and there are doubtless thousands of rocking stones to be found among these hills. The granite, being felspathic, decomposes easily, giving rise to great sand-slides or tali of fine *débris*, while the road, which is only a track worn by the wheels of the stage, is deeply covered with coarse granitic sand. The flanks of the hills are sparsely clothed with pines which huddle together in the sheltered ravines, and climb slopes almost too steep for the foot; while the wayside is carpeted with dwarf grasses and pear-shaped cactus.

After a drive of thirty-six miles, occupying seven hours, we looked down upon Estes Park, a flat, grassy depression, about four miles long and half as wide, dotted over with pines, bisected by a brawling stream, and entirely surrounded by mountains, some timbered to their summits, others rising above the timber line and streaked here and there with snow. The park evidently occupies the site of an ancient lake whose waters have escaped; but it now forms a natural amphitheatre where peak and plain, forest and stream, are combined, almost theatrically, to form a picture having the charm of a park with the sublime features of a mountain range.

The volatile member of our party, a man of pre-eminently social nature, had diluted the heat and industries of Chicago with hopes of being shortly "alone with nature among the everlasting hills;" and even the cynical balance of the expedition expected solitude as well as cool air in the Cordilleras. It is well known that Estes Park was purchased some years ago by Lord Dunraven, and we unconsciously presumed that his lordship became the proprietor of this remote estate in the character either of Timon or Nimrod. We were certainly told that besides the earl's cottage there was a good hotel in the park, but we thought this was probably a hospitable provision for his lordship's sporting friends and occasional English tourists. Commercial enterprise however grows rank on American soil, and even a child of primogeniture becomes a land speculator in the West. The hotel at Estes Park is a large establishment, and what the Americans call a "health resort," having a resident doctor and a regular *clientèle* of invalids, who not only derive great benefit from the air of this mountain sanatorium, but carry away, and therefore presumably spread, most favourable impressions of the location, thanks to the judicious management which makes every guest acquainted not only with the beauty of the park but all its natural advantages whether for sport or agriculture. Hence, instead of being alone with nature, we found ourselves in a gay and crowded house, the company comprising several invalids, a few fishermen, a number of American tourists, and some foreign waifs and strays like ourselves. The host, to our intense surprise, greeted us with the cultivated voice and manner of a thorough English gentleman, and we found later that he was Lord Dunraven's partner in the purchase, who, with his pretty American wife, lives in a charming cottage near the hotel, and manages the affairs of the Estes Park Company, Limited, into whose hands the estate has now passed. For the first time since leaving New York we wondered whether we ought to dress for dinner; and this in the Rocky Mountains! But the war-paint of civilization had been forwarded with our heavy luggage to San Francisco, and both cynic and socialist searched their hand-bags in vain even for a linen collar.

IN THE ROCKY MOUNTAINS—ESTES PARK.

Our host was indefatigable for the amusement of his guests. Yesterday he drove a party of us round the park in his four-in-hand, and the journey was interesting as much from the superb driving over roadless hill-sides as from the wild beauty of the scenery. To-day he gave a picnic in Clear Creek, when the toilettes were as pretty and the lunch as good as if we had been under the trees of Cliefden Woods. To-morrow, a fishing party starts for the Big Thompson, where if any fishermen are as lucky as ourselves, they may take, as we did, a hundred and twenty trout in a short afternoon. In the evenings the saloon was full and the piano never idle, while flirtation flourished on the verandah, as rapid and rank of growth as on the stairs of a London house in the season. Such was our introduction to life in the Rocky Mountains!

Estes Park is rather more than seven thousand feet above sea-level, and the hotel stands in the centre of a vast semicircle of hills, some of which are among the highest in the Rocky Mountains. Long's Peak, only a little lower than Mont Blanc, lies on the left; Olympus and Ida—the latter named after our host's wife —face the hotel; and thence the range trends away northward, becoming lower as it goes. There is no definite snow-line, and what little snow remains lies in the gullies and among the higher timber. The timber-line however is clearly defined at an altitude of about twelve thousand feet, and above that the summits are bare rock. This absence of snow in summer from heights of nearly fifteen thousand feet, in latitude 41°, and during winter, from plains more than seven thousand feet above the sea, is very surprising. But the great dryness of the atmosphere which it bespeaks gives to the enclosed parks of Colorado one of the most beautiful and exhilarating climates in the world. The air is deliciously cool although the sun is hot; every day breaks with a cloudless sky, and the sunrises offer startling spectacles of pure colours; a cool breeze rises every morning at ten o'clock, and blows fitfully till sunset. At night every star looks out of a deeply blue sky, and the Milky Way throws a broad and brilliant band across the heavens. It is never too hot for exertion during the day, nor too cold at night, and the atmosphere is so clear that we can distinguish all the details of Long's Peak from base to summit. In this dry air the nails become brittle and the hair harsh, food dries up, and bread becomes biscuit in a very short time. Lightning is always playing about the horizon, be the sky never so clear, and electric sparks are given off on approaching a knuckle to metal after shuffling across the floor in woollen socks. Our friend the doctor once produced an explosion like that of a rifle by pulling some woollen drawers quickly out of a pair of trousers, and the latter were covered with a sheet of flame.

Climbing is difficult at first on account of the dryness of the air, but after getting acclimatized fatigue is hardly felt. One of our party being out of condition, we gave up with regret the ascent of Long's Peak, with the intention of "doing" Pike's Peak, a slightly higher mountain, later on, and meanwhile we found some fine scrambles among the lower hills. One of our pleasantest excursions was to the Black Cañon, which brings a considerable stream of snow water to the Big Thompson River, and leads over a divide, somewhat higher than the timber-line, into Middle Park. This gorge is densely clothed with pines, and an Indian trail sometimes conspicuous, sometimes obscure, but always traceable leads through the forest. The ascent is rough and toilsome, and we tyros were always a little anxious about missing the trail, which would not be easily found again when once lost. On the way we got splendid occasional views of Long's Peak and the range, and finally rose above the timber-line. Here full-grown pines give way very suddenly to bare rock, covered with large patches of granular snow. The air was piercingly cold at this elevation, and, wonder of wonders, we had a rainstorm, showers being common and heavy about the crests of the hills though rarely extending to their feet. We saw no large game on the way, the elk being among the timber at this time of year, and only descending into the park when driven from the higher feeding-grounds by the winter-snows, but we started a few grouse

—large birds like a pheasant, who let you walk up to them before they rise. Coming home by the Big Thompson river, in whose rapid stream the trout were rising fast, we found two beautiful kinds of wild flowers growing in the moist bottoms—a small tiger-lily of brilliant red colour, and a lovely wild cyclamen, the latter thickly clustering on the banks of the creek close to the water's edge.

It was pleasant, returning tired after our daily tramps, to find an excellent dinner of trout and mountain sheep, together with pleasant society, at the hotel; and it was amusing to study Western manners in the billiard-room after dinner. Here a party of ladies and gentlemen, whose toilettes would have passed muster at a suburban garden-party, played pool at one table while a second was occupied by the ranchmen and servants of the estate; the room, which contained the bar, being usually filled with men dressed in canvas " pants " and wide hats, lounging, chewing, and drinking cocktails.

The American artisan assumes equality with the higher classes with perfect *naiveté* and good humour. No operative, especially in the West, doubts that the sale of labour stands on the same level with the sale of dry goods or "notions;" and if we were startled on the night of our arrival at Estes Park to find ourselves seated at the same table with the stage-driver at dinner, he at least proved an amusing and well-informed companion. The American working man is a very different being from his English *confrère*. He is usually the better educated of the two; but those who have mixed with the cream of the latter class know that they are better informed, and more interesting companions than the prejudiced or frivolous sections of our middle classes, in comparison with whom, if they have not easy manners, it is because they are made to feel like social inferiors. The American artisan on the other hand is not sharply separated from the class above him either by dress or by manners. It is only in the workshop that he wears clothes suited to his employment; at home and in the streets his appearance is like that of his employer or any other citizen. This distinction may seem trivial to some people, but the case is one where trifles denote much, and the gap between the skilled artisans of the two countries is far wider than is indicated by differences in a coat. Fresh from England, I once offered a dollar to a New York mechanic who had given me a long and intelligent explanation of a certain process; but I was soon politely given to understand that I had made a mistake, and, while tendering an apology, I wished that such an incident could occur in England. Nothing but the British theory of caste prevents this. Our skilled artisans, would accept nothing, in such a case from an equal, while they are ready to pocket a shilling which, if it comes from a "gentleman," implies no insult, although it pays for no equivalent service. I once asked one of my own workmen, who had reappeared in the workshop when I thought he was in America, why he had come back. "Only to visit my friends," was the reply, "but I took a job to lessen expenses." "Do you earn better wages in the States than here?" "Well, I think about the same, for times are dull on the other side, but it costs me more to live in the States because I have a standing to keep up." "And is that why you are going back?" "Well sir, that is the only reason; I can do about as well in England, all things considered, as in America, but I am a respectable member of society there, and here I am only a moulder." Necessity and custom have given manual labour—inadmissible among the higher classes of the Old World—a new character in America. Every one becomes a handicraftsman on occasion, willingly and without false shame. Hence the operative suffers scarcely any disabilities from labour, while he may avail himself of intellectual and material enjoyments which are reserved for the upper classes in Europe. For sensitive men bred in the refinements of the best European society, the less exclusive habits, less elegant life, and less polished manners of the States form a purgatory; but the country is the paradise of the artisan.

The "earl's cottage" is a pretty boarded house, which would however be more in keeping with its surroundings if built of logs like our host's house. The latter is charming both without and within; a home with the air of an English country house, but decorated with the spoils of nobler game than ours, and graced by the refined taste of an American lady; seated in whose exquisite little drawing-room it was difficult to believe that we were in the heart of the Rocky Mountains. It was easier to recognise the fact however while talking with Hank Farrar, the hunter, who was usually to be found on the piazza of the hotel in the evening. Hank is the guide, philosopher, and friend of every stranger who comes to Estes Park in search of sport; and it was pleasant to listen to his slow good-humoured talk of elk and elk-hunting, and to admire his word-pictures of the chase and camp. Elk is much less abundant in the park than formerly, and a man must now work hard to find his game. In this regard Farrar makes no secret of the fact that he prefers hunting with Englishmen rather than with his own countrymen. The latter he accuses of being lazy; they will not do their fair share of work in camp, or slave all day for a shot. An Englishman on the other hand takes his full half of the labour in caring for and picketing the horses, camping, cooking, and breadmaking, while he is always earnest about his work, and will spare himself no fatigue to get his elk or mountain sheep. This was not said to please an English listener,—that is not an American fashion; and Farrar illustrated his views with so many stories that I fully believe his statement.

Good society, scenery, and trout-fishing had already detained us for a fortnight among the mountains, when we tore ourselves away from kind friends and excellent quarters and started for Longmont, *en route* for Denver, the capital of the west. The stage carried a much heavier load this time, needing a six-horse team; and the skill of the driver, which had not struck us so much on the lighter coach, became very conspicuous—disagreeably so at times — on the return journey. On three occasions we came as near capsizing as it was possible to do without failing; twice when the driver's attention had been diverted from his horses for a moment to accept a chew of "Navy plug" from a friend; and once when the off middle leader hitched his hind leg up in the whippletree while descending a hill where pulling up was impossible. In the last case the horse was so stimulated by the thunderstorm of oaths which broke out upon the instant, that under its influence he continued to canter on three legs till we reached level ground, and thus averted an accident which was inevitable if he had fallen. It is difficult to make the reader understand the character of these mountain roads by any description without appearing to exaggerate their dangers; but I may say that the stage-driver's worst enemy is sideling land, traversing which the heavily loaded coach, with its high centre of gravity, often hangs over at dangerous angles. Labour again is so dear that mountain road-making cannot afford much assistance from art, and small gulches are consequently filled up with a minimum quantity of boulders or pine stumps. In these cases it is really necessary to drive to an inch, which, with six horses and a heavy rolling coach, requires great coolness and skill. The bridges over streams or wide gulches are made by throwing two stout pines across the gap and laying smaller pines across these again, forming a corduroy road, whose loose timbers rattle and shake under the passing stage, or it may be break, as happened to us at one such place, though fortunately the team was landed before the pines cracked, and the horses were able to drag the stage up the gradually sinking incline.

We changed horses three times in the thirty-six miles. The stables are shanties of rough pine boards buried among the mountains. At one of these the young fellow in charge, handsome, active, but in very fine-drawn condition, was addressed by the driver as follows:—"What do you live on here Tom anyhow?" "Wal, I get a few flies mixed up sometimes, I guess." "Haow do they go with mountain scenery?" "Pretty wal I reckon, but I hev to live most of the time on the scenery." From this point we started before the stage on foot, and, the road rising, did seven miles before we were picked up again. Making a short cut in the course of this walk, we turned a point whence the plains became suddenly visible. At first sight we could hardly persuade ourselves they were not the sea, stretching away, flecked with the purple shadows of gliding clouds, to an horizon yellow and dim with dust haze. It was a beautiful scene. High granite towers hemmed in the way on either side and framed two glorious pictures. Looking southwards, we saw the blue-black gorges and sterile summit of Long's Peak, streaked here and there with snow, while to the north lay a mimic ocean, still, sunlit, and boundless. A fortnight in the mountains amidst cool air and clear skies had made us critical, and we grumbled a good deal as the stage emerged from the St. Vrain cañon into the heat and dust-laden atmosphere of the plain. Our hearts turned to the pleasant party of sudden friends we were leaving, and our eyes to the beautiful hills, wrapped in diaphonous garments of azure and purple air, through which, as through a Coan robe, the range, half hiding, half displaying her beauties, showed herself to her lovers.

CHAPTER XVI.

DENVER.

July 14-16.

THE railroad from Longmont to Denver runs almost due south over the plains, skirting the range at an average distance of fifteen miles, but approaching it more nearly now and then. On the right are the blue hills, capped as we pass with pink sunset clouds, while to the left stretches an apparently boundless desert of yellowish drift, arid, treeless, and, except for patches of cactus, entirely bare; the home of chipmunks—small striped squirrels—and prairie dogs. The mountain outlines are extremely sharp and jagged, showing no signs of glaciation, and they probably were never covered to their summits by the continental glacier, of whose extent and action so much has been said; but vast terraces of drift run out from the flanks of the hills into the plain, looking like unfinished railway embankments. Massive as the range is, it does not impress the traveller as much as the mountains of Switzerland. There is hardly any snow, and the clearness of the air leaves nothing to the imagination, which, always taking the unknown for the magnificent, creates for itself the sense of size out of clouded peaks and gloomy gorges. The air of Colorado is so transparent that it is impossible to estimate distances; instead of fifteen miles away the hills look close at hand. A couple of Englishmen once started, so they say, from Denver for the foot hills, judging them to be four miles off. After walking eight miles and finding themselves apparently no nearer to the range, they came to the Denver irrigation ditch, about four feet wide. One of them stopped on the bank and began to strip, his companion exclaiming, "Why, what are you going to do?" "I am going to swim this river." "Why man, it's a ditch and only a yard or so across." "How the deuce do I know it isn't a quarter of a mile? We've been fooled enough already, and I'm not going to risk a wetting; you can jump if you like." This atmospheric transparency not only impairs the power of judging distances, but seems to dwarf the size of objects as well. A line of hills nearly two hundred miles long is in view from the cars; they are high, massive, and occasionally snow-capped, yet we are obliged to tell ourselves that they are part of one of the great mountain ranges of the world. The plains on the other hand are almost painfully impressive, so wide and desolate are they. There are no mountain streams between Longmont and Denver; and no strips of cultivation therefore break the monotony of the desert landscape; but here and there the derrick and engine-house of a coal-mine rise like a black island out of the plain. The glacial drift is thinner here than it is further north, and the cretaceous strata below it contain beds of lignite which are worked wherever the overlying mass of sand and pebbles is not too thick.

The cars of the Colorado Central Railroad are filled for the most part with miners or men connected with mining interests, and we observed that most of them carry arms. Opposite me a young giant in a blue flannel shirt and canvas trowsers stretched himself, now this way, now that, in search of a comfortable position for a nap, and as he rolled sleepily about a pretty little revolver dropped from his pocket. I picked it up, and gently waking the young Hercules, suggested that if the pistol was loaded it would be better not lying around loose. With a mixture of thanks and oaths he re-pocketed the weapon and took another awful reach after comfort; but the thing was on the floor again within a few minutes and I thought it best to secure it until my friend should awake. As we neared Denver, the giant, refreshed with slumber, took the revolver once more from my hands and, wishing I suppose to repay my attention, said in a hoarse voice finely flavoured with whisky, that he would show me the "All-firedest hotel in Denver," if I would put myself in his charge. We declined the offer with many thanks and left him playing with his pretty toy, and looking very sorry not to be of service.

The Platte river on which Denver is built, was rolling at head-long speed on our arrival, a mad, muddy torrent, through the bridge just outside the town. Men and lights were moving about the abutments, which were evidently considered in danger of being washed away, and the train crawled over to the other side at a snail's pace. My neighbour in the car was returning from a short journey and had left Denver only four hours before, at which time there was hardly a drop of water in the bed of the Platte. Floods like these arise from heavy rains on the range, where the clouds sometimes discharge their burden like the breaking of a waterspout, and every cañon then carries a boiling stream to the plains. At such times, as upon this occasion, the water rushes in a solid mass five or six feet high down the almost flat and usually narrow bed of the river, spreading right and left to a great distance and wrecking bridges and dwellings in its course. Men on horseback race the flood from higher to lower levels and give what warnings are possible in advance; but little can be done on these occasions beyond watching the railway bridges, and within a few hours the Platte is again empty. At the moment of our arrival, rain was the question of questions in Denver. There had been none for more than a year; the Platte was pumped dry, and the mayor had issued a proclamation enjoining the most rigorous economy in the use of water. Now, every one is cheerful. The wrecks are forgotten, and if the flood had carried away a quarter of the town it would have been welcomed in Denver. The thunder was roaring loudly, and the sky over the range was intensely black as we walked from the depôt to our hotel, but though a drenching rain looked imminent, not a drop fell, and so it is throughout the rainy months. The hill-tops are swathed in clouds, lightning flashes, thunder rolls, and torrents fall on the range, but only an occasional shower wanders out into the plain.

Denver, the capital of Colorado, is one of the peculiar creations of the swift tumultuous advance of American civilization, originating in and sustained by the thirst for gold. Lying out in the plain at some miles' distance from the range, it possesses no mineral wealth itself, but its position makes it the natural metropolis of the Rocky Mountains, and every new mining discovery is a fresh stimulus to its growth. The first settlement of white men within the limits of Denver was made by a party of prospectors who, attracted to Colorado by the reports of gold, camped here in 1857–58. The camp soon grew into a city, and in 1859, not only had a child been born within its walls, but municipal government had been established, a mayor elected, a newspaper published, public worship performed, and a theatre opened. Four years later Denver was almost destroyed by fire, and within another twelvemonth the new wooden houses rising from the ashes were swept away by a great flood. Such events are but episodes in the history of these strange mining towns, and the city now contains twenty thousand inhabitants, thirty hotels, many great commercial houses, a branch of the United

States Mint, fine churches, schools, a splendid opera-house, and, streets of elegant private residences. All this in the heart of the desert.

The town is rectangular in arrangement, as usual; the streets are wide, and the roads—wonder of wonders!—excellent. The citizens are proud of these roads, but without reason, for they have had nothing to do with there being so good; the plain hereabouts consisting of a mixture of loam and gravel which forms hard and durable tracts without artificial aid. But the Western man is apt to take credit to himself whether fairly or unfairly, and in his higher flights would persuade you, if not himself, that the blue mountains themselves and all their mineral wealth are creations of the great republic. Every street is planted with cotton-wood "shade trees," which are watered from ditches lining the side-walks. The shops are excellent and beautifully kept. About half the houses are of brick, the other half being of wood, and the pavements are of planks badly nailed down as usual. The drinking saloons are numerous, tastefully fitted up with walnut-wood and graceful draperies, whose Parisian elegance contrasts strangely with the company frequenting the bars. Handsome horses and equipages are common in the streets, especially in the late afternoon when all the world goes "buggy-riding." This is the time for seeing the ladies of Denver, who are not less fond of dress and jewellery than their New York sisters, and like to display both in their daily drive. The absence of women is a most striking feature of Denver. The streets are full of men, but one rarely sees a woman, and the men themselves appear to form a very fugitive population. A *queue* forms daily at the post-office, waiting for letters addressed "till called for," and seldom numbers less than a hundred people, among whom fresh faces are seen every day. Almost all these men wear the blue shirt denoting a miner's occupation, and this crowd of "transients" forms a strange feature of Western life to our unaccustomed eyes.

The Chinese form an important element in the population of

Denver. Hitherto we have seen but few Chinamen, although they are present in all the American cities. In New York they have superseded washerwomen, while there are factories in Massachusetts—notably a large boot and shoe works at North Adams—"run" by Chinese labour. At Estes Park several Chinamen were employed about the hotel, and they are always to be seen in the cars of the transcontinental railroad; but it is only in Western America that the yellow race assumes any numerical importance. So far as we can judge, the Chinaman seems to fill his humble place in an exemplary manner, and our sympathies are already enlisted on behalf of this well-behaved and industrious worker. But the public clamour against him is loud, and we have as yet had so few opportunities of observation, that we shall reserve our judgment in regard to the Chinese question until we reach California, where the Mongols are most numerous and most unpopular.

Public order has been established in Denver for some years past, but only, as in so many other western cities, by violent means. At the present moment the "rowdies," though strongly represented, are afraid of the respectable element of society, knowing that if a steady citizen were to shoot a rough in the course of a "difficulty," a jury would not convict; whereas if a rowdy is taken red-handed, or only suspected of foul intentions, no mercy is shown. But though the town is generally speaking orderly, outrages sometimes occur. A tram car was attacked in Larimer Street, one of the chief thoughfares, during our short stay, by two fellows, who tried to make away with the cash-box. We were in the street at the time and heard the shots which the conductor discharged from his revolver at the thieves, but being near a small shooting gallery at the moment, we had no notion that highway robbery was being attempted within a few hundred yards of us. The newspapers mentioned the incident next morning but without any comment! On the other hand I have patrolled Denver late at night, and though I saw many picturesque figures, who might be either miners or brigands, lounging at the corners of streets, I was never molested, and the town seemed as quiet as an English village.

One evening we attended a "social hop," to which, in common with all the world, we were invited by public placard. Not knowing whether a social hop might or might not be given by the social evil, but presuming that the city hall would only be lent to respectable people, we paid our fifty cents entrance money and found ourselves among about a hundred persons of both sexes who were waltzing, polking, and quadrilling to the music of a good band. The ladies looked like "helps," and the men like mechanics, but both the dancing and behaviour were excellent. The girls were simply but tastefully dressed and the young men inclined to dandyism. Dance programmes hung from every man's button-hole, and introductions were as ceremonious, and etiquette as strict, as in a London drawing-room. Seeing we were strangers, a polite steward found us partners, and whether for good waltzing, animated conversation, or thoroughgoing enjoyment, we would back the social hoppers of Denver against even a London "small and early."

"There are more flies in Denver than anywhere else in the world and they stick more." Such is the dictum of the natives, and it is true so far as our present experience goes. I have never seen flies thicker or more affectionate. If the waiters did not fan one during meals, only a few fragments of any dish would remain many seconds after the cover is removed; and if the creatures did not sleep at night, life would be a burden.

Colorado is English almost as much as it is American. We knew more about this state ten years ago than the Americans themselves, who regarded it as little better than an arid wilderness. Englishmen early settled here in some numbers, taking up land for cattle ranches, digging irrigation ditches, investing money in real estate, building hotels in Denver, and mining in the range, until they are now quite a commercial power in the state. Among American enterprises in Colorado, Senator Hill's smelting works are the most important. They are situated at

Argo, just outside Denver, and reduce the chief part of the ores mined in the state, turning out about one ton of silver and fifty pounds of gold weekly. The process of silver extraction consists in first crushing and roasting the ores to expel the sulphur; the residue is melted to get rid of the silex and earthy matters, and a metallic "mat" results, which is reduced to a fine powder and gently heated, when the remaining sulphur combines with oxygen from the ore, producing sulphuric acid. This attacks the silver, forming a soluble phosphate, while any gold that may be present remains in the "mat." The silver sulphate then flows over copper plates, which take metallic silver from, and give up copper to the fluid by interchange. The sulphate of copper is sold as such, while the silver, which appears in a white and spongy condition, is dried and finally run into ingots. The gold in the mat is reduced by a secret process known only to Mr. Hill and his manager, and upon this secret the prosperity of the Argo Works is built. Ores differ enormously in value—a lean one, located where transport is easy, being often better worth mining than much richer lodes less accessibly situated; but the average yield of the precious metals at Argo may be taken as sixty ounces of silver and one ounce of gold to the ton of ore. The dry air of Colorado has a curious effect on the sulphurous vapours that issue from the roasting furnaces of the Argo Works. In Swansea, as is well known, vegetation is killed by similar fumes evolved in the reduction of copper, and chimneys are sometimes carried to the tops of hills in order to discharge the copper smoke high up in the air. Here however the sulphurous acid diffuses into the atmosphere and no condensation takes place in consequence of the absence of aqueous vapour.

The range, always in view from Denver, dressed in hourly changing garments of pink and purple, gold and azure, tempted us to return to its cool glens every time our glances sought the west. The attraction was too powerful to be long resisted, and at length our hand-bags were gleefully stuffed a day before the time appointed for our next move up to the mountain towns, or "mining camps" of the Rockies.

CHAPTER XVII.

THE MINING CAMPS OF THE ROCKY MOUNTAINS.

July 17-20.

WE left Denver for Central City, one of the most important mining camps of Colorado, by the Colorado Central Railway, retracing our steps across the plains for fifteen miles to Golden, a small smelting town close to the foot of the range. Here a mountain stream called Clear Creek debouches from a cañon and enters the plain, seeking the Platte river. Golden, though standing on drift, is nearly six thousand feet above the sea, while Central is eight thousand three hundred feet in elevation; and the railway which connects the two places rises therefore two thousand five hundred feet in its course of forty miles. A narrow gauge of three feet six inches has been chosen for the mountain railroads of Colorado, both on account of its lower first cost and because it is better suited for steep inclines than a wider gauge with heavier rolling stock. Our train consisted of six passenger cars, a freight car, and an "observation" car—the latter an open truck from which we got capital views of the scenery, though we were terribly bombarded on the upward journey by ashes from the labouring engine.

The cañon is narrow, and for the most part filled with a thick level deposit of detritus, through which the stream, evidently much smaller now than at some former period, flows or leaps in a channel always steep and sometimes precipitous. The rails

K

occupy the left bank of the "crick," and rest for the most part on the floor of detritus; but here and there the gorge narrows, the *débris* disappears, and the river foams between strait rocky walls which rise precipitously on either hand to heights varying from a thousand to two thousand feet. Nevertheless the stream winds like a river flowing through flat meadows, and the train rolls around curve after curve at a uniform speed of eighteen miles an hour, until after passing many stations once busy with "gulch mining" it reaches Black Hawk, thirty-seven miles from Golden and seven thousand three hundred feet above sea-level. Here the valley is wide enough to hold a considerable town full of foundries, stamping-mills, and smelting works. The distance between Black Hawk and Central is only a mile and a half as the crow flies, but there is a thousand feet difference in their levels, so the railroad zigzags up the hill-side, the train travelling now forward, now backward, over a series of dizzy inclines, having a total length of about four miles. The position is a remarkable one for a railway traveller. Around him are the peaks of the range whose sterile summits gleam with occasional snows. Right beneath his feet is the busy little town of Black Hawk, whose chimneys shoot their pointed flames from among rolling clouds of smoke. Lower still the white thread of foaming Clear Creek slips in seeming silence through hidden eyes in pointed needles of rock. And at this great height he steps from the cars into Central City, a flourishing mining camp of three thousand souls, perched at an elevation of more than three hundred feet above the Alpine line of perpetual snow.

The little town consists of a straggling collection of wooden shanties dotted all over the steep hill-sides, but clustering more closely at one spot where a short street contains a number of excellent shops, three banks, three hotels, and several churches The bare brown hills are burrowed everywhere with seeming rabbit-holes, from whose mouths run out little embankments of bright-coloured mining rubbish, while here and there horses are seen treading the mill round of windlasses or whimseys. The streets are deserted during the day, but all the world is astir in the evening, presenting faces of a type which is very familiar to us. Two-thirds of the miners in Central are Cornishmen and the balance either Norwegians or Germans. Native Americans are seldom found underground; they "prospect," and sell their "claims," generally preferring the manufacture of balloons to the founding of solid industries, and having little stomach for the hard work of a miner's life.

Nothing was known of the existence of the precious metals in the mountains of Colorado before 1852, but in the summer of that year a Cherokee cattle-dealer found gold in an affluent of Clear Creek, and members of the tribe continuing to prospect, they finally obtained a moderate quantity of the precious metal. The first party of American prospectors entered Colorado in the early part of 1858, but their success was only partial, and it was not until 1859 that the first gold-bearing lode found in the state was discovered by a man named Gregory. This was a true "fissure vein," as it is called in America, of auriferous quartz very rich in gold. It crosses the valley now called "Gregory's Gulch," between Central and Black Hawk, and, although the first, has proved the richest find in this neighbourhood. Many similar discoveries followed that of Gregory, and two years afterwards it was estimated that the new mining camps of Colorado contained together a population of twenty thousand souls. The pioneer prospectors, seeking gold only, never thought of silver, and finding it without recognising it, threw it on one side as worthless; but in 1864 a Central assayer, named Dibbin, detected silver in some ores sent him for analysis, and since that date the mining history of Colorado is chiefly a record of silver discoveries on the one hand, and the introduction of scientific processes of reduction on the other. Gold, which is found exclusively in quartz rock, and in a "native" or pure metallic state, is often accompanied by silver, usually in the form of a sulphuret. The inexperienced eyes of the early miners failed to recognise these silver ores, and in some cases lodes which have been abandoned on account of their poverty in gold are now being worked as silver mines. Gold as well as silver is still sought in Colorado, but the prosperity of the mining camps rest chiefly on silver.

"Gulch mining," the earliest form of gold-digging, consists in washing the sandy detritus of river valleys, and collecting the free gold which subsides by virtue of its specific gravity. The erosion of a mountain glen in rocks containing mineral veins, constitutes a gigantic natural process of quartz-crushing and gold-washing, whose operations have been continued over enormous periods of time. As frost and rain slowly carve out the valley, the fragments of rock falling from time to time into the stream, are converted by its action into sand and pebbles. In the course of this operation, the quartz parts with its gold, whose flakes and scales are however too heavy to be carried away like sand, so that they remain scattered among the detritus left in the gulch and accumulated chiefly in the upper valleys and at the lowest levels. Gold in fact can neither be destroyed nor removed far from its original position by natural means. It has come into the quartz we know not how, but it is inoxidizable, so that the atmosphere cannot consume it as it would any other metal under similar circumstances, while its high specific gravity prevents its distribution by water.

In some valley then whose gravels have been proved by preliminary washing to be auriferous, the gulch miner sinks a shaft down through the detritus to the bed rock, and upon this floor runs a tunnel or gallery up stream. Water percolates freely through the loose roof and sides of the burrow, but is kept under by pumping. A portion of the stream, diverted from its bed higher up the valley, turns a rude water-wheel, which operates the pump and raising windlass. The mine is worked by two "pardners" who dig and wash by turns, the former employment being wet and heavy work. The contents of the bucket are emptied on a platform and shovelled thence into the "sluice box." This is a long wooden shoot, supplied at its upper end with a constant stream of water and discharging into the creek. The shoot is provided with "riffles," or strips of wood nailed at short intervals across the bottom, which serve to retain a charge of mercury placed there for the purpose of amalgamating the finer particles of gold which might otherwise escape. The riffles are "cleaned up" at regular intervals, the amalgam being squeezed in a linen bag for the recovery of free mercury, while the heavy sand which they contain is transferred to the "pan," a saucer-shaped tin vessel, where the larger pieces of gold are separated out by hand-washing. Gulch mining has almost ceased to exist now that all the auriferous gravels of Western America have been washed. Only the patient Chinese practise it, at the present moment, working over again gravels which the white man considers exhausted.

In "fissure vein" mining, quartz outcrops are sought among the mountains by prospectors, who, when they find a promising "lead," drive in eight stakes, enclosing a space of fifteen hundred feet by one hundred and fifty feet, and this is called a "miner's claim." To convert such a claim into freehold property it is needful to put five hundred dollars' worth of labour into the mine within one year, and this being done the United States Government issues a title. The professional prospector rarely carries his operations beyond this point, but tries to sell his claims, and it is probable that as much money has been fooled away over bubbles blown very big by "smart men," and glowing with iridescent lies, as has been made by honest mining.

Fissure vein mining is carried on in the same way as copper and tin lodes are worked in Cornwall. A shaft is sunk, and galleries constructed, striking the vein at different levels; and the ores on reaching the surface are sorted and crushed, after which they are for the most part sent away to Argo, to be reduced as already described. No great lodes have yet been found in Colorado, the quartz veins varying from a few inches to a few feet in thickness, whereas in Nevada, lodes occur which are two or three hundred feet thick. The mines are small, carried on without adequate capital, and in the rudest way. There are fewer people engaged in mining in Colorado than we were led to expect from the exaggerated statements made to us in Denver, and the mining camps of the Rocky Mountains cannot for a moment be compared with the great and organized operations which we have yet to see in the Sierra Nevada.

These, however, are by no means the opinions of the Coloradans. They believe, or would have you believe, that their claims are all El-Dorados, and their shares priceless. We were fortunate enough to make the acquaintance of a Mr. Fillmore, "attorney and mining agent," whose office, a small wooden shanty, was fitted with shelves filled with specimen ores from every mine in the neighbourhood. One wall was covered with photographs of bare hill-sides, pierced here and there with tiny burrows and dotted with shanties, the pictures representing the "richest mines in the state." Mr. Fillmore himself was a glib man with an enthusiastic manner, roving eyes, and long grey hair, who sold town lots and mining shares in earnest, and called himself an attorney apparently in jest. Thinking probably that an Englishman in Central City could only be explained as a possible investor, he took us into his "prettiest little parlour" of an office, and sidling from shelf to shelf, showed us the world and all the riches thereof. His eyes glowed and his white hair floated as if electrified by excitement while he delivered an eloquent address on the potential wealth around us, describing mines which were all Golcondas, and "town lots" which were paradises. His ardour was infectious, and made us feel so rich that we determined to take some stock in the "richest mine in the state" as soon as Fillmore could make up his mind which that was. But the last lode was always the best, and finally the "attorney and mining agent" piled it up so high that the entrance of a fourth party was a relief from an excitement which was getting too much to be borne—seriously. The new-comer was a Mr. Bozey, to whom we were ceremoniously introduced as "one of our earliest prospectors, a gentleman who has found and sold more good mines than any man in this state, and who is now resting on his oars."

Mr. Bozey was a fat millionaire, dressed in shirt sleeves, and evidently resting even from the labour of washing his hands; but he enjoyed Mr. Fillmore's dish of melted butter exceedingly, swallowing it in silence, and remaining a perfectly dumb oracle to the end of the interview. When the great man was gone, the mining attorney looked at us with benevolence beaming from his glowing features and flying hair. His face said plainly, "Gentlemen, I can make Bozeys of you both;" but we felt in want of a little fresh air after the millionaire, whose well-timed entrance and exit had thrilled us like a melodramatic situation, so we said *au revoir* to our apostle, and left him preaching the gospel of gold in the doorway, and half hoping that the seed had fallen on good ground, half fearing, from an untimely smile on the socialist's face, that we had received the word with the wrong sort of gladness.

Idaho Springs is another mining town distant six miles from Central, lying on a branch of Clear Creek, the divide which separates the two valleys being seventeen hundred feet above Central City or ten thousand feet from sea-level. Driving over this ridge we experienced a curious electrical phenomenon. Daily at this season of the year clouds cover the summits of the range about two o'clock and heavy showers fall; these are accompanied by thunder and lightning and usually last about half an hour, when the sky clears again as suddenly as it clouded, but the rain extends only a very little way from the hill tops. It was raining but without lightning as we neared the divide, when I felt a tickling sensation on the back of my hands like what one experiences when standing on a glass stool and in connection with the conductor of an electrical machine. Judging that a discharge was taking place from our persons I tried to increase its intensity by holding one of the wet umbrellas point upwards above the waggon. This at once produced a distinct sensation in the hand and arm, and on mentioning the matter to the driver he exclaimed, "I guessed you felt it when I saw you looking at your hands. It's common enough here, though many don't know what it is, and others don't notice it." This man was very nervous about crossing the divide while it was thundering, and plainly said that if there was lightning he must wait for fair weather. He declared that the ridge is constantly struck and very unsafe during thunderstorms, a moving horse or buggy being very liable to accident, while once in the gulch, no matter how little below the summit, there is no danger.

The approach to Central City by the Colorado Central Railway is, as we have already seen, a succession of frowning precipices and bare mountain slopes; but the valley of South Clear Creek is hemmed in by less rugged hills, the barren crags are replaced by pine-decked slopes, and the stream is no longer a torrent but a gliding brook, while the gulch is almost too open to be called a cañon. Idaho was first settled in 1859 by a party of gold-diggers, who commenced gulching where the town now stands. In the same year a small log cabin was built by a man named Beebee, who catered for the miners' physical wants, but this has now grown into a great hotel—the "Beebee House," for Idaho possesses soda springs and has become a health resort as well as a mining town. Two years after the camp was first pitched, Clear Creek Cañon was alive with gold-diggers, and gold dust was the universal medium of exchange in this then remote spot. In 1864 came the discovery of silver, followed first by a new excitement for fissure vein mining, and then by the gradual decadence of gulching. Several mineral springs were discovered in sinking the earliest shafts at Idaho; and these having been exploited by an enterprising medical man, the place now attracts a number of Americans, always great valetudinarians. The Beebee House is yearly crowded with these real or fancied invalids, who drink the waters or lounge in the sun on the piazza, weighing themselves daily to see whether they are improving.

The deserted bed of a creek which has once been the site of active gulch mining is a curious sight. The stream flows between banks composed entirely of great heaps of washed pebbles, clean and bare of any vegetation. Wrecks of waterwheels, flumes, and sluice-boxes lie here and there, accenting the desolation of the scene; and if a group of Chinamen should be seen, their blue frocks, conical hats, and pig-tails give the last touch of outlandishness to the picture.

A mass of detritus with a surface flat as a floor, through which the creek meanders, fills the bottom of Clear Creek Cañon to a depth of about seventy feet. It consists of sandy soil, thickly stuffed with boulders varying in size from stones as big as a piano to pebbles. All of them are water-worn and free from glacial scratches, but there are trains of boulders lying on the shoulders of the hills at heights of two and three hundred feet, where they could only have been left by ice, and many of the blocks in the river-bed are so large as to preclude the idea of their being water-borne. The stones differ from the local rock, having travelled, as we afterwards found, from a point twenty miles further up the stream, and the whole must have been deposited during a state of things totally different to that which now prevails. The erratics which line the hill-sides up to heights of more than three hundred feet, and the tumultuous assemblage of sand, stones and boulders in the bed of the stream, point to a time when Idaho Valley was nearly abrim with ice, as well as to a later period when the melting glacier poured a roaring torrent of water down the gulch which now carries only a comparatively tiny stream.

A branch of the Colorado Central Railway follows South Clear Creek from its point of junction with Clear Creek to Georgetown, fourteen miles above Idaho, and the highest mining camp in the Rocky Mountains. Georgetown lies in a perfect amphitheatre of hills, at an elevation of eight thousand four hundred feet, or five thousand feet higher than Chamounix. It is considerably larger than Central, and notwithstanding its elevated situation has all the appearance of an old settled place. Its streets are numerous, wide, and busy; it has capital shops, and many hotels. The snow does not often lie for more than twenty-four hours in winter, and the sun is warm and pleasant in January;—this at the height of the perpetual snow-line in Switzerland. Mining towns, like Western cities, are soon seen, and we were now pretty familiar both with the wooden homes and burrows of the miners; so giving Georgetown a passing glance, we started up another branch of Clear Creek in search of the granites whence the Idaho pebbles were derived, and to visit Green Lake—a small sheet of water dammed by moraine, at a height of sixteen hundred feet above Georgetown, or ten thousand feet from sea-level.

The narrow gorge is very fine. The stream falls so rapidly that for the first mile its course is an unbroken sheet of foam. Its bed is cut through enormous lateral moraines lying on the flanks of the mountains, and containing boulders of stupendous dimensions. Some of these are as big as a moderate-sized house, and where they have fallen the stream is put to shift after shift to outflank the tremendous obstacles in its path, while the valley is cumbered with such a confused mass of blocks as defies description. We were fairly staggered by the dimensions of the boulders, and scarcely less surprised by the elevation and mass of the lateral moraines, whose presence showed that the continental ice-sheet had once stood here at least ten thousand feet above the sea. The hills around us were pierced to their very summits with little burrows and seamed with white, yellow, or grey mining tips, while delicate, zigzag lines, betokening trodden paths, branched downwards to the valley, and stretched from mine to mine. Green Lake is a small basin hidden among tall pines, holding water as green as grass, and full of mountain trout; but this moraine-dammed pond was tame indeed compared with the superb views of the range which now presented themselves in every direction. The hills bend round Georgetown in three-fourths of an almost perfectly symmetrical circle—Mount Evans, Gray's Peak, and James's Peak, some of the highest summits, being included in the view; while they are seen without reference to the plain, which elsewhere seems to partially bury and consequently dwarf their masses. The afternoon storm had lingered longer than usual, lightning flashing and thunder growling during the whole of our walk; but just as we turned to descend, great indigo wreaths gathered themselves together in the south, capping Mount Evans with almost terrifying gloom, while the sun shone brightly over the pines and crags of the most inspiring view we had yet seen in the Cordilleras.

The train swept us rapidly down the grades and past the precipices of Clear Creek Cañon to Golden, and thence across the hot and dusty plain to Denver, where we dined before starting for South Colorado by the Denver and Rio Grande Railway. I mention this dinner because it was made remarkable by the fact that we accidentally sat down, six Englishmen, at one table in the Windsor Hotel. Three of the six were settled in the state, and whatever may have been their temptation to belong to the Yankee nation, they certainly all remain enthusiastic Englishmen. This fortuitous concurrence of atoms fraternized and made itself merry, and whether by good-fellowship or champagne I do not know, but we got the national balloon which burst at Washington repaired, and took in a fresh charge of patriotic gas, sufficient we hope to float us to the misty portals of the Golden Gate.

CHAPTER XVIII.

MANITOU—PIKE'S PEAK.

July 21-29.

EIGHTY miles south of Denver lies Manitou, a mountain "health resort," famous for its mineral springs, and the point whence the ascent of Pike's Peak is usually made. It is six thousand three hundred feet above sea-level and stands among the tilted strata which everywhere rest against the eastern flanks of the Rocky Mountains, whose granite core has intruded through the once level beds of mesozoic and tertiary age which lie beneath the drift of the plains. Manitou is quite a fashionable little place, always crowded during the summer with American tourists and invalids ;

it has several large hotels, and the native exquisite of both sexes is seen here in full bloom at this time of the year.

Certainly American ladies dress in a very *prononcé* way. Their breakfast toilets are good enough for the dinner-table, while for dinner they dress as we do for the opera. They are great on ornamental hose and tiny French shoes, and having pretty feet are quite disposed to let the world know it. Their jewellery, if too abundant, is costly and beautiful in its design, which stands between the lightness of French and the solidity of English work. American ladies never walk, but they go out " buggy-riding" in dancing shoes and ball dresses, or amble about on ponies in highly ornamental riding habits. All this seems very odd among the mountains, where the surroundings, as at the Riffel or upon Dartmoor, would suggest serge walking dresses and stout Balmoral boots to Englishwomen. The men too are curiously lazy about walking; both tourists and invalids sit about the piazza, talking dollars, smoking, and spitting almost all day; but no one treats his holiday as an occasion for taking exercise. If athletics were a cult in America, as with us, there would probably be fewer men here who, though in the prime of life and having no specific ailment, suffer from some "trouble," usually of digestion, often of nerves, and spend their time drinking mineral waters, weighing themselves, and discussing their daily progress.

Men and women are never seen to advantage in a fashionable watering-place, and neither at Scarborough nor Trouville is society at its best. But fashionable life in Manitou seems more frivolous, not to say faster, than at similar places in the Old World. It may be that what appears to us licence is only the natural result of women's greater freedom, and certainly social propriety is as rigidly observed in the States as in Europe, but while the men are more solemn and shoppy, the women are decidedly gayer and more openly anxious for attentions than with us. The billiard-room and the bowling alley are brilliant with beautiful toilettes every evening, and there are as many ladies as gentlemen with cues in their hands. Representing domestic duties by business cares, men and women seem to have changed places; the woman is the pleasure-seeker, while the man gravely revolves his home affairs.

Although parties of Americans make the ascent of Pike's Peak almost daily in the summer they characteristically prefer riding to walking, and we astonished our guide by declaring our intention of going up on foot. He on the other hand said he "wouldn't take twenty dollars to walk it," and rode. This mountain is fourteen thousand two hundred feet above sea-level, and its summit is occupied by a United States meteorological station, where two observers are constantly stationed. Such an arrangement would of course be impossible at a similar elevation in Europe; but here there is seldom snow enough to block the trail which leads to the signal station, and men can live there very comfortably in the winter. Besides the Government trail as it is called, a second route leads to "Seven Lakes," where, at an elevation of eleven thousand feet, there is a small mountain ranch, and here we determined to sleep for a night, so as to be ready to attack the peak in time to see the sun rise, returning to Manitou on the evening of the second day.

The trail is very steep for the first three miles, rising thirteen hundred feet in the mile, and following Ruxton Cañon, the bed of whose roaring stream presents a scene of the wildest confusion. The gorge is very narrow, having precipitous flanks covered with patches of pine, but cumbered at the bottom with masses of fallen rock, many of which are as big as a large house. The rock is granite, which has all the appearance of being bedded in lines crossing the valley at a moderate angle. These "beds" are very variously affected by the weather, some crumbling readily, while others waste but little. On the side of the valley where the beds hang towards the stream, the wear of the softer strata leaves vast overhanging masses of rock, which, when undermined beyond a certain point, break off and fall into the cañon. Where the rocks are most friable the flanks of the valley and the hills themselves are covered with great "sand-slides," or tali of granitic *débris*, and the juxtaposition of softer with harder granite gives rise to most fantastic weathered forms, which line the sides and crown the precipices of the cañon with spires and pyramids, quaint profiles, and the images of strange beasts. The daily storm burst upon us about two o'clock, and instead of clearing as usual, stuck by us for the rest of the day. The lightning playing among the pines around us was very fine, and the thunder reverberated, as it seemed for minutes. The ascent became much less steep after the first four miles, and thence to Seven Lakes the trail, though difficult to find in places, was little more than a long and toilsome walk in the wet.

These mountain cañons are all alike in one respect; their beds are steepest and their sides most precipitous near the plain, but at elevations of about nine thousand feet their flanks widen, becoming like those of an ordinary river valley, and the ascent sinks to an easy grade; often indeed the cañon leads up into smooth and level basins many miles in extent. The narrow and precipitous gateways of the cañon however are clearly no accidental cracks convenient for the escape of water flowing from above, for, when viewed from such a distance that general characters prevail over particulars, they have each the appearance of having been cut by the stream itself. When this first began to flow over the hill-side it must have been dammed in many places by irregularities of surface giving rise to lakes of greater or smaller area, the overflow from each of which never ceased cutting its way backwards, through the retaining bank until the lake was drained. The beds of such old lake-like expansions of the stream are found in the upper reaches of every cañon, and sometimes afford space enough, as in the case of Idaho Springs, for the building of a town.

The pine is very characteristic of American mountain scenery, and gives it a peculiar tone which is not agreeable at first. Seen from a distance the hill-sides appear to be clothed with scaffold poles, while a cold grey, rather than a green tint distinguishes the forest, unless the trees are thickly massed in ravines, when they look almost black. Within the forest itself the pines are still more like scaffold poles; all of them are bare of branches up to a great height; many are dead, and fallen trees are so numerous as seriously to impede the way whether of horseman or pedestrian. Burnt patches frequently occur, and the charred trunks and blackened underwood give a repulsive character to the scene.

The Seven Lakes are a series of large ponds, dammed by glacial moraine, and occupying a depression which is almost entirely surrounded by bald peaks, rising from five hundred to a thousand feet above a well-defined timber-line. Here we found comfortable quarters in a log house built by a man named Welch, who, with a strange taste for isolation, has taken up land in this remote spot and is stocking the lakes with mountain trout, in order to supply the Manitou hotels with fish. Meanwhile he entertains such tourists as prefer to make the Pike's Peak trip in two days rather than in one, and we had to thank him and his wife for much kindness during our stay, which was unexpectedly prolonged by the indisposition of one of our party. Three days indeed were thus thrown on the hands of half the expedition, who whiled them away by tramps to Bald Mountain in search of topaz; in fruitless pursuit of deer-trails across the sand-slides; in rowing a crazy boat over the lake, which was crowded with great external-gilled newts; in playing quoits with old horse-shoes; watching the tricks of the half-tame chipmunks, or painted squirrels; playing euchre; or listening to Indian stories told by the guide.

At length—the invalid riding—we were able to start for the summit, which was reached after a few hours' stiff walking, and here we were welcomed by the signal service observers. These men are soldiers, well-educated and intelligent fellows like the privates of our Royal Engineers. They live in a stone hut where, if luxuries are absent, there is no want of substantial comfort. The station is connected with Washington, and therefore with all the world, by a telegraphic wire which serves to despatch observations as soon as they are made. There is a capital library, and if the position is lonely in winter, there are daily visitors from

Manitou all through the summer. The men are frequently relieved and seem to like the service. As might be expected from the great elevation, there is little electrical equilibrium between the summit and the lower levels, and the telegraphic instruments were constantly snapping like the excited conductor of an electrifying machine.

Many of the highest peaks in the Rocky Mountains occur quite independently of the watershed, and Pike's Peak is several miles eastward of it, rising indeed only just without the upturned strata which flank the range and lie in great "hog-backs," as they are called, against the granite uplift of which the peak is a part. A heavy snowstorm accompanied with thunder and lightning signalized our arrival at the hut and threatened for a long time to deprive us of any view; but after a couple of hours the cloud was withdrawn, displaying the beauties of the scene in quite a theatrical manner. The whole of the northern and western horizon was filled with the serrated profiles of hills, many of them still nameless, belonging to the Continental Divide. These merged in the south-west into the Sangre de Cristo range—a spur of sufficient importance to have been separately named. In the south rose the "Spanish Peaks," conical hills almost as high as Pike's Peak itself; while eastward the eye ranged over the sea-like plains, flecked with the purple shadows of a thousand clouds. Immediately at our feet lay a wide expanse of tumbled mountains, bare for nearly two thousand feet below, and clothed with dark forests thence to the plain. It was a beautiful picture; but in spite of their immense mass, the mountains have not the sublimity as they have none of the grace of the Swiss Alps.

The country between Denver and Manitou forms a low divide, separating the streams flowing towards the Platte and Arkansas rivers respectively, and the "Fontaine qui bouille," which runs through Manitou, finds its way by the latter route to the Father of Waters. This "boiling spring," so called from its turbulence, rises on the flank of the granite upheaval only a few miles west of Manitou and in its course towards the plain crosses at one place the edge of a hogback lying against the hill-sides. The latter consists of a thin bed of extremely hard sandstone, which, stoutly resisting weathering, gives a peculiar and interesting character to the cañon. Throughout that portion of its course which lies among the granite, the stream flows in an open valley flanked by low and gently sloping hills; but it traverses the hogback in a deep, precipitous gorge and in a series of cascades. It is clear that the hard capping has determined the section of the cañon by preserving the friable rock beneath it from degradation. If the protecting bed were absent, these rocks would have weathered, as they have done higher up the stream, into an open V-shaped valley; but the tough sandstone has prevented their wasting, and hence the deep U-shaped gorge, whose precipitous sides contrast so strangely with the undulating country immediately above. Here then we have a cañon still in course of excavation by means of an overflow which is cutting its way backwards in the manner already suggested; together with an example of the influence which the juxtaposition of hard and soft rocks may exercise in producing widely different profiles of river valleys.

The hogbacks of mesozoic and tertiary rocks lying against the granite core of the range are turned up at all angles. Those which lie immediately on the core itself partake of its slope, but a little further off others are seen which are quite perpendicular. The effects produced by erosion among these vertical beds are very remarkable. The "Garden of the Gods" is a fanciful but inappropriate name given to a little valley where rock pillars and needles, some of which rise to a height of three hundred and fifty feet, abound. One of these is a hundred and twenty feet high, while its base is not more than ten feet in any direction; but this obelisk-like form is exceptional, the beds usually rising from the ground in wall-like masses which must be viewed edgewise to look like aiguilles. Thus seen, especially at sunset, these columns of red sandstone have a singularly artificial and weird appearance as they flame out like copper in the red evening light.

But bizarre as they are, these examples of erosion are surpassed

L

in strangeness by the columns of "Monument Park," situated among undisturbed tertiary strata some ten miles from the foot of the hills. Here the plain, consisting of a loosely compacted white sandstone, is dotted with tapering pillars, from six to fifty feet high, each capped with a flat overhanging stone of dark colour. They stand sometimes in closely associated groups, sometimes alone, and look like sugar-loaves wearing college caps. They are of the same material as the soil, from which they have evidently been shaped; and the flat stone at top is a fragment of a thin bed of similiar sandstone, indurated by the percolation of water containing iron. Here and there the ferruginous layer is continuous, though for the most part it is broken up into plates more or less separated from each other; but however it occurs, it locally stops that degradation of the surface which is constantly going on under the influence of wind. Whenever this blows it scatters the slightly coherent sands of the soil to great distances, and thus gradually degrades the plain; but as the surface beneath a protecting plate cannot be carried away, a pillar necessarily results from the lowering of the surrounding soil. The pillar again assumes a tapering form because the erosive forces have been at work longer upon its neck than its base, and the former indeed becomes in the course of time a mere stem upon which the widely overhanging flat stone appears to totter. Finally the latter falls, and the pillar, no longer protected above, moulders down and disappears, while beneath the fallen cap, now protecting another spot, a new and similar column begins to grow. When the hard bed is continuous it gives rise to cliffs, and the groups of columns are usually found on their flanks; the question of column or cliff being determined by the continuous or broken condition of the hard vein. Examples of every stage of growth and decay abound, and the simple process can be traced from its first to its last stage, while its apparently artificial results excite the liveliest interest.

When Monument Park and the Garden of the Gods have been seen, and Pike's Peak ascended, there is nothing to be done at

Manitou beyond sitting on the hotel piazza, admiring the brilliant and ever-changing toilettes of the gay American girls, and wondering at the portentous gravity of the men. But for two pedestrians in good condition this was tedious work, and our worn tweeds and heavy walking boots seemed out of place in the well-dressed crowd. Already this charming state had held us much longer than we had anticipated, and the Grand Cañon of the Arkansas, together with Leadville, the last mining miracle and a really "rough" camp, had to be seen before Southern Colorado was exhausted. Within an hour after coming to this conclusion we had said good-bye to more than one pleasant table friend, and were *en route* for the stupendous gateway by which the Arkansas river breaks through the range and enters on the plain.

CHAPTER XIX.

THE GRAND CAÑON OF THE ARKANSAS—LEADVILLE.

July 30–August 2.

THE Arkansas river rises on the flanks of the continental watershed, and after a course of more than a thousand miles pours its water into the Missouri. For the first hundred miles of its existence this stream is a mountain torrent, fed by the snows of the range, from whose foot-hills it issues to the plain through a narrow gorge, having precipitous sides nearly three thousand feet in height. This is the "Grand Cañon" of the Arkansas, to reach which from Manitou the traveller skirts the mountains, following the southward course of the "Fontaine qui bouille" to its junction with the Arkansas at Pueblo, and then turns due west along the valley of the latter river to Cañon City. Before Pueblo is reached the drift which covers the plain everywhere to the northward begins to thin out and finally disappears, revealing the underlying cretaceous rocks, which are here composed of a white, friable limestone. At a distance of a few miles from the range these beds lie horizontally, but on the flanks of the hills they have been tilted upwards by the granite upheaval like the rocks of mesozoic age at Manitou. Streams traversing the level beds of the plain give rise to peculiar valleys, whose flanks are formed by flat-topped cliffs called "mesas," to which the horizontal lines of stratification lend the appearance of masonry. The mesas are deeply buried in the rubbish which falls from their sides, and look exactly like railway cuttings capped with dwarf walls. The valley of the Arkansas is bounded on both sides by these natural walls whose remoteness from the present river-banks shows how widely the stream has wandered since it first began to flow. But stranger appearances are presented by the vertical beds of the tilted series as the train approaches the range. The edges of the soft strata have been worn down to the level of the plain, while the hard beds stand up exactly like artificial walls. These walls again are not continuous, but have been breached here and there by streams, and the approach to Cañon City has consequently all the appearance of having been once defended by military works which are now in partial ruin.

Cañon City lies on the plain but is very near the hills, and viewed from one of the neighbouring hogbacks has a strangely Oriental aspect. A group of white, flat-roofed houses occupies a small space in the midst of a yellow desert, sparsely covered with tall branching cacti. A green streak, representing the cottonwood trees which line the river Arkansas, winds across the plain and through the town, being finally lost in the distance. Bare, serrated peaks, rising from the shoulders of mountains, themselves deeply sunk in the sea-like plain, carry the eye to a far-distant horizon. The air is full of a yellow dust haze which seems to add to the glare of what might well be a Syrian sun. It is the East itself reproduced in the deserts of the West. In the early days of gulch mining Cañon City flourished wonderfully. Standing in the gateway of the hills, it formed a base of operations for the diggers who were working in every mountain valley of the Arkansas river, and was the point where the rush from the plains concentrated. It became quite suddenly a town of six thousand inhabitants; but the gravels were soon washed out, the Ute Indians "made trouble," and Cañon City, like so many other western mining centres, burst like a bubble. Coal and oil however have brought back men whom the failing gulches could not keep; the river has been tapped, land irrigated, farm produce and fruit raised; a brisk trade with Leadville, the new mining camp on the headwaters of the Arkansas, established, and a fair amount of prosperity still attends the little town which now numbers about two thousand souls.

Five miles west of Cañon City the Arkansas issues from the hills, and the last six miles of its course among them is justly called the "Grand Cañon." Throughout the whole of this distance the river flows between precipitous rocky walls which tower in some places as much as three thousand feet above its bed. One part of this extraordinary channel, called the "Royal Gorge," has absolutely vertical sides two thousand feet high and not much more than fifty feet apart. From above the traveller can look directly down upon the river foaming through the narrow chink; while below he could jump, if he dared, across the deep but narrow stream. Although so trench-like at first, the cañon widens after a few miles into a comparatively open valley, but even its straitest and deepest portions give evidence of having been excavated by the action of water.

Originally the work of streams, all the cañons of the Rocky Mountains have been partially shaped by the ice which filled them during the glacial period. That they were so filled is amply proved, as at Idaho, by the lateral moraines still lying on the flanks of their upper valleys, and by the huge travelled blocks which cumber their beds; and, this being so, it is not a little surprising at first to find so few of the ordinary marks of glaciation in these rocky gorges. But the friable granites, universally present in the Coloradan hills, weather so rapidly that grooves and striæ must soon have disappeared, and only a hard bed here and there now retains the scratched and polished surfaces which undoubtedly characterised every valley in the Rocky Mountains at the close of the great ice age. Glaciated rocks occur at intervals throughout the Grand Cañon, sometimes so smoothly polished that they reflect the sun's rays like a mirror; and everywhere the hog-backed outlines of ice-worn surfaces appear, bespeaking the passage of a glacier as plainly as if grooves and striæ were present.

Walking leisurely through six miles of this astounding scenery, astonishment grows with every step at the stupendous character of the work which has been accomplished by means apparently so feeble. The tool and the finished job stand side by side, only the chips have been swept away; but looking from one to the other of these, it seems impossible to believe that a thin thread of running water has ploughed out this tremendous trench. The mountainous portion of the Arkansas Valley is however very remarkable. Its western flank is formed by the continental watershed, and its eastern flank by a parallel range or spur, equalling the great ridge itself in elevation and distant from it about twenty miles. At the junction of these two great chains of hills stands Mount Lincoln, fourteen thousand three hundred feet high, upon whose sides the Arkansas river rises, and the vast depression in question, forming the mountain bed of the stream, is more than a hundred miles from source to mouth. That mouth was once dammed by a cross range of hills which retained, as with an embankment three thousand feet higher than the plain, all the water above it, and, where that water found an overflow, the work was begun which did not end until the cross range was cut through from flank to flank, and the Grand Cañon completed.

Near the head-waters of the Arkansas and standing almost upon the Continental Divide, at an elevation of more than ten thousand feet above the sea, is the city of Leadville, the greatest mining marvel in America. Four years ago its site was a bare mountain side, but to-day its population is variously estimated at from fifteen to thirty thousand souls. At the time of which I write the Arkansas Valley Railroad had reached within a few miles of the town, and so rapidly was the line advancing that though I staged three miles from its terminus to Leadville on a Saturday night I left the city in the cars on the following Monday. Of the railway journey from Cañon City to Leadville it is difficult to speak without appearing to exaggerate its beauties. Leaving the wall-like scenery of the cañon, we entered upon an open valley, whence, rosy and golden long after we were in shadow, the peaks of the range came successively into view as we swept rapidly past their feet, while later, when the moon had risen, their cold white cones glittered in the silver light. It was a journey never to be forgotten. Contrary to what would be supposed until the character of cañons and their higher valleys is understood, mountain railroading is much easier at its highest than at its lowest levels. In the cañon proper the track must be blasted out of wall-like rocks, while at higher elevations open valleys and gentle grades make the work almost as easy as on the prairies, and certainly easier than over ordinary hilly country.

California, Stray Horse, Evans, and Iowa Gulches—all famous in the early mining history of Colorado—are situated near the head-waters of the Arkansas. The first was prospected in 1860, and, the gravels proving very rich in gold, a rush followed, which, in the course of a short time, crowded all the gulches in question with gold-diggers. The tiny affluents of the river, feeble because so near their sources, hardly furnished water enough for the sluices, and, extensive methodic workings being thus prevented, the surface washings were soon exhausted, so that six years after the rush these gulches were almost deserted. In 1874 however water was brought from the Arkansas itself, a distance of twelve miles, by two miners, for the purpose of systematically working their claims in California Gulch. Operators in this valley had always been troubled by the presence of very heavy sand in the sluices, which filled the riffles without yielding gold; but it never occurred to anybody to have this unwelcome deposit assayed until 1876, when one of the men in question, named Ward, proved it to be carbonate of lead carrying a great deal of silver. Thus for sixteen years had the gold-diggers of California Gulch, like the miners of Georgetown and Central, failed to recognize silver in the rubbish which they abused for the trouble it gave them in the sluices. Finally, in the ridges which separate the gulches in question, and at no great depth from the surface, the lead carbonates themselves were found *in situ*, not occuring in fissures as mineral veins generally do, but disposed in thick horizontal, or rather undulating, layers of considerable extent.

The value of this find was not at once apparent, and by January, 1878, there were not more than three hundred men working in the "Sand-Mines," as their claims were contemptuously nicknamed by the fissure-vein miners. In that month however a meeting was called to organize a town, and was attended by eighteen men who, after considerable discussion, selected the name of Leadville, and a fortnight afterwards, a mayor and recorder having been elected, the infant city came to the birth on January 26, 1878. Six months later two prospectors, named Rische and Hook, being at the moment completely hard up, asked the new mayor, who sold groceries in the camp, to supply them with the necessaries of life while opening a new claim, upon condition of his sharing with them anything they might find. The mayor's name was Tabor, and a short time after breaking ground Rische and Hook struck the mine now known throughout the world as the "Little Pittsburg." Within two months they had sold out their joint interests for half a million dollars, while Mr. Tabor stuck to the mine, became a millionaire and is now the Governor of Colorado State. All the fat was in the fire; other lodes were found, and, though the new town was a hundred and twenty miles from any railroad and without a stage line, the latter was at once established, the former was commenced, and the daily arrivals were soon counted by hundreds. In the twinkling of an eye Leadville has become a city. Two railways have reached it, spite of its remote and elevated position; substantial houses have arisen; banks, hotels, even a great opera-house, built by Mr. Tabor, have been opened; churches have been erected, waterworks and fire stations organized, and newspapers started;—and this at an elevation of two thousand feet above the Alpine snow-line, and where all supplies must be drawn from the plains, a hundred and twenty miles away.

The Leadville carbonates occur in so abnormal a manner that it is doubtful whether they will prove permanently valuable. It is thought that they merely occupy pockets, and the recent failure of one mine after another seems to favour this view. In the mean time the Leadville find is the most astounding incident which has yet occurred in the history of mining for the precious metals, as the rush which followed it surpassed all that had previously taken place.

The social aspects of Leadville are as extraordinary as its situation and history. It is a "hard" mining camp, but it is not lawless. All the restless elements of western life are present, curiously blended with eastern method and perseverance. The crowd which throngs the streets is like no other crowd in the world, it is so rough yet so very much in earnest. Only a few women are visible, and the men might be taken for ruffians but for their conspicuous look of self-reliance and self-control. The first of these qualities, the child of self-help, is almost universal among the pioneer population of the west; while the last comes perhaps of every man knowing that the revolver in his pocket shoots no straighter and is reached no quicker than that of his neighbour. Take a ruffian then with a character modified by respect for the weapon of another, and dignified by self-confidence; dress him in a wide-brimmed felt hat, a blue flannel shirt, brown canvas "pants" tucked into high-heeled Wellington boots which have seen neither blacking nor brushes since their birth; put a broad leather belt round his waist; give him long and dusty hair; fill his mouth with tobacco juice and extravagant profanity;—and you have a picture of the men who crowd the streets and saloons of Leadville from morning till night, or rather from morning till morning, for night, as a season of rest, is almost unknown in this wicked town, where there are perhaps six or seven thousand men actually engaged in mining and prospecting, and an equal, if not larger, number of gamblers, rowdies, gaming-house and saloon keepers, thieves, and prostitutes assembled to prey upon them.

The American miner is a gamester *pur sang*. Keno, faro, and roulette are his favourite games and these are openly played in public gambling-houses on the main street. All three are games of pure chance, and seemingly very poor amusement; yet the rooms are nightly crowded with the characters already described, who play in perfect silence (barring a "difficulty") well into the morning hours. In the side streets are "dance-houses," where girls in ballet costume perform within a ring, outside of which a mob of miners looks on. Sometimes the women "rope in" a few male dancers from among the spectators and then the fun grows fast and furious. Elsewhere, standing at the open doorways of a whole street, women, sometimes in stage costumes and painted up to the eyes, solicit passers-by; while the gaping front doors and brilliant lighting of other houses bespeak the homes of a higher grade of the prostitute's profession. Music halls, where fast songs are sung, abound, and there are several theatres giving variety entertainments, chiefly of an indecent character. At the Tabor Opera-House highly coloured melodrama sometimes finds a home for a few weeks, but this sort of thing must be mixed with a good deal of firearms in order to attract. At all these places the audience is alike—a crowd of slouch-hatted, independent men, full of strange oaths, and having a freedom of manner which is very striking to a stranger. Every man drinks whisky, smokes a cigar (never a pipe) and spits as freely as he swears. Drunkenness, though by no means absent, is not conspicuous, and I saw no quarrelling. The various amusements go on till three o'clock in the morning, and the traveller arriving, as I did, at two o'clock a.m., finds the town brightly lighted and as much alive as at noonday. The stores are open and newspapers are published on Sundays, when, however, a number of well-dressed people, sprung one knows not whence, attend the various places of worship. I went alone into many of the saloons, gaming and dance houses, and found them orderly; but lest I should take away too good an impression, there was a "man for breakfast" on the morning after my arrival, making two such repasts served up within a week.

The city itself lies in an open, park-like valley, once heavily timbered but now entirely bare of trees, which have been felled for house-building and smelting purposes. It is circled with snowy-peaks, and the air is keen, although the sun is hot, while it freezes at night even in midsummer. There is but one street of substantial houses, all the rest consist of rough log huts, and the stumps of the primeval forest still stand in the roadways. To drive a buggy through such a *chevaux de frise* seemed impossible, nevertheless I found myself in the trap of a new friend, threading Leadville streets at a brisk trot, within a few hours of my arrival. The mines lie to the north-east of the town, among the ridges of which I have already spoken. The "Little Pittsburg" and the "Chrysolite" are the most famous lodes, but there is so much talk about exhaustion that strangers are rigidly excluded from the workings, possibly lest they might be spies sent out to ascertain whether the land be naked or no. A characteristic sight occurs near the town, where a wide space of ground, several acres in extent, is entirely covered by empty meat-tins. The mining camps of the west depend on canned provisions, but, in spite of a now intimate personal acquaintance with this useful form of food, the stretch of tin-drift, glittering like a great mirror in the sun, and diversified with blackened tree-stumps, was a surprising spectacle.

Georgetown, Central, and Idaho, are quiet, humdrum old places in comparison with Leadville, which reproduces the old Californian days of '49, though shorn of their wickedest features; and it is the only place in the world at the present moment where that most strange and characteristic sight, a rough American mining camp, can be seen. Leadville is booming at the time this is written, but already the geologist thinks he sees the handwriting on the wall; and it may be that, after the pockets of the mountains are once emptied of their carbonates, the city will wither as it rose, in a night; and the tourist of a few years hence, following the Arkansas to its mountain sources, may find the "roaring camp" of to-day absolutely deserted, and slowly strewing the lonely shoulders of Mount Lincoln with its ruins.

The railway was completed to Leadville during my stay, and I steamed out on the first train that ever left the mountain city, returning direct to Denver by the Denver and South Park Railroad—a line which, leaving the Arkansas Valley at Buena Vista, climbs a low pass in its left flank and, crossing South Park, falls into and follows the narrow and tortuous cañon of the South Platte river, running thence across the plain to the Coloradan capital. Like all mountain railroad trips, this journey had its own peculiar attractions. South Park is another Estes Park in its structure, being evidently the bed of an old lake once imprisoned among the spurs of the range but now drained by the Platte river. Its wide levels are, however, tame and uninteresting, and I was glad when we left them to clamber over Kenosha Summit, and drop into the cañon of the South Platte. Kenosha Summit is ten thousand one hundred feet above sea-level, and the highest ridge yet scaled by the railway in North America. The descent winds down by a series of zigzags, and from the car one sees below the road to be travelled, while above is the one already traversed; and far, far down, the river valley, into which it seems as if the train might fall at any moment. It is a magnificent ride, but exciting, on account of the many mishaps that have occurred on the road; the curves are very sharp, and it is no uncommon occurrence for the engine to leave the rails. But we reached the bottom safely and then twisted for many miles through the narrow cañon, shut in by high walls of granite and gneiss, and accompanied by the brawling Platte; till, reaching the plain at sunset, and unwillingly breathing once more its hot and yellow air, we sped over the desert flats to Denver.

CHAPTER XX.

SALT LAKE CITY.

August 3-9.

THIRTY-SIX hours spent in a Pullman car carry the traveller from Denver to Salt Lake City. The Union Pacific line is rejoined at Cheyenne, soon after leaving which town the train crosses the watershed of the continent, eight thousand feet above sea level and about two thousand feet higher than Cheyenne. This is no ridge, but a wide plateau, reached by gentle grades, and, but for a painted board on which the railway company have thoughtfully inscribed the words "Summit of the Rocky Mountains," there is nothing to indicate that the Continental Divide has been reached. The rocks are composed of the same friable granite as in Colorado, and fantastic weathered shapes abound. Snow-sheds are built in the depressions to protect the line from drifts, but the snow-fall is so small that the winds clear the hills, and cattle range in search of open ground, or drift before the severer storms, during the whole winter. After crossing the summit the railroad descends gently into the "Laramie Plains," which are covered with short nutritive grasses and tenanted by innumerable herds of cattle. If Wyoming is, as our friend the ranchman declared, "God's own footstool for cattle," then the Laramie Plains are its cushion. The eastern and western flanks of the Rocky Mountains are strongly contrasted in regard to vegetation, the former being brown and bare while the latter are green and fruitful. Game, of which we saw nothing in Colorado, was plentiful on these plains, where, from the train itself, we saw many antelopes and "grouse." By-and-by the granite gives way to mesozoic rocks, sometimes jurassic, sometimes cretaceous, and these are succeeded by level beds of eocene age, which, being soft and horizontally bedded, weather into the strangest castellated shapes. To these, as to the mesas, the stratification gives the appearance of masonry, while the erosion, as in the case of Monument Park near Manitou, is almost entirely due to the action of the wind, which scours the country in tremendous gusts, sweeping away the loose soil, or flinging it, like a sand-blast, against the crumbling cliffs.

Echo Cañon is a valley cut through these soft beds, and its sides are carved from end to end with fantastic forms, sometimes monumental, sometimes architectural, the whole having a singularly artificial appearance, in consequence of the level bedding. Echo Cañon leads to Weber Cañon, where a series of beds ranging from the top of the jurassic to the bottom of the coal measures, is exposed, rising more or less vertically from beneath the flat tertiaries, and reposing on the flanks of the Wahsatch range. The train runs for many miles through the picturesque and varied scenery to which this uplift gives rise, and presently issues from the cañon into an open country of level meadows, once evidently an old lake-bed, across which, in company with the Weber river, it approaches a magnificent mountain wall standing square across the path and seeming to bar the way of both road and stream. This is the Wahsatch range, whose snow-capped and serrated profile stretches away north and south until its outline is lost in the hazy distance on either hand. On its farther side is Salt Lake, into which we know the Weber falls, but we look in vain for indications of the spot where the stream breaks through the apparently continuous rampart before us. Finally we are close upon the "Devil's Gate" before we see it, and acknowledge that the name has been appropriately given to the narrow portals of shattered gneiss, through which the river has forced a passage. This mountain gateway opens on a plain which is at once recognized as the bed of a vanished inland sea, of which indeed Salt Lake is but the bitter and dwindling dregs. The western flanks of the Wahsatch range are terraced to a height of nine hundred feet above the plain, each terrace marking a pause in the gradual subsidence of the water. The lake-bed itself looks as if it had been drained yesterday, no vegetation in this arid climate having yet covered its deposits of loess. The line runs across its levels for fourteen miles, to Ogden, where the Union Pacific Railroad ends and the Central Pacific begins, and where also is the junction for Salt Lake City, which lies about forty miles south of the transcontinental route.

The City of the Saints is like no other in America. Seen from a distant standpoint in the hills, it wears the same quasi-Oriental aspect as Cañon City, but in all other respects it is *sui generis*. It stands at the feet of the mountains, on the edge of an apparently boundless plain, with Salt Lake shining in the sun twelve miles away. The plain is cultivated near the hills; but only a few miles beyond the city, it becomes a desert, where nothing grows except wild sage and great sunflowers. Detached white houses, each standing in a garden of its own, gleam from among thick foilage which is furrowed here and there by rectangular lines of yellow dust, marking the courses of travelled streets. The oval dome of the great tabernacle, and the rising mass of the new temple, dominate the town, which is overarched by a sky of the tenderest blue and enveloped in an atmosphere of indescribable purity. On a near approach the Saints' houses are found to be surrounded with orchards and trees, which almost entirely hide them from view. They are built for the most part of "adobe," or unburned bricks; and architectural taste is conspicuously absent even in the most ambitious residences. The same may be said of the tabernacle, which is a hideous oval building, crowned with a kind of shingle dish-cover; while the new temple, built of a beautiful local granite, is hardly worthy of a carpenter in design. In fact it may be taken for granted that cultured taste, whether in architecture or decoration, does not exist among the Mormons. The wide streets are bordered with "shade trees" of cotton-wood, and in every gutter a swift little stream of mountain water bustles gaily along. Only the shops thrust themselves on the notice of passers-by, and these are numerous, well-stocked, clean, and, wonder of wonders in America, cheap. No American towns, except Philadelphia and Washington, can compare with

Salt Lake City for cleanliness; its roads are excellent, and there is evidently no slackness in the performance of their municipal duties by the saints. Perched on the hill-side, high above the town, is Fort Douglas, a small stronghold built by the United States Government after the Indians had been driven out from Bear Creek in 1873, ostensibly to guard against their further incursions, but really to overawe the Mormon capital. When the fort was first located, Young sent word to the lieutenant that he forbade him the flanks of the Wahsatch, and got a curt reply from that officer, whereupon the prophet followed his message with a threat. The lieutenant's second answer consisted of three shells, which, entering the roof of the tabernacle, finally closed an argument that has not since been reopened.

Joe Smith, the founder of Mormonism, was born in Vermont in 1805, and received his first "revelation" at the age of eighteen. Four years later he became, according to his own account, miraculously possessed of the Book of Mormon, a collection of metal plates, engraved in "Egyptian" character, which the seer translated by the supernatural aid of the "Urim and Thummim." It need hardly be said that this book is a farrago of nonsense, but it formed a basis for the organization of a Church of the "Latter-Day Saints" which was first established in 1830 at the town of Fayette in the state of New York. Affiliated Churches soon arose in other states, and a considerable Mormon settlement was formed in Missouri, which was however attacked by a mob and destroyed in the same year. The fugitives made a second home at Clay, in the same state, whence they were again violently driven in 1836 by a mob, and the same thing was repeated in another county two years later. At length, in 1839, the exiles fled to the then remote state of Illinois, where they found a friendly home, took up land, built their city of Nauvoo, and enjoyed religious freedom for a time. In 1844 however they were again threatened by a mob and the prophet Smith was imprisoned, but before he was brought to trial, a band of men, with blackened faces, surrounded the gaol, and, overcoming the State authority, shot Smith and his brother Hyram dead, and wounded Taylor, the present Mormon president, who was confined with them. Previously to this, Smith had been brought before judicial tribunals nearly fifty times, but had always been acquitted, and, from first to last, he and his community suffered nothing at the hands of the law, but everything from violence. The assassins were brought to trial but were acquitted, and the Mormon persecution went on until, in the fall of 1845, a mob, which the Sheriff of Hancock County vainly tried to control, commenced house-burning at Nauvoo. Shortly after this the Mormons agreed to quit the state, and asked to be left unmolested while they made their preparations for departure. The exodus began in February 1846, when more than a thousand families crossed the Mississippi Valley on the ice, hoping by their timely flight to allay the excitement against those who were not able to leave in the winter. Brigham Young, who became president on the death of Joe Smith, directed the operations of the emigrants, and having established a temporary town in Nebraska and a great waggon encampment on the Missouri, he, with a hundred and forty pioneers, started west in the spring of 1847, seeking a permanent settlement. By midsummer, the pioneer party, "led by the inspiration of the Almighty," camped in the great Salt Lake Valley, but the main body of Mormons did not arrive until the fall of 1848, and winter overtook them still at the foot of the Wahsatch range. Young's original intention undoubtedly was to reach California and establish the saints in Mexican territory, but during the halt at Salt Lake the Mexican war had ended in favour of the Union; California, as well as Utah, had been ceded to the Americans, and further advance became useless. In the spring of 1849 therefore a provisional government was organized under the name of the "State of Deseret," and the foundations of Mormon power in the west established. In the following year Utah became a "territory" by Act of Congress, and such it still remains, although the population has long been large enough to justify its conversion into a state. This step the United States Government, in spite of Mormon pressure, have hitherto refused to take, wisely preferring to retain the power of appointing the governor, land agent, and judges, instead of surrendering all control into the hands of a purely Mormon state legislation. There is no question that the same policy will continue to keep the saints in check, and safeguard the growing Gentile interests of Utah until either Mormonism itself dies of inanition, or is dealt with by American law. Such is an outline of the history of the Latter-Day Saints from their establishment by Smith to the foundation of Salt Lake City, which, commenced in the year following the arrival in Salt Lake Valley, has grown to a town of twenty thousand inhabitants, nine-tenths of whom are Mormons, and become the capital of a territory having a population of a hundred and forty-three thousand, of whom no more than twenty thousand are Gentiles.

Before regarding either the theocratic government or religious character of the Mormon community, it will be useful to examine what it has accomplished from the point of view of material progress, and learn something of what these men are from what they have done. It is the boast of Mormon leaders that they have made the "wilderness blossom as the rose," replacing sterility with fertility in a quite exceptional manner, and that the Church swells in numbers as no other religious body has ever done. But, touching cultivation in the first instance, the new-comer from Colorado cannot fail to be struck with the difference between the irrigation works of this state and those of Utah. The Mormons have watered the fringe of land lying at the very feet of the hills, using the simplest means for this purpose, but they have undertaken no important works such as should long ago have spread cultivation over the still desert area stretching between the city and Salt Lake. In Colorado, on the other hand, organized ten years later than Utah, immense sums of money have been spent on scientific irrigation, with the result that while less than a million acres of land have been taken up in Utah during the last ten years, nearly two millions have come under the plough in Colorado in the same period. Still more striking results appear on comparing the

Mormon territory with Kansas and Nebraska, where, though both these states were settled four years later than Utah, thirteen million and nine million acres were taken up respectively between 1870 and 1880. Mormon theocracy boasts of its desert roses, as if the saints alone could raise flowers in the wilderness, but for every bloom which Utah has put forth, Colorado shows two, Nebraska eight, and Kansas ten.

And if we push economic inquiries in various directions a similar answer attends them all. Thus, while the total population of Utah, settled in 1850, is a hundred and forty-three thousand; that of Colorado, settled in 1861, is a hundred and ninety-five thousand; of Nebraska, settled in 1854, four hundred and fifty thousand; and of Kansas, settled in the same year as Nebraska, nine hundred and ninety-five thousand. Or, reducing these figures in each case to show the annual increase of population, while Utah grows at the rate of four thousand eight hundred souls yearly, Colorado gains ten thousand; Nebraska twenty-eight thousand; and Kansas thirty-nine thousand per annum, and this in spite of polygamous competition. Similarly, while Utah has made six hundred miles of railway, Colorado has built twelve hundred, Nebraska sixteen hundred, and Kansas three thousand miles. Or, turning from material to intellectual progress, it appears that Utah spends nine-tenths of a dollar per annum per head on the education of her school population, Colorado and Kansas spend each one dollar and a tenth, and Nebraska two dollars and a tenth for the same purposes. The traffic returns of the Utah Central Railway, by which all exports and imports leave or reach the New Jerusalem, are equally significant. In the year 1873, a total of one hundred and nine thousand tons of goods were received and twenty-seven thousand tons despatched by the line in question; while the imports fell to a hundred and one thousand tons and the exports to twenty-three thousand tons in 1879, in spite of the yearly increasing consignments of metals which are now being made by Gentile miners.

The day after our arrival, being Sunday, we visited the

tabernacle, a huge and hideous building, large enough to hold several thousands of worshippers, but containing no more than fifteen hundred on the day of our visit. We placed ourselves where a good general view of the congregation could be obtained, and found the Mormon faces even more commonplace in character than we had anticipated. The American type was not to be seen anywhere, but the people looked like, what they indeed are, the dregs of Britain and Scandinavia. In form, the service was similar to that of an English Nonconformist chapel, both prayers and sermon however being extremely commonplace, though free from any special Mormonite doctrine. A curious feature of the ritual consisted in handing the Eucharistic elements round to the whole congregation, exactly as if they were refreshments, during the progress of the sermon.

Enough has perhaps already been written about the theocratic government and religious aspect of the New Jerusalem, which, together with its prophet, has been treated too much as a prodigy. It is no doubt an extraordinary fact that Brigham Young should have succeeded in creating and upholding in the very centre of the American continent, a state of things which is entirely opposed to the ideas of our race and our time, but this result has really been reached by very simple means. It must be admitted that Young was a man of vast ambition, a great organizer, fertile in resource, selfish, unscrupulous and a born tyrant. But he possessed the magic of cordiality, and a magnetic presence which controlled while it seemed to persuade, and inspired devotion among people who were really his slaves. It must also be remembered that, after the last exodus from Illinois, the Mormon community was not again disturbed in its remote mountain home, and had already consolidated into an *imperium in imperio* before America had any ground for thinking that her deserts were destined to be brought within the fold of civilization. This immunity from external interference, while giving scope to Young's powers and leading him to developments little dreamed of at first, has ended in presenting the Mormon difficulty to

America in an aggravated shape; a disagreeable, if not, as some think, a dangerous legacy from the unwise violence of 1844-45.

Contrary to what is usually supposed, polygamy formed no part of the Mormon faith as preached by Joe Smith. Smith himself had but one wife, and the same thing was true of Young for some years after the settlement in Salt Lake. Brigham was "no saint," as the phrase goes, but it was not until he was firmly established as the inspired prophet, absolute sovereign, and military chief of the Mormon community that he ventured on promulgating the "Revelation on Celestial Marriage." It was in 1852 that Young first produced a document, bearing the above title, whose contents he declared had been revealed to Joe Smith a year before his death. Smith's widow and son denounced the story as apocryphal, but such was the influence of the prophet at this time, that the "revelation" was accepted at a meeting of Mormon delegates, and its doctrines became the leading feature of the Mormon faith from that time. Polygamy however was not the bait by which proselytes were in the first instance attracted to the New Jerusalem, nor indeed did it become so even after the promulgation of the "Revelation on Celestial Marriage." Young's want, like that of America at the present time, was labour, and in order to procure this he established missions in almost every European country, in Australia, and even in India and China. The last were soon abandoned, but religious labour agencies were prosecuted with the utmost energy in Britain and Scandinavia, whence, especially from Wales and Denmark, a constant stream of emigration flowed to the head-quarters of the saints. Only the lowest classes were sought by the Mormon missionaries, and to these poor toilers the gospel of "labour and faith" sounded attractive enough when the New Jerusalem, painted in glowing colours as a land flowing with milk and honey, was declared free to all and within the reach of all. Such a message, backed by material assistance, and delivered with enthusiasm by men selected for their devotion to the prophet's person, could have but one result, and emigrants, drawn from the lowest and consequently most credulous classes, repaired by thousands to Salt Lake Valley. The movement had no specially religious stimulus whatever, but the proselytes were simply led, as in the case of other emigrants, by the hope of improving their condition in life. They were for the most part penniless, and of course utterly without the means of cultivating the portions of land on which they were settled upon their arrival in the Far West. It was Young who supplied every want of the new-comers, whether for building houses, or breaking up the soil, taking payment in liens on the various farms. Thus, from the moment of his settlement, the emigrant became the debtor, and practically the slave of the prophet, whose powerful character, aided by unfailing *bonhomie*, established an extraordinary influence, half fear half faith, over the partially developed minds of his people, who thought of him, not as a creditor, but as a beneficent being of supernatural powers in direct communication with the Almighty.

As a matter of fact however Utah became a prison; for though, by dint of constant labour, the Mormon farmer gained a livelihood, it was rarely indeed that he succeeded in discharging his obligations. To leave the valley, even if he wished it, was impossible without money; and purchasers of farms in a community burdened with debt and deprived of any surplusage by heavy Church tithes were few indeed. Young riveted these chains in many ways. The administration of justice, ostensibly a function of the Church, was practically in his hands and, like all spiritual tyrants, he wielded a secret system of espionage which kept him informed of everything passing even in the obscurest households. He disposed absolutely of a considerable military force and of the devoted services of a mysterious body called the "Avenging Angels," who secretly executed his decrees. Discountenancing the use of money, he made it a matter of religion to conduct all commercial transactions by barter. He prohibited mining in the neighbouring mountains, declaring that the tilling of the soil was the only work approved of by God. He even tried to introduce a

Mormon language, in which if he had succeeded, the children of the original settlers would have lost the power of reading anything but Mormon literature. No schools, properly so called, were established, but only "ward-meeting houses," where the Book of Mormon formed the whole educational curriculum. While however the prophet aimed at producing mental stagnation among his people, he took care that they were both occupied and amused. "Labour and faith" was the creed he unceasingly preached, but he made leisure agreeable by amusements and the drama. The theatre played a *rôle* only inferior to the tabernacle in New Jerusalem, where they worked, believed, and laughed, but did not think.

Given then, on the one hand, an isolated, credulous, and ignorant community, bound almost equally in the chains of superstition and poverty, and on the other, an able, suave, and unscrupulous autocrat like Young, whose hand of iron was never ungloved with velvet except openly to strike the foes of the commonwealth, or secretly to smite where he feared private danger, there is little to excite surprise in the general phenomena of Mormonism. With regard to its special feature, polygamy, Brigham created a fanatical community in spite rather than by means of this doctrine; and his ascendancy would perhaps have remained more unquestioned if he had never promulgated the "Revelation on Celestial Marriage." For the bulk of the Mormons were after all too poor to have more than one wife, and though the prophet probably pleased the priesthood, who lived in comparative wealth on the tithes, and whose co-operation was essential to his superstitious system, by the institution, his hold on the masses did not depend on the doctrine of plural marriage. The commonplace clay of which his bishops, elders, and prosperous traders were made, was no doubt well pleased to gratify passion under the sanction of religion, but Mormonism as a system was weakened, not strengthened, by the introduction of polygamy. Within twenty years after its establishment there was serious insubordination in the camp. Young girls made vows against marrying polygamous husbands, and the children of first marriages treated the issues of later unions as illegitimate. Force and fear entered the community, creating a crisis whose gravity Young himself appreciated, and whose end he perhaps secretly dreaded. After his death polygamy became a less prominent feature of Mormon faith, apart from which tenet however it would be difficult for any man intelligibly to formulate this strange creed.

All the world asks "What will be the end of Mormonism?" and some say "Why does not the American Legislature interfere to put an end to this scandal?" But, during the time when distant Utah was treated with the natural neglect already referred to, a great population of ignorant, bigoted, and credulous people has arisen, whom the Americans of to-day are much too wise to treat, whether lawfully or unlawfully, in the spirit of persecution. The soul of Mormonism died with Young, and its body is rotting. Gentile miners, whom Brigham hated, and while he yet had power forbade the territory, are raising twenty thousand dollars' worth of bullion a day in the Wahsatch range. Gentile traders have settled under the protecting guns of Fort Douglas, to supply the wants of these men. Gentile newspapers are published. Gentile schools have been opened. Money has taken the place of barter. The rich mining men of Idaho and Montana come here to spend their winters agreeably, crowding the hotels, spending money freely, and unconsciously distributing ideas. Railways to the mining camps will follow, and by-and-by it will be found that the bottom has dropped out of Mormonism, before the world, or the Mormons themselves for that matter, are aware of it. Such is the view of the practical average Yankee, who has a boundless, if not noisy, faith in the gospel of selfishness, and who cannot conceive of a superstitious creed proving stronger than dollars. America believes that railroads, newspapers, and schools will prove more than a match for polygamy and priestcraft, and on this occasion will undoubtedly "let all things grow together till the harvest" which common sense will one day reap, even in Salt Lake Valley. But for the follies committed in Illinois in 1844 and 1845, a crowd of inconsequent sectaries could never have become important, or Brigham Young have risen to be a power in the state; but man, especially fanatical man, is so much wiser than his Maker that he always tries to improve on the methods of providence.

A dip in the dense brine of Salt Lake is a curious experience. Swimming is difficult, for the heels float above the surface and strike at the air, but one can sit in a natural posture in the water without making any movement. A bathers' train runs daily to the lake, giving magnificent views of the Wahsatch range on the way, and carrying a crowd of saints, together with some sinners, who, in all sorts of becoming and unbecoming costumes, splash about in the limpid blue water till the locomotive shrieks a summons to the bank.

The hill-sides around Salt Lake are scored, like the Wahsatch range, up to great heights with many terraces, some conspicuous and others obscure, but all suggesting that the vast inland seas which covered Central America after the close of the glacial period have disappeared by gradual evaporation, the arid climate of a later period being even now engaged in draining the last drops of sweet water from the ever brinier depths of the great Salt Lake.

CHAPTER XXI.

LAKE TAHOE—VIRGINIA CITY.

August 10-19.

LEAVING Salt Lake City, the railroad enters upon the great American desert, those desolate plains so well characterised by Bret Harte—

"Alkali, rock and sage,
Sage brush, rock, and alkali, ain't it a pretty page?
Sun in the east at morning, sun in the west at night,
And the shadow of this 'yer station, the on'y thing moves in sight."

From Ogden to the feet of the Sierra Nevada the cars traverse a succession of old lake-beds, whose floors, now dry, are covered with a thin crust of alkaline efflorescence derived from the moisture of the sub-soil, which, creeping upwards by capillary attraction and loaded with saline matter, evaporates on reaching the surface and leaves the deposit in question. Vegetation entirely fails in the desert basin, save for scattered bunches of sage brush, whose roots, holding the earth together, preserve the soil here and there from erosion by wind, and give rise to great hummocks, sometimes five or six feet high, upon whose leeward slopes the ragged sage branches huddle together. Life, like vegetation, totally disappears, not even ants or prairie dogs being able to pick up a living in such a wilderness. The surface of the ground is parched and yellowish-brown in colour; there are no streams and great rivers, like the Humboldt and Truckee, which, rising in the snows of the Eastern Sierran slopes, lose themselves in the bitter and thirsty levels of the desert basin. The desolate scene is margined by high mountains, whose waterless flanks, bare of all vegetation, are terraced for hundreds of feet above the plain, every terrace marking a pause in the process of desiccation which has deprived Western America of its ancient inland seas. A fine white dust, disturbed by the passage of the train, rises in clouds and covers everything within the cars with a thick alkaline coating, penetrating into trunks and portmanteaux, while dust-storms, shaped like water-spouts, travel slowly across the plain, looking like great whirling columns of smoke. Still, the desert basin is far from uninteresting to the traveller with an eye for geological changes. To him the dry sea-floors and terraced hill-sides suggest a far-distant time when Western America consisted of a group of islands, the summits of the present ranges, which, enjoying a moist and moderate climate, lifted their steeply sloping and densely wooded sides from a sea whose waters mingled with those of the Arctic Ocean.

After leaving Ogden, Indians were seen at almost every depôt, and the train was never without a few red-skinned passengers during this part of the journey. These were chiefly Shoshones and Piutes, contrasting most unfavourably in appearance with the clean and intelligent-looking Sioux whom we met in Chicago.

The men were degraded-looking wretches, plentifully smeared as to their faces with red and yellow ochre, and dressed for the most part in blankets; while the women who, with babies strapped to their backs, squatted on the platforms begging, and eating such food as was thrown them from the cars, were as much like monkeys as human beings in their ways and movements.

The future of the American Indians is not difficult to divine. Everything favours their extinction, and nothing tends to prolong the life of this unhappy race. War, fire-water, disease, and cross-breeding with whites, perpetually diminish their dwindling ranks. America on the other hand is careless and unjust in her dealings with the red man, and too often allows the "agent" charged with his protection to become the grave-digger of his race. It is notorious that these officials grow rich by withholding from the natives goods which it is their duty, in execution of treaty obligations, to distribute. Annoyed at such treatment, a tribe, it may be, makes a formal complaint, and an inquiry is ordered at Washington. Under these circumstances and determined that no investigation shall take place, an agent has been known to represent the intervention of government as an act of hostility directed against the tribe. An Indian attack or outrage follows, whereupon troops are ordered into the district, and a "little" war ensues, in the course of which a number of white men are scalped, and some white homes destroyed, but in the result the tribe is nearly exterminated, and the inquiry abandoned.

Twenty hours from Ogden the ascent of the Sierra Nevada commences, the railroad in the first instance following the course of the Truckee river, whose valley opens into smiling meadows soon after the desert plain is left, while pines again begin to cling to the mountain-sides. Before rising far, and when still some fifty miles from the summit, we stopped at Reno, and diverged thence to Carson City, lying about twenty miles south of the transcontinental route. From the desert levels surrounding this town we could see the bare brown summits of the Washoe chain, and beyond and above them the snowy peaks of the Sierra Nevada itself. On the other side of the nearer range lies Lake Tahoe, for which we took the stage at Carson, and clambering first to the Washoe summits, wound down thence through forests of magnificent Californian pines to the lake-shore. The axe, which has already stripped so many hills to supply the wants of Nevada mines, is busy among these glorious trees, and in a few years the green frame now encircling the lake will be destroyed, and one of the most beautiful bits of scenery in the world robbed of half its charm. A great saw-mill has been established on Tahoe, and timber is being transported in immense quantities by a mountain railroad to the Washoe summit, where it is thrown, stick by stick, into a snow-fed flume, or trough, which winds along the mountain-sides, sometimes by gentle slopes, sometimes in steep inclines, to Carson City. A constant stream of logs is thus delivered to the great lumber-yards of that town, twenty miles distant, and, as the flume follows the stage road for the greater part of that distance, the operation is frequently in view from the top of the coach. It is curious to observe that upon the steep inclines the logs travel faster than the water in the flume. The falling fluid is retarded by friction against the sides of the trough, but the baulks of timber, travelling with the water, suffer no such retardation, and consequently, where the descent is rapid, drive the lagging liquid in a wave before them, spilling it over the edges of the trough.

A famous mountain driver, named Hank Monk, handled the lines on the day of our making the journey; the same man who once gave Horace Greeley a terrific ride from the summit of the Sierra down to Placerville, a mining town in the western foot-hills, where the philosopher-politician was going to give an address. The road was bad, the time short, and Greeley became not a little anxious about his arrival, as the stage crept slowly up the mountain-side, but once on the down grade, Monk drove at such a headlong pace that his distinguished passenger thrust his head again and again out of the window to remonstrate; Hank's only answer to every caution being "Keep your seat, Horace, keep your seat; I'm agoing to get you there on time."

Lake Tahoe is perhaps the most beautiful sheet of water in the world. It lies on the eastern flank of the snowy range, about six thousand feet above the sea, in an oblong trough-like bed, parallel with the axis of the mountain chain; a very unusual position for a valley. To say that Tahoe is embosomed in mountains would be to use a figure better suited to the lakes of Italy than to this, which is more correctly described as buried in the range, whose crests rear themselves as much as three thousand feet above its surface on either side. The lake is a sheet of transparent water, green where shallow, and azure blue where deep, set like emerald and turquoise in the glittering silver of snow-clad peaks. The sky that overhangs it is cloudless, and rain in summer is unknown; the surrounding rocks are of grey granite which give a cold look to the scenery, except when the last rays of sunset, or the first of sunrise, light them up with the splendid tints of the "Alpen-glow." The great pines which fringe the shores and clothe the mountains give a peculiar beauty, but add little grace to the landscape, their foliage, though dark green near at hand, looking ashy grey on distant hill-sides. Many of these glorious trees are seven or eight feet in diameter and tower up to heights of two hundred feet and more, while the largest of them cannot be less than a thousand years old.

We quartered at the head of the lake in a rough but comfortable hotel kept by a character named Clements, universally known throughout the neighbourhood as "Yank." He came here more than twenty years ago, when both California and Nevada were full of Indians; took in land, and built himself a board house, which, now that Tahoe is visited for its beauty, has grown into a rambling tumble-down hotel, standing on the edge of the lake and surrounded by gigantic pines. Among the last, the white tents of summer "campers" are scattered, and at night, when a score of camp fires are lighting up the red stems of the trees, it is both picturesque and pleasant to stroll, always a welcome guest, from one forest home to another, admiring the fickle illumination of the trees, and chatting, here with a trout-fisher, there with a grouse-shooter, or again with a family party spending its holiday under canvas.

Once a week Yank gives a "ball," when people who look like artisans, but may be mining millionaires, arrive with parties of gay wives and gayer daughters, in wonderful buggies, drawn by still more wonderful four-horse teams. As evening approaches, neighbouring ranchmen; folks from the saw-mill; others from Tahoe City—a town on the lake, of at least a dozen houses—and Yank's male helps appear, "fixed" for the occasion. The dignified young person who waits at table in a wide hat and Dolly Varden dress gets into her war-paint, while guests like ourselves rummage their portmanteaux for something more becoming than tweed suits; and the band, arriving in excellent time, is importuned to take drinks. The ball-room is built expressly for dancing, having a spring floor which plies in the centre, while a fixed margin, three or four feet wide, is left for the chaperones, if such things are in the West, where they may sit "solid" while the gay crowd is gently heaving like ships on a quiet sea. Etiquette, as at the Denver "social hop," is strictly observed, and behaviour is as punctilious as in a London drawing-room; while for real enjoyment I would back these light-hearted pleasure-loving westerners against even the French themselves.

We take our meals at Yank's in a bare boarded room, and sleep on bare boards cunningly disguised with blankets; the kitchen and Chinese cook are conspicuous parts of the establishment, and we see our dinner daily cut from a tough buck hanging on a pine branch outside. The ranch-helps and grooms, lounge independently, and spit casually about the piazza. The campers, in shirt-sleeves and high boots, drop in now and then for drinks and friendly conversation, and Yank himself lays wait for us in the bar, to tell for the fiftieth time an endless yarn beginning with "I settled this valley two and twenty years ago," at the sound of which words experienced men have been known to leave the most seductive cocktail and fly. But life is a thing to be thoroughly enjoyed at Yank's landing. A morning swim in the cold blue water, is followed by a tramp to some neighbouring Sierran summit, or to one of the smaller lakes with which the district abounds. Or we shake out a sail and troll for great trout, or, boarding the pleasure steamer which calls daily at the primitive pier, make a tour of the whole lovely lake. At night, failing a "ball," we stroll through the lighted forest, or chat with the campers, lying on couches of odorous pine needles, with eyes that wander from the flashing camp fires up the dark shafts of stately trees to the quiet stars shining out of a violet-black sky.

From Yank's we made the ascent of Mount Tellac, a peak ten thousand two hundred feet above sea-level, lying east of the Sierran summit and somewhat lower than the crest of the range. This mountain is glaciated from the bottom almost to the top, exposing in some places acres of bare white granite, polished like a mirror, and reflecting the sun's rays dazzlingly. From its shoulders, two lateral moraines, gently graded and symmetrical as railway embankments, sweep down to Lake Tahoe. No model, contrived for the purpose, could better illustrate the former existence of a glacier on the flanks of Tallace, while, as if to make the picture of what has been more complete, masses of snow lying between the dark walls of the lateral moraines, simulate the vanished ice-flow. The number of butterflies, and variety of wild flowers met with during the ascent surprised us not a little. The former were fluttering gaily on the very summit of the mountain, and we gathered no less than thirty species of flowering plants, to say nothing of ferns which were almost equally numerous, on the way. Such snow as remained unmelted varied from a few feet to a few yards in thickness, and was tinted here and there at the higher elevations with bright pink patches, for which, in the probable absence of the Arctic snow fungus from such a locality, we could in no way account. The view from the crest, looking west, embraced a magnificent line of the Sierran peaks, while southward we were hemmed in by lower, but still snowy, spurs of the main range, and eastward, the eye ranged away to the Carson Desert. Although the sun was extremely hot we suffered no inconvenience from his rays, so cool and dry is this mountain air, but a natural spring of sparkling soda water, occurring by the way, found favourable critics both on the upward and downward journey.

Nevada is the greatest mining state in the Union, and Virginia City, its capital, the greatest mining city in the world. It lies among the foot-hills of the Sierra at an elevation of six thousand two hundred feet, on the eastern face of Mount Davidson, whose summit is seven thousand seven hundred feet above the sea, and is separated from Tahoe by the Washoe range, over whose crest we climbed on our way to the beautiful lake. The city clings so closely to the flanks of the lower hills that the Sierran summits lying to the westward are hidden, but eastward, the landscape is made up of innumerable interlocked mountains, conical in outline, red-brown in colour, and perfectly bare of all vegetation. These stretch as far as the eye can reach to where the snowy tops of the Humboldt peaks stand against the sky, and the terrible sterility of the scene is enhanced, rather than relieved, by the thin meanderings of the Carson river, whose course is marked by a narrow green line, looking like grass from the city, but really consisting of cotton-woods. This is the only sign of water visible in the arid panorama, whose bare red cones are steeped all day in dust haze, and lighted for a few moments at sunset by an "Alpenglow" which dyes the countless peaks in as countless gradations of rosy light. Through this labyrinth of interosculating hills the railway from Carson to Virginia City is built; not following the course of a valley as railways usually do, but skirting the hill-sides like a contour-line on a map, and sweeping around them in great S-like curves, which sometimes almost return upon themselves in joining two points, scarcely more than a gunshot asunder, but parted by a valley perhaps a thousand feet deep. The valleys are as dry as the hills, and though the country has evidently been shaped by the action of running water, the streams have all completely disappeared. The mountains are of volcanic origin, and the railway cuttings expose rocks of the most varied and brilliant tints, sometimes dark purple, sometimes bright red in colour.

Virginia City began to be a town in July 1859, when silver was first discovered by two Irishmen in the Ophir Mine, and the rush from California which ensued, on the find becoming known in that state, soon made the now world-famous Comstock Lode a busy place. A straggling village of canvas houses, tents, and brush shanties grew up at once; before a year had passed, adobe and brick buildings began to make their appearance, and the bare slopes of Mount Davidson were soon whitened with the dwellings of a great camp. This was totally destroyed by fire in 1875, after which the place was systematically rebuilt, and is now a handsome town numbering about twenty thousand inhabitants. Virginia City is more orderly, cleaner, and better kept than many eastern cities; while the crowd which fills its well-paved streets, though cosmopolitan to the last degree, is prosperous, well dressed, and well behaved. It comprises keen-faced Americans, in store clothes and stove-pipe hats; Chinamen, in pig-tails and blue and black blouses; Piute and Washoe Indians, in paint and rags; hard-headed Cornishmen, with, here and there, a wild Mexican; but totally unlike Leadville, Virginia City looks as finished as New York or Philadelphia, its dwellings and the mills connected with the silver-mining industry being remarkable for a neatness and order, which is quite foreign to mining districts generally.

The Comstock Lode extends through the whole length of Virginia City and for some miles on either side of it. This great "fissure vein" varies from twenty feet to three hundred feet in thickness, and yields quartz containing both silver and gold. The shafts are very deep, averaging from thirteen hundred to fifteen hundred feet, but there are some which are sunk vertically as much as two thousand five hundred feet below the surface. The mineral vein is the richest in the world, having yielded more than £60,000,000 worth of gold and silver since its discovery in 1859; and two shafts in particular, the Consolidated Virginia, and California, called the "Bonanza" mines, yield together nearly six and a half millions of the precious metals annually.

The operations of the Comstock Lode are unusually interesting on account of the extraordinary perfection of the appliances used, both above and below ground, which, together with an admirable organization, offer a striking contrast to the primitive machinery and unsystematic management of mines in general. Excellent permanent buildings contain the hoisting machinery and engines for winding and pumping. The former consist of large drums, provided with well-considered arrangements for indicating the position of the cages throughout their ascent and descent, together with scientific signalling apparatus; the whole being of excellent workmanship. The winding-engines are the best that can be procured; powerful, easily controlled, and trustworthy. Ordinary pumping-engines have proved unsatisfactory in raising water from such great depths, and, as "a stop costs more than an engine" in these deep mines, the ingenuity of the best American engineers has been taxed to produce the splendid motors in use for this purpose. The only fuel in Virginia City is wood, and, the sources of supply being distant, this is dear, so that all these fine engines have been built as much for economy as efficiency, and are provided with scientific valve-gear for reducing the expenditure of steam to a minimum. The miners descend the shafts in iron cages, each of which carries twenty-seven men. These are fitted with safety catches, and lowered by wide iron bands, instead of ropes or chains, and so perfect are all the arrangements for this important service that no accidents have ever occurred. Indeed it is impossible to admire too much the overground machinery of the Bonanza mines, and the same remark applies underground, where compressed-air engines, steam and air drills, blowers for ventilating heated drifts, and every device that skill can suggest, whether for the easier extraction of ore, or the miners' safety, is found in operation.

The Comstock mines form a sort of underground city, whose numerous drifts and cross-cuts intersect each other like the streets of a town; and, like them, they are paved with planking, and lighted by lamps. The heat in the workings is very great, averaging 130° and reaching in some places 157° Fahr. Labour in these temperatures is extremely exhausting, and for new hands painful; but the men get acclimatized after a few weeks and remain in the mines for the four-hour shift without serious discomfort. They drink large quantities of iced water while at work, and four or five tons of ice a day are consumed in the Consolidated Virginia Mine alone. Large and convenient dressing-rooms, fitted with baths, are provided for the miners, each man has a locker for his clothes, and everything in this department is kept in "apple-pie" order. At the time of a shift, the men congregrate from the dressing-rooms in the hoisting-houses, and, at a given signal, file with soldierly regularity by threes into the cage. When a cage has received its full complement of twenty-seven, a bell rings; the great winding-engine begins to turn, and the cage sinks rapidly down; while the mouth of the shaft, which is guarded by a substantial railing, is closed at the same moment. For the visitor who does not object to losing a few pounds' weight by perspiration, a trip to the lower levels is interesting. There is not much to be seen, but the pit is "full of noises;" and the reports of blasts fired in rapid succession, the bark of the air-engines, the roar of the blowers, the rumble of the cars, the rattle of the pumps, and heavy falls of ore in the chutes, lend an air of mysterious activity to the dim scene.

The quartz of the Comstock Lode contains both silver and gold, and is called "free milling ore," because it does not require to be desulphurized by roasting, but goes at once to the stamps. These convert it, by pounding with water, into liquid mud, which, after being strained through fine wire gauze, runs by a long wooden flume to the "pan-mill." This is an independent establishment, where the precious metals are recovered by amalgamation, and run into "unparted" ingots, or blocks containing a mixture of silver and gold, in which condition they are sold to the mint. The silt flowing from the stamps is ground for several hours between iron millstones with sulphate of copper and common salt, and when the silver sulphurets of the ore have been desulphurized by the action of these chemicals, mercury is added to the mass, and the grinding continued until the precious metals have amalgamated with it. The semi-fluid mud is then transferred to a "settler," where the amalgam, by reason of its greater weight, sinks to the bottom of the vessel. Thence it is drawn off into canvas bags, through which the free mercury is squeezed by hydraulic pressure, leaving a semi-solid residue, composed of one part bullion and four parts quicksilver, in the bag. Finally, the amalgam is heated in a retort until all the mercury has been driven off in vapour, and the pure bullion is then melted and run into ingots; the quicksilver being recovered in a metallic condition by condensation.

The pan-mill works for hire, receiving nine dollars a ton for milling, and being bound to return seventy per cent. of the declared assay value of the ore operated upon. In practice it usually returns eighty per cent., and, if the pan-miller takes great care that his operatives do not steal his amalgam, he nets large profits from the business. The larger mills grind from three hundred to five hundred tons of ore per week, and employ from seventy to a hundred hands, each of whom earns from three and a half to four dollars a day. Like everything else connected with the Comstock industries, the pan-mills are models of efficiency and order. Their engines and equipment are of the highest class, the shops and yards are neatness itself; even the rubbish-heaps are tidy, while the operatives, whether in the mills or the mines, are an orderly, respectful, and self-respecting body of men.

Virginia City does honour to the rich mine-owners who direct and control the operations of the Comstock Lode. They have imparted a spirit of enterprise, economy, and order, both to the municipality and the workshop, such as I have never seen in any other industrial town, rarely in any private establishment, and which certainly does not exist in any other mining district in the world. The credit of all this belongs to the "Bonanza kings" Mr. J. W. Mackay and Mr. J. G. Fair, gentlemen who, although they probably do not know how many millions of dollars they are worth, are as energetic and attentive to business as if they were struggling men. There is perhaps no industry whose methods and appliances are generally so rude and unscientific as those of mining, and it is therefore all the more a delightful surprise to the engineer, to find how royally his craft is entertained by the silver kings on the remote hill-sides of the Sierra Nevada.

CHAPTER XXII.

SAN FRANCISCO.

August 20-31.

RETURNING from Virginia City we slept for a night at Truckee, a station on the Central Pacific Railroad, fourteen miles from the summit of the Sierra Nevada. Here the night was cold and frosty, but the sun rose hot and bright as usual. The Truckee river runs out of Lake Tahoe, and, flowing eastward through a deep picturesque cañon, is finally lost in the sands of the desert basin. The railway follows its course to "Summit," the ascent beginning at Wadsworth, where, as already mentioned, the alkali plains are exchanged for mountain slopes, diversified by streams and scattered groups of pines. Between Truckee and summit, and for many miles beyond the latter point, the track is covered by snow-sheds, which are almost continuous for nearly forty miles on one or the other side of the divide. Summit is not more than seven thousand feet above sea-level, but so much more snow falls in the Sierras than among the Rocky Mountains, that the railroad not only requires protection from avalanches but is obliged to avoid the cañons, which are liable to be blocked by heavy drifts. Hence, as in the case of the road from Carson to Virginia City, the track descends from Summit by skirting the hill-sides, thus giving magnificent views of densely wooded mountain slopes, and affording occasional dizzy glimpses into gorges, two and even three thousand feet below the road.

The Sierra Nevada is by far the grandest of the many mountain chains which, folded in broad corrugations, form the western margin of the continent of America. In the words of Mr. Clement King, it is "a long and massive uplift, lying between the arid deserts of the great basin and the Californian exuberance of grain-field and orchard; its eastern slope is a defiant wall, plunging abruptly down to the plain; the western, a long grand sweep, well watered, and overgrown with cool stately forests; its crest a line of sharp snowy peaks, springing into the sky and catching the 'Alpen glow' long after the sun has set for the rest of America. For four hundred miles the Sierras are a definite ridge, broad and high and having the form of a sea-wave. Buttresses of sombre-hued rock, jutting at intervals from a steep wall, form the abrupt eastern slopes; irregular forests, in scattered growth, huddle together near the snow; the lower declivities are barren spurs sinking into the sterile flats of the great basin. Long ridges of comparatively gentle outline characterize the western side, but this sloping table is scored from summit to base by a system of parallel, traverse cañons, distant from one another often less than twenty-five miles. They are usually two or three thousand feet deep, falling at times in sheer smooth-fronted cliffs, again in sweeping curves, like the hull of a ship, again in rugged V-like gorges, or with irregular hilly flanks, opening, at last, through gateways of low rounded foot-hills out upon the horizontal plain of the San Joaquin or Sacramento. Every cañon carries a river, derived from constant melting of the perpetual snow, which threads its way down the mountain—a feeble type of the vast ice streams and torrents that formerly discharged the summit accumulation of ice and snow, while carving the cañons out of the solid rock.

"The western descent, facing a moisture-laden aerial current from the Pacific, condenses on its higher portions a great amount of water which is piled upon the summits in the form of snow, and is absorbed upon the higher plateau by an exuberant growth of forest. This prevalent wind strikes first on the western slope of the coast range, a chain of hills of no great elevation, skirting the very margin of the Pacific, and there discharges a very great sum of moisture, but, being ever reinforced, it blows over their crests, and hurrying eastward, strikes the Sierras at about four thousand feet above sea-level. Below this line the foot-hills are oppressed by an habitual dryness, which produces a rusty tone throughout the large conspicuous vegetation, scorches the red soil, and during the long summer, overlays the whole region with a cloud of dust. Dull and monotonous in colour, the oak-clad hills of this lower zone wander out into the great plain-like coast promontories enclosing bays of prairie. Above this zone of red earth, with its softly modelled undulations and dull grey groves, its chain of mining towns, and scattered ranches and vineyards, rise the swelling middle heights of the Sierras, a broad billowy plateau, cut by sharp, sudden cañons, and sweeping up with its dark, superb growth of coniferous forest to the feet of the summit peaks.

"Strikingly contrasted are the two countries bordering the Sierra on either side. Along the western base is the plain of California, an elliptical basin four hundred and fifty miles long by sixty-five broad; level, fertile, well watered, half tropically warmed; chequered with farms of grain, ranches of cattle, orchard, and vineyard, and houses of commonplace opulence, towns of bustling thrift. From the Mexican frontier on the other hand, up to Oregon, a strip of actual desert lies under the east slope of the great chain, and stretches eastward, sometimes as far as five hundred miles, varied by successions of bare white ground effervescing under the hot sun with alkaline salts, plains covered by the ashy-hued sage plant, high, barren, rocky ranges which are folds of metamorphic rocks, and piled-up lavas of bright red or yellow colours; all overarched by a sky which is at one time of hot metallic brilliancy, and, again, the tenderest of evanescent purple or pearl." Between these two regions, lifted equally above the bustling industry of the plains and melodramatic mining theatre of the foot-hills on the one hand, and the stark, glaring desert, with its chains of bare and corpse-like hills on the other, shine the white peaks of the High Sierra, their heads bathed in the ethereal blue, their feet swathed in dark luxuriant woods.

At last, the summit of the Sierra Nevada crossed, we were in California, the land of romance, whose treasures are guarded by entrances as wonderful as the gates of a true fairyland. From

Summit to Sacramento is rather more than a hundred miles, and, within that distance, the train descends from an elevation half that of Mont Blanc, almost to sea-level; passing successively through the splendid forest belt of the Sierran flanks, the arid foot-hills of the range, and finally emerging into the valley of the Sacramento river, whose wide flats form one great grain-field. At Summit the traveller shivers in an overcoat, but he learns how shrewdly the sun of California bites before reaching the plain, where, however, the transparent air and vibrating light of the great altitudes disappear; the horizon becoming lead-coloured, and the sky soft, while the atmosphere recalls the pearly air of Holland.

The valley of the Sacramento is thickly dotted with wealthy homesteads, well built and comfortable looking, like the farmhouses of Lincolnshire, and frequent wind-mills help to remind us of the English fen country. Harvest is over, and wheat in bags lies at every railroad depôt, or piled in the fields where, though not under cover, it is safe from rain which is quite unknown at this time of the year. Here and there, lie the great "headers," or reaping-machines, twenty feet wide, which take off only the ears of the grain and deliver them to the thrashing-machine while the cutting proceeds. Elsewhere stand immense mounds of straw, useless except as fuel for the straw-burning steam-engine, and waiting a favourable calm to be fired and destroyed. The cultivation throughout the Sacramento Valley alternates between wheat and lucern, or "alfalfa" grass, but grain is often grown for many years in succession. The soil is a rich alluvium which carries heavy crops sometimes amounting to fifty or sixty bushels per acre. The farms, contrary to the rule in America, are very large, holdings of twenty and even forty thousand acres being no uncommon thing. These great tracts of land are for the most part held under Mexican titles, many of which have doubtless had rather shady origins, but at the close of the Mexican war the United States Government respected the rights of owners in possession, and great farms remain the rule in the valley of the Sacramento.

The San Joaquin and Sacramento rivers enter the harbour of San Francisco together by the Straits of Carchenas, across which the train is ferried, a distance of nearly three miles, on a huge steamboat. This vessel is four hundred and fifty feet long and a hundred and thirty feet wide, and on her deck are laid four lines of way which can accommodate as many as fifty cars at a time. The train is put on board so easily, and the transit made so quietly, that a stranger, crossing at night, would hardly be aware of anything beyond a long stoppage having taken place. Leaving the Carchenas Straits, the railway skirts the eastern shore of San Francisco harbour, a long, narrow, and lakelike expanse of water, landlocked by the hills of the coast range, except at one point, where the Golden Gate opens its narrow and rocky portals to the Pacific. On the southern jamb of this continental doorway stands the city of San Francisco, facing the enclosed harbour, and climbing thence backward up the steep slopes of the hills which separate the anchorage from the ocean.

Arrived at Oakland, a flourishing suburb of the western metropolis, situated on the eastern side of the harbour, we left the train, which pursued its way southward to San José, and crossed, in a great ferry-boat, to the city. A fleecy fog was flowing in through the Golden Gate, the sun, no longer brilliant as at the great altitudes, or glaring, as on the plains, shone with a soft delicious lustre, the air was cool, almost cold, and the white buildings of the city of romance stole out of the mist as we advanced. We had good reason, as we well knew, to enjoy the temperature. Fifty miles inland the cultivated plain was reeking in tropical heat; fifty miles farther back, the arid foot-hills were lying, like the corpses of a once living land, buried in hot red dust; and still fifty miles farther eastward, the white teeth of the Sierra were chattering in the snow. Meanwhile, for us, a cool exhilarating wind was blowing, and a sun, as much silver as gold, shone from a sky of pearl. The westerly wind blows steadily and continuously from the Pacific, loaded with fog, with which the sun struggles daily at San Francisco, sometimes with more, sometimes with less success.

The solar rays are thus tempered during the summer, while, in winter, the aerial current brings the warmth of the Pacific to the city, which then enjoys the temperature of an English May. Fires are not needed at any time of the year, but an overcoat is pleasant both morning and evening all the year round. Frost is almost unknown, and the whole city turns out to look at a hailstorm.

The history of San Francisco covers a period of only thirty-five years. A house was built where the city now stands in 1835, around which, in the course of time, a small Californian village, called Buena Yerba, sprang up. The Americans changed this name to San Francisco in 1847, and the population in 1848, just prior to the discovery of gold, was a thousand souls. About half of this number were Americans, who, on the termination of the Mexican war, came here either to trade or take up land in the Sacramento Valley; the rest were Californians. The native houses were of unburnt bricks, and their owners were quite Spanish in appearance, wearing high steeple-like hats, jackets of gaudy colours and velvet breeches. Cattle-breeding was the only industry, and the surrounding hill-sides were dotted with scattered ranches, whose white buildings and garden patches were the only visible signs of man in an otherwise desolate country. The farmhouses were built of stakes, driven into the ground, and interlaced with boughs, plastered with mud, and whitewashed. The interior was bare and cheerless, the soil, beaten hard, formed the floor, the furniture comprised only the simplest necessaries of life, and a few gaudily coloured prints of saints were the only ornaments.

In 1848, Colonel Mason, the first American Governor of California, was stationed with a few troops at Monterey, a small town upon the coast south of San Francisco, whence he directed the affairs of the newly acquired and sparsely populated territory. On the 8th of May in that year a rumour came to San Francisco that gold had been found in the American river, a tributary of the Sacramento, about a hundred miles inland. For two days nothing was talked of in the little place but the new gold "placer," as the half-Spanish natives called it, and, on the 10th, some ardent spirits had already started, pick and pan in hand, for the diggings. Before a week was over San Francisco was in a *furor* of excitement. All the workmen had struck, ships in the harbours were deserted by their crews, and storekeepers, merchants, lawyers, mechanics, and labourers alike, were making preparations for moving on the American river. By the end of another week the fever reached and decimated Monterey, Colonel Mason's soldiers deserting and joining the rush. It was at first supposed that Mason would take possession of the mines on behalf of the United States Government, but, if such a course was ever contemplated, it could not have been carried out because his force was insufficient, and he could not keep his men together; while, in addition, it was soon ascertained that the gold occupied many miles of ground, and was not confined to any particular place. Within a fortnight of the news first arriving in San Francisco, the town was practically emptied of its inhabitants, only a few of the longer heads remaining to organize means for supplying the various wants whose early growth and immense extent they had the sense to foresee.

The actual discovery of gold was made by a Mr. Marshall who had built a saw-mill on the American river, a few miles above its junction with the Sacramento, for a settler named Sutter, whose farm lay on the banks of the latter stream. In May, 1848, Marshall had occasion to widen the tail-race of the mill, and, with this view, he let the whole of the water in the dam through the channel at once, thus enlarging the passage-way, and carrying off a mass of detritus by the force of the torrent. Next morning, while walking along the newly crumbled bank, Marshall saw something glittering among the rubbish, and, to use his own words, " I debated within myself whether or not I would take the trouble to bend my back and pick it up. I had decided on not doing so when another glittering morsel caught my eye which I condescended to pick up, and, to my astonishment, found it was a scale of what appeared to be pure gold." While beginning actively to dig and wash for the treasure thus discovered, Sutter and Marshall vainly tried to keep the find a secret, but the report soon spread, and crowds of people flocked from San Francisco, Monterey, and the various ranches, to the Sacramento and American rivers. A pioneer party of Mormons entered California just as the affair became known, and, halting at once, commenced operations which were soon reported far to the eastward of the Sierra Nevada. What followed on Marshall's discovery is now a matter of history. The adventurers of both worlds rushed to the new El-Dorado, and, whether across the then trackless deserts and mountains, or by the gate which opens seaward on the golden land, a surging stream of turbulent men of all nationalities overflowed California, which had hardly yet passed into the hands of the United States, and was still so distant and dissevered from the central authority that executive government was powerless to control its new subjects. If, under these circumstances, anarchy prevailed for a time, and life and property were held by the pistol, it is not to be wondered at. The marvel is, that out of such elements as constituted society in the "early days" of California, order ultimately, and, to a very great extent, spontaneously arose.

In the mean time San Francisco, the natural centre of the territory, grew rapidly. At the time of the gold discovery its population, as we have seen, was not more than a thousand, but two years later, when the influx from the east and Europe had fairly commenced, it contained twenty-five thousand inhabitants. Since that date (1850) it has doubled its numbers in every succeeding ten years, and now contains nearly three hundred thousand souls. The city was incorporated in 1850, but municipal government was for some years so bad, and the administration of the criminal laws so corrupt, that vigilance committees were at length organized who summarily executed or banished the worst offenders without judicial formalities. Judge Lynch, however, resigned in favour of lawful tribunals in 1860, and, at the present moment, but for some acts of violence against the Chinese, too much in vogue unhappily elsewhere, San Francisco might be called one of the most orderly towns in America. The gold which created it has long since been washed out of the Californian foot-hills, and the successors of the lawless "forty-niners" are peaceful growers, of wheat, wine, and fruit, and importers of lumber, coal, coffee, tea, rice, and sugar, while local manufacturers already begin to supply their general wants.

The city is beautifully situated with its back resting on the hills of the Coast range which separate it from the Pacific, and its face turned towards the lake-like harbour, beyond which rise the mountains of the Contra Costa range. The streets are rectangularly arranged, as usual, and the houses are generally of wood, painted white, and always furnished with bay windows, to catch as much sun as possible. All of them have some pretensions to architectural beauty, and there are a number of mansions, belonging to wealthy men, which, though built entirely of pine, rival the finest dwellings of London or Paris. No American city is so un-American as San Francisco. Its population is extremely cosmopolitan, and contains only a small proportion of native Americans. The people speak without a nasal twang, and, new as it is, the town is more finished and home-like than the older but cruder eastern cities, which interest, but do not charm, the visitor from Europe. If a delicious temperature, abundance of fruits and flowers, dainty cleanliness, streets quaintly diversified by Chinese houses and dresses, shops displaying, in addition to much excellent native art, the treasures of Japan and the far East—if these things make a city pleasant, San Francisco is a pleasant town. Then the place is redolent of mining romance. The neighbouring foot-hills are still dotted with camps such as those which Bret Harte has invested with a melodramic interest. The palaces of California Street, to which reference has already been made, belong to men who were miners yesterday and are millionaires to-day. A sanguine, light-hearted, and courageous people, who know how to *reculer pour mieux sauter*, throng the streets. The very nursemaids hope to become rich by lucky investments of their savings in mining stock. There are no old men or women, but every one is in his first youth, and the "Queen's English" is spoken more generally than usual in the States.

The Coast range, to which allusion has already been made, forms the extreme margin of the continent, and stands with its feet in the Pacific Ocean. It is the western, as the Sierra Nevada is the eastern wall which flanks the valleys of the Sacramento and San Joaquin; but it is neither so high nor so massive as the Snowy Range; its loftiest peaks being under five thousand feet in elevation. The two ranges join both towards the north and south, and completely enclose the plain of Central California, which has already been referred to as an elliptical basin of fertile flats nearly thirty thousand square miles in extent. The Coast ranges were elevated at a later period than the Sierra Nevada, and have suffered great disturbance in very recent geological times. None of their rocks are older than the chalk, and most of them are composed of soft tertiary deposits, which have weathered into mountain forms possessing outlines of peculiar softness and delicacy. These are made conspicuous by the general absence of vegetation, which hides in the cañons, or sometimes crowns the crests of the hills, but leaves the hill-sides quite bare.

While such is the character of the scenery surrounding the bay of San Francisco, no pen, and scarcely any brush, could faithfully represent the peculiarly beautiful atmosphere which invests the landscapes of the Coast range with an altogether indescribable charm. On days when there is no fog, the panorama from Telegraph Hill, one of the highest points in the city, is magnificent. The lake-like bay, lost at either end among the windings of the hills, lies at the observer's feet, and joins the misty Pacific by the narrow opening of the Golden Gate. This rocky portal is a precipitous gash in the Coast range, whose bare, red, and softly outlined hills run north-west and south-east, meeting at either extremity of the bay the mountains which hem in its opposite and not distant shore. The latter constitute the Contra Costa range, at whose feet, fronting San Francisco and lining the water's edge, shine the white houses of Oakland, San Antonio, Alameda, and San Leandro, forming an almost continuous line of towns more than ten miles in length. Behind the Contra Costa range rise the twin cones of Monte Diablo, bounding the eastern outlook; while westward, at the back of the observer, the city itself reposes on the flanks of the Coast range which narrowly separates it from the ocean. The scene, fine in itself, is informed with magical beauty by the colouring, to attempt a description of which is like trying to seize the very atmosphere whose peculiar quality gives to each distance a new tint of amethyst or opal, softer and sweeter than any words can paint.

Gold, as we have already seen, first led the Californian "forty-niners" into a country which well repays cultivation. Of its vast wheat-fields I have already spoken, but wine and fruit are only second to breadstuffs in commercial importance on the Pacific slope. The vine thrives admirably in California, and, although native Americans are too impatient of careful industries and deferred profits to become wine-growers, the Germans are on the way to make the valleys north of San Francisco rivals of France and the Rhine. Excellent white and red wines are already grown in the Napa and other districts, and the demand, which is constantly increasing, is already larger than the supply. It would become overpoweringly so if the Americans themselves drank native clarets, hocks, and champagnes; but it is the fashion to prefer foreign wines to the home productions. This state of things, based as it is on mere affectation, will only be temporary, but in the mean time the Californian wine-grower has to seek a European market. As, however, a great deal of his wine goes to Hamburg, there is probably more of it drunk, under French names, at ostensibly fastidious Eastern dinner-tables, than is generally supposed. We visited the well kept and extensive cellars of Mr. Lachman, and found his hocks and clarets excellent, but the ports and sherries were as luscious as liqueurs; these however find a ready sale in Central America, though they are much too cloying for our taste. The grape was introduced into California by the Spanish Jesuit missionaries who, like the French in the north-west, were early labourers in this field for the conversion of the natives. Wine made from the "mission grape" is however thin and poor, and a vine much better suited to the soil and climate is now generally grown. The wine trade suffers at present from the characteristic American hurry to get rich. The growers are not capitalists, and neither care, nor can afford, to mature their wines before throwing them upon a greedy market. The growth of a home demand will remedy this evil by stimulating with high prices the practice of keeping wines, and nothing but American consumption is wanted to give an enormous development to this already important Californian industry.

Fruits and vegetables of all kinds grow most luxuriantly on the Pacific slope. Peaches and apricots were selling wholesale at twopence a pound during our visit, but the former in good years are not worth more than a halfpenny a pound. "Bartlett" pears, similar to our jargonelles, cost three halfpence a pound, and black Hambro' and Muscat grapes twopence a pound, melons of seven pounds weight are sold at twenty-five shillings the hundred, and water-melons may be had for asking.

With fruit at such prices, canning has become an important trade, and, although confined chiefly to peaches, pears, and apricots, employs nearly three thousand people in California. This industry is carried on in factories, sometimes employing several hundred hands. Women peel and halve the fruit in the first instance, and throw the slices into tubs of water, which is constantly being renewed. Other women pick up the slices, rejecting all the bad ones, and pack them carefully in tins which, when full, are hermetically closed and boiled for ten or fifteen minutes. Leaky cans are discovered by their bubbling during this process, and the sound ones are pierced, each with a tiny hole in the cover, from which steam and air rush violently out together in a small jet. The hole is closed with solder while vapour is still issuing, and, a vacuum being thus secured, the cans, when cool, are ready for labelling and despatch. There are ten large fruit-preserving establishments in San Francisco which confine their attention solely to canning, leaving the French in possession of the trade in high class "glass goods," no fruit being put up in bottles in California because there is no fine white glass made in the western states, or indeed, thanks to the protective system, in America.

Six miles from San Francisco is the "Cliff House," a favourite pleasure resort of the citizens, standing on the shore of the Pacific immediately opposite the famous "Seal Rocks." The road to it lies over great hills of blown sand, now being reclaimed and converted into a beautiful park, but the Pacific coast when reached proves extremely disappointing. The sea horizon is rarely visible on account of the fog, and mild waves of by no means translucent water break on a desolate shore whose sandy levels stretch tamely away on either hand into misty obscurity. The ghosts of ships steal out at intervals through the Golden Gate, but neither these nor the curious Seal Rocks, with their strange population of basking and roaring sea-lions, give animation to the "vicinity of a melancholy ocean."

Newspaper advertisements soon make a visitor aware that spiritualism is a great cult in San Francisco, the number of clairvoyants, mediums, and "spirit healers" who parade their supernatural powers being legion. Many of these people have a regular *clientèle*, who attend their *séances*, especially on Sunday evenings, just as a congregation might meet for religious service. The handsome rooms and residences in which these reunions take place testify to the profitable character of the spiritual business, while the attitude of the medium towards his, or her, visitors, proves how much consideration the profession enjoys. We joined a noted circle one Sunday evening, and found about thirty respectably dressed people, sitting round a large and handsomely furnished room, and looking very serious, not to say devotional. The medium, who was a lady, sat at a green table, and commenced the *séance* by asking each visitor to write the names of dead friends or relations on slips of paper, which were then folded and thrown in a heap on the table. Taking up one

O

of these, apparently at random, she asked of the air, "Is this spirit present?" and was answered either by silence or by three raps on the table. If by raps, the paper was opened, and the writer requested to put any questions he pleased to the spirit who was present. The devotees, with almost all of whom the medium seemed on intimate terms, had usually a whole string of inquiries written out and numbered which were propounded to the unseen presence as Question No. 1, No. 2, and so on; the answer consisting of three raps for "yes" and two for "no." Whether this system was arranged to secure privacy for the questioner, or an easy time for the medium, we could not determine, but it certainly did away with any need of intelligence on the part of the oracle. Ours was a "writing medium," whom the spirits, when exceptionally powerful, and sufficiently well educated, can "control to write" their replies, which are rapidly traced in inverted characters by a pencil held in the wonder-worker's fingers and operated by the spirit. The audience, seemingly aware that it is the practice of the unseen world to write backwards, accepted this *tour de force* as a convincing proof of supernatural agency, and asked, in simple good faith, for advice on personal or family matters with the evident intention of acting on the hints of their ghostly, and therefore presumably omniscient, relatives. It is hardly necessary to say that when, towards the end of the *séance*, a spirit invoked by one of our party appeared, it proved extremely incoherent and incorrect in its statements; but it was a little remarkable to find the medium's accustomed circle anxious to help her out of her difficulties, and ready to lay the blame of the spirit's fatuity at the door of our want of faith. There are hundreds of these quacks driving a flourishing trade in San Francisco, and it is not many years since a wave of spiritualism rolled over the United States, puzzling Europe, as we were puzzled, to reconcile the easy credulity we witnessed with the proverbial 'cuteness of the American character.

The Chinese problem, whose consideration has been purposely deferred, presents itself to the traveller at every step of his progress throughout Western America. There is a large Mongolian population in all the western towns, where the whole of the humble, and much of the skilled labour is performed by men of the yellow race. They are largely employed as labourers on the Central Pacific Railroad; they are scattered broadcast throughout the Californian gulches, washing over again the gravels left by the whites; they raise fruit and vegetables with much success on the Pacific slope; and household work is a Chinese monopoly throughout California, where every dinner is cooked and every shirt washed by Chinamen. The Chinese question is one of great moment for the United States, and in view of its importance I reserve for a separate chapter both a description of "Chinatown," the Mongolian quarter of San Francisco, and any discussion of the rights of the Chinese in America.

Once more, and for the last time, we turned our faces towards the Snowy Range upon whose western flanks we had yet to seek the famous "Big trees," and the Yosemite Valley. This was our last American trip, and, as the Pacific mail steamer would receive us immediately on our return to San Francisco, to start was like taking a farewell of the city, which it would be ungrateful to leave without a few kind words for its people. The lawless origin of Californian society has already been glanced at, but faithfully to paint the pandemonium which existed on the Pacific coast for ten years after the first advent of the gold-seekers would need a palette full of the darkest colours. "For a few years the solemn pines looked down on a mad carnival of godless licence, in whose picturesque delirium human character crumbled and vanished like dead leaves."* If the genius of Bret Harte has found some traits of humanity among the reckless populations which thronged the gulches of the foot-hills from 1849 to 1860, it is because, like the miners so skilfully depicted in his stories, he knows how to sift a few grains of pure gold from a mass of rubbish. But the inferno of '49 has gone, and scarcely a flicker of its old flames lights the mining camps of to-day, while California now contains a popula-

* "Mountaineering in the Sierra Nevada," by Clarence King.

tion which respects law and order as much as any other state in the Union. In estimating the people it is a mistake to link the past too closely with the present. The lawlessness, if not the crime, of the "early days" was the result of circumstances, but the establishment of order was the act of the people. Meanwhile, as Bret Harte touchingly shows, society, even at its worst, was never without some salt, and at least one virtue, that of generous hospitality, flourished throughout the foot-hills. In addition to this a certain gaiety and cheerfulness characterized the camps, as it now characterizes the whole state. The Californians are a gay, light-hearted people, among whom the long faces and sedate manners of New England are unknown, who love to "seize the day" and bask in the sunshine of life. Their delicious and stimulating climate, rather than their reckless ancestry, is the cause of this pleasant characteristic, which, for a stranger who himself drinks exhilaration with their air, makes the West much pleasanter than the East. It may be that there is little intellectual aspiration, and less desire for cultivation than for wealth; but the East also worships dollars, while it is less able than the West to enjoy what dollars bring.

Although civilization, properly so called, is not more than twenty years old on the Pacific slope, the West has already produced a number of original and imaginative writers of quite exceptional powers. There are also artists in San Francisco, who are painting the peaks and forests of the Sierras with extraordinary vigour and feeling. In matters of business the Californians are distinguished by an energy and splendid audacity which is all their own, and if, socially, there is room for the criticisms of over-fastidious Bostonians and New Yorkers, the foreign visitor loses sight of such trifles, in view, not only of what these bold bright people are, but of what they promise to be.

CHAPTER XXIII.

THE CHINESE IN AMERICA—CHINATOWN.

THERE are a hundred and twenty thousand Chinamen in the United States, of whom about twenty thousand live in San Francisco, while the remainder are widely distributed throughout America, being thickest in California, where they form a conspicuous part of the population, and thinnest in the eastern states and cities. There is a manufactory in Massachusetts which is run entirely by Chinese labour, and the Chinese have almost a monopoly of the laundry business of New York, but the traveller does not see many Mongolians until the Rocky Mountains are passed, after which they appear in increasing numbers all the way to the Pacific. The Chinaman is usually only a humble worker, who thankfully eats of the crumbs which fall from the rich table of white labour; but in San Francisco there are Chinese merchants, manufacturers, and brokers, as well as washermen, artisans, and labourers.

The Mongolian quarter is called "Chinatown," and consists of half a dozen blocks of houses, abutting on the best part of the city, and exclusively occupied by Chinese warehouses, manufactories, shops, and dwellings. Chinatown is a fragment of the Celestial Empire itself, planted in the midst of an American city. The influences which absorb Teutons and Celts alike into the national life of the New World leave the Chinaman absolutely untouched. Such as he is in the streets of Canton, he remains in Chinatown, while he transforms the wooden houses of America into excellent imitations of those he has left behind him. All this makes a ramble through the Chinese quarter of San Francisco a most interesting experience, and it may be undertaken alone and at night by any visitor who has the courage to disregard the absurdly alarming cautions which he is sure to receive as soon as he begins to make inquiries on the subject. The city police are in the habit of chaperoning strangers who desire to see the Chinese quarter, and have an interest in giving the worst possible impression of it. Fortified against a host of imaginary dangers by an escort which cost us five dollars, and prepared for seeing all sorts of horrors, we were led through the slums of Chinatown without experiencing a single thrill of disgust, or finding anything half so shocking as we should have done in similar quarters of London or New York.

The Chinese give a national character to their streets by adding balconies of carved wood to the houses, which they cut up into small sections, and by hanging up handsome vertical sign-boards, lacquered with vermilion, and carrying the name of each merchant and shopkeeper in gilded Chinese characters. The provision shops display an extraordinary variety of strange eatables, including dried fish from Japan, sea-slugs, edible seaweed, split ducks, and duck cutlets, eggs preserved in black earthy envelopes, and tiny portions of strange green vegetables. Above the roofs of such shops hang strings of thin mottled sausages, drying by thousands on high wooden frames. Here is a fraction of a house, forming a tailor's shop, behind whose tiny window a grave Chinaman is at work upon blue and black calico garments. Below is a cellar occupied by a barber, who is busy with his narrow razors and tweezers taking every hair from the scalps, ears, and nostrils of his patient customers. Opposite, is a restaurant, decorated with quaintly carved wooden screens, and full of gay company, busy with bowls, chopsticks and tiny tea and samsu cups. Next door is a merchant's warehouse, piled with tea-chests or packages of rice, and in charge of two or three spotless and serious clerks who calculate with a little frame of sliding wood buttons, and make entries in stitched books of filmy yellow paper with a camel's-hair brush and Indian ink. Then comes a jeweller's shop with three feet of frontage, and within, the art craftsman, whose long, flexible fingers, each ending in an inch of nail, are cleverly twisting gold and silver wire into filigree, or who sells a pair of green jade ear-rings to the passing *belle Chinoise*. Here is a joss-house, or temple, from whose open door comes the heavy scent of incense, and here a curiosity shop, crowded with carved ivory, china dragons, curious silks, and nameless nicknacks. Along the side walks steals a silent but considerable stream of sedate pig-tailed Mongolians, dressed in blue blouses and black calico pants, gathered in at the ankle upon white hose. They are for the most part workmen; but how quiet, intent, and methodic is the crowd! No white men are to be seen, and the visitor might easily suppose himself in Canton, so entirely national is the picture before him.

From such a street we dived in the first instance into a basement forming a pawnbroker's shop, where goods, we were told, are pledged for a song by that inveterate gambler the coolie, and sold, in case of non-redemption, at profits of a hundred per cent. The place was dark and dirty, but it was very orderly, and "my uncle" looked like a quiet man of business, and was probably no worse than some of his London brethren. Thence we were taken to an "opium-den," a small room with two tiers of bunks running around it, as in a ship's cabin. These were about six feet square, carpeted with clean India matting, and furnished with a couple of little footstools serving for pillows. In the centre of each stood a large tray carrying two opium-pipes, a small oil lamp, a little horn box, holding the drug, and a few wires like knitting-needles. The pipe-bowl is of earthenware, shaped like the rose of a watering-pot, but having only one central hole, and mounted on a bamboo stem. Two men reclining at length, with the tray between them, occupy each bunk, and the smoker commences operations by dipping one of the knitting-needles into the opium-box and taking up a small quantity of its viscid contents. He heats and reheats this over the flame of the lamp, rolling it cleverly between whiles on the convex surface of the pipe, until he has fashioned it into a tiny cylinder which is finally stuck concentrically on the hole in the bowl, and then lighted. Over this delicate process of preparation the smoker lingers lovingly, but two or three slow, voluminous puffs exhaust the opium, and the operation of modelling a new pellet recommences. After five or six such doses, sleep supervenes, and the man lies for an hour or so enjoying his dreams. Then he gets up and goes about his business, apparently none the worse for the indulgence, and certainly a much more respectable person than the dram-drinker. I am credibly informed that not more than ten per cent. of the Chinamen in San Francisco are habitual opium-smokers, but the majority drop into the "den" now and again for a smoke just as the whites take a drink. The name of "opium-den" seems to be singularly misapplied. There is absolutely nothing to shock the most sensitive person in a roomful of silent and recumbent figures quietly enjoying the Chinese equivalent for a "whiskey straight" without the latter's common accompaniments of rowdyism and profanity.

From the opium-house we adjourned to a restaurant kept by a very business-like Chinaman, named Sam-Li, who spoke English well and was a man of considerable property. Sam-Li entertained us with cigars and tea and showed us over his establishment with some pride. In one large room a number of working men were supping together in celebration of some feast-day. The guests sat around a table where, while each convive had his own tiny cup of scalding tea and another of samsu, the company ate with chopsticks out of a common bowl, replenished at every course with mysterious delicacies. Here we were pledged in samsu and tea, the latter being delicious and the former like a sweet and fiery sherry. We were much struck with the air of enjoyment shown by these people, who seemed as happy as children in their social intercourse. In a smaller room was a select supper party of six, three of whom were girls, magnificently dressed, but looking like children, with hair elaborately banded and faces delicately painted bright rose and white. The women were probably high class courtesans, but the utmost propriety reigned, and there was the same appearance of simple enjoyment as characterized the larger party of men. We left our smiling host

Sam-Li to visit one of the lodging houses, where operatives and domestic servants sleep. A dwelling had been partitioned off into a number of small rooms, in each of which were wall-shelves arranged like the steerage bunks in a ship. Here the men lay, closely packed indeed, but not more crowded than in an emigrant vessel, while, beyond a scanty supply of air, there was nothing to shock the most fastidious person. The Chinese do not care for much light, whether natural or artificial, in their dwellings. Although gas and petroleum are both cheap, they prefer, as still cheaper, their own lamps, little open vessels of oil, whose smoking wicks blacken the walls and ceilings of the houses, giving our anti-Chinese guide occasion to remark on the dirty habits of the people. In the matter of cleanliness, however, the Mongols are not nearly so black as they are painted. They wash themselves all over daily; the cooking is done in the open air outside of the crowded rooms, and they dispose of sewage matters in the practically cleanly, though offensive, national manner.

From the lodging-house we walked through a narrow street entirely given up to a low class of prostitutes. Here the subdivision of houses appeared to have reached its limit, the women inhabiting rooms which are little better than cells. Each door opening on the street is fitted with a wire grill through which the painted tenant stares at the passers-by. Even this quarter exhibited nothing worse than what may be seen in low districts of American and European cities, while the total absence of drunkenness and rowdyism, was distinctly in favour of the Mongolian. The number of Chinese prostitutes in San Francisco, though grossly exaggerated by the anti-coolie party, does not exceed two hundred and fifty, a surprisingly small total among an adult male population of nearly twenty thousand.

Every street in Chinatown has its Buddhist joss-house, or temple, usually consisting of a room in a tenement house, containing half a dozen shrines, with the god of peace, wealth, or plenty in place of a Virgin or saint. Before each image burns a "joss-stick" of incense and a small swinging lamp. The attendants, as in the Christian churches of Italy, make a profession of begging, and, from the poor appearance of both priests and temples, it seems that there is not much religious enthusiasm in Chinatown.

We visited the theatre, of which there are two, and found a large building, decorated externally with great lamps and quaint Chinese devices, and crowded within by a shaven and pig-tailed audience, grave, quiet, and orderly. The back of the stage, whose proscenium was ornamented with strange paintings, was occupied by the "band," consisting of two agonizing Chinese fiddles, and several tom-toms or drums. "Music" accompanied the action almost continuously, and a great many intolerably tedious solos were sung, the play appearing to be some kind of musical farce, very monotonous and seemingly very stupid, for the audience neither laughed nor applauded. The *ars celare artem* is quite disregarded in the conduct of the Chinese drama. Scene-shifting, such as it is, was accomplished before the audience, the stage-carpenter making his exits and entrances when and where he pleased. Tea was brought to the musicians and actors in the same unceremonious way, and when the place grew too full, the crowd overflowed on to the stage, which seemed almost as much at the service of the public as of the actors. Our presence was hardly noticed, and, if I compare this concourse of Chinese coolies, drawn for the most part from the humblest, not to say lowest, ranks of society, with the audiences of the theatres in Leadville, candour compels the confession that the Mongolian audience shines by the contrast. The Chinese operative is no rowdy, and as he drinks nothing stronger than tea, his behaviour is excellent; perhaps similar classes among whites would be as orderly if their diet were as simple and drink as harmless as the Chinaman's.

Apart from the white working classes with whom the Chinese compete, and who hate them cordially, no unprejudiced person has a word to say against the yellow race. On the contrary, the universal testimony of American merchants, municipal officers, ministers of religion, and employers of labour declares that, while their mercantile men are exceptionally able and honourable, the masses are no less moral, while they are cleaner, more orderly and more industrious, class for class, than the whites. Crime is less frequent in Chinatown, disease less fatal, and the death-rate lower than among the native population of San Francisco. The Chinese have built railways, reclaimed land, and established a number of manufacturing industries in California which would have been quite impossible in their absence, while the character of American home life has been raised, to the great satisfaction of San Franciscan housewives, by their universal employment as domestic servants. In a word, the Chinese operative in America is distinguished by the possession of the very qualities whose rarity among our own working classes we are always so pathetically deploring. He is abstemious in regard to food, an abstainer as to drink, industrious to the last degree, requiring no supervision when he knows his work, docile, clean, patient, quiet, and respectful. His honesty, so recklessly impugned, is negatively proved by the City police reports, and positively by the uniformly favourable testimony of those who employ Chinese servants in their houses and about their persons. The Chinese merchants and manufacturers of San Francisco bear the highest character among their American *confrères*. They are noted for fair dealing, prompt payments, correct accounts, truthful statements, and aversion to litigation. The word of a Chinese merchant is thought as good as his bond. Many of these men are wealthy, and their charity is evidenced by the fact that the number of poor Chinese seeking public alms is very small indeed.

This favourable picture of the Chinese in America is no fancy sketch. By the joint action of the two Houses of Congress a special committee was appointed in July 1876 "to investigate the character, extent, and effect of Chinese immigration to America, with power to visit the Pacific coast for that purpose." This committee sat at San Francisco, and, as might be expected in a city the bulk of whose voting population is violently anti-

Chinese in feeling, the evidence received was of the most contradictory character. Disregarding, however, the statements of politicians and aspirants for public offices, who trim their sails, no less in America than in other countries, to catch the wind of popular favour, unprejudiced minds will receive the independent evidence of judges, bankers, merchants, manufacturers, farmers, clergymen, physicians, missionaries, and consuls as indisputably favourable to the Chinese.

Such then are the immigrants whom, in defiance both of humanity and treaty obligations, a Californian mob assaults with impunity, and Californian law oppresses. The report of a select committee, appointed by the state of California to inquire into the Chinese question, states it as "a well-known fact, that there has been a wholesale system of wrong and outrage practised upon the Chinese population of this state which would disgrace the most barbarous nation upon earth." This was in 1862, but matters had not mended in 1876, when the following uncontradicted statement was made by Colonel Bee, an American spokesman for the Chinese, before the Congressional Committee already referred to :—" Acts of brutal violence against the Chinese which are a disgrace to civilization, have transpired in the streets of San Francisco. No country and no government in the world has ever permitted indignities to be cast on any race such as those which are permitted by the government and municipality of San Francisco and the state of California."

In view of these admissions, it is needless to describe how the Chinese in America have been murdered, assaulted, and maltreated with impunity; the facts are not disputed, and they cannot be stigmatized in stronger terms than those which have already been quoted from official sources. But the acts of rowdies and mobs have been almost paralleled by those of the state and municipal authorities of California, who at various times have harried the Chinese with oppressive ordinances, some of which have since been set aside by the superior courts as in contravention of treaty obligations, and unconstitutional. Such were the capitation, and foreign miner's taxes, the tax on the export of embalmed bodies, the tax on the handbaskets in which Chinamen carry home washing, and the hair and queue ordinances. Of the two last-named acts, the former made it illegal for any one to sleep in a room containing less than five hundred cubic feet of air per man, and the latter ordained that the hair of every person arrested for any offence should be cut within two inches of his scalp. Under the first of these shameful ordinances, which, though ostensibly of general application, only touched the Chinaman, the gaols were suddenly crowded to overflowing with unoffending men whose only security against a loss which they considered a bitter and lasting degradation, was the payment of a heavy fine.

The persecution of the Chinese in California is ostensibly directed against paganism, filth, a lower civilization, the depletion of American wealth, and the danger of Mongolian supremacy. Three-fifths of these charges concern matters of fact, and have already been sufficiently answered by American evidence, but the remaining two, which are purely supposititious, have been so dressed up with fancy and exaggeration that many people in America believe they are serious national dangers instead of mere bogies. In an address to the people of the United States, issued by a committee of the Californian legislation, it has been stated that the Chinese labourers of California have abstracted the equivalent of a hundred and eighty million dollars from the money wealth of the state, while they have contributed *nothing* to the national wealth. This statement was bandied about the halls of Congress, and the eastern cities, and, coming from an official source, was widely believed, although its absurdity can easily be demonstrated. It is the custom of the Chinese to send a large part of their savings home, but, as the whole number of Chinamen in California has never exceeded ninety thousand, to credit them with having abstracted the sum in question from the state, is to allow at least two thousand dollars for the remittance of each individual. But it is not long since the Chinese became numerous on the Pacific coast, and, if each labourer saved so large a sum as two thousand dollars from his wages in a few years, it must be confessed that these people far surpass other nations in economy and thrift, qualities which are highly esteemed in a population. The grand total of precious metals sent to China since the gold discoveries to the present time does not exceed seventy millions of dollars, and it is ridiculous to assert that ninety thousand Chinese operatives have remitted a hundred and ten millions more than was required during this time to balance the entire Chinese trade with the Pacific coast. With regard to the statement that the Chinese have contributed *nothing* to the state or national wealth, it has been already stated that railroads have been made, land reclaimed, and industries established which would have been impossible without their abundant and cheap assistance. Americans themselves admit this, and the Congressional Committee's report avers that "the resources of California and the Pacific coast have been more rapidly developed with the cheap and docile labour of the Chinese than they would have been without, and so far as material prosperity is concerned, it cannot be doubted that the Pacific coast has been a great gainer." The Chinaman earns a dollar a day, the white operative from two to three dollars a day, and as there are, at the present moment, about seventy-five thousand Chinese in California, the state clearly gains a sum of at least a hundred thousand dollars per diem from the presence of the yellow race. Is this nothing added to the state or national wealth? But, granted that the Chinaman sends his surplus earnings home, they are his own property, which he may dispose of lawfully as he will. If the Chinese are depleting America, how much more are the Irish, who, during the last fifty years, have sent home millions upon millions of dollars? It has been estimated that twenty millions of dollars have been spent in Europe by rich American tourists during the last ten years, but no one accuses these gentlemen of depleting the country of wealth.

The last bugbear, that of Mongolianization, is finely portrayed in a message of Governor Irwin, delivered on the 6th of December, 1877. "It is unnecessary," says his excellency, "that I should make an argument to demonstrate the evils of Chinese immigration. In this state, and everywhere on this coast, they are universally conceded; nor are these evils of any ordinary character. The presence of the Chinese in this state in large numbers, with steady additions thereto from the exhaustless hive of China, not only threatens an irrepressible conflict between the American and Chinese civilizations, but has already initiated such a contest. If the right of unlimited immigration, conceded under the Burlinghame Treaty, is continued; if Chinese immigrants are guaranteed the same rights that immigrants from the most favoured nations are, as is the case under this treaty, what is to prevent the triumph of their civilization in its conflict with ours? I go further and say that this triumph is as certain as any event can be which is yet in the future if the Chinese are to enjoy perfect and absolute protection here." These are strange words from a high official of a country dedicated to the proposition that all men, irrespective of race or colour, are born free and equal. Admitting, however, that national policy must be governed by expediency rather than by theory, let us endeavour to see how far the fear of being swamped by the Mongolian is a reality or a sham. If you should ask any merchant or manufacturer in San Francisco, not a politician or an office-seeker, whether he is afraid of Mongolian supremacy, he would laugh in your face. He regards the Chinese simply as labour-saving machines, and he would as soon expect to be dominated by steam-engines or reaping-machines as by this race. Like the Jew, who requires a country already settled for the practice of his useful national callings, and who would perish to-day, as of old, in a wilderness without supernatural aid; so the Chinaman may subserve white schemes of development but cannot initiate them. Hence the Chinese flow, whether towards America, Australia, or the Straits, not as a dominant race, but as the servants of the dominant race. Chinese immigration to America, again, has hitherto been confined to the single province of Canton, and every emigrant has sailed from the British port of

Hongkong. Their numbers have been grossly exaggerated, but it is a well-known fact, easily verifiable by the customs returns of arrivals and departures at the port of San Francisco, that the Chinese have been coming forward for some years in smaller numbers than they leave. The immigrants, who are almost exclusively adult males, do not indeed come to the States intending to remain. They have for the most part left behind them either parents, wives, children, or friends whom they look forward to rejoining after having put by a little money, while, so well informed and sensitive is the Chinese labour market, that whenever trade is bad in America the returning stream outnumbers the inflowing one.

The Chinaman's real offence is that he works for a dollar a day, and he can afford to undersell his white competitors because he is more abstemious and economical than they. Impelled by the fear that his accustomed luxuries are threatened, the American labourer thinks—

> "We are ruined by Chinese cheap labour,
> And he goes for that heathen Chinee"

with arms which are a disgrace to Christianity and civilization. Meanwhile the politicians mount the stump, and fan a convenient flame, with the result that Chinese treaty rights have been totally disregarded and justice has leagued itself with popular violence to oppress an industrious and unoffending race.

By the treaty of 1844, confirmed by the Burlinghame Treaty of 1867, America and China mutually guaranteed complete protection of life and property, entire freedom of religion, education, and sepulture to subjects of either power resident in the other's country. This treaty, like our own with China, was not sought by, but was forced upon the Chinese, for Asia desires seclusion from the Western nations while these desire commerce with Asia. When Mr. Burlinghame returned from San Francisco to Pekin in 1866, he reported to the Chinese that a million of labourers could find employment on the Pacific coast. The Pacific Railway was not then completed, and capitalists engaged in that and other public and private works were eager to obtain labour from China at a cheap rate. Everything in fact was done on the part of America to encourage and regulate the immigration of the Chinese, while the latter, who have been immigrating for centuries to the Straits and elsewhere, were willing to come, the more so as they were protected by solemn treaty engagements. The Chinese were treated well in California as long as American citizens could make money out of their cheap labour, and when the hopes of getting a large portion of the China trade were encouraging, but they have since been abandoned to the mercy of the mob.

Still sheltering myself behind the highest American authorities, I close this too lengthy discussion by quoting from an address on "Our Relations with the Chinese Empire" by the well-known Dr. Wells Williams, late Secretary of the American Legation at Pekin. "One cannot but feel indignant and mortified at the contrast between the way in which the Chinese have treated us in their country, into which we have forced ourselves, and the way in which we have treated them in this country, into which we have invited them. We have used them as if they had no rights which we were bound to respect, and refused that protection as men and labourers which the existing treaties guaranteed them. Is it necessary in order that we should carry out our own treaty obligations that we wait for a Chinese minister at Washington to officially inform the Secretary of State how they have been violated; or for a Chinese consul at San Francisco to complain to its mayor that his countrymen are stoned, robbed, and set upon, and no one punished, no one arrested for such deeds? Is our Christian civilization not strong enough to do right by them?"

CHAPTER XXIV.

THE "BIG TREES"—YOSEMITE VALLEY.

September 2-13.

IN the spring of 1852, a man named Dowd was engaged in supplying meat to a party of canal excavators who were bringing water to the gold-diggers of Murphy's camp, a productive but dry gulch in the foot-hills of Calaveras County, California. Dowd's hunting camp being pitched one night about sixteen miles above Murphy's, and near the Stanislaus river, his attention was arrested by the immense size of some of the forest trees, which towered for a hundred feet or more above even the gigantic yellow and sugar pines to which he was accustomed. He carried such a wonderful account of these vegetable monsters down to Murphy's, that the miners laughed at him, but on his story being verified, it soon spread through the newspapers, and was reported, for the first time in Europe, by the London *Athenæum* in 1853. Through some unaccountable remissness on the part of American botanists, Dr. Lindley was the first to publish a scientific description of the big tree, of which specimens had been imported to England by Messrs. Veitch, and he named it *Wellingtonea gigantea*. A subsequent examination by M. Decaisne showed that the tree was not generically new, as Lindley supposed, but a species of redwood, a genus already known to botanists under the name of sequoia. Properly speaking therefore the Californian big tree is called *Sequoia gigantea*, although in England the name of *Wellingtonea gigantea* still clings to the numerous specimens which have been planted in the British Islands.

The sequoias never form groups by themselves, but are always scattered among a much larger number of other trees. They are strictly confined to the great pine belt which clothes the western flanks of the Sierra Nevada, and occur only between the thirty-sixth and thirty-eighth parallels of latitude, never descending below five thousand, or rising above seven thousand feet of elevation.

Only eight groups of the big trees have yet been discovered, all in the state of California, and, of these, the groves of Calaveras and Mariposa counties are the most important and best known. The former, which is most northerly in situation and contains the largest trees, was chosen for our visit because it can be taken *en route* to the Yosemite Valley.

Leaving San Francisco then, a party of three—for the cosmopolite, newly arrived from the Yellowstone Park, had now joined the socialist and cynic—we took train to Stockton, a town in the San Joaquin Valley, not far south of the capital. Here we lay the first night, closely besieged by a combined force of mosquitoes and small water-beetles, the latter being so numerous that playing billiards was impossible without crushing them by hundreds on the cloth. Next day the railroad carried us to Milton, on the very edge of the cultivated plain of Central California, where we took stage for the big trees, distant about fifty miles. This ride occupied the whole day, the road, after leaving the San Joaquin Valley, ascending, in the first place gently, through the foot-hills of the range, whose low volcanic ridges "wander out into the plain like coast promontories enclosing bays of yellow prairie." Hills and plain are both oak-covered, the trees standing in clumps, as if arranged by a landscape gardener, and giving a park-like aspect to the scene. The road, like the soil, is carpeted with a thick layer of fine red or yellow dust, which rose in clouds from under our wheels and flowed steadily with the wind towards the range, so completely enveloping the stage that it was sometimes impossible to see the leaders. On the way we met three large flocks of sheep which, as they passed, were quite invisible from the top of the coach, but their dust was seen, like a column of smoke in the air, more than a mile away.

When we had risen about a thousand feet, pines began to mingle with the oaks, the first species to appear being the digger, or nut pine (*Pinus sabiniana*), the seeds from whose cones are eaten by the Digger Indians. Its foliage is pale and parched looking, evidencing the arid climate, and the tree, like the oaks which keep it company, seems to exist with difficulty in so dry a region. At two thousand feet elevation the oaks and nut pines alike disappear, and the scattered vegetation gives place to the true forest. This in the first instance is chiefly composed of yellow pines (*P. ponderosa*), magnificent trees five or six feet in diameter and two hundred feet high. These are soon joined by the sugar pine (*P. Lambertiana*), which, appearing first at three thousand feet of elevation, becomes perfectly developed at five thousand feet, and dies out at seven thousand feet, while the hardier yellow pine endures up to timber-line. The sequoias apart, it is impossible to imagine a more beautiful conifer than the sugar pine. Its smooth, brown shafts, six or eight feet in diameter, rise with a gentle taper to a height of two hundred and twenty feet, while from its far-reaching and graceful branches hang great cones fifteen inches in length. Masses of exuded resin, sweet to taste and golden in colour, cling to its trunk, and through its resonant needles the wind sings a grand woodland air. A little higher we come upon the Douglas spruce (*Abies Douglasii*), which thrives throughout the main pine zone, attaining a diameter of six or seven feet and a height of two hundred feet. The white pine, the silver fir, and the arbor vitæ now help to swell the forest which, at this elevation, displays a vigour, symmetry, and distribution that is absolutely perfect. The trees are neither crowded nor in too open order, but each has room to display its stately beauty without ceasing to be a member of a group. There is no undergrowth, as in tropical jungles, but the enchanted traveller may wander at will through the half-shaded, half-sunlit aisles of this glorious natural colonnade, satisfying three senses at one and the same time with beauty, odour, and music.

Such is the character of the great pine belt, more than four hundred miles long and forty miles wide, which stretches from end to end of the Sierra Nevada; its lower margin formed of scattered and thirsty oaks and pines, its centre a zone of profuse luxuriant life, and its upper edge a ragged rank of hardy trees struggling for a foothold with the snows of the summit peaks. Lengthwise, as transversely, the forest is distinguished by zones which fade into one another by imperceptible gradations, through possessing well-marked characteristics at either end. Towards the south, it is more open, and single trees reach their greatest perfection. Northward, it grows gradually denser, until on the shores of British Columbia the pines are crowded as closely as canes in a jungle, and become wandlike in growth. It is in the centre of the belt, both along and across it, that the forest is finest, and here, as if nurtured by a combination of conditions most favourable to vegetable life, the big trees are found.

Only on good soil amply supplied with moisture is such a natural phenomenon as the pine belt in question possible, and it is not, at first sight, clear how these conditions have come together in arid Western America, and upon the stark granite flanks of the Sierran uplift. But the prevailing westerly wind, which blows continuously from the Pacific, is deflected upwards by the hills of the Coast range, whose feet, as already mentioned, stand in the ocean; and the moisture-laden current of air, passing over Central California and the foot-hills, strikes the Sierra Nevada at a point about four thousand feet above sea-level, and distils in rain and snow upon its flanks and summit. With regard to the soil, a close examination of the forest discloses the fact that its pines are everywhere rooted in morainic *débris*. As the glaciers which, in a colder age, poured out of every Sierran glen, crept slowly backwards before the advent of a warmer climate, their terminal moraines were left by the retreating ice at successively higher and higher levels upon the flanks of the range. This process took place so slowly that the glacial detritus became pretty evenly spread over the hill-sides, ending however at the base of the summit peaks; often at the feet of abrupt, bare rocks, which still retain the grooves and polish left by the passage of ice. Wherever this old moraine extends the forest follows, where it terminates the pines end also, and where, within the moisture belt, its drift soils are richest and deepest the trees are finest.

Darkness fell before we reached the hotel in the Calaveras Grove, and never shall I forget the impressions received during the last few miles of this drive. The night, as usual, was still and starlit; the road, carpeted with odorous pine needles, and shrouded with gloom, seemed to open as we advanced, leading one knew not where, through avenues of dark columns whose unseen capitals were hidden in star-spangled obscurity. Balsamic aromas filled the air, which stirred at intervals in soft pulsations, half scent, half music, along the mysterious aisles. Suddenly the enchanted forest opened to a clearing, and we pulled up before a wooden hotel, sentinelled by two magnificent sequoias, where, though buried in the heart of the pine belt, we were registered and lodged as promptly and prosaically as if we had been in New York or Philadelphia.

The valley, or rather depression, in which the Calaveras Grove of big trees is situated, contains nearly a hundred sequoias, not including those of from one to ten years' growth. They occupy a space about a thousand yards long, and two hundred and fifty yards wide, and are accompanied by hundreds of sugar and pitch pines of astonishing proportions, which, anywhere else, would be regarded as vegetable monsters, but are here completely dwarfed by the big trees. The grove is nearly five thousand feet above the sea, and occupies in this respect a point where the Sierran Forest finds its highest development. In 1853, shortly after Dowd's discovery, one of the largest trees was cut down. Five men worked twenty-five days in felling it, boring the trunk through with closely apposed auger holes and toppling the tree over with wedges. The stump was then smoothly levelled, six feet from the ground, and a pavilion built over it. This room is twenty-seven feet across and has accommodated thirty-two dancers. Theatrical performances have been given in it, and, in 1858, a newspaper called the *Big Tree Bulletin* was printed within its walls. The diameter of the trunk itself is twenty-four feet, but the bark, which has been removed, was eighteen inches thick. The age of the tree, as determined by the annual rings of growth, is more than thirteen hundred years. A step-ladder of twenty rounds leads to the summit of the fallen log, whose dimensions, as compared with ordinary timber, begin to be appreciated while mounting this staircase. On top is a bowling alley, or rather two alleys side by side, stretching along the levelled upper surface for eighty feet, while from the point where these terminate it is a walk of nearly a hundred yards to the end of the stem. The largest trees in the grove are named after American and other celebrities. Four of them, viz., "Keystone State," "General Jackson," "Mother of the Forest," and "Daniel Webster," are more than three hundred feet high, Keystone State being three hundred and twenty-five feet, and the tallest, though not the stoutest, of the group. The biggest tree now standing is Mother of the Forest, three hundred and fifteen feet high and sixty-one feet round at six feet above the ground, measured without the bark, which was stripped for exhibition several years ago and perished in the fire at the Crystal Palace. The Keystone State is the tallest tree yet measured on the American continent; there are stories of trees having once stood in this grove over four hundred feet in height, but when we observe, as Professor Whitney has pointed out, how regularly and gradually the trees diminish in size, it becomes evident that no sequoia has ever overtopped all the others by seventy-five feet and more. The average elevation of the mature trees in the Calaveras Grove is two hundred and seventy feet and their average girth, measured six feet above ground, is forty-one and a half feet. The sequoia is beaten in age by some English yews; in height by the Australian eucalyptus which, though slenderer, overtops it by a hundred and fifty feet; and in diameter by the baobab, whose height however is insignificant; but no tree except the blue gum, height and thickness both considered, approaches the sequoia in magnificence.

The foliage of the big tree is very thin for its vast size, and looks totally inadequate to the nourishment of its enormous product. The cones also are insignificant, and it is upon the trunk of the sequoia that Nature seems to have spent all her art. The shafts of these trees are simply perfect for symmetry, texture, and colour. Where twins or, as in some cases, triplets occur, the tapering parallel shafts are grouped with indescribable grace. The wood is light and dry, strong and straight grained, coloured like cedar, and slightly scented, while the bark is very thick and of a soft spongy structure. There are many fallen trees in the grove, one of which, "The Fallen Monarch," has been down for centuries. It is still eighteen feet in diameter, though not only the bark but much of the wood of the trunk has decayed. What is left is perfectly sound, but the upper half of the tree, shivered into fragments by the fall, has mouldered away, and sequoias nearly a hundred years old are growing where the top fell. The "Father of the Forest" is another fallen tree whose trunk has been hollowed by fire into a great tube, or tunnel, through which one can walk for two hundred feet, finally emerging at a knot-hole, big enough to admit the stoutest man. Some trees, which are still flourishing above, have been completely gutted by fire below, and in one of these, "The Miner's Cabin," we spent Sunday morning writing and reading, our party of three having ample room for chairs, tables, and accessories.

Fully to appreciate the magnificence of the Sierran Forest, one should live, as we did, for a few days among the trees themselves. To watch the light of sunrise adding a rosy tint to the chocolate columns of the scattered sequoias, a purple to the close-knit brown shafts of the sugar pine, and a flaring red to the great flakes of the pitch pine bark; or to lie, in the starlight, on the scented needles, letting one's eyes climb little by little up the long tapering masts into the very vault of heaven;—that is the way to realize the grandeur and beauty of the big trees.

We left the Calaveras Grove with much regret, and taking the stage, drove again for a whole day down through the forest belt to Murphy's, the mining camp already mentioned, where we slept a night before starting for the Yosemite Valley. The aspect of the country around Murphy's, where many square miles of the surface have been washed for gold, is very curious. All the soil has been stripped from the bed rock, which consists of curiously weathered limestone, honeycombed into fantastic crypts and arches by the action of water. The earth's very ribs seem to be bared, and a ghastly skeleton of stone lies bleaching under the glaring Californian sun where once was a park-like country, sprinkled with live oak and nut pine. Nature does her best to repair damages, and has already thrown a thin green covering over the naked rock here and there, but such growth is slow in this arid climate, and it will be long before these mining scars are hidden.

Next morning, the stage started at six o'clock, and, keeping to the foot-hills, crept southward along the range all day, passing through country almost the whole of which has been washed for gold. Hardly any mining is now in progress, for the gulches were practically exhausted within half a dozen years after the first discovery of gold, and the precious metals, as we have seen, are now obtained almost entirely from the lodes, or "fissure veins," of Nevada and Colorado. Here and there, however, a group of patient Chinamen is seen, working old gravels over again; or banks of detritus, too poor to pay for hand-washing, are being attacked by powerful jets of water, issuing from nozzles like those of a fire-engine. Hydraulic mining, as it is called, is the most effective means ever employed for washing auriferous gravels. It requires an ample supply, and a great head of water, together with a disposition of the ground favourable to the escape of vast masses of rubbish. Where these conditions are combined, the melting snows of the Sierra are caught and tanked high up in the mountains, and great pipes, strong as steam boilers, bring the water down into the valley. The nozzles employed are sometimes as much as six inches in diameter, and from them issue streams having the solidity of an iron bar, and the strength of gunpowder. Before their attack high cliffs of *débris* give way like sand, and great boulders are tossed about in the stream like leaves in the wind. The gold is saved, as in ordinary gulch mining, by allowing the turbid water to escape through sluices furnished with riffles, charged with mercury for amalgamation.

But not even hydraulic mining, which, in the hands of the "forty-niners," would have cleared the gold from the foot-hill valleys in six months instead of six years, can revive camps now dead or dying. The stage passes through towns of weed-grown streets and empty houses, whose doors swing wide, whose windows are broken and unshuttered, and within whose desolate rooms furniture too bulky for easy removal still stands. Here is the post office with dusty racks holding a few unclaimed letters, and there the saloon with its billiard tables still in place, but abandoned as if a sudden panic had driven away the people. Such a scene of desolation is often accented by a Chinese occupation of some outlying street, whose houses have been divided into dark and smoky boxes, where yellow men and women pack close, while poverty, pigs, and foul smells haunt the filthy roadway. So the day passes, driving through a stripped and corpse-like country, or towns from which enterprise has drifted away to more prosperous mining centres, and where the helpless few who remain look like fishes stranded by an ebb tide. Things have changed vastly in the Californian foot-hills since the "fifties," and the sights and sounds of to-day are strangely contrasted with those of the "roaring camps" in the "early days."

After fourteen hours' staging we arrived at "Priest's," where we passed the night, and, starting next morning at four o'clock, turned our faces from the foot-hills towards the range, reaching the lower edge of the pine belt in about three miles. Thence to the Yosemite Valley the road leads through forest, now a succession of open plantations, and again a thick grove of magnificent pines. At an elevation of about six thousand feet, a group of sequoias occurs which, though less important than that of Calaveras, comprises some splendid trees. One of these, named "The Dead Giant," is actually traversed by the track, the stage passing right through the trunk, a third of whose bulk remains untouched on either side of the way to form the walls of this strange tunnel. Through this fitting gateway we finally passed away from the big trees, and continued roughly bumping upwards, over rocks of grey granite, till we reached the divide between the Tuolumne and Merced rivers, from which point, nearly seven thousand feet above sea-level, the road descends for the rest of the way, giving occasional glimpses of the Yosemite precipices, grouped by distance into a single beautiful and astonishing picture.

The Yosemite Valley is a great trough, hollowed in the western flank of the Sierra Nevada nearly at right angles to the trend of the range. Its floor is a level area, six miles long, and varying from half a mile to a mile in width, sunk almost a mile perpendicularly below the general level of the region in which it occurs, and its sides are vertical or almost vertical walls of white granite. This trough, in the words of Professor Whitney, "is quite irregular, having several square and angular recesses let back as it were into sides, and at its upper end it divides into three branches through either of which we may, going up a series of gigantic steps as it were, ascend to the general level of the Sierra. . . . Down each of these branches, or cañons, descend streams, forks of the Merced coming down the steps in a series of stupendous waterfalls; while at its lower end the valley contracts into a narrow gorge," through which the river foams on its way to the San Joaquin.

The stage approaches this extraordinary depression from above, and, descending the face of its northern wall by a dizzy winding road, finally turns the traveller out at the doors of one of three hotels built on the floor of the trough. Here the stupendous character of the cliffs which hem in the valley is first realized, the eye vainly trying to estimate their height, which, relatively to the width of the depression, is enormous. These walls, for such they are, look smooth and white, no vegetation clings to their sheer surfaces, and the pines which cap them might be blades of grass, so dwarfed are they by distance. The floor of the valley is covered with magnificent pitch pines and cedars, springing from an undergrowth of manzanita and wild raspberries; the riverbanks are thickly set with alders, spruce, and fragrant white azalea; and the steeply sloping banks of rock piled against the feet of the cliffs are clothed with live oak, maple, and Californian laurel.

Cascades, without rivals in the world, pour over these wonderful walls, swelling into mad torrents when the sun begins to melt the winter snows, but shrinking almost to nothing after the summer's heats are over. Of the five chief falls in the valley the lowest is four hundred feet and the highest two thousand six hundred feet high, the last, or "Yosemite Fall," surpassing in vertical height any cascade in the world, and possessing accessories of grandeur and beauty which neither pen nor pencil can adequately describe. The "Bridal Veil" is another fall, perhaps even more beautiful in general effect than the "Yosemite," but having a drop of only nine hundred feet; while the "Vernal" and "Nevada" waterfalls are two of the plunges, one four hundred, the other six hundred feet deep, made by the Merced river on its way down the "gigantic steps" leading up from the valley to the Sierra, and are probably, all things considered, the grandest cataracts in the world.

All the famous points of which one hears under the names of "El Capitan," the "Half-Dome," "Cathedral Spires," "Cloud's Rest," and others, are simply the most striking or loftiest features of the Yosomite walls. El Capitan is a single block of granite which projects from the cliff into the valley, like a squarely cut stone with a sharp and almost vertical edge, three thousand three hundred feet in elevation. It is quite impossible to realize the enormous dimensions of this rock, which can be seen in clear weather from the San Joaquin plains, a distance of fifty miles. The Half-Dome is even more astonishing than El Capitan. It is a crest of granite nearly five thousand feet high, shaped on one side like a helmet, but cut down sheer on the other for nearly half its height, and falling off thence in a very steep slope to the bottom of the valley. This slope, which looks exactly like a talus of fallen rubbish, is really solid rock, and the mass appears to have been originally a dome-shaped elevation, one-half of which has been split off and disappeared. These are but two among a hundred other salient features of precipices, which are everywhere stupendous, and often sublime, in the combination of their spires, domes, and buttresses, with forest, and waterfall. From a particular spot, called Inspiration Point, all the striking features of the valley are seen at one time, and perhaps there is nowhere in the world a more astonishing view, yet, in spite of the extraordinary character of each element in the picture, something is felt to be wanting. Rocks, pines, and waterfalls have done their best, but the walls of white granite are grim; the summits are cold in colour, and the ridges which sweep upwards from one to the other are bare and forbidding. The forest itself is dressed in greens so pale that they look grey in the distance, and the mind, recovering from its first thrill of wonder, yearns for the subtler charm of the Alps.

The parapets of the Yosemite walls are accessible from below at several points, and the whole valley can be circumambulated above. We climbed the northern rampart at Glacier Point, three thousand five hundred feet above the Merced river, and, arrived at the top, lay with our heads over the sheer cliff, looking down upon pines which, though nearly two hundred feet high, appeared like the trees of a Noah's ark; horses which were moving specks; and the hotel which seemed a toy house. If, from such a point on the summit of Yosemite walls, the eye turns from the dizzy brink towards the Sierra, it travels over a region of rolling ridges, and great granite domes, the hollows between which contain shallow layers of soil, nourishing scanty forests of pine; above and beyond which long bare ridges stretch upwards to the snowy peaks of the range.

The dome-shaped mountains which specially distinguish the Sierra Nevada, form one of the most curious and notable features of the region around Yosemite. The granite composing them is arranged in concentric layers, like the coats of an onion, and the domes, while accurately circular or elliptical in plan, have semicircular, or nearly semicircular profiles, so steep as to be perfectly inaccessible to an unaided climber. Such a cupola is the North Dome, a rounded mass of rock, rising three thousand five hundred feet above the valley, made up of huge concentric plates of granite ; and such is, or rather was, the Half-Dome already mentioned, once a dome-shaped mountain, towering five thousand feet above the Merced river, but now a helmet-shaped crest, whose western half has been split off and removed.

This extraordinary mass, which is unique in the Sierra Nevada, and probably in the world, cannot fail to suggest the question, asked almost as peremptorily by the Yosemite walls everywhere— How has this trough-like valley been formed? The cañons which seam the flanks of the range at every few miles of its length, have nothing in common with the Yosemite. These are all more or less V-shaped in section, and their sides never present such angular forms, such squarely cut re-entering angles, as those of the valley itself; while the Half-Dome is a perfectly inconceivable product of erosion by running water. It is equally impossible to suppose that the work was done by ice, for the passage of glaciers results in rounded surfaces and smoothly flowing outlines, of which there are none here. Professor Whitney has offered a singular explanation of this interesting problem which, strange as it sounds, is probably the true one. Dismissing erosion, whether by water or ice, as out of the question, and, having conclusively shown that the valley is no mere crack in the rocks of the range, he says, "In short, we are led irresistibly to the adoption of a theory of the origin of the Yosemite in a way which has hardly yet been recognized as one of those in which valleys may be formed; probably for the reason that there are so few cases in which such an event can be absolutely proved to have occurred. We conceive that, during the process of upheaval of the Sierra, or possibly at some time after that had taken place, there was at the Yosemite a subsidence of a limited area, marked by lines of fault, or fissures, crossing each other somewhat nearly at right angles. In other and more simple words, the bottom of the valley sank down to an unknown depth, owing to its support being withdrawn from underneath, during some of those convulsive movements which must have attended the upheaval of so extended and elevated a chain, no matter how slow we may imagine the process to have been. By the adoption of this theory we are able to get over one difficulty which appears insurmountable with any other. This is the very small amount of *débris* at the base of the cliffs, and even, at a few points, its entire absence. There is no way of disposing of the vast mass of detritus which must have fallen from the walls of the Yosemite since the formation of the valley except by assuming that it has gone down to fill the abyss which was opened by the subsidence which our theory supposes to have taken place. What the depth of the chasm may have been we have no data for computing, but that it must have been very great is proved by the fact that it has been able to receive the accumulations of so long a period of time. The cavity was undoubtedly occupied by water, forming a lake of unsurpassed beauty and grandeur, until quite a recent geological epoch. The gradual desiccation of the whole country, the disappearance of the glaciers, and the filling up of the abyss to nearly a level with the present outlet, where the valley passes into a cañon of the usual form, have converted the lake into a valley, with a river meandering through it."

The most elevated region of the Sierra Nevada, called the High Sierra, where the passes exceed twelve thousand feet, and the peaks rise to nearly fifteen thousand feet, occurs about a hundred miles south of the Yosemite, but the mountains which border the valley are hardly less imposing than those of the culminating portion of the range, and these Californian Alps offer every inducement to mountaineers for a visit. There are peaks, many of them still unscaled and unnamed, as difficult to conquer as any in Europe, and there is a type of scenery totally different to that of Switzerland to be seen. On the other hand, the summer climate of California is perfect for mountaineering expeditions, the sky is always serene, the sudden storms and vexatious delays so common in the Alps are unknown, and camping at elevations of eight thousand to ten thousand feet is easy and agreeable. The most striking contrast between Swiss and Californian mountain scenery consists in the absence from the Sierra of glaciers, and snow in large quantities. The Sierran flanks are also wanting in the grassy slopes which occur in Switzerland between timber-line and the snow; those high pastures, with their scattered châlets, where the Swiss cattle feed through the summer months. In place of these, the forest in California stretches right up to the snow, the hardiest pines only dying out at elevations of more than twelve thousand feet. The slopes of the Alps have no timber which can compare with the forest belt of the Snowy Range, but the Swiss pine, with its brighter colour, gives more animation to a mountain-side than the grey needles of the great Californian conifers, so sombre in tone, and monotonous in their general effect. The lower valleys of the Sierra too, though often beautiful with grassy meadows, are not numerous or important enough to form a conspicuous feature in scenery of so grand a type as that of these Western Alps, while in Switzerland, on the contrary, these green, flower-spangled meads, have a never-failing charm for the mountaineer.

The High Sierra, in short, is sublime, but without the charm of the Swiss Alps. It has aspects of beauty, due to its clear skies and transparent air, such as no mountains in Europe exhibit; but it awes more than it attracts. Except for its belt of splendid pines, it might seem as if the Sierra Nevada, like the deserts around its feet, had perished of thirst, and that a grisly skeleton, rather than the living body of a great chain of mountains, lay prone along the Pacific shore. The range indeed is a sublime sarcophagus of cold grey granite, capped with silver, banded with a single wreath of luxuriant foliage, and steeped in opalescent sunlight; the grave of a mountain beauty, which departed with the beneficent vapours that once wrapped it in a living vesture of leaves and flowers, and for whose return the thirsty deserts and stark hills alike wait, dead and still.

We left the valley by the Madera stage which, after traversing the pine belt, descends, instead of skirting, the foot-hills, and then crosses the San Joaquin plains to Madera, a station on the Southern Pacific Railway, a hundred and eighty miles south of San Francisco. Although this journey involves a hundred miles of staging, seventy of which are accomplished in one never-to-be-forgotten day, the Madera route to the Yosemite is much to be preferred to any other, and will supersede them all long before the commission agents who sell tickets for the valley have learned to speak the truth about the roads which they respectively recommend. The drive, whether through forest, foot-hills, or plain, was one long delight to us, now case-hardened against mountain roads and springless coaches. Our driver was a handsome and powerfully built man of colour, whose handling of a six-horse team over difficult ground was almost worth a trip to the Sierra to witness. Stage-driving in America is unmistakably high art, and, exercised as it is in mining and mountainous regions, where the stage is pioneer for the railroad, requires great courage, skill, and readiness. Before the completion of the Pacific Railroad the mining population of Nevada was supplied with all the necessaries of life from the Pacific coast, and the range was daily crossed, chiefly by way of the Sonora and Carson passes, by immense trains of waggons, which were linked together in threes and fours, and drawn by ten or a dozen horses. The driver rode one of the wheelers and managed the whole team by his voice and a single line, the latter being used to signal one of the leaders, by an understood series of jerks, either to turn to the right hand, the left hand, or to stop, all the other horses being trained to follow his movements. Deserted shanties, now falling to ruin in isolated spots among the mountains, mark the old resting-places of this service, where passed masters of the twin arts of teaming and swearing drank many a "whiskey straight" in the good old "early days."

We landed, after a long and terribly dusty drive, at Madera, a little town on the very frontier of the wheat-growing industry which encroaches farther every year on the desert plains of the

San Joaquin. Begrimed as we were, we gladly paid a dollar for a bath at the barber's shop, and then made our way through vast outworks of wheat-bags, piled around the railroad depôt, to a Pullman car which waits nightly in a siding at Madera for travellers from the Yosemite. We were sound asleep when the night train took us in tow, and the next morning found us once more in San Francisco.

Our American trip was over. A few days later we watched from the deck of the Pacific mail steamer, *City of Tokio*, the portals of the Golden Gate sliding from sight in the fog, and as the great ship rose and fell on the waves of a strange and misty ocean, scarcely knew whether to look with more interest back to the New World with its restless civilization, or forward to the sight of cities, older than history, and the long-settled polity and culture of the mysterious East.

PART II

EAST

PART II

CHAPTER I.

THE PACIFIC.

September 20—October 12.

YOUNG as the port of San Francisco is, two lines of steamers already connect the far East with the far West; while a third, started and owned entirely by Chinamen, was daily expecting the arrival of its pioneer steamer, the *Ho-Chung*, at the moment when we left America. We chose the Pacific mail route, and found the *City of Tokio* a splendid vessel of five thousand tons, built in America, and, probably in consequence of this, combining the luxurious saloons, roomy berths, and many smaller comforts of the great river steamers, with excellent sea-going qualities. True to her time to a minute, the ship left the wharf at San Francisco, and, starting without the slightest fuss, her decks perfectly clear and every rope in place, turned her face towards the Golden Gate, so completely prepared for the voyage that it was difficult to believe ourselves already launched on a journey of five thousand miles.

The *City of Tokio* is not a fast ship, the day's run averaging less than two hundred and thirty miles, while crack Atlantic steamers make three hundred and fifty miles or even more in twenty-four hours; but competition is not severe on the Pacific, and ships only hurry when they are bringing back tea to the American market; there is no object in wasting coals on the outward voyage. If the ship is slow, she is perfect in every other respect, from a passenger's point of view. She is well officered, with men who give themselves no airs and are frankly at the service of the people they carry. The crew, the cooks, and the stewards are all Chinamen, and whether on deck, in the saloon, or in the cabins, the ship's work goes on with an automatic smoothness which is surprising. The vessel is as trim as a lady from stem to stern, and scrupulously clean both above and below, yet one looks in vain for the agency which keeps everything in order, and wonders, as in an American hotel, how the great machine is run so noiselessly. Never have I seen decks so clear, ropes so faultlessly coiled, or berths so snowy white; never before have I occupied a cabin, with a bell which I have only to ring to find excellent and immediate service; never have I sat at table so well waited upon as by the silent Chinaman in blue blouse, spotless linen cuffs and hose, and pigtail falling from under a close cloth cap crowned with a red button, who stands behind my chair. Our skipper, Commodore Maury, with his handsome wife, heads a table in the saloon, and each of his officers another, but all of them are in plain clothes, as indeed they are upon deck, and, with true American ease of manner, these gentlemen encourage their passengers to feel that the ship is made for them, and not they for the ship. We are at sea, and yet not at sea, appearing rather to live in some great hotel, surrounded by comforts usually quite unknown on board ship.

We carry about thirty saloon passengers of very various nationalities. The majority are Americans, naval officers joining their ships in Japanese waters, ladies returning to their husbands at Yokohama, merchants, missionaries, and tourists. The minority consists of half a dozen travelling English, a German, also a traveller, a Japanese diplomatist, a Japanese manufacturer, and a young Chinaman returning home from school and college in the States. Forward are some five hundred coolies, their numbers an example of the fact already mentioned, that the Chinese exodus from California is greater than the immigration at the present moment. The ship, her officers, passengers, crew, and cargo, are all very different from anything we have seen before, and remind us that we are now in a strange new world, where, across a still half-mysterious ocean, the white and yellow races have begun to amalgamate upon a new basis of liberty and equality.

Our weather for the first ten days of the voyage was perfect. The sea a deep azure blue in colour, more like a melted solid than a fluid in appearance, and the air clear and balmy both by night and day. On the 1st of October, however, there being no wind, we met a very heavy swell, the ship rising over great rounded hills of water some fifteen feet high and about five hundred feet apart; and two days later we encountered the tail of a true cyclone. This storm, which whirled through every point in the compass within an hour or two, raised so lumpy and confused a sea that the water was quite white as far as the eye could see in any direction; but the ship, beyond rolling slowly and regularly through an arc of nearly forty degrees, and shooting inexperienced passengers from side to side of the saloon, behaved remarkably well, and shipped very little water. We watched with interest the behaviour of the Chinese sailors when, our squaresails being blown away, they proceeded to secure the flapping ribbons of canvas. The work was well, but not very quickly done, too few men being sent aloft at first; had the force been adequate, I think the yellow men would have proved as smart as whites. During the gale the coolie passengers threw overboard thousands of "joss-papers," or gilded leaves, which fluttered like birds around the ship but without bringing the fine weather they were sent to seek from the gods.

The Chinese quarter of the *City of Tokio*, whether on deck or below, was always, like Chinatown at San Francisco, a picturesque and amusing scene. On fine days the forward decks were densely crowded with men, for the most part squatting in groups, playing cards or dominoes, the players themselves being surrounded by interested and laughing spectators. A Chinese pack of cards consists of some hundred slips of paper, not more than half an inch wide, and printed with strange devices. The dominoes are like our own, but are dealt to the player and held in his hand like cards. The games were apparently interminable, but the gamesters, enthusiasts; it is only when thus engaged that the serious Mongol face shines with smiles, and the usually silent tongue is unloosed. One withered and ugly old man was a fiddler, who sometimes played for hours together to approving audiences on a tiny instrument like a wiry banjo, scraping shrill and agonizing sounds from the thin strings; while, a little removed from both art and amusement, sat industry, tailoring black and blue garments with long-nailed and flexible fingers. As meal hours approached every one became busy, some cutting up dried fish, or washing bunches of strange vegetables, others shelling preserved eggs of their black earthy coating, or preparing split ducks and stringy sausages for the galley fire. Below, the five hundred were packed at night, not more closely than immigrants on the Atlantic, but in bunks which were almost hidden by a varied mass of personal baggage and household goods, lashed to every available post and support between the floor and the deck. These articles were for the most part so national in character as to defy classification, but, from among bamboo baskets and packs of Mongol clothes, there sometimes peeped that entirely unmistakable article, an American trunk, or the equally characteristic outfit of the Californian miner. One of the largest forward cabins in the *City of Tokio* is fitted up for opium-smoking, with the same matted bunks, pillow-stools, and paraphernalia already described. This is a wise concession to Chinese habits, without which the ship would run a great risk of fire—the one enemy that is most carefully guarded against on this long voyage. The "den" is under strict surveillance, and is open only at certain hours, but the Chinese, having a place provided for them, do not attempt to smoke in their own bunks, as they might otherwise try to do in spite of the closest watching.

Our saloon passenger of the yellow race is a young Chinese gentleman, returning home after nine years spent in the States. He went to America at thirteen years of age, being one of a number of Chinese boys, the sons of men in good positions, who are annually sent abroad at the expense of the Chinese Government to be educated in the schools of America, England, and Germany. There are a hundred and twenty such boys now in the States, thirty in England, and thirty in Germany, and they are looked after by a commissioner resident in each country, who selects their schools, places them in good families, and, at the end of their school career, enters them at some university, where they graduate and afterwards return to their homes. The Chinese Government took this step at the instance of the liberal party in the empire, and begins apparently to regret its action; for every foreign student is found to return to his country an advanced liberal, bitterly opposed to the existing Tartar dynasty, and desirous above all things for a national government.*

The feudal system of China, with its great lords on the one hand, far richer and more powerful than any individuals in Christendom; and on the other, its people, sunk for the most part in abject poverty,—exists by virtue of a tyranny which is nevertheless taxed to the utmost to keep the great feudatories in subjection. Feudality is at once the curse and weakness of China, pauperizing her industrious population, and so dividing her strength that every instructed Chinaman foresees and fears the day when an unscrupulous foreign foe may make the million soldiers of the empire count for nothing, because they belong to the great feudatories, who might be divided by the skill of a new Clive or Cortes. Yet the Chinese Government, by its education policy, is creating intelligent and irreconcilable foes both to the feudal system and its own existence. My friend Mr. Tsoy indeed predicts a revolution and the fall of the Mantchus within ten years; at the same time declaring that we entirely failed to understand, not only the national wrongs of China, but our own trade interests, when we lent the weight of English power to crush the Tai-pings.

* Since the above was written, the Chinese Government have recalled the boys who were being educated in Western schools and colleges.

Cum-Chiong-Tsoy has a critical eye also for the failings of the United States, and examines, shrewdly enough, what is the height and depth of American freedom, in view of the treatment of the Chinese in California. I quote verbatim a few of his remarks on the "Inconsistencies of the American People," illustrating on the one hand the excellent use which the Chinaman makes of European education, and, on the other, how keenly he feels the wrongs of his compatriots in the States. "It would be amusing if we could ascertain with what extravagant expectations the thousands of Europe and Asia, leaving their destitute and oppressed homes, sail for America, that land of liberty, where the equality of mankind, without regard of colour or race, is the fundamental principle of government. But this we do know, that they find the same state of things, only under different names, there as at home. Human nature is the same everywhere. In the United States is a president instead of a king or emperor, and the ignorant masses have the privilege, though they do not know how to exercise it, of voting. There are as many classes of society in a republican as in a monarchical country. The aristocracy, although not hereditary, is quite as arrogant and unapproachable, and the poor man might as well expect water to run uphill as to enter its circles without money. Republican girls are as crazy after titles as any European maidens, and generally there is little consistency between the professed principles and actions of the American people. By the constitution of the United States all nationalities are allowed to enter her territory, yet a law was passed in the Senate to prohibit Chinese immigration, and would have become law, in direct violation of existing treaties, but for the veto of a clear-headed president. The Americans are zealous in sending out missionaries to convert the heathen, but when the heathen come to their threshold they threaten to expel them from the country for the criminal offence of being willing to work for low wages. Is it strange that the heathen, receiving such treatment at Christian hands, should regard Christians as wolves in sheep's clothing? The United States is a free country, so free in fact that the 'hoodlums' and mobs can do whatever they please; but it is not free for certain unoffending and peaceful foreigners."

The *Gull of Tokio*, from which the above extract is made, was a "semi-weekly journal, devoted to literature, social and physical science, the three R's, and the news of the day." This amateur newspaper appeared regularly during the voyage, and was read aloud in the saloon on certain evenings, when music, mock trials, and similar devices for passing the time accompanied the reading. The fun of such things is usually too fugitive for reproduction, but the following communication, selected from a bundle of "Intercepted Letters," gives a portrait group of our passengers, set in a frame of incidents, slight indeed, but characteristic of most voyages:—

"On board the *City of Tokio*,
"September 30, 1880.

"DARLING EDIE,

"Of course I couldn't keep the promise which I made in London, to write a line every day while on board, and here we are, ten days at sea, before I touch my pen. The first few days of our voyage were simply delicious, the sea calm, the weather exquisite. The commodore's wife is my chaperone, as you know, and she is the dearest creature in the world. Fancy a very pretty young woman, with the *loveliest* white hair dressed high up on her head. She looks like a bit from Watteau or Greuze, and, like all these dear American ladies, she is the most indulgent of sheep-dogs. If I *wanted* to flirt, I think she would let me to my heart's content. The commodore himself is delightful, perfectly devoted to her; but I am a little afraid of him, for he says clever things in that cool American way, which gives me a little shiver, half nice, half horrid, when I speak to him. There are two ladies on board, going to their husbands in Japan. One is a brunette, piquante, awfully well read, and all that sort of thing, but *much* too clever for poor me. The other is a blonde, very sweet and kind. I *do* think it is *such* a shame to say there are more grass widows in America than anywhere else, and as for *flirting!* I give you my word, dear, that though Lieutenant Barry and Mr. Gardiner read nice new books to them on deck all the morning, they are *always* down in that horrid saloon in the evening, no matter how delicious it is on deck. *We* aren't half so good in England, my dear. There is a group of Englishmen on board, very thick with one another, and, just as they are at home, *always* in the smoking-room, getting up pools, or playing whist all day. They see very little of my *beaux yeux*, I can tell you. There is a mysterious little fellow whom they call the 'Pasha,' who wears a fez, and looks rather nice. I am dying to know whether it is true that he is a Turk, with a harem at Constantinople. One of the Englishmen told me so, but he is one of those horrid men you know so well at home, always laughing at girls, and chaffing, so that you don't know what to think. The 'Pasha' is always with the Englishmen, and my chaperone thinks he borrows money of them. *The* man of the ship is the purser; he is delightful, with a long, drooping moustache, and *such* eyes, full of fun and feeling at the same time. I had the greatest fun with him at first, until some of those horrid *clever* people, whom I hate, started a stupid thing they call the *Gull of Tokio*, a kind of amateur newspaper, and since then not a girl in the ship can have the least bit of fun without every one knowing it. I was behind the wheel-house to-day for a few minutes with Mr. Darby, a dark, *distingué*-looking man, and very interesting, when I saw one of those wretched *clever* people peeping round the corner, so I suppose that even that will be in the next week's issue. It's perfectly horrid, dear, and soon only the missionaries will dare show their faces on deck after dark for fear of this stupid *Gull*. There goes the purser, and I promised him a stroll at three. I will resume to-morrow."

It was a never-failing pleasure to watch the great gulls, more than a score of which followed the ship from San Francisco, evidently intending to accompany us to Japan. They wheeled around the steamer all day, deserting her only at night, to sleep, if they sleep at all, on the waves. In the morning they were with us again long before the passengers were astir, watching for the earliest refuse of the galley, and floating, when hungry, over the quarter-deck itself. The flight of these birds is apparently accomplished without any expenditure of muscular energy. They keep abreast of the ship, although their wings are scarcely ever seen to flap, and dart hither and thither in the pursuit of food by almost imperceptible movements. During the storm they left us to play about the great rollers, up whose sides they skimmed, resting for a moment over each crest, obliquely poised, and with the tip of one wing almost touching the foam. They were not hunting, for there is no fish in this deep ocean; they seemed to be only revelling in their powers of flight, waked to activity by the strife of wind and sea.

If a traveller, starting from the longitude of Greenwich to circumnavigate the globe sails west with the sun, chronometer in hand, this, upon his reaching the hundred and eightieth meridian, will of course declare that it is midnight of any given day, while the sun says it is noon; and *vice versâ* if he sails eastward, or against the sun's path in the heavens. Or, to put it in another way, if he starts say at noon on Monday, and could travel westward, as fast as the sun, for twenty-four hours, the clock would say it was midday Tuesday, although Monday's sun had not begun to decline. The day which is thus lost between America and Japan was thrown overboard as we crossed the hundred and eightieth meridian of longitude, and if any of my readers fail to understand the simple reasons for its burial given above, I fear that the following extract from the *Gull's* answers to correspondents will not make the matter any clearer :—" Yes, it is quite true, we have lost a day. To-day is yesterday as well as Tuesday, but at the same time yesterday is Monday as well as Sunday, though the day before yesterday was Saturday. Take our advice, and do not venture into east longitude any more."

Long as the Pacific voyage is, we did not tire of it. The days were amply filled with exercise, reading, writing, and conversation, while at night the beautiful heavens tempted us to lounge for hours on deck, watching the glowing stars or the luminous ribbon of the Milky Way. The storm excepted, our daily passage through the calm azure water was so monotonous that we could not realize our approach to Asia. We seemed to be sailing over an interminable ocean, seeking no other haven than the setting sun, straight for whose disc our bows pointed night after night. At length, however, I was roused, early on the morning of the 12th of October, by my companion jumping suddenly from the upper bunk and exclaiming, "Japan is in sight!" and a moment afterwards our faces were framed, one in each of the open port-holes of our cabin. The view which met our eyes was at the same time strange and familiar. Conical hills, covered to their summits with dense foliage, descended abruptly to a plain which, wider here and narrower there, bordered the ocean. Every inch of the level land was cultivated, not in wide fields of grass or grain, but in parti-coloured slips and patches. Villages of tiny brown houses, with thatched roofs and wide eaves, planted along the ridges with lilies, clustered thickly on the plain, while detached dwellings, recalling the pagodas on a willow plate, peeped here and there from the foliage covering the hill-sides. The sea was alive with the "sampans" of fishermen, quaint boats of unpainted wood, with high bows and square sterns, sculled by living bronzes, standing erect in scanty drapery, their shaven heads tied around with blue and white handkerchiefs. It was like a picture by Meissonier, of a quaint and beautiful toy-land, utterly new to all European experience.

CHAPTER II.

YOKOHAMA—FIRST IMPRESSIONS.

October 12–13.

THE early Japanese, who looked eastward over an ocean which even to their boldest seamen appeared shoreless, might well believe that their country was truly the "Land of the Rising Sun." They called it Ni-Hon, or the Sun-source, a word which we usually spell Niphon, but, following a national custom, which still prevails, they wrote it, in Chinese characters, pronounced Ya-pan. The Portuguese, who first of Europeans, visited Niphon in the sixteenth century, were already settled at Macao and, being acquainted with the Chinese language, naturally gave the Chinese pronunciation to these characters which they found on the native maps, so that, Ni-Hon, the Land of the Rising Sun, has been Japan for Europe ever since.

The engines of the *City of Tokio* stopped for the first time since leaving San Francisco, at half-past ten on the morning of the 12th of October, after being incessantly in motion for twenty-two days and nights. The steamer was no sooner anchored than she was surrounded by "sampans," the strange boats already described, each propelled by two men who stood erect and back to back "sculling" with long crank-handled oars. The figures in the boats were stranger than the craft. It was raining heavily on our arrival, and the men appeared to be literally thatched with conical straw hats as big as an umbrella, while their bodies were wrapped in mantles of thatch which made them look like so many yellow porcupines.

Yokohama is purely a settlement town. It had no existence prior to 1859, when the site was placed at the service of Europeans by the Japanese Government, in partial fulfilment of their obligations under the Anglo-French Treaty of 1858. The Japanese had indeed agreed to open Kanagawa, the port of the capital, but their fear of strangers was stronger than their sense of duty, and, at the risk of seriously offending the foreign envoys, they changed the promised site for the settlement to Yokohama, then a poor fishing village, standing in the midst of a salt-water marsh, two miles from Kanagawa, and quite out of the line of traffic between that port and the capital. The object was to locate the foreigners where their trade could be controlled and themselves watched, or, if need be, shut up, as the Dutch had been in the small island settlement which they alone of all other nations had been permitted to occupy for two hundred years at Nagasaki. The envoys protested vigorously against this breach of faith, but, while they negotiated, the merchants established themselves in such numbers at Yokohama, that the question was taken out of the hands of the diplomatists, and the site accepted in spite of its drawbacks.

The irregular Yokohama of the first settlers was entirely destroyed by fire in 1866, and has been succeeded by a comparatively regular city, containing at the present time twelve hundred foreigners and a hundred and twenty thousand natives. Viewed from the road-stead, the town occupies a shelf of low and level land bordering the sea, and behind it rise hills of no great height, whose steep slopes are diversified here and there by cliffs, horizontally stratified, and of recent age. The hills are covered from base to summit with a dense growth of small conifers, above which in the west rises the sacred mountain Fusiyama, a white and symmetrical cone, shining with subdued lustre through some seventy miles of pearly air. On a nearer approach, the shore is seen to be lined with a row of good houses, each with a small garden in front, and bordered by a wide road protected by a substantial sea-wall. This is the "Bund," containing some of the best residences, and several large hotels. To the right are the low brown roofs of the native town, while to the left of the settlement, and separated from it by a small stream, are the "Bluffs," picturesque and densely wooded cliffs, once the site of the foreign legations only, but now thickly sprinkled with the residences of merchants, who enjoy some of the prettiest imaginable scenery from their windows. At the foot of the Bluffs is the English Naval Establishment, a Portsmouth Yard in miniature, whose trim roads and buildings are set in a slope of the same luxuriant foliage as that which clothes the Bluffs from the sea to their summits. Behind the Bund are the streets in which the business of the settlement centres. Here are the merchants' "hongs," or blocks of substantial stone buildings, and here are the banks, the offices of the steamship companies, the retail shops, and some factories.

On landing we found the pier lined with "jinrickishas," the light "man-power carriages," like a Bath chair with shafts, which, within a few years, have spread over Japan in vast numbers, almost entirely superseding the "kango," a kind of palanquin, in which the natives formerly travelled. The horse is a coolie, short but muscular, with legs of polished bronze, and dressed in a blue cotton gown, gathered about his loins and tied round the waist with the "obi," or sash. Over his shaven crown curves the short national queue, while his feet are protected by sandals of plaited rice straw fastened by strings of the same material.

What a pleasure it was to sit once more on a firm floor, at a well-appointed table in the Grand Hotel, discussing an excellent *déjeuner* and a bottle of good Bordeaux, while, through the open windows, our eyes roamed over Yokohama Bay with its crisp blue waves and misty shores, its shipping, and moving sampans! But we were not long the guests of the Grand Hotel. My companion had letters to a German mercantile house of high standing in Yokohama, where we were welcomed with all the characteristic hospitality of the far East. The visitor fresh from Europe is received all the more cordially, perhaps, because he breaks the monotony of settlement life and brings with him a whiff of the old country, never forgotten by the men who seek fortune at the antipodes. Certainly it was a charming circle that we joined. The pioneers of commerce in the far East, as in the far West, are almost always young, ardent spirits, without prejudices, intelligent, and being recruited chiefly from the higher commercial classes of Europe, well-educated and cultured gentlemen. The Western man, on the other hand, exhibits the same characteristics, but springs from another social source, a fact which makes a wide difference between pioneer society in California and Japan. Tiffin, as in China, is the meal of the day in Yokohama; dinner is only a ceremony, often taken very late, after an evening already far spent at the club, so it is at lunch that we usually listen to narratives, explanations, and anticipations concerning this interesting country. For, whether consuls, merchants, or travellers, the settlers talk perpetually of Japan. Europe is so distant that events occurring there have lost their importance before the

R

outlines of telegrams are filled in with details, and meantime, these men are surrounded by social and political problems which still have all the attraction of the unknown, and their acute minds naturally turn from useless considerations of European affairs, to attempt the solution of many yet unguessed riddles in the national character of the people with whom they live and trade. For two travellers with eyes and mouths full of questions, what position could be more agreeable? The easy luxurious life was charming too; the servants were Chinese, and therefore excellent, the table was good, and the elasticity of the whole establishment, so far as entertaining is concerned, reminded us of the elephant's trunk, which picks up a pin or a timber tree with equal ease.

Around the European settlement lies the native town, consisting of low wooden houses, seldom more than one story high, with heavy tiled or thatched roofs, having wide eaves turned up like the brim of a felt hat. These dwellings are quite open during the day, being divided into apartments only by sliding paper panels, and enclosed at night by external slides of wood. They are seldom more than twenty feet square, and are griddled by frequent streets, some wide, some narrow, but always clean and with well-made roadways. Main Street, the chief of these, is occupied almost exclusively by dealers in curios, china, lacquer, and jewellery. In the less important avenues one finds the tea and silk merchants' establishments, shops for the sale of the bronze vessels in which charcoal is burnt (the domestic fireplaces of Japan), pipes, books, umbrellas, fans, toys, and paper. Remote streets are even more national in character. Here is a "saki"-shop with its rows of wooden tubs cased in plaited straw, holding the wine of Japan, distilled from rice and tasting like a sickly spirituous hock. Dried fish are sold next door; and then comes the shoe-shop, piled to the ceiling with "geta," the wooden clogs in universal use. Hard by squats the tobacco-cutter; then comes a cook-shop, where fish are stewing in oil; and there is a sweetmeat-maker, rolling up rice, sugar, and seaweed into sticky, cigar-shaped packets. Here is a shop buried in big paper lanterns painted with bizarre designs; and next door one may buy cheap petroleum lamps from Birmingham, or domestic utensils, such as pails, rice-boxes, and dippers, beautifully made of pine or bamboo. The shops are entered on the level of the street, and a portion of the floor, where the wooden clogs are left, is formed of the soil beaten hard, from which rises the true floor, a wooden platform about fifteen inches high, covered with fine matting. Upon this the stock is displayed, the proprietor squatting among his wares, teapot and pipe at hand, laughing, chatting, and smoking by turns. The merchants and high-class shopkeepers reserve a small floor space for the cashier, who sits with his books and calculating-machine behind a tiny screen, giving an air of privacy. By his side is the "tobacco-bon," a small square box, containing live charcoal in a china pot and a short cylinder of bamboo, the one to light the pipe and the other to receive its ashes. No other article of domestic use in Japan is so universally conspicuous as this little firepot. If you sit but for a moment, whether in a tea-house, a shop, a private house, or a public office, it is instantly pushed towards you with graceful gestures and beaming smiles; it is what the snuff-box was between friends in the days of our grandfathers. The lower class shop is a dining-room as well as a mart, where the family eat their rice and fish, with chopsticks, out of lacquered wooden bowls, in view of all the world, and the same thing takes place, scarcely hidden by a paper screen, in the houses of the wealthier native merchants and shop-keepers.

But what pen can describe the appearance of the streets, filled with gay and graceful crowds, or give the reader any real idea of the groups which enliven these half-seen, half-unseen interiors? A thousand sketches have made us all acquainted with the costumes of the Japanese; we know that both men and women wear tunics of silk or cotton, with hanging sleeves, and confined around the waist, in the one case by a girdle of *crêpe*, and in the other by a wide and brilliantly coloured silk sash, with bows behind so big that they cover the greater part of the back. Japanese fans and photographs have made us all acquainted with those smooth bands of ebony black hair, which shine with tea-oil, and bristle with handsome hair-pins, over the faces of the charming, though not strictly beautiful, Japanese girls. But the best descriptions of shops and costumes are pigments without a painter—fragments from which it is as difficult to construct the *coup d'œil* of a Japanese street as to restore the aspect of Pompeii from the frescoes on its walls. The busy crowd, the smiling faces, the courteous greetings, and graceful inclinations of the body; the flying but noiseless jinrickishas, with their bronzed and muscular men-horses; the half-grotesque, half-charming children, with their bright parti-coloured garments, shaven crowns, and quaint tufts of hair; the naked coolies, bearing heavy loads, slung from their shoulders by long bamboos, sweating, and shouting a measured chant; the avenue of open shops, with their heavy roofs and painted paper lanterns, their stores of art and curiosities, and their squatting proprietors, smoking or taking tea;—all these combine to form a picture, whose colour and movement, grace and grotesqueness cannot be matched in the world, but which no pen or pencil can bring before eyes that have not looked upon the thing itself.

One of the prettiest walks in the neighbourhood of Yokohama is to Mississippi Bay, a deep indentation in the coast-line, on the further side of the Bluffs, whence, better than from the town itself, may be seen the wide, land-locked, and lake-like expanse of Jeddo Bay. The country around Yokohama, and indeed, as we are told, almost the whole sea-board of Japan, consists of steep, wooded, and closely-grouped hills, which rise to an almost uniform height of a few hundred feet above the level of the sea. They are carved out of soft, recent rocks, horizontally bedded, and are evidently the weathered remains of a plateau of detritus, which has been elevated in late geological times, probably by volcanic movements. Their feet stand on a low plain, the beach-mark of a recent sea-level, which everywhere skirts the ocean, or winds far inland, forming flat-bottomed valleys between the interosculating hills. These valleys, now wide, now narrow, are cultivated exclusively with rice. The lower shoulders of the hills are planted with millet, sweet potatoes, buckwheat, egg-plant, cotton, and "daicum," the last a curious vegetable like an elongated turnip, which is largely grown, and is drying now in quantities around every cottage that we pass. Higher up, the hills are covered with a thick growth of coniferous timber, which gives way to cultivated terraces here and there, where, in the immediate neighbourhood of Yokohama, European vegetables are raised for sale in the settlement. The rice was ready for the sickle as we passed, and the blue-clad peasants were already cutting it with small hooks, The men stood nearly knee-deep in the mud of the flooded fields. and neither crop nor reapers had a picturesque appearance; the former looked like wheat badly laid by storms, and the latter like scarecrows. Rice should be seen in the spring, when it paints the ground with a bright emerald green; its colour at maturity is rusty, and the soil which the harvest-man exposes is a swamp. The hill side forest, or rather jungle, is everywhere penetrated by narrow footpaths, a close network of which, they tell us, covers all the inhabited portions of Japan. These are bordered by flowers and ferns, the latter being very abundant. It was pleasant to find such old friends as the harebell, flowering trefoil, and common pteris fern, intermingled with a hundred wayside plants entirely new to us. Scarcely a bird was heard or seen throughout our walk, and there were no sheep, cows, or horses in the fields.

Arrived at the crest of the hill which overlooks Mississippi Bay, we came quite suddenly upon a view of extraordinary and fairy-like beauty. The seeming lake of Jeddo Bay spread away before us, a sheet of dusky silver, to distant, irregular shores of sloping foliage, only half lighted by a sun shining through the pearly mists of the Pacific. Beneath us and lining the water's edge, lay a fishing village, a cluster of brown, lily-grown roofs of thatch rising from among trim gardens, while the sampans lay ready for sea on a wide beach lapped by tiny waves of palest silver. A tangle of pines fell steeply from our feet to the shore, where nestled these remote and peaceful homes, and from the foliage peeped here and there a few steps of wide stone stairways leading to temples hidden among the trees.

A sort of fair is held in the native town of Yokohama one night in every week. Several of the most important thoroughfares are then occupied by stalls, which display a most extraordinary variety of useful and curious little articles, sold for trifling sums. The scene is strikingly picturesque. The long and crowded streets are lined out by rows of glowing lanterns. A thousand strange sounds rise from the stall-keepers crying their wares, and across the hum of talk come frequent gusts of laughter. The crowd flows slowly hither and thither, each dusky figure bent a little forward, as the use of the wooden geta demands. The parti-coloured tints of the costumes are lost in the clear obscurity of the night, or imperfectly displayed when a group of laughing girls clusters around a favourite stall. Look at the picture well; to-morrow it will be a memory, a dream of graceful movement and subdued colour, thrown on the magic background of the half-tropical night, and scarcely lighted by the mysterious glow of scattered lanterns.

The Chinese are the Scotch of the East. Wherever there is a commercial opening, a Chinaman is ready to fill it; and, in Japan, he takes the very bread out of the native mouth by his superior qualifications for business. The coasting trade of Japan was not long since confined to British vessels; but it passed away from our flag, first into the hands of the Germans, and then into those of the Chinese. Chinese exports to Japan are very considerable, sometimes rivalling in value the combined shipments of Europe and America to that country. The chief clerks of every bank in Yokohama are Chinese. Every European merchant of standing has a Chinese cashier, and in every well-organized household the head servants are Chinese. There is a Chinatown in Yokohama as well as in San Francisco, where these singular people live in the same self-contained way that they do in the United States; mixing little with the Japanese, and bearing themselves as if fully aware of their superiority to them in affairs. The Chinese question seems always growing in importance as we proceed, and we clearly have not left it behind us in California. It is a complete surprise to find the Japanese, whom we have been taught to regard as, next to the white races, the cleverest and most advanced people in the world, distanced by Chinamen in their own country. We commonly think of the Japanese as a people who have made good their claim to a high place in the comity of nations by the intelligence with which they have appreciated our ideas, and the courage they have shown in destroying a feudal and absolutist system with the professed object of unshackling trade. Of the Chinese, on the other hand, we have no high ideals; yet the traveller has hardly landed in Yokohama before he begins to doubt whether the views of Japanese character current in England are correct, and to question whether the yellow race is not superior to the other in many important respects.

Certainly the trade of Japan, which was expected to make rapid strides under a government ostensibly devoted to material progress, and eager to imitate European models, has progressed very slowly. The total imports for the year 1870, when the country had hardly recovered from the civil war of 1868, or adjusted itself to the great political changes which followed it, were thirty-one million dollars. Five years afterwards, they were twenty-five millions; and if, ten years later, they were thirty-six millions, 1880 is the only year whose totals have exceeded those of 1870. Exports, it is true, have largely increased during the same time, as they were bound to do with the opening of railroads, however limited in their extent, to say nothing of the new American demand for Japanese tea. But the wants of the people—that sure test of advancing civilisation—have not grown since the establishment of the reformed government, and, looking now at Japanese progress from a totally different standpoint to that taken above, we already begin to doubt whether the rulers of Japan are as sincerely anxious for the extension of intercourse with Europe as we have been led to suppose.

It is arranged that we make Yokohama our headquarters during our stay in the country. The settlement is a much more convenient centre than the capital, and we look forward with pleasure to returning again and again, from such inland trips as we may make, to our circle of hospitable friends and to the pleasant European town which has taken the place of the old Japanese fishing village "across the seashore."

CHAPTER III.

A JAPANESE "AT HOME."

October 14.

ONE of our fellow-passengers across the Pacific was a Mr. Okowa, son and partner of a Japanese paper manufacturer, who, formerly a member of the military caste, devoted himself to business on the abolition of the daimiate and consequent dispersion of the "samurai." Okowa spoke English well, having just spent a year, studying American processes of paper-making, in the States, where my companion had known him intimately, and he was good enough to arrange his return home so as to coincide with our visit to his country. This not only gave us an opportunity of acquiring a few useful Japanese words and phrases on the voyage, but opened the doors of Japanese family life to us as well, a fact of which we took advantage almost immediately on our arrival. Mr. Okowa's house and mill are situated at Oji, a charming village about seven miles from the capital, where we paid our friend a visit, and were most agreeably entertained in purely native style.

A railway, opened in 1872, connects Yokohama with Tokio, situated at the head of Jeddo Bay, and still, perhaps, better known in Europe by its old name of Jeddo (The Sea-gate) than by that of Tokio (Eastern Capital), which it has borne since, on the close of the civil war in 1868, it became the residence of the Mikado, as it had formerly been that of the Shogun, or Tycoon.

The line is eighteen miles long and skirts Jeddo Bay, whose shore is, as we have already seen, a wide shelf of low and level land, once evidently the sea-bottom, but now upraised. An English railway at last! What a pleasure to see again the finished details of permanent way, points, crossings, and signals, after so many thousand miles of rough-and-ready railroads in America! Everything looked solid and good; the iron bridges as if they would carry the train, the stations brick-built, and the very ballast so neatly laid that we were half ashamed of throwing our cigar ashes on the tidy track. Track! that is the very word for an American railroad. No people name things so aptly as the Yankees. Going "gunning with a smell-dog" is good Yankee, and truer description than "shooting over a pointer," and the American who first called "the line" "a track," had a sense of the fitness of things.

On our right hand was the Bay of Jeddo, shimmering in the sunlight, crowded with native and foreign craft, and with the mountains of Kadzusa and Awa provinces bounding its opposite shore. On our left stretched a wide and cultivated flat, covered almost exclusively with rice-fields, and ending in toy-hills, behind which rose the symmetrical cone of Fusiyama, faintly seen through the misty air. The fields were dotted with blue figures, some reaping, others carrying the rice crop, for there are no horses or carts employed on the land in this part of Japan; while, elsewhere, men and women were digging, manuring, and planting the soil. The villages are close together, and we made many stoppages, always finding the stations crowded. Our fellow-passengers in the first-class carriage were, for the most part, native merchants, going up to town by the early train on business. Each of them was reading, or, to speak quite correctly, intoning his morning newspaper, a quaint little sheet about the size of a concert programme, and taking breath at measured intervals with a sound like a loud and long-drawn sigh. The costumes were very mixed, sometimes entirely European, sometimes purely Japanese, but oftener a comical mixture of both. The first article of clothing which a Jap adopts from foreigners, is a hat; the last, a pair of boots. Reforming thus, from the head downwards, he is found in every stage of the transformation, sometimes covered with a "bowler," or a straw hat, but wearing his own handsome and dignified dress; sometimes in coat and trousers, but retaining the "geta," or wooden clogs, because he cannot give up the habit of squatting, a thing impossible with dirty shoes. The effect of all this is truly ridiculous. Native Japanese costume is dignified, becoming, and picturesque. It suits a short race of people admirably, and seems to add a cubic to the stature of men who appear insignificant in our garments. Europeanized Japanese look as if they were wearing each other's clothes.

We compassed the eighteen miles between Yokohama and Tokio in an hour, and drove in jinrickishas straight to Oji, passing rapidly through the crowded streets of the capital. The men-horses are marvellous little fellows. They ran the seven miles within an hour, and arrived quite fresh, perspiring, of course, but with their wind in perfect condition, and ready for a return fare. We paid them each twenty-five sen, equal to tenpence in English money, or something less than three halfpence a mile.

Mr. Okowa's mill at Oji is a large establishment, built about seven years ago on the European model, fitted throughout with English machinery, and about to receive the latest American improvements. Within the walls of this great manufactory we seemed to be again in Europe, and as the workmen have for the most part adopted our costume, better suited than their own for industrial occupations, little remained to remind us that we were in Japan. Yet only just without, the half-naked coolies who trotted with us from Tokio were eating their morning rice with a pair of chopsticks, in a neighbouring tea-house, within hearing of the noisy engines and machinery. The pictures are sharp contrasts. Which of them, we ask ourselves, foreshadows the future of Japan?

From the mill we adjourned to Mr. Okowa's private house, a large, handsome, one-storied building, constructed, as usual, of wood, with a heavy tiled roof, and standing in the midst of extensive ornamental grounds. These occupy the summit of a hill, which overlooks a flat but lovely country, cultivated here and wooded there, and, spite of the different character of trees and shrubs, singularly European in appearance. There is no such thing as a front door or hall, but the house is open on one side to the garden, being closed at night by wooden slides, like the shops in Yokohama. Similarly, the interior consists of one very large room, capable of division into chambers, by sliding partitions of paper-covered lattice-work, while the domestic offices, as we should call them, form a separate, but, so far as construction goes, similar establishment on a smaller scale. We left our shoes among a number of wooden geta on the garden-path, and stepped thence on to the raised and beautifully matted floor of a spacious room, entirely without furniture, whose paper walls exhibited bold and beautiful drawings of storks and other birds. Some folding screens stood here and there, decorated with grotesque paintings of gods; these and a handsome vase, filled with growing crysanthemums, were the only ornaments in the apartment. The ceiling of this simple chamber was made of a beautifully figured brown wood, which, together with all the other woodwork, was without paint, polish, or varnish. No nails, screws, or fastenings of any kind were visible, and the finish of the joinery work was absolutely faultless. Everything was light, almost toy-like, in design, and it is positively difficult to give an adequate idea of the cleanliness which prevailed throughout the house. The woodwork looked as if it had just left the plane, the matting might have come from the loom only an hour before, and the screen paintings seemed fresh from the artist's brush.

We were greeted on entering by a kneeling man-servant, who prostrated himself repeatedly till his forehead touched the ground, smiling graciously the while. He was handsomely dressed, spotlessly clean, and wore on his tunic the family crest, or, "mon." Throwing cushions of blue *crêpe* silk on the floor for the newcomers, he gently pushed towards us, still on his knees, a handsome tobacco-bon, blew the charcoal till it glowed, and placing his master's pipe by his side, withdrew, after further prostrations, to prepare refreshments. Every Japanese carries a pipe-case and tobacco-pouch, hanging by a silken cord from a "netsuki," or carved ivory figure, tucked in the "obi," or waistbelt, and the whole paraphernalia, like everything else in common use among the Japanese, is a tasteful work of art. The tobacco is cut as fine as sewing cotton, and is very mild, while the pipe-bowl is a tiny metal thimble, hardly large enough to hold a good-sized pinch of snuff. After two or three puffs, discharged from the nostrils, the smoker taps out the ashes into a little bamboo cylinder, which always accompanies the tobacco-bon, and having refilled five or six times, puts his pipe back into the case. We had hardly learned to smoke *à la Japonais*, when the manservant returned, accompanied by three girls, beautifully dressed, with smoothly banded hair shining like polished ebony, and naked feet peeping beneath their long robes. Kneeling when within a yard of us, they gently pushed towards each person a lacquered stand, or tray, carrying beautiful bowls of lacquered wood, beside which lay the chopsticks. On a separate tray stood bottles of saki of various brands, and a number of tiny China cups, in delicate silver stands, while a great bowl of water was placed near us on the floor. It was some minutes before we learned to manipulate the chopsticks, the girls meanwhile smiling frankly at our difficulties, as indeed they did at every mistake we made. The dinner occupied a very long time, and we smoked or strolled in the garden between some of the courses. These were served slowly, with many removals of the trays, and were not eaten in any given order. It is good manners to take a little of everything, but it is *de rigueur* to eat twice at least of rice. Here are the dishes. Fish soup, fish of many kinds, dressed in many ways, chestnuts, sweet potatoes, three kinds of seaweed, green ginger, prawns (as big as little lobsters), a gelatinous fish-cake, pounded chicken, mushrooms, lily seeds, plums and rice. Saki, served hot, was handed as required, the man filling, while one of the girls held the little cup, not in her fingers, which would never do, but by the silver saucer. This was then gently pushed, with deep obeisances, by the kneeling waitress along the floor, till within a foot of the guest, who was expected to take the cup leaving the stand. Although the service was extremely ceremonious, the relations between master and servant seemed quite friendly, and their intercourse politely familiar. As the dinner progressed, Okowa handed a cup of saki now to one attendant, now to another, who received it with beaming smiles and a profusion of prostrations, while they chatted with him at intervals, just as happy children do with grown-up people, laughing perpetually. The handing of the cup is a complimentary act, like our health-drinking, and a complicated etiquette governs this ceremony in company, but it is at all times indispensable that the person to whom a cup has been given should rince it in the bowl of water already mentioned before returning it to the convive who paid him the compliment of handing it. The smiling faces of the girls told us how far we fell short of ideal Japanese good behaviour at table, and certainly our long legs, sprawling uncomfortably in search of an easy position, and our awkward fingers, flirting morsels with the chopsticks, more by good luck than skill, into our mouths, gave them plenty of food for amusement.

In view of their gracious smiles, pretty manners, and ceremonious politeness, one would think that the Japanese are a very social people; but this is by no means the case. Their daily life is regular and monotonous, and there are no such things as dinners, evening parties, *conversaziones*, or balls. Family connections sometimes dine together, and young people are educated to play a graceful part in matters of the minutest detail on these occasions, but, beyond this, the Japanese never "entertain." A Japanese day begins about seven or eight o'clock in the morning, with a meal of rice and tea; a second similar meal, with fish added, is taken at midday; and a third about seven in the evening. The last is such as that which I have described, and is eaten, except among the masses, by ladies and gentlemen separately. While the day has been devoted to work, the evening passes in talk and story-telling, or the girls of the family take their "samisens," a kind of tinkling lute, and sing. The people are great believers in ghosts and witchcraft, and the long evenings and dimly lighted rooms lend themselves well to the wildest stories of superstition. At nine o'clock comes the bath, when the family assemble, irrespective of sex, and stew together in water hot enough to cook a European; this lasts an hour, and at ten o'clock every one is in bed.

Society, in our sense of the word, does not exist in Japan; men meet frequently, but always to discuss affairs or arrange business, and visits of ceremony are paid at certain times, but that is all. No Japanese asks his friends to his home for the sake of social enjoyment, but if he wants to entertain them, goes to some tea-house, provides saki, musicians, dancers, or what not, and makes a riotous night of it. The position of woman whether as wife or maiden, though far superior to that of Orientals generally, is not high. A girl is taught to read and write, to play the samisen, dance, and behave with extreme politeness, and is free to go, whether to the temple, the shop, or the visit, alone; enjoying, in fact, in this respect all the liberty of Europe. But she remains the slave of her parents, who can dispose of her services absolutely, and sell her, if they so please, even into a shameful life, without the interference of law on her behalf. Marriage is an affair *de convenance*, arranged by the father without reference to the girl herself, and indeed woman in Japan attains to no dignity until she has become mother and manager. Even then she plays a part very inferior to that of the man, being quite ignorant of her husband's affairs, and never, as with us, a centre around which the family groups itself, but a toy during youth, and an upper servant in middle age.

CHAPTER IV.

ENOSHIMA—KAMAKURA—DAIBUTZ.

October 15—17.

October 15.—We left Yokohama, accompanied by our Japanese friend, to visit the island of Enoshima, famous for its beauty, and with the intention of seeing Kamakura, the ancient capital of the Shoguns, and Daibutz, the colossal bronze image of Buddha, on our way back to the settlement. As our route lay for some twenty miles along the Tokaido, the great highway of Japan, we hired a carriage and pair, in preference to taking the long ride cramped in jinrickishas; and found ourselves provided with a buggy, evidently of American origin, but now dying of old age, and a pair of ragged China ponies, piloted, I cannot say driven, by a Japanese coachman. The trap looked good for another twenty miles, and the horses had apparently been fed within a few days, so we made the venture, encouraged by the triumphant confidence of the driver in himself and the outfit. The buggy belied its appearance of senility at starting, our Jehu carrying away a whole row of scaffold poles in the first street we turned, and this without damage to the trap. As the sticks fell—behind us, fortunately—we glanced at our man, who sat smiling, evidently proud of his work, a picture of self-satisfaction. After this we gave ourselves no more concern, feeling that we were in the hands of Providence, and having no legal responsibility for damages.

Following Okowa's counsel, we launched upon this, our first expedition, without any of the preparations usually made by Europeans when travelling in Japan. We had made up our minds to eat, drink, and sleep like the natives, and took neither cook, canned meats, wine, nor bedding with us. We had indeed found the dinner at Mr. Okowa's house very palatable, and our friend assured us that, with him as caterer, should fare no worse in the tea-houses; so we started, prepared to obey the Japanese proverb—one of the many identical with our own—and "enter a village ready to follow its customs."

The villages touch one another along the Tokaido, and, saving their poorer appearance, the houses are just like those of Yokohama. A Japanese house is only a shelter, whether its roof covers the emperor or a coolie. A few poles, a straw covering, a raised floor, and some paper slides satisfy the wants of all classes. The dwelling is a tent rather than a home, having none of the privacy, as it has none of the cherished joys, of the family hearth, such as we know it in Europe. Great fires visit these temporary towns at intervals, sweeping away miles of their flimsy buildings, but even such calamities are powerless against the instincts of a people, descendants of a nomadic race, and hereditary camp-builders.

Japan is a paradise for children, where they swarm in numbers which appear quite phenomenal to travellers fresh from childless America. Though petted by every one, and inordinately indulged by their mothers, who appear devoted to them, they are neither *exigeant* nor quarrelsome. A stranger has ample opportunity to form an opinion on this point, for they live out of doors, and from the tenderest age wander at their own sweet will about the streets, playing games, flying kites, or sucking sweeties; while every foot-passenger and horseman is as careful of their safety as if they were his own. The last comer is carried on the mother's back, but older members of the family have no sooner learnt to walk than they are taught to carry their younger brothers and sisters in the same manner. The wide sash which every child wears serves to secure the living burden to the young back, but the bearer's arms are free, and it is a comical sight to see youngsters of seven or eight, playing with all the energy and activity of youth, darting hither and thither, jumping and shouting, apparently quite unconscious of the baby tossing behind them. Children are suckled for a very long time in Japan, and it is a common thing to see urchins run from their games to the maternal bosom, and thence back, with fresh vigour, to their companions. It seems probable that this practice is the cause of sore head, which is almost universal among children in Japan, who depend too long on a food which becomes insufficiently nourishing.

At the first steep descent in the road our coachman produced some ropes of rice straw from beneath his seat, and proceeded to tie the hind wheels of the venerable buggy securely to the body of the trap. About half-way down the hill this patent drag gave way, and the ponies being at last pushed into a moderate trot by the weight of the carriage, it was not long before we heard a loud "crack," and for a moment feared that the last hour of both the waggon and expedition had arrived. It was only a part of the fore carriage, however, which had been carried away, and European skill managed to patch the wound with bamboo and straw-rope lashings; but the pole now pointed so uncertainly, first to this and then to that side of the road, that we wondered for a long time what would go next.

As we got further from Yokohama, the coolies, whom we met drawing loads and jinrickishas, wore nothing but a waistcloth. The jinrickisha coolies, when in the country, stow their clothes under the seat of the vehicle, and only resume them on nearing the town, where, since the Europeanization of the Government, the police have orders to prevent nudity. This is a pity, for *naturalia non sunt turpia*, and semi-nudity is perfectly natural to Japan, where, as in the tropics, the work of a coolie would be insupportable in clothes. Certainly nothing can be finer than the view of these bronzed and muscular bodies, the smooth, clean skin shining with healthy perspiration, and condition visible in every pose and movement.

The traffic of the Tokaido is carried on solely by manual labour. Sometimes one meets a cavalier, but never a horse between shafts. Merchandise and produce of all kinds are loaded on large hand-carts, drawn by four or six coolies, and travellers now universally ride in jinrickishas. The highway itself, on the other hand, although the chief commercial artery of Japan, is what Americans would call a "dirt road," and would be cut to pieces in a week by carts and horses. There is scarcely a bridge in good repair, and streams are crossed by all sorts of temporary and unsafe makeshifts—a state of things which has evidently lasted a long time, as the weather-beaten notices on the closed bridges testify. Again the question recurs—Are these people, whom we think so progressive, in earnest, or merely playing at civilization? Are they men seriously bent on works of improvement, or children giving a great entertainment in a doll's house? They have built a railroad from Tokio to Yokohama and another from Kioto to Hiogo, connecting the old and new capitals of the empire with their respective ports. But the united length of the two lines is not more than sixty miles, and it is nearly ten years since the first was opened with an immense flourish of trumpets,—but they build no more. Meanwhile the Tokaido remains in the same state as in the feudal times, with broken bridges and unrepaired roadway, a route which might serve for the retinue of a great daimio going to court, but totally unfit for the traffic which struggles along it in hand-carts. Aside from this highway of princes, there is hardly a road, probably so called, in Japan, the country remaining in the same condition as in remote centuries, covered with beaten tracks, seldom wide enough for wheeled carriages, often too narrow for a jinrickisha, and generally mere paths for pack-horses and foot-passengers. Evidently the wish to imitate Europe falls short of a desire to develop the country. The Japanese have indeed spent vast sums on naval and military preparations, and, interested by temperament, like the Athenians of old, in anything new, have endowed the teaching of our physical sciences and constructive arts; but it hardly needed to be fresh from America, where the road-maker is the pioneer of civilization, and the railroad breeds towns in deserts, for an English engineer and German man of business to find in the Tokaido itself a proof that the Japanese Government have no real desire either to open the country to foreign capital or encourage its development by native enterprise.

There remains then the problem—never absent from our minds—With what objects have the leaders of New Japan, the destruction of the old feudal system having been accomplished, entered headlong on the path of Europeanizing the institutions of their country? For us, at present, this is an inexplicable puzzle. Our assurance grows daily that, in regard to commercial progress, the Japanese have not got the root of the matter in them, and meanwhile we await such further lights as experience may afford us on this, the most important of all questions connected with the country.

We pulled up at a tea-house to water the horses, and were immediately greeted by a crowd of girls, with handsome dresses and carefully banded hair, who came forward with beaming smiles and a thousand welcomes. We did not alight, so they brought us hot weak tea, in tiny cups, laughing and chattering, like a lot of polite and sweet-tempered children, while the driver gave the horses a drink. Simple as life is in Japan, its accessories are complicated enough. There is a special apparatus for every little want, and even a horse is not allowed to drink out of a pail, but the water is thrown into his mouth by means of a wooden ladle, the animal having learnt to take his refreshment as cleverly as a Christian eats soup with a spoon.

Katase, where our drive came to an end, is a small village, standing on the shore of Odowara Bay, separated from the Bay of Jeddo by a considerable promontory. The Tokaido, leaving the shore at Yokohama, cuts across the base of this long triangle of land, and strikes the sea again a little beyond Katase. The route, on leaving the settlement, winds through flat valleys, and between toy hills, climbing a shoulder of the latter now and then but being for the most part level. The wayside scenery and cultivation is exactly like that around Yokohama; the flats everywhere covered with rice, the hill-sides with the various cereals, roots, and tubers already named, and the hill-tops with conifers and bamboo grass.

Enoshima is accessible from Katase by a tongue of sand at ebb tide, and is reached by boat on the flood. It is a mere islet, steep and densely wooded, the home of fishermen and the site of some famous shrines. We landed under a "torii," the gibbet-like framework of wood which marks the entrance to every Shinto temple, at the foot of a steep street of stairs, lined on either hand with gay tea-houses and shops, and deeply sunk in a mass of luxuriant foliage. Darkness was already falling when we settled in for the night at one of the largest tea-houses, where a crowd of bowing and smiling girls made ready our room in the twinkling of, an eye, dividing us from a party of native guests by a paper screen, lighting a wick, floating in a vessel of oil, and closing the wooden slides which form the outside wall of the house. Okowa ordered supper, and we heard with satisfaction that some of the delicate fish, for which, together with lobsters, Enoshima is famous where, in the larder, or, I should say, in the tub, waiting their death. Tea, sweatmeats, and the inevitable tobacco-bon, made their appearance at once, followed within half an hour by a meal of rice, fish, seaweed, prawns, and saki, the double of that which we had eaten at Oji. Stewed "haliotis," the "ormer," or ear-shell, of Guernsey, was added to the *menu* at my particular request, but proved so much like savoury shoe-leather, that, with the seaweed, it was neglected. The fish, prawns, and rice, were excellent, and we agreed that life might at least be sustained upon native regimen until our return to Yokohama. Supper over, the "nasans" returned with the "futons," or beds, and having laid these on the floor, set the tobacco-bon, furnished with fresh charcoal, in a dish; placed a tray, with teapot and cups, on the floor; lighted an oil wick within a square paper lantern on legs, the "andon," or nightlight of Japan; and with many smiles and prostrations wished us "Saionara," or good-bye. Meanwhile our friend had gone to stew for an hour in the native hot bath, and we saw him no more that night. A Japanese bed consists simply of two thin cotton mattresses, of which one forms the bed, and the other, furnished with wide sleeves for the arms, the coverlet. A pillow of wood, like a rolling-pin on legs, called the "makura," tucks under the poll, and completes the outfit. Replacing the last instruments of torture by our travelling bags, and enervated by the as yet unaccustomed air of the Pacific, we sought our hard couches, and slept, in spite of the floor and the fleas, the sleep of the weary.

October 16.—We were awakened early by the girls, who walked in, quite unconcernedly, to open the house and make preparations for breakfast. Modesty kept us under the bedclothes for some time, but presently it became clear that, if we meant to get up at all, we must "adopt the customs of the village," and dress in public. But how? There was nothing in the room except two big, half-ashamed men, and the busy nasans; not a washstand, towel, or looking-glass. Once on our legs, however, a great deal of pantomime on one side, and smiling chatter on the other, ended in our finding water, a shallow brass dish, and a bamboo dipper, in the narrow gallery which forms a feature of every Japanese house between the outer (wooden) and the inner (paper) slides. How the girls laughed as we cunningly arranged these panels in the interests of international modesty! but whether at the figures we had cut negotiating in our nightshirts, or at our needless blushes, we did not know, and could not inquire. Suffice it, that we got through our first toilet in a tea-house without any breach of the proprieties, and meanwhile the nasans cleared away the beds, set the floor for breakfast, brought the burning tobacco-bon, and finally left us, squatted on the matting with agonized calves but excellent appetites, waiting food and drink. Rice, fish, and seaweed soon became monotonous, and, as we now began to find, are not very "filling;" while chopsticks have a way of getting unmanageable in inverse proportion to a man's hunger. Already we were beginning to hanker, though neither would confess it, for the flesh-pots of Yokohama, and thinking of canned corned beef, as the Israelites in the wilderness thought of Egyptian mutton.

The island of Enoshima, which we started to explore on full, yet craving stomachs, had a wonderful origin. "In the sixth year of Rai tua," a Mikado who reigned a hundred and fifty-two years before Christ, "a great storm arose at night off the coast of Sagami; black clouds covered the sea, and the waves mounted to heaven. In the morning celestial music was heard, and there appeared in a rift in the clouds a lovely lady of divine form, accompanied by two boys of surpassing beauty. The storm ceased, the black clouds lifted, and the island of Enoshima, upon the top of which sat the heavenly lady, appeared. Then all the inhabitants of that coast worshipped her. She was Benten." Now, anciently, in Sagami, there were great marshes, where lived five dragons, whose lair no man durst approach; but, after Enoshima appeared, the dragons ceased from ravaging. Benten had subdued them. The people lived in peace, and though these events occurred so long ago, that, like the old lady, shocked at the tragedy of the Red Sea, we may think the story is not true, the goddess is still worshipped as the dragon-tamer, and her shrines are scattered all over Japan. Of these the original and chief is here, consisting of a damp, dark, and tortuous cave, the work of the Pacific waves, to reach which we crossed the island, passing many temples on our way, and resting for a few moments on the summit, to admire the long curve of Odowara Bay, with its hilly and embowered shores, half hidden in the ocean mists, and to glance thence inland where, over a billowy sea of green slopes, Fusiyama reared its white and graceful cone.

Benten's cave was full of candle-smoke, and the bonzes who show it were quite as happy with a few coppers as if we had penetrated to the innermost of its many shrines; so we strolled about the ebb-tide rocks, breathing the fresh, or rather lukewarm, air of the Pacific, and looking for shells and zoophytes. Some familiar forms of each were present, among them a periwinkle (*Littorina saxatilis*) and the daisy anemone (*Actinia bellis*), both common British species, whose occurrence here, at our antipodes, forcibly suggested to our minds those interesting questions which have yet to be resolved by the naturalist—From what centre of origination did these widely distributed species radiate? and by what route did they travel to habitats now separated by impassable barriers? Two naked bronze fellows, impatient of our researches, were waiting to dive for lobsters, or rather for *cash*; and an importunate boy was begging Okowa to tell us what wonderful things he could do in the water. The former, after two or three plunges, brought up some small crustaceans from the rocks below, remaining below, in one case, for twenty-nine seconds; while the boy turned summersaults in the warm transparent water, and revolved like a paddle-wheel with great energy but little skill.

After a second edition of rice, fish, and seaweed at the tea-house, we took boat for Kamakura, intending to reach the Daibutz while the light lasted, and sleep at the village of Noshima. Kamakura lies in a valley enclosed by hills, and was for nearly four hundred years the political metropolis of Japan. It was here that Yoritomo, the first Shogun, or Governor-General of the Mikado, established his capital in the last years of the twelfth century, his master, the emperor, continuing to reside in the ancient Mikadonal capital of Kioto. The Shoguns, as we shall see hereafter, early became the actual rulers of Japan; the Mikado's authority, though theoretically supreme, being completely overshadowed by their rule, and so remaining until our own times, when the revolution of 1868 destroyed the Shogunate, and restored the government of the country to its theoretical head. Yoritomo's twenty-fifth successor, Yeasu, finding his city outgrowing its narrow and hilly site, removed the capital to Jeddo, then only a village, in A.D. 1600, and Kamakura has since declined; while such is the temporary character of Japanese architecture, that scarcely anything now remains of a town which the Portuguese Jesuits of the sixteenth century describe as containing two hundred thousand houses. The spot, however, is classic ground to the Japanese, the scene of the most stirring incidents in their history, as it is of nearly all their romances, and, so far as fighting is concerned, the very cockpit of Japan. The chief place of interest now is the Shinto temple of Hachiman, the Japanese god of war, where the priests show a variety of warlike and ecclesiastical relics, among which are the swords of the early Shoguns, including that of Yoritomo himself. The last are extremely interesting examples of the high state of art in Japan seven hundred years ago, the oldest Shogunal sword being an exquisite production, rivalling, in the quality of its blade and the beauty of its decorations, the best work of any subsequent age.

About a mile from Kamakura stands the famous Daibutz, a colossal bronze figure of Buddha, situated in the middle of a lonely valley, and approached by a beautiful avenue of evergreens. This image, rather more than forty feet in height, was erected in the thirteenth century, and sits on a pedestal of granite, with legs crossed and hands folded in the well-known attitude of meditation, the suave and handsome face being evidently borrowed from the Hindoo type. The figure has been so popularized that any lengthened description is out of place, and I limit myself to noting one interesting point in its construction. Daibutz appears to be cast in a single piece, having no visible joints anywhere, whether within or without. Probably the metal was run, it may be in sections, between a central core and an outer shell, as bronze vases are now made in Japan; but in any case, the work remains a triumph of the founder's art, and is such as no native foundry could produce in the present day. Inside the figure is a little Buddhist chapel, the very double in all respects of a Catholic shrine, lighted by tapers, and adorned with flowers and offerings.

Shinto and Buddhism—already these twin religions of Japan have challenged our attention many times in the course of this short trip. The temples of both cults are thickly scattered over the whole length and breadth of the country, to the number of more than a hundred thousand " miya," or Shinto, and a hundred thousand " tera," or Buddhist shrines, with a priesthood numbering twenty thousand and seventy-five thousand respectively.

The teachings of Sakya-Muni, the Buddh of India, promulgated six hundred years before the Christian era, are well known. He declared that the unhappiness of human life arises from the "thirst" (trishna) of men for earthly things, from their wants, desires and passions; that such unhappiness could only be escaped by the eradication of the thirst, to accomplish which was the true object of life, and, this task completed, man, no longer the victim of "trishna," entered upon "Nirvana," and became absorbed into the infinite. The six hundred millions of men who profess the religion of Buddha to-day have wandered in many directions, and very far from the "eightfold path" of various virtues which Sakya preached as leading to. Nirvana. Every Buddhist country has twisted this pure, if somewhat sad, doctrine into various corrupt forms, grotesque enough sometimes, as in the North of India and Thibet. In Japan, the idea of paradise, to which true Buddhism does not lend itself, has been introduced, together with a hell for evil-doers, and a whole pantheon of gods; while a splendid and ceremonious ritual, singularly analogous to that of the Roman Church, is very attractive for the Japanese character. Hence, Buddhism is essentially the popular religion of Japan, where it was first introduced, by way of China and the Corea, about the middle of the sixth century of our era; and where, after a long, stormy, but never apparently bloody struggle with the older faith, it now runs peaceably alongside its former rival, no longer an enemy.

Shinto, on the other hand, is in effect Confucianism, introduced, like Buddhism, from China, and corrupted like it, but originally consisting in Japan, as in its birthplace, of purely moral teaching. The Chinese philosopher upheld the natural rectitude of the soul, and the sufficiency of conscience as a guide for human action, laying down certain precepts of "dsin," virtuous life; "gi," justice; "re," politeness; "tsi," good government; and "sin," a pure conscience,—to be meditated upon and applied to the daily conduct of life. The noble system of Confucius, disregarding as it does the spiritual cravings of mankind, could never attract the masses, and its offspring Shinto, though the State religion of Japan, has few followers, except among the nobles and gentlemen. But the original features of Shintoism, like those of Buddhism, are now entirely concealed under corruptions which have converted its high doctrines into the mere worship of tradition, ancestry, and constituted power. Its ceremonies are formal and meaningless, its ritual bald and colourless, and its hold on the hearts of men *nil*.

Strange as it seems to us, these two religions run side by side in Japan, so completely confounded, one with the other, that the people pay their devotions indifferently, whether at Shinto or Buddhist shrines; both of them now little better than temples of almost Indian idolatry. Nor is it difficult to find the reason of this confusion in the religious indifferentism of the Japanese character, for an example of which it is only necessary to watch the worshippers at their prayers. A young girl, or perhaps a young man, arrives before the shrine. He claps his hands, bows slightly, claps his hands again, throws a small piece of copper into a great wooden chest, and goes his way. His prayer is probably for some personal benefit, or it may be that he only recommends himself generally to the god as a deserving young man. Sometimes, having a sick relative, he deposits an *ex voto*, a picture, or a lock of hair; sometimes makes a vow; and often he buys a printed prayer of the priest, chews it into a pulp, and flings it at the idol of the god whom he implores. If the pellet sticks, that is a good omen, so he usually chews long and throws hard. Such is popular devotion in Japan. As to public worship or private prayer, both are alike unknown, and the notion of a man communing with his Maker, if one should try to put it before a Japanese, would be a hopeless puzzle to his mind. The higher classes, whether Shintoists or Buddhists, are sceptics, who smile at the superstition of the people, and deride their gods. The masses are formalists, whose religious exercises, such as they are, have their root solely in that vague fear of the supernatural powers which is part of man's nature. Religion, in fine, properly so called, does not exist in Japan; but the true popular cult consists in religious *fêtes*, or "matsuri," held on certain days of the year in honour of the gods; but of these purely secular festivals I shall speak more at length by-and-by.

The Shinto temple (miya) and Buddhist (tera), when pure, are quite distinct in appearance. The former is always approached by an avenue spanned at its entrance by the torii, or perch for the sacred birds, while the shrine itself is perfectly simple, containing only a polished metal mirror, and some notched strips of white paper (gohei) as symbols. Buddhist temples, on the other hand, are usually situated on hill-sides, among handsome groves of trees, and are crowded with images, candles, bells, drums, books, and ornaments, while outside both miya and tera hang *ex votos* and paper prayers on wooden racks. At the present day, however, there is little distinction between the respective shrines, Buddhist idols elbowing the Shinto mirror, while priests of both religions officiate in the same temple, the people worshipping without discrimination of creeds.

Darkness fell before we reached Noshima, where we spent the night, repeating all our tea-house experiences of yesterday, but finding the beds harder, the fleas hungrier, supper less appetizing, and sleep more coy, than at Enoshima. I did not know how much a man could long for a chair and a table, until I had sprawled without either on a matted floor for two days and nights. But we shall reach Yokohama and civilization before our friends have taken tiffin to-morrow.

CHAPTER V.

TOKIO (JEDDO).

October 21-24.

RAPID as was our passage through the capital of Japan on our way to Oji, we saw enough of this lately mysterious city to convince us that, so far as Jeddo is concerned, the unknown is not always the magnificent. The European houses of Yokohama form an island of solid but unpretentious masonry, lying in a sea of low brown roofs, from which spring no temples, towers, or pagodas; but then Yokohama is only a settlement town, and one does not expect to find palaces, where godowns and counting-houses began to rise only twenty years ago. But Jeddo—the capital for nearly three hundred years of a populous, wealthy, and art-loving country; the home of a rich and proud nobility; the centre of the pompous popular religion; the head-quarters of the military system, and now, since the abolition of feudalism, the residence of the Mikado himself,—that will be a very different affair. At least there will be great gates, handsome streets, imposing palaces, splendid temples, and who knows what besides of strange magnificence, in so vast and ancient a city! So people thought ten or twelve years ago, when the veil which had always hidden this mysterious capital from the eyes of Europe was withdrawn, and so, even now, the traveller's imagination paints it.

A low, undulating plain, bathed towards the south-east by the Bay of Jeddo, is crossed at right angles by a great river, the Sumidagawa; and Tokio, a parallelogram nine miles long by eight miles wide, lies in the corner formed by stream and sea. From the centre of the plain rises a circular eminence, crowned with a building of cyclopean masonry, the "Siro," or ancient castle of the Shoguns. This is surrounded by a vast open space, called "Soto Siro," containing the palaces (yashickis) of the old feudal lords, one of which is now occupied by the Mikado, and others by court personages and ministers of State. Here, in the Shogunal days, the great feudatories, or daimios, were compelled to live for half of every year, and their wives and children always; the latter in reality hostages for the turbulent clan-leaders, whose loyalty could not be trusted during the visits to their territories and armed retainers. At a distance of a few miles from this *mamelon*, the plain is encircled by a belt of low hills, two of which, one in the north and the other in the south, are capped by the Castle of Uyeno and the famous Temple of Shiba respectively, both of them burial-places of the Shoguns. Between these hills and encircling the Siro, spreads the city, a sea of brown roofs, out of which rise here and there the heavy and sombre eaves and ridges of temples, tall pagodas, some large European buildings—the work of the reformed Government, and here and there the brick chimney of a new manufactory. The plain is cut by many streams, canals, and castle moats, and variegated with pretty parks and gardens. In the south-east is Jeddo Bay, shining in the sunlight, while in the south-west rises Fusiyama's white cone.

It is a striking picture, but the only one of Tokio that charms. Siro, Shiba, and Uyeno apart, the capital of Japan is little better than the native town of Yokohama. The streets are irregular and ugly, bordered by low wooden buildings, blackened by time, and spreading like an interminable and labyrinthine village over a wide monotonous plain. A great boulevard has indeed been cut right through the town, but the shops on either side of this avenue are like those in poorer streets, with the addition of a cloistered walk, having flat groins of plastered brick, supported by mean columns —the style debased European, and the work bad and flimsy. There is less character about the shops than in Yokohama, and we wander for miles past displays of silks and saki, rice and porcelain, arms and woodware, curiosities and lanterns, tea-houses and toy-shops, all confusedly mingled, and making no better show than the wares of a village on the Tokaido. The temples hide themselves among the low houses, and must be carefully sought in the labyrinth of streets, where one happens too often, on canals, filled with sluggish black water and smelling like an open drain. Everything comes into and goes out of Tokio by water, the largest junks floating easily in the wide canals, and passing with lowered masts under the frequent and high-arched bridges.

But, if the city itself disappoints the traveller, the life in the streets rivets his attention and piques his curiosity far more than that of the settlement. Its elements are the same, but the dresses are brighter, the movement brisker, the people gayer, and the *tout ensemble* more national than at Yokohama. How crowded the great boulevard is! Yet the countless jinrickishas circulate at a trot through the press. And how polite every one is! The very coolies in the shafts warn you to move, with cries that are compliments; no one jostles his neighbour, but each makes way for the other with smiles and gentle inclinations of the body, and a harsh word is never heard. Here is a beggar, posted on a crowded bridge, making a hideous noise with a battledore of raw hide; and there is a strolling story-teller, shaking a jingling toy, followed by a crowd, as he makes his way to some open space of ground, large enough to seat an audience. Yonder, on the sidewalk, sits a fortune-teller casting the horoscopes of two pretty girls by means of magic sticks; and here again is a naked wrestler, struggling with and overcoming an imaginary opponent. What true and powerful poses! It is difficult to believe that he is not actually engaged with an invisible person. Every day there is the festival, or "matsuri," of some god in Tokio, and in one quarter or another, gaily dressed processions parade the streets, preceded by high bamboo frames, which flutter with flags, and are clothed in rice and flowers. Sometimes, on summer nights, there is a water *fête*, when fireworks go up from the great bridge, and the river and canals are crowded with boats filled with well-dressed, laughing girls, or sober citizens and their wives. From the dainty masts hang great paper lanterns, swaying in the evening breeze, or moving hither and thither in the distance like meteors, while the tea-houses on the banks are gay with bright hangings, floating flags, and brilliant company. Such are the streets of Tokio, the same, probably, to-day as when Yeasu first settled here in 1600; and the home then, as now, of a people, gay, polished, careless, and lovable.

No one has really seen Tokio without having visited the Yoshiwara. This word means "good plain"—a strange title for the prostitutes' quarter, and a still stranger place. Picture a long street, bordered on each side by large houses, not open to the road as we have hitherto seen them, but enclosed by railings of upright wooden bars, giving them the air of great cages. In front of each house hangs a huge paper lantern, and a frame containing a number of photographs, usually of handsome faces with carefully dressed hair. Behind the wooden grills are the originals of these pictures, squatting around spacious and elegant rooms, dressed in magnificent robes of scarlet and gold, sipping tea, smoking the tiny Japanese pipe, and chatting. Of immodest display, gestures, or solicitation there is none; on the contrary, so formal are the groups, so set the attitudes, and so gorgeous the superabundant costumes, that an Englishman is infallibly reminded of Madame Tussaud's exhibition of wax figures. It seems to be generally supposed that prostitution is less repugnant to public opinion in Japan than in the West, and that the social position of a prostitute is less disgraceful. So far, however, as I can gather from Europeans who have lived for a long time in the country, this is hardly a correct statement of the case. Men are loose livers in Japan; but there is no country where the lives of unmarried girls are more strictly regulated than this. The freedom which, as we have seen, a Japanese girl enjoys does not extend to her thoughts and wishes. In respect of these, as of her person and services, she is absolutely under parental control, and her life before marriage is even more strictly fenced about than that of a girl in France. Hence, in Japan, writers of popular plays and romances are obliged to look outside of the loves, hopes, fears, and emotions of youth, which form the basis of nearly all our dramas and novels, for interesting or even intelligible themes. Their heroines must be sought among the demi-monde, and intrigue becomes the motive both of comedy and romance. The woman of loose character is consequently brought into undue prominence both upon the Japanese stage and in Japanese literature; but one might easily reach erroneous conclusions by arguing from this circumstance to the status of the prostitute. While, however, prostitution is far from being the respected institution in Japan which some would have us suppose, public opinion undoubtedly judges the Yoshiwara leniently, and for the reason that so many of its members have been sold into the life, against their will, by greedy and unscrupulous parents. The helplessness of such victims is so well understood that no obstacles are put in the way of women who, having enfranchised themselves by payment of their taskmasters, wish to return to a well-regulated life.

In every Japanese town one sees private houses which are distinguished at night by a very large, balloon-shaped paper lantern. Within the passer-by hears sweet voices and laughter, or catches a glimpse of a group of girls putting, it may be, the last touches to a toilette, brilliant, but rather exaggerated; adding a flower to the already over decorated hair, or a streak of brighter carmine to the lips. One of these butterflies calls two or three jinrickishas, and the pretty, painted creatures, perching in pairs behind the bronzed coolies, are soon lost to sight in the dusky street. These women are "gueshas," musicians, singers, and dancers, on their way to some tea-house to give an entertainment, either private or public, and where, presuming the latter to be the case, we will follow them. The brilliant little group have already disposed themselves on the matted floor of a large and well-lighted room. Two of them are provided with samisens, a kind of tiny guitar, thrummed with a triangle of ivory; the third has a "kokiu," another kind of samisen, played with a bow; and the fourth, a mere child, a pair of small drums. They are eating, as we enter, a meal exactly like the elaborate dinner we partook of at Oji, and we notice that they are served no less ceremoniously than ourselves on that occasion. The cup of saki goes round; they smile, bow and chatter; and finally, the bowls and chopsticks being removed, they take their instruments gracefully from the ground. Great Heaven! is it from those pretty butterflies there rises this discordant and monotonous song—whose intervals and harmonies are new to European ears, and where of melody there is none? The "tink-a-tank" of the samisen, the long and but slightly inflected wail of the voice, give us a nervous shiver;—and they tell us this will last for hours! Ah! the drums break in now, with the effect of an exploding shell, and the place is filled with a discordant uproar. If they are going on for ever, shall we be of the men who go? We think so—and yet there is something fascinating about that drummer-girl of twelve. What accurate movements! What daring and bizarre poses of the body! What wonderful legerdemain with the flying sticks! It is not a living girl, it is a mechanical figure come from another world, where the body expresses itself in terms unknown to us, at once grotesque and precise. But the tiny automaton has dropped her drumsticks, the samisens are jangling an agonizing accompaniment, and now it is some pantomime we are watching. The figure is telling us a story with its lithe little body, and it is a love story without a doubt. Mimicry, grace, and suggested emotion seem to have said their last word. Gestures, poses, movements, all are slow yet full of "go;" free, yet restrained, graceful, yet bizarre; now timid as childhood, now extravagant as folly; but always controlled by a perfect and natural good taste. The drama is over, and it has ended sadly, for the painted little *poseuse* is lying on the ground, in despairing yet comical tears, but not before she has made us feel the fascination of her art. The dancers of Japan know nothing of the lively movements or bold postures of our stage. Their long robes permit no leaps and bounds, but they make up for violence by expression, and for rapidity by grace. Dancing is an art for which girls are trained from their childhood, and, like all the other arts of Japan, it is distinguished by such refined taste and perfect execution that one fails to notice its want of spontaneity.

Through the kind offices of the German Minister at Tokio we obtained admission to the Insetz Kioku, a great national establishment, whose spacious walls enclose a number of Government manufactories. The official introduction procured us much polite attention, which took rather an odd turn at starting. Prevised of our arrival, the manager met us, and ushered us, after many pretty speeches, first into the laboratory. Here we were asked to be seated, when a shrewd-looking little Jap made his appearance, and ran through a short programme of dazzling chemical experiments, ending in a time-honoured "flash, bang, and stink." Bowing our way out from the demonstrator's polite presence, we next visited the Treasury buildings, where we found a large factory,

T

busily employed in the production of "kinsatz," the paper money of Japan. There is so much to be said hereafter on the financial situation in Japan, that I limit myself, for the moment, to an expression of surprise at the activity of which we were witnesses at this great kite manufactory. Kinsatz were quoted at a discount of sixty per cent. on our arrival at Yokohama, and were rapidly falling in value. The Government, alarmed, was loudly proclaiming its intention to limit the paper issue, inviting the Europeans to inspect its silver reserve of fifty million "yen," and the public to see a bonfire of redeemed Treasury notes. Yet all the time the Insetz Kioku was hard at work turning out fresh paper, while the Government credit was dropping day by day. We next ran, in quick succession, through a soap works, a wall-paper factory, a type foundry, a chemical works, an engineer's shop, a printing-office, and various other minor industries. These were all small affairs, models rather than mills, where the production was on much too trifling a scale to be profitable, and where, be the wages what they might, it was clear at a glance that nothing was made as cheaply as it could be bought of European importers in Yokohama. At the same time, the Insetz Kioku, taken collectively, is an immense concern, raised and equipped at great expense, and directed by a numerous staff of officials. The last are samurai, or the sons of samurai, members of the old military caste, impoverished by the disestablishment of the feudal chiefs, their former employers and paymasters, and who, too proud to trade, are hungry for the humblest Government employment.

Such is the character of the new industrial life of Japan, and such are the parodies of serious business which prove, as we are told, the desire of the people for commercial progress and their aptitude for the reception of Western ideas. At present the Government is cultivator, manufacturer, shipowner, spinner, miner, and merchant, but most of these enterprises pay a yearly loss, and their chief use is to find employment for the samurai class. Commerce, like the living organism, can exist only in a suitable environment, which it is the function of governments to create, instead of themselves becoming manufacturers and traders. The Japanese ministers know this; but do they build new roads or repair old ones? Do they reform the civil law, or give foreign merchants equal rights with the natives? Do they initiate a commercial and industrial legislation? Do they offer foreign capital the necessary guarantees of proprietorship, and power to prosecute affairs in its own way, and in freedom? No—these are the very things which the Government of Japan will not do at any price.

We lunched most agreeably at the German Legation and witnessed, during the meal, a scene very characteristic of Japanese life. The minister, like all the European residents, is an art collector, and lunch is the hour at which he receives the dealers. Three or four of these men were already kneeling in the room when we entered, and bowed their heads to the ground, with loud sighs, as we took our seats, while, at intervals in the conversation, one or another of them pushed forward a bronze, a piece of lacquer-work, or an ivory carving for inspection. These were handled and criticized when we had nothing better to say or do, while the merchants sat patiently by, silent and seemingly a quaint addition to our entertainment rather than tradesmen pushing their wares.

Shiba Uyeno contain the tombs of the Shoguns, who were buried at these two places alternately from the beginning of the seventeenth century down to the abolition of the Shogunate in recent times. Each mausoleum consists of an outer court, a temple, and, behind the temple, the tomb,—all characterised by that magnificence and display which the Shoguns affected both in life and after death. The temples of Shibar are among the most beautiful in Japan, and Uyeno is the twin of Shiba; but I defer a description of the Shogunal tombs until we reach Nikko, a village about a hundred miles north of the capital, where it is universally conceded that the splendour of these monuments and of their surroundings culminates.

Asakusa is the most popular temple in Tokio, and the most famous in Japan. It is approached by an avenue, bordered on each side by booths filled with all sorts of gay ornaments, dolls, toys, votive pictures, and holy images. Behind the booths are the shrines, and behind these again are theatres, shows, and shooting galleries. A matsuri, or religious festival, was in progress at the time of our visit, and the avenue was densely crowded with gaily dressed people and children carrying field rakes of bamboo, decorated with rice, flowers, and masks of Inari Sama, the Japanese Ceres. We pressed forward, with slowly moving throng, until we reached a large open square, the courtyard of the temple, where multitudes of tame pigeons, to whom every one threw peas, ran about, so confident and importunate that they had actually to be pushed aside with the foot. Arrived at the shrine, each worshipper clapped his hands, made a bow, muttered a momentary prayer, threw a copper coin into the grated boxes, and then turned to enjoyment. The scene was something like an English fair, the pleasure-booths being crowded with eager sightseers, who were clearly determined to make the most of their holiday. Among the shows, a peculiarly horrible sort of waxworks draws crowds of spectators. Miraculous scenes are represented, apparitions of gods, fights, and legendary stories. The figures are made of bamboo and *papier-mâché*, and, if the events represented are bloodthirsty and revolting, still, one cannot but admire the skill with which the artist has reproduced the expression of violent emotions; and the powerful, if exaggerated, attitudes of his personages. Shooting galleries, where tiny bows and arrows take the place of guns, are much frequented; the tea-houses are crowded, so are the numerous theatres and saki-shops; a whole quarter, in fact, is swarming with pleasure-seekers rather than religious devotees. For the children, who are very numerous, there is no diversion more attractive than the "ameya's" stall. This clever stroller's stock-in-trade consists of a little bench, furnished with a lamp, some plastic sugar, red and blue pigments, a few twigs of split bamboo, and a pair of scissors. Taking a lump of the sugar in his hands, he makes a funny speech to the parti-coloured little crowd, and ends by asking what it is their pleasure he shall produce. " A dragon," shouts some bold little beauty, while a murmur of approbation arises, and every eye is fixed on the artist. Little by little, the terrible creature grows out of the paste, a collection of unrelated details at first, which a few sudden touches complete as if by magic. Now some one calls for a gourd, another for a tortoise, a third for a man on horseback, and a fourth for a monkey swinging by its tail. It is a contest between the children and the old man, but they cannot nonplus him, try how they will. No matter what they call for, the ameya is equal to the occasion, and, within three minutes, his dextrous fingers conquer every difficulty which his audience may propound.

Such are the diversions of a matsuri, beginning early in the morning with a noisy street procession, for which the quarter pays, while the houses along the route are gay with flags and banners, and men, women, and children, all in gala dresses, crowd the shops and house-galleries, to see the pageant pass. It is a religious *fête* only in name—a survival, in fact, of ceremonies once full of meaning, but preserved to the present day only by the strong national love of traditional customs.

Notwithstanding its vast extent, and a population numbering three quarters of a million, the capital of Japan can scarcely be called a city from the European point of view. There are no squares, or public buildings, not even a town hall or an exchange ; no columns, statues, quays, great bridges, or aqueducts, but only a gigantic village, dominated by the walls of a fort, rather than a castle, and scarcely relieved by temples and pagodas. The famous nations of the world have always been great builders, and the wish to leave behind them proofs of their pride and power was felt as strongly by such states as by their individual citizens. The stones of Rome, Athens, and Venice are eloquent of national grandeur, and we credit the unknown peoples of Egypt and Assyria with a high place among cultured races on the strength of their architectural exploits alone. The Japanese, on the other hand, have built no great cities. It is true that Japan, the contemporary of

Greece and Rome, has not only seen the decay of these states, but remained to the present day without a dynastic break, and with an inviolate country; yet no European can turn from the Partheno., the Coliseum, or the Duomo of Saint Marc to the sea of undistinguished roofs which circles the old Shogunal stronghold of Jeddo, without feeling assured that, in regard to the elements of national greatness, there is no question of superiority between the Mongolian and Hellenic or Latin races.

CHAPTER VI.

MYANOSHITA—HAKONE.

October 24–28.

October 24.—On starting for our second trip, we agreed to give up the idea of living à *l'indigène*, and took a native with us as cook and guide. This little man was named Kobé, and he proved a treasure. We paid him a dollar a day, and, leaving every arrangement in his hands, found ourselves perfectly served, while he was also an intelligent guide and a capital walker. Our first objective was Myanoshita, a village in the Hakone mountains, picturesque in itself and surroundings, and only three hours from the Otomitonga Pass, the lowest point in a chain of hills which hides the greater portion of Fusiyama from the west, but from whose summit the sacred mountain is seen from base to cone.

Very little is yet known of the geology of Japan, but the backbone of the various islands is said, by Baron von Richthofen, to consist of metamorphic rocks of Devonian, or Silurian, age. These are everywhere interpenetrated by old volcanics, chiefly of a porphyritic character, which cover the bulk of the country, and sweep through the whole group of islands, from Yesso in the north to Kiusiu in the south, as a continuous mountain chain, whose watershed may be said to coincide with the centre of

Japan. These rocks, again, are overlaid by new volcanics, basalts, and trachytes, forming the summits of the range, and embracing a large number of volcanoes, either extinct or nearly so. From this great ridge, running centrally throughout the whole length of Japan, radiate countless lateral spurs, upon whose flanks, as they approach the coast, lie beds of alluvium, two or three hundred feet in thickness, the deposits of ancient rivers, which have been elevated, and then eroded, forming the little hills already so often alluded to as characterizing the shores of Japan, and whose feet stand upon a narrow plain, which everywhere skirts the ocean and marks a recent sea-level.

Fusiyama itself, though the highest mountain in Japan, is not situated on the watershed of the country, but rises near the southern coast, about seventy miles west of Yokohama, giving off two lofty spurs, one of which curves away towards the north-east, while the other runs south, projecting far beyond the general coast-line in the form of a narrow and rocky peninsula, called Idzu. This mountainous bar is thrown right across the Tokaido, just after it leaves Odowara Bay, and is threaded by the Hakone Pass, where the royal road, of which Japan is so proud, becomes a mere mountain track, paved with great stones, as a protection against the heavy rains, but impassable for a jinrickisha, and difficult for horses. A little north of Hakone lies Myanoshita, perched high on the western flank of the spur in question, from whose summit we hoped for a near view of the sacred mountain.

We left Yokohama with the same outfit as that which carried us safely to Katase on the occasion of our visit to Enoshima, and drove thirty-five miles along the Tokaido to Odowara, repeating the roadside experiences of the previous expedition, but finding the road and bridges in worse and worse condition as we advanced. We crossed two large rivers by ferry-boats, the bridges having been carried away more than a year ago, and still remaining unrepaired. The Japanese islands are so narrow and ridge-like in structure that the rivers have only short courses, and descend very rapidly towards the coast, being for the most part torrents in winter and dry in summer. Owing to this circumstance, and the easy disintegration of the volcanic rocks, the beds of streams silt up rapidly, and very few of them are navigable except for shallow craft. Serious inundations follow every heavy fall of rain, and the frail native bridges are constantly being carried away; an event for which the builders prepare by stapling each plank of the roadway to a strong cable, whose end is secured ashore, thereby preventing the timbers being lost when the catastrophe occurs. When one starts on a trip in Japan it is always a question of returning. If the weather keeps fine, all will be well; but heavy showers in the mountains may shut the tourist off from his desired haven, by an impassable torrent, for a week or more.

The Tokaido skirts the sea along the head of Odawara Bay, where, although the day was quite calm, magnificent waves were rolling in from the Pacific. Looking seaward, the green and beautifully indented coast hemmed in the greater part of the misty horizon, while, inland, our eyes met the bold and broken outline of the Hakone range, behind which rose Fusiyama, whose graceful cone became more beautiful with every mile of our approach. We left the buggy at Odowara, giving orders to the driver to meet us on our return, and jinricked to Tonosawa, where the road becomes a mere trail, and baggage has to be packed on the shoulders of coolies, of whom there were plenty waiting for employment. Japanese porters do not snatch at the traveller's traps, as in more civilized countries, but draw lots for a job with a rope of many strands, the lucky fibre being distinguished by a metal ring. A frail bamboo bridge carried us across the stream, a wide mountain torrent, brawling between beautifully wooded hills, whose left bank we had followed from Odowara; and on the other side of which lay the village of Tonosawa, famous for its thermal springs and boasting a tea-house more than ordinarily attractive by reason of its many pretty nasans. From this village to Myanoshita it is five miles, by a wooded hill-side path, which became lighted with glowworms as the daylight failed us.

We found a capital tea-house at Myanoshita, furnished with chairs and tables, washstands and looking-glasses; and, within half an hour of our arrival, Kobé served up a good European meal, the trout and fowls which he had bought on the way being supplemented by many of the cunning luxuries which civilization has learned to preserve in bottles and tins. Being valet and butler as well as cook, Kobé gave the nasans less to do for us than usual, but this seemed to suit them even better than work, and the pair told off to our room loafed around and laughed with the greatest enjoyment, while pouring tea or tending the tobacco-bon. One of them, called O-Kea-Sun, spoke a few words of English—Myanoshita, as the furniture witnessed, being much frequented by European travellers—and was insatiable to learn more. Dinner was accordingly enlivened by some naïve studies of English phrases, the girls competing with one another in pronunciation; and it was the most comical thing in the world to hear O-Kea-Sun's triumphant laugh when we, at last, entirely approved of her " How do you do?" and "Not at all!" She was particularly proud of the latter phrase, the equivalent of a polite Japanese commonplace, and we heard her muttering "Nodd-ad-all, nodd-ad-all!" while opening the paper slides next morning, and shouting with laughter at her own cleverness. When we left the house for our daily tramp, little O-Kea-Sun was the last to wish us *bon voyage*, with her everlasting "Nodd-ad-all!" and when we came back at night, she was the first to welcome us with the musical "Ohaio, ohaio! oka danna sai, oka danna sai! Nodd-ad-all, nodd-ad-all!" Then how they all laughed!—the inn-keeper, with his head in the dust; the black-toothed old dame, his wife; and all the crowd of painted butterflies behind them! There never were such people as the Japanese for laughing.

October 25.—The morning toilet furnished no occasion for blushes at Myanoshita, where we were lodged in European style; and Kobé's breakfast being as good as last night's dinner, we started at eight o'clock, morally and physically "fit" for the Otomi-tonga Pass. The trail leads for a short distance over level country, and then rises along steep hill-sides, clothed to their summits with trees or tall bamboo grass, while the view was at first bounded on all sides by volcanic hills, some three or four thousand feet in elevation. At three hours out, we reached the top of the pass, whence the ground slopes rapidly away to an extensive plain, out of which Fusiyama rises, its mass displayed from base to summit. Although the mountain-top was quite clear when we started, we caught but a momentary glimpse of it from Otomi-tonga, the clouds covering it deeply soon after our arrival. The very absence of the hidden peak, however, directed our attention more particularly to the lower slopes of the volcano, which would hardly have been noticed if the snowy cone had been visible. These rise from the plain with an inclination so extremely slight that it was almost impossible to believe such gentle grades could end in a lofty cone. They might be the first heave of a low mountainous ridge, but not the foundations of a towering peak. Fusiyama is a beautiful example of the modification which the outlines of volcanoes undergo from the undermining of their bases by the ejection of matter from below. But for this, volcanic cones would slope steeply like a railway embankment, from top to bottom; and, if they do not, it is because the centre sinks while the heap is accumulating. It is with the utmost regret that we have given up the project, cherished from the day we left the Golden Gate, of ascending Fusiyama, but the mountain became covered with snow on the day after our arrival in Japan, and snow, in this latitude, is quite fatal to climbing. The trip is not a difficult one in July and August, and it is a great disappointment, especially to that half of the expedition which has scaled the Matterhorn, not to have had the summit of the sacred mountain under our feet, and to have looked down into its exhausted crater.

On our way back to Myanoshita, we encountered several small snakes and a number of little land-crabs, the latter living in the damp wayside vegetation; but, favourable as the country seems to land-shells, I only saw two helices during the whole day. We passed many villages on the trail, surrounded by irrigated patches of rice, and picturesquely embosomed in densely wooded hills, whose foliage was brightening with the tints of autumn. Thermal springs abound among these volcanic mountains. Myanoshita itself is a kind of Japanese Buxton; while the neighbourhood is thickly scattered with village watering-places, quite as much in vogue with the Japanese as among ourselves, for the cure of disease.

October 26.—A wet morning put a stop to our projected trip to Hakone Lake and the sulphur springs north of it, so we strolled about the village, which straggles up the hill-side by a crooked street of rock-cut stairs. Wood-turning and ornamental box-making form together quite an extensive industry in Myanoshita, and the work finds its way in large quantities to the shops of Yokohama. The turning-lathe in use is an extremely primitive machine, consisting of a small iron spindle, twirled by two pieces of string wrapped round it for a few turns in opposite directions. The spindle revolves alternately backwards and forwards, the cutting tool being applied only while it is turning towards the workman; but it is surprising to see what accurate work is produced in this way.

Returning after a short walk through a lovely valley, cultivated with tea and ginger, we came suddenly upon one of the great bathing establishments, of which there are so many among these hills, frequented by the Japanese in summer for the sake of their hot mineral waters. The house looked deserted; but in one of the galleries was a pretty girl, towelling after the bath, who fled, like a flash, behind the paper slides when she saw us. We could only suppose that she disappeared in search of her clothes, which were certainly not outside; but, had we been her own countrymen, it is probable that it would never have occurred to her to move.

The tea-house where we are lodged possesses a characteristic Japanese garden. It is very tiny, but its centre is occupied by a lake, through which flows a winding river. The latter is crossed by several bridges; and on the banks of the former are a Shinto and Buddhist temple. In the north rises a range of mountains, with hill-paths and wayside shrines, while gnarled pines and cedars, hundreds of years old in appearance, but only a foot or two in height, are scattered over the hills and plain. It is a country to explore; but its area is only a few square yards. The lake is full of great fat gold-fish, which come to the surface for food, at a peculiar cry from the girls; and the river-bank is lined by a dozen pots of blooming chrysanthemums, seeming tall forest trees by comparison with their toy-like surroundings. The chrysanthemum is very commonly grown in Japan, but the rage is rather for dwarfed trees and trained shrubs than for flowers; though the native gardeners, when they wish, are no less skilful in producing specimen blooms than monstrosities.

October 27.—We started early for Hakone Lake, rejoicing in a brilliant day, and with good hope of a fine view of Fusiyama from Hakone village. The trail was steep for the first hour and a half, which brought us to Ashinoyu, another Japanese Buxton, whence there is a magnificent prospect. Beneath us, at some miles distance, lay Odowara Bay, stretching towards the northeast, its deeply indented and densely wooded shores being half hidden by misty air. Seaward, the Pacific was shrouded as usual in light vapours; while inland, an irregular chain of volcanic hills crossed the picture diagonally, falling almost to the plain as it neared the shore, but rising again in a castellated prominence before finally sinking under the waves.

On the way to Ashinoyu we passed a rock-cut Buddha, which is said to be twelve hundred years old, or coeval with the introduction of the religion of Sakya-Muni into Japan. The figure was heaped with small stones, lying wherever they would rest. Each stone represents a prayer, which the worshipper thinks likelier to be heard if the pebble he throws remains on the image. All the sacred statues around the temples in Japan are in this way heaped with stones, which no one ever attempts to disturb.

From Ashinoyu the trail was easy to Hakone, which was reached in three hours after starting. Here we got a perfect view of Fusiyama, the lake forming a foreground, while wooded hills opened widely enough on the right and left to show five or six thousand feet of the cone, glittering white in the sunlight, and outlined with indescribable clearness against an azure sky. Taking a sampan at Hakone village, we sailed to the northern end of the lake, whose scenery vividly recalls that of the Scottish Highlands; and, having landed, an hour and a half of stiff climbing brought us to the sulphur springs. Thence we got our best view of Fusiyama, displayed from summit to base—a picture such as that which Japanese artists are never tired of repeating.

The sulphur springs were curious, but not impressive. Jets of steam issued from the ground in all directions, and small basins of boiling mud were sputtering vigorously; the air was full of sulphurous vapour, and the ground covered with beautiful yellow crystals. Some ruinous and deserted bamboo sheds told us that the place had been worked for sulphur at some time. It was already late, and the mountain paths are so dark at night where they cross tracts of forest, that we cut short our adieux to the sacred mountain, and hurried homewards down the steep and stony track. Reaching Myanoshita soon after sundown, we wallowed for half an hour in the warm water which flows from a natural source by a bamboo pipe through the baths of the teahouse; while Kobé was busy in the kitchen.

A long tramp, a warm bath, a good dinner, and good digestion, make men enjoy a good cigar, and thus solaced, we sat, wrapped in the Japanese robes which we had already learned to use when *en deshabille*, and discussing with much interest the events of the day. Suddenly O-Kea-Sun appeared, leading by the hand a hideous old blind woman, with black teeth, shaven eyebrows, and wrinkled skin, who approached my companion, saying something in Japanese, and laying a hand with an entreating gesture on his shoulder. All the Joseph in my friend's nature was roused in a moment, and a good German oath rolled round the room like a prolonged peal of thunder. O-Kea-Sun screamed with laughter, while the unabashed old scarecrow remained unmoved and imploring. "What does she mean, O-Kea-Sun?" shouted the cosmopolite. "What does she mean? I'm afraid your friend is not a good old lady." " Nodd-ad all, nodd-ad-all!" laughed the little nasan, without an idea of what he was saying. But by-and-by she found English and pantomime enough to make us understand that this was one of the blind "amas," the professional shampooers, or rubbers, of Japan, who earn a modest living in every city by the practice of this truly national and, as they declare, most remedial art.

October 28.—We quitted Myanoshita and our attentive entertainers with considerable regret. The scenery was charming, the mountain air invigorating, the tea-house chairs and beds comfortable, and the study of native life amusing; but we left all these delights for the sake of the Yokohama races, and reaching Tonosawa on foot, jinricked to Odowara, where we found the evergreen buggy duly awaiting us, and, threading all day the interminable villages of the Tokaido, reached Yokohama in time to join a charming party at our host's dinner-table. To-morrow we shall see with what energy these ardent young spirits prosecute the sports of home, which they carry round the world, and acclimatize under every meridian.

CHAPTER VII.

SETTLEMENT LIFE AND VIEWS.

October 29–31.

NOTHING strikes the traveller more forcibly in passing through America than the variety of industries, men, and manners which he encounters. Every state is in course of active development, according to its natural capacities, and new objects of interest present themselves at each stage of the journey. Japan, on the other hand, is absolutely without variety. Its natural features, people, cities, and occupations are alike from one end of the country to the other; and, when a fortnight has rubbed off the novelty of his surroundings, the tourist begins to find native men and manners a little monotonous, and the life of his compatriots in the settlement a pleasant change.

The races were in full swing on our return to Yokohama, and "everybody" was to be seen on the course. What a motley crowd it was sauntering up the sunlit hill to the wide stretch of turf which commands so splendid a view over sea and green hills! Here comes an English pony-chaise, with madame, splendidly attired, driving, monsieur beside her, and a pair of rosy-cheeked English boys behind them. Skimming the ground in front of the horse is the running footman of Japan, dressed in black tights and loose sleeves, clearing the way for the quality. Here, are two grave Chinamen in blue, with close caps and long pigtails, packed in one jinrickisha, drawn by a little Jap one-fourth their combined weight. There, are a pair of pretty "nasans," under a bright paper umbrella, with painted faces and newly banded hair. Near them, is a group of Japanese mammas, with polished black teeth, and babies at their backs, laughing and chattering as they mount the hill. Jack Tar follows in a jinrickisha, at a fast trot, and with something better than saki on board. Next comes a native swell in a Newmarket coat and race-glasses; then a shop autocrat in a silk hat and light *paletôt*, and last, not least, the favourite, a vicious-looking Chinese pony, with half a dozen "bettos," or grooms, around him. We reach the grand stand, to be dazzled by a blaze of unaccustomed European beauty; and surveying the scene from above, find it, saving the native crowd outside the ropes, and the native racing swells in the paddock—Japanese princes, some of them—very like a racecourse at home. Certainly the clerk of the course is a jovial merchant, the judge is a banker, the horses are wild little China ponies, and the jockeys are the men we meet every night at dinner or at the club; but in other respects the scene is too familiar for description, and it is only the longitude that makes it remarkable.

But life in the settlement is not always so vivid as it is to-day, although these exiled Aryans sweeten it as much as possible with the pleasures of sport and society. Of the two thousand Europeans in Japan, twelve hundred live in Yokohama, and our "hong" represents very fairly the homes of the wealthier section of this little foreign community. To a large dwelling-house, with spacious and handsomely furnished rooms, are added great "godowns," or warehouses, the business offices, and a compound, surrounded by the houses of the "comprador," and several of the domestic servants. The forenoons are given to business, and at noon comes tiffin—a substantial dinner in reality, when there are almost always a few guests. Mail days excepted, the afternoons see a great deal of riding, rifle-shooting, cricket, or pic-nicking, and five or six o'clock finds the clubs full of whist-players. All the world dines at eight o'clock, and forgets the drooping prices of silk and the paper money, while enjoying a dinner which, though cooked by a native, is equal to anything one gets in Europe. A cigar follows as a matter of course; and, as three-fourths of the homes in Yokohama are bachelor establishments, a game of billiards at the club, a stroll through the native town, or perhaps a visit to the native theatre, finishes the evening.

There is a street full of theatres in Yokohama, where long streamers, floating from tall masts, and large pictures of scenes from popular plays, sufficiently advertise the home of the drama. Entering a low door, paying a few *cash*, and passing a great pile of ticketed wooden shoes, the visitor hires a cushion to squat on, and takes possession of one of the boxes, shallow little matted pens, without seats, disposed in a single row along either side of the house, and accessible to the vendors of refreshments, who move about continually, crying their wares in the intervals of the acts. Each box holds four people, and, as the representation begins in the morning and continues all day for two or three days running, one sees a family meal in progress here and there, and the floors of the boxes littered with rice-bowls, saki-bottles, tea-cups, and the ubiquitous tobacco-bon. The house is large, and square in plan, while the stage is prolonged by a narrow platform, running all round the building, without, and a few feet above which, are the boxes, and within, the pit. The actors make their entrances and exits by these platforms, as well as from the side-scenes, and much of the action takes place upon them. The drama embraces tragedies, the tales of Old Japan, which relate, in a tedious way, stories of family feuds and vengeance; and comedies, which, we are told, are admirable sketches of real life. It was a comedy that we went to see, and so excellent were the actors that, though we knew nothing of the language, their pantomime enabled us partially to follow the plot. There are no actresses in Japan; but the women's parts are played by men, who gave the coquettish witcheries of a beauty and stiff proprieties of a duenna with extraordinary skill. The scenery is good; and if the stage machinery is a little crude, it is at least better than what satisfied our forefathers a hundred years ago. One convenient expedient is very funny. A figure, dressed in black from head to foot, the face covered with a conical cap having eyeholes, occupies the stage throughout the whole performance. If the actors want anything, the figure hands it; and if they leave the stage for the side platforms, the figure follows with a candle on the end of a long stick, to light up the group. This useful but comical dummy, presumed to be invisible, forms one of the most curious features of the Japanese stage for European eyes.

In the course of after-dinner talk, we soon became aware that there is great present stagnation in the trade of Japan, and a good deal of disquietude among Europeans, not only as to the future of business, but with regard to the political situation and prospects of the country as well. The days of large profits have long passed away; and, of the five treaty ports, four are already almost deserted by foreign merchants. The first comers of 1859 made fortunes, chiefly by supplying cannon and rifles to the feudatories, who were crazy to give their little armies weapons of precision;

and by land speculations in Yokohama, which proved enormously profitable. These exceptional sources of wealth soon dried up, but enough money was made in the early days to attract a large number of traders, while the legitimate wants of the Japanese people increased very slowly. Manchester and Bradford goods find a market in the interior, and there is a large demand for window glass and iron rods; but the chief, if not the only, customer for other European manufactures is the Japanese Government, which, rather than the people, is engaged in every kind of business. These are no foundations for a solid trade, and at the present moment, indeed, the Government is trying to sell the imperial factories, in the interests of an economy which the decreasing stock of silver and drooping value of the paper money peremptorily require. Meanwhile, competition between the European merchants has become ruinously keen, and there have been some failures and many departures. Nagasaki, once a busy port, is deserted; Hiogo is little better off; while Hakodadi is a name without commmercial meaning. The imports have hardly increased at all during the last ten years, and the exports, consisting chiefly of tea and silk, have remained stationary for four years past. During that period, the average annual value of imports and exports has been eleven millions sterling, or not quite seven shillings and sixpence per head of the population, taking the latter at thirty millions. The gross trade of India for 1880, on the other hand, was ten shillings per head, while that of Russia, the most backward of European states, was forty-five shillings, and of Australia six hundred and forty-four shillings per head.

But, while the wants of the *bonâ fide* consumers of Japan are so small and continue so nearly stationary, the unbusiness-like character of the native dealers forms a further obstacle to trade. The Japanese have no talent for affairs, and the merchant—a member, we must always bear in mind, of a low and despised caste—is a timid buyer, without the courage to pursue any enterprise which does not give immediate results, and always a chicaneer. I have known these men spend days in the office, hesitating over trifling transactions which a Chinaman would despatch off-hand, and I have seen, in the godown, what laborious precautions a silk inspector must take against being grossly cheated in the quality of his purchases. Add to this that the word of a Japanese merchant is of little value, and—significant fact—that all business is done only against cash payments. One cannot fail to be struck here, where the two races elbow one another, with the contrast between the Japanese and Chinese in commercial matters. The latter is a merchant by nature, intelligent, enterprising, and reliable; while the former is a born huckster, without foresight, timid, and untruthful.

Such is a sketch of the commercial situation, not, I believe, too darkly painted, but looking still more gloomy when viewed from a political standpoint. Every one agrees that the remedy for the present stagnation in trade lies in further opening the country. Japan, though politically open, is practically closed, and the merchants of Yokohama are little better than retail shopkeepers, supplying the tiny wants of the people through a grill. They are strictly confined to a distance of thirty miles around each of the five treaty ports, and require passports, which the Government may grant or not, as it pleases, to travel beyond the "treaty limits." They cannot become freehold owners of house or land anywhere, and, outside of the settlement concession, they are subject to Japanese jurisdiction, although, within the concession, consular rule is supreme. On the other hand, the whole country is rich in all sorts of natural productions; but these cannot develop in native hands, the man of business being such as I have described him; while the cultivator, though of much higher character than the trader, has few aspirations beyond the satisfaction of his daily wants. Not more than a tenth part of the soil is cultivated, and the population, dense as it seems to the traveller, does not extend far on either side of the public highways. The forests are full of magnificent timber, useless for want of roads, and minerals, such as sulphur and petroleum, abound, but are not exploited for the same reason.

In view of these resources on the one hand, and a stagnant condition of business on the other, the Europeans naturally clamour for the opening of the country. "Let us travel freely," they say, "investigate the interior, judge for ourselves, and make the soil produce what it can. Give us power to hold property, equal rights with the natives, and a civil and commercial legislation such as that of Europe. Wants will follow the wealth which we will create, and Japan will then really march with the times." There is certainly nothing illogical in preferring such requests to a Government which poses before the world as a convert to the civilization and commercial ideas of the West; but how are such appeals answered? When it was a question, in 1874, of revising the treaties of 1858, the Powers formally asked for the "suppression of all the fetters on free relations in the interior of the empire," or, in other words, for the opening of Japan. The Government of the Mikado answered by a refusal, except upon condition that the consular jurisdiction in the concessions should be abolished—a proposition which, in the entire absence of justice, in our sense of the word, from Japanese courts, it would have been a waste of time for the Powers to discuss, and whose only effect, if it were carried out, would be to close every foreign house of business in the treaty ports. The negotiations consequently broke down, and, since that time, each party to the discussion blames the other for the present unsatisfactory state of affairs. "Open the country," says the one; "Accept our jurisdiction," says the other. It is a dead-lock.

The truth is that the Japanese Government has no intention of opening the country to the foreigner on any conditions. It desires to have the moral equality of Japan with Europe acknowledged, and to preserve the national independence; but does not want to see Japanese resources exploited, no matter how profitably to the population, by European, possibly by Chinese enterprise. If Japan has partially unclosed her doors, it is only because events* have taught her that the Powers could break them open at any moment; but she dreads, as she always has done, lest intercourse with other nations may ultimately lead to foreign domination. An Oriental of Orientals, she took a necessary step, with an attitude of so much courtesy towards our superior knowledge, that Europe received the new member of the family of nations with compliments and open arms; but she keeps her back as firmly as she dares against her half-open gates, though there are words of welcome on her lips. Meanwhile, that Aryan race, which will never be denied when material advantages are in view, knocks louder and louder, and no man can say what the end will be.

For my own part, I believe that the foreigner will yet have an ally within the gates. The Japanese people themselves have always been a docile and inert mass, too nearly slaves to have any political opinions, and ruled, as much since the abolition of feudalism as before, by the territorial aristocracy; *Enfants charmants, gouvernes par des enfants terribles*, as they have been most aptly called. Society is divided into castes, now abolished in law but surviving in fact, at the head of which stand the "samurai," or feudal soldiery, followed by the farmer, the artisan, the trader, and the coolie. The samurai number about a million men, all of whom were practically ruined by the destruction of the clan system which followed on the revolution of 1868. It is true that they have been compensated for the loss of their lords' support by "pension-bonds," but the capital value of these does not exceed £40 per man, and even in Japan one cannot live on the interest of £40. These men know nothing of trade, which they consider the function of a despised caste, and, being still, although disfranchised, a privileged class, they crowd the Government offices, and terrorize the ministers by their cabals. For them the opening of the country means the supremacy of the

* The bombardment of Kagoshima took place in 1863, and of Shimonoseki in 1864.

"barbarians," and the fear of being ousted from their places by better men, and told to earn their own living.

The farmers, who form three-fourths of the whole population of Japan, are a hardy, intelligent, and industrious race, without ambition it is true, but not altogether blind to the main chance. Under the feudal system these men were the mere vassals of the daimios, who could rack-rent them at will, and whom they dare not approach except on bended knees. Now they are tenants of the Government at fixed rents, owing homage to no man, and their sons, not unfrequently, enter the new and Europeanized imperial army, thus becoming the equals of the old military caste, and raising the sense of independence throughout the class to which they belong. For the Japanese agriculturists the advent of the foreigner means a better market for their produce, and payment in cash instead of in kind; but, thanks in part to the absence of communications, in part to the inertia natural to the cultivators of the soil, they are slow to understand the situation or appreciate their new opportunities. They are taught that the Europeans are ruining the country; causing the disappearance of silver and the depreciation of the paper money; and, as yet, they make no demand for communication with the outside world and freedom to dispose of their tea, silk, and rice to the best advantage. But some of them have already felt the advantage of the railway; native newspapers begin to distribute new ideas, in spite of a strict censorship, and self-interest will yet make the farmer a partizan of the foreigner, if human nature in Japan is the same as human nature elsewhere.

As for the artisans, traders, and coolies; the great native town which has arisen around Yokohama sufficiently proves that they would benefit by the further opening of the country; but these classes stand even further from the throne and nearer political nonentity than the cultivator. It is on the birth and growth of public opinion among the latter class—healthy, honest, industrious, intelligent, and numerically overwhelming—that the foreigner must found his hopes for the future trade of Japan.

That the political welfare of the country depends upon the same condition, I shall hope to show hereafter, but the consideration of this question is out of place in the present connection, except so far as the character of the Japanese Government is concerned. This is a factor equally in the commercial and political state of affairs, but, for the present, it must suffice to say —what will, I hope, become clearer by-and-by—that the Government of Japan is an oligarchy, distracted by self-seeking factions, without any central authority, and having no unanimous policy beyond that of preserving the national independence. Meanwhile the people of this ancient and, in its own way, highly cultured nation, are simply a flock of sheep, driven by the same masters now as in the feudal times, which, indeed, have disappeared on paper, but not from the habits of the country. If the masses, hardly conscious as yet of their emancipation, ever come to have opinions—ever, in fact, become a nation, Japan may have a new birth. What she has passed through lately is only revolution.

CHAPTER VIII.

A TRIP TO NIKKO.

November 1–7.

November 1.—Nikko is a village about a hundred miles north of the capital, situated on the slopes of the volcanic range, and containing tombs and temples of such beauty that the Japanese say, "Who has not seen Nikko, cannot say, 'Wonderful!'" Arriving early at Tokio, we found our guide, philosopher, and friend, Kobé, waiting at the station, prepared at all points for a week's trip, and our little train of four pair-horse jinrickishas started immediately. For the first half of the distance to Nikko the road is perfectly level, crossing the old sea-shelf, so often alluded to, which spreads very widely north of Jeddo Bay. Afterwards, it rises gently, approaching the range, which lies on our left, and striking it at Nikko, where the hills shoot up suddenly, like a wall, out of the plain. The flat country is one great rice-field, carefully cultivated, and teeming with people, now busy with the harvest. The plain is ruled all over with long lines of light bamboo frames, upon which the rice sheaves are drying, like towels on a clothes-horse; while the cleared ground is a quagmire, dotted with the blue figures of reapers knee-deep in the mud. The wayside villages are not so numerous as on the Tokaido road, but much more prosperous in appearance, with better shops, and better-dressed inhabitants. We passed some good farmhouses, with large and pretty gardens, hedged with clipped camellias, forming great green walls, thirty feet high, which must look splendid when in flower.

While the fields along the Tokaido are universally tilled with a hoe, like that employed for the same purpose in Northern Italy, the farmers in this part of Japan use a large iron-tipped wooden spade, with which the soil is thrown out sideways, as if by the turn-furrow of a plough, to a depth of nine or ten inches. Up to the present time we have seen no carts, ploughs, or horses in Japan, farm operations of all kinds being carried on entirely by hand labour. The absence of cattle, sheep, and pigs is no less remarkable; even dogs are scarce, if one excepts the wolf-like curs which haunt every village, but these creatures are not worthy the name of dogs.

The rice-stripper, winnowing-machine, and rice-pounder are busy, just now, in every village. The first is simply a comb, made of iron plates, and the grain is stripped by pulling the heads through it. Rice was formerly winnowed by a pair of large paper fans, but a simple winnowing-machine was introduced from Europe a few years back, and has run like wildfire all over the country. The rice-pounder is one of the most conspicuous objects in Japan, and its whereabouts in a village is always indicated by a screen of cords which hangs in front of the rice-pounder's shop. Through this blind, one catches glimpses of a man, naked but for the waist-cloth, who steps perpetually backwards and forwards from the ground on to one end of a long lever, whose further extremity is armed with a pestle weighted with a heavy stone. This overhangs a large wooden mortar full of rice, into which the pestle falls every time the man jumps off the end of the lever, and thus, in the course of time, the grain is decorticated. This worse than tread-mill labour goes on day by day throughout the length and breadth of Japan, while any amount of water-power is running to waste; but the Jap, though a skilful workman, is not a mechanic, and has no idea of labour-saving appliances.

À propos of handicraft, it should be said that a Japanese workman is almost as clever with his feet as with his hands. The tailor holds his thread, and the carpenter his wood while planing, with his toes. I have seen a file-maker using both feet, squatting with the soles apposed, holding one end of the steel blank with the toes of each foot, and sliding the work along thereby, while using the hammer and chisel with the hands. The blacksmith also squats at his work, and pushes a piston backwards and forwards in a square box with one foot instead of using bellows. It seems a pity that the Western nations have abandoned the industrial use of the foot, especially as, in limiting its functions, they have also deformed its beauty.

We are now among those Japanese agriculturists about whom something was said in the last chapter. It seems doubtful whether these men are or are not the owners of the soil which they till. In the feudal times, they paid the lord a land tax in rice, and this, when the crop failed, was either remitted, or its payment was spread over a number of years; but their tenures seem to have been indefeasible. Since the dispossession of the daimios, the farmer pays the Government two and a half per cent. per annum on the value of his holding, as determined by the State surveyors; rice-lands being usually assessed at £20, and unimproved lands at about £16 an acre. A rent of ten shillings per acre for rice-land sounds moderate; but it appears that as much as £20 an acre is sometimes paid for possession; fixity of tenure being so firmly established a custom, that the farmers deal in land as if it were their own, although there is every reason to believe it is, and always has been, the absolute property of the Mikado. *La petite culture* is the universal rule in Japan. A farmer rarely employs any labour beside that of his own family, and no one keeps more than three or four coolies at work. Yet this country, of whose hundred million acres not more than eleven millions are cultivated, feeds a population of thirty millions, and has rice to spare in good years. The land-tax furnishes three-fourths of the entire revenue of Japan, while the farmers form three-fourths of the whole population, clinging closely to the soil, and setting a high value on their rights. There can, I think, be little doubt, the spirit of change having once taken possession of the country, that these are the men who will ultimately shape the destinies of New Japan.

November 2.—We slept last night at a village called Nakada, thirty-five miles from Tokio, leaving which, the road, hitherto perfectly level, begins to rise gradually, and is bordered on either side by pines and cedars. The former are fine trees, each a hundred feet or more in height; while the latter are magnificent, having straight tapering stems, often a hundred and thirty feet high, and a dense foliage, almost exactly like that of the Californian big trees. The typhoon of October 3, whose tail touched us in the Pacific, did immense damage in this glorious avenue. Many pines were uprooted, and cedars, which stand better than pines, were broken off and twisted around in the most remarkable manner. We reached Utsonomiya, an old daimio town, in the afternoon, the coolies having run forty miles since the morning, apparently without fatigue. Europeans are evidently not everyday visitors in Utsonomiya, for we were followed through the streets by a little crowd of laughing children. The town was full of soldiery, quartered here to overawe some discontented agriculturists, and it sounded odd to hear familiar European bugle-calls while eating our dinner in a Japanese tea-house.

November 3–5.—This morning every one asked, " Did you feel the earthquake?" It woke us at 3 a.m., shaking the house violently, while a loud rumbling sound was heard, lasting two or three seconds. Shortly afterwards, came a second shock and rumble, and, after that, quiet. There was nothing alarming about the event, but we wished it had occurred when we were sufficiently awake to take notice of details; the natives seemed to treat the matter with complete indifference. I am told that Mr. Milne, an English professor at Tokio, has ascertained, by means of the seismograph, that earth-movements, which suffice to throw down Japanese houses, are of surprisingly limited extent, and do not exceed a quarter or three-eighths of an inch even in very severe shocks.

The avenue of cedars becomes still finer between Utsonomiya and Nikko, the trees completely over-arching the narrow road, their grand dimensions, straight shafts, and sequoia-like foliage, recalling to our minds the glorious pathways through the forest belt of the Sierra Nevada. By this route the Shoguns used to come in state to pay their devotions at stated intervals to the shades of their ancestors; and under these trees hundreds of Japanese pilgrims from the most distant parts of the empire still annually pass, to pray before the tombs. At Nikko, the volcanic range lifts itself suddenly out of the plain, rising into peaks from six to eight thousand feet high, separated from each other by steep rocky ravines, carrying swift mountain streams. Hills and valleys are alike clothed with foliage, and among these picturesque solitudes lie the Shogunal shrines and tombs which are the boast of Japan. To describe in detail the Nikko temples, every square inch of whose surfaces is loaded with the most delicate art workmanship, is out of the question; but, generally, the reader may picture vast groups of religious buildings, scattered among stately cedars, the growth of centuries, which clothe with sombre forests some of the most beautiful and romantic scenery in the world. While no single shrine at Nikko can compare with the Cologne Dome, Milan Cathedral, or indeed with any great Gothic pile, in the power of exciting religious emotion; there is probably no other scene in the world which could furnish the imagination with such pregnant suggestions of a once splendid religious establishment and ceremonial. Every dark avenue in these solemn cedar groves, carries the eye to some gorgeous shrine, a perfect work of strange and delicate art, or lifts it upwards towards some hidden tomb, by wide flights of granite stairs, winding through the trees, till their summits are lost in the shadows of the foliage. Standing at the foot of the great staircase which leads thus, through mysterious aisles of red-brown shafts, to Yeasu's mausoleum, one expects, at every moment, to see a long procession of shaven, yellow-robed priests, approaching through the sun-spangled shadows of the cryptomerias, with swinging censers and monotonous chants. But the silence of these mountain solitudes is unbroken, save by the sound of streams and waterfalls; all the religious enthusiasm, if such it was, that built these high places and planted these sacred groves has departed, leaving us to wonder why a race, which covered its country with shrines only a few centuries ago, has become so indifferent to its old cults. The majority of the temples are Buddhistic, but there are some Shinto shrines, and both are kept in good preservation at the national expense. In one of the latter, which was pure of all Buddhist symbols, the "kagura," or sacred Shinto dance, was in progress during our visit. A white-robed girl sits all day on her heels before the mystic mirror, except at certain hours, when she rises, and begins a slow, graceful dance; genuflecting and waving her arms, while in one hand she holds a fan, and with the other shakes a group of jingling bells. This lasts for a few minutes, and then she kneels again, motionless, before the symbols. Among the many artists who helped to decorate Nikko was a certain Hidari Jingoro, the Pygmalion of Japan, who once painted the picture of a lady so surpassingly beautiful that he fell in love with his own work. By the kindness of the gods, whom he implored to that effect, the canvas came to life, married the artist and lived happily with him ever after—of course. It was curious to light upon this old myth in the far East.

Although an artistic temperament is the common heritage of every Japanese, art has passed its prime in Japan. It culminated during the seventeenth century, but its aims, even in its golden age, were never high; while, now, it has ceased to create, and only reproduces. Architecture, with which, at Nikko, we are chiefly concerned, has, strictly speaking, never existed in Japan. Temples, castles, palaces, and private houses are all alike in general character, and the most sacred shrine, like the humblest shop, is built of wood. There is a raised floor, some vertical posts, and a heavy roof. The outer walls of the building are wooden shutters, and the interior simply an open space, divided by slides; but that is all; whether the dwelling be that of a god or a coolie. It is because of the exquisite decoration which the art-workman lavishes on buildings, in themselves only worthy of a camp, that Japanese architecture escapes condemnation for its want of constructive power. The eye looks in vain, in Japan, for the aspiring grace of Gothic outlines, the classic beauty of Greek construction, or the strong and sensuous work of Rome.

Japanese sculpture and painting are devoid of ideality equally with architecture. The great bronze images of Buddha, of which the Daibutz at Kamakura is the best example, have a certain sublimity, due in part to their great size, in part to the expression of ineffable serenity which characterizes the faces of these idols, but the figure is in all cases formal in treatment and conventional in attitude. The native gods, whose statues guard the temples, are hideous monstrosities, designed apparently to terrify the multitude, but without any pretensions to art. It is extraordinary to find these ugly images tolerated among a people possessing so much natural good taste. In secular works, such, for example, as those at Asakusa, the human figure is treated with great power, but without the least feeling for the beautiful. Emotion is portrayed with the utmost skill, but always extravagantly, and in a humorous spirit. Tragedy itself is so highly accented as to seem cynical and untrue; it is as if a story of human agony were told by a man with a grin on his face. While the Greeks elevated the beauty of the human form into something half divine, giving the world statues which seem to link man with the gods, Japanese sculpture, with the nude always before its eyes, has had no similar inspiration. For it, the human body remains, like that of beast or bird, a thing to be reproduced, skilfully, it is true, but only better worth representation than the bird or beast because it lends itself more perfectly to vivid expressions of pleasure and pain.

Painting in Japan is of two kinds—the heroic and the familiar. The former represents feats of arms, and the chase, the figures being shown in violent action and unnatural contortions, while of grouping and perspective there is none. It is in the painting of familiar subjects, and in decoration, that the Japanese artist is seen at his best. Without ideals, and sometimes with low aims, he covers screens, fans, and "kake-mono," the rolls of silk or paper which hang even in the poorest houses, with designs, either commonplace, humorous, or simply pretty, but always charming and effective. These may illustrate the operations of the rice-farmer and tea-grower, or exhibit a procession of pilgrims in the snow, a street crowd, a river scene, a solitary crane flying through infinite space over sea, a dragon whose coils envelop the screen, and must be sought, half on one side of it, half on the other, or a wary tortoise, baby on back. Be the figures what they may, they are designed with exquisite taste, are often extremely humorous, and always a little extravagant, but for delicacy of execution and happy choice of colours they are simply unrivalled. Landscape painting is not understood, composition, perspective, half-tones, and the play of light and shade being all absent from Japanese reproductions of nature. They pile houses on the sea, mountains on the house-tops, and clouds on the mountain-tops, without distinction of distances; while, in regard to composition, everything is thrown *pêle-mêle* upon the canvas, like dice from a box. The Japanese artist is positively perverse about perspective. Given a room, with company seated at table, which a European would naturally represent from the point of view of a spectator standing on the floor; he will regard the scene from the ceiling, and present a bird's-eye view of the table, surrounded by heads and shoulders, the latter grotesquely contorted by the use of the knife and fork.

Art is assiduously cultivated by both sexes of the upper classes in Japan, not seriously, but as an accomplishment, having a few clever *tours de force* for its object. For the professional artist, there are neither schools, exhibitions, nor picture-dealers; but painting, like sword-making or lacquering, is an hereditary occupation, whose traditions and methods pass without change or development from father to son. Japanese art, in fine, still wears the fetters which bind every form of human energy in a feudal country. As in Europe, during the Middle Ages, distinguished by a condition of society not unlike that of Old Japan, ideals do not exist; man's life is bounded by his wants and pleasures, and the pursuit of the good, true, and beautiful is not only impossible, but inconceivable. That *renaissance*, whose gestation occupied centuries in the West, is now to be carried to Japan, so we are told, by the steamship and locomotive engine; but the need of Japanese art, like that of Japanese religion and politics, is a soul, in whose absence the gifts of civilization are not benefits, but which cannot be packed in a boiler or sent along a telegraphic wire.

November 6.—Refreshed by a few days' rest at Nikko, our coolies offered to show us their powers on the return journey, and run back to Nakada, a distance of fifty-eight miles, in one day. As this journey promised to be an interesting example of what these sturdy little fellows can accomplish, I took careful notes of their performance, with the following results:—Leaving Nikko at 7.45 a.m., the men ran twenty miles in two hours and fifty minutes without a stop. Then they rested twenty minutes, taking a bowl of rice and some weak tea. The rest of the journey was made by ten-mile stages, with stops of a quarter of an hour between each, and the fifty-eight miles were completed in ten hours, including stops, or eight hours and a quarter, exclusive of stops, being at the rate of 7·03 miles per hour while running, and 5·8 miles per hour including stops. The whole party arrived at Nakada in capital condition, laughing and chatting gaily. They ran, almost naked, at an even trot, with a long springy stride, and took nothing but rice, a little fish and tea by the way. Their feet were protected by straw sandals; but if these wore out or gave way, they were not particular about replacing them with others. Their consideration for one another was remarkable. The man between the shafts has the hardest work, and the strongest coolies were always ready to take more than their fair share of this position, while the weaker never shirked it. It rained hard during the last third of the journey; but whether they dripped with perspiration or with rain made no difference to these plucky little fellows, who, after completing fifty miles, ran the last eight miles into Nakada within an hour.

November 7.—The rain, which continued nearly all night, had made the roads very heavy, but our men started, apparently none the worse for their long journey of yesterday. The weather was fine and the air clearer than we had ever seen it in Japan, designing the outlines of the range with extraordinary sharpness against a sky of the tenderest blue. All the higher summits had gathered a mantle of snow during the night, and Asamayama, a high and still smoking cone, looked like a smaller Fusiyama. But the sacred mountain, though more than a hundred miles distant, still dominated the view, and, together with the long serrated line of white peaks, delighted our eyes as we rolled almost noiselessly along the lake-like levels of the plain, with its endless rice-fields, prosperous villages, and simple, happy, industrious people. We caught the five-o'clock train at Tokio, actually beating a party who started from Nikko at the same time with us, in our old friend the Yokohama buggy, and took our departure for the settlement amid the bows and smiles of the eight fine fellows, our coolies, for whom we had conceived a well-grounded respect, and who were brimming over with satisfaction at receiving a sum equal to £7 10s. English money for their seven days' work, or 2s. 8½d. per day per man ! nothing found, except a few well-earned bottles of saki as a *douceur*.

CHAPTER IX.

HIOGO—KIOTO—NAGASAKI.

November 17-23.

WE divided a week, after our return from Nikko, between our friends at Yokohama and Tokio, being always sure of a kind reception at the latter place, either from the German Minister or our friend Herr von Siebold, Secretary of the Austrian Legation. The time passed pleasantly in sight-seeing, sociality, and discussions, some of whose conclusions have already been noted, and it was with sincere regret that we drank our last glass of champagne with the friends who gathered round us for a farewell dinner at the Yokohama hotel on the 16th of November. The following afternoon we left the settlement for Kobé, in one of the Japanese "Mitsu Bishi" steamers, our parting view of Fusiyama being lighted by a full moon, which seemed to shine upon the white ghost of the sacred cone. On the 19th we reached Kobé, as the settlement of the treaty port of Hiogo is called, situated on the western shore of Osaka Bay, another great landlocked inlet, like that of Jeddo. Opposite Hiogo is Osaka, the commercial capital of Japan, and seat of the silk trade, built upon the Yodogawa river, but on the shallow side of the bay, where only boats of light draught can lie, although great steamers anchor within a stone's throw of Kobé.

The settlement is a little semicircle of European houses and gardens, prettily disposed around a charming bay, and overhung by bold waterworn hills, which rise almost immediately behind

x

the town to considerable heights. The native town of Hiogo is much more Europeanized than that of Yokohama, and its shops contain the finest art-work we have yet seen anywhere in Japan ; but the prices asked are exorbitant. A railway, forty-five miles in length, joins Kobé with Kioto, and we only waited to obtain our passports before starting by this route for the old Mikadonal capital. Soon after leaving Kobé the hills recede, and the old sea-shelf, narrow at the site of the settlement, widens into a vast plain. This is crowded with villages, and cultivated with the utmost care, the fields seeming alive with people ploughing and preparing the land for crops to follow the rice. Here they use a wooden plough, drawn by a single bullock, and bullock-carts are common both in the fields and on the roads. Rice, as usual, prevails, but a good deal of cotton and "daicun," a kind of long turnip, is grown. For these "dry" crops the land is thrown up into carefully shaped, flat-topped ridges, in each of which two grooves are trodden for seed-beds, and served with human manure, which is carried in buckets depending from a shoulder-yoke, and distributed by means of a bamboo dipper. No European garden is more minutely tended than a Japanese farm. The railroad crosses a number of streams, or rather their beds, whose great breadth tells of sudden and heavy floods in the wet season. Graceful groves of bamboo occur at frequent intervals, the villages are embowered in foliage, and have a substantial, prosperous appearance, in keeping with that of the country and people.

Kioto is said to have been the residence of the Mikado ever since the eighth century, and, before the recent transfer of the court to Jeddo, it held four hundred thousand souls, a population now reduced by one-half. The imperial palaces are in partial ruin, and the temples seem deserted by both priests and worshippers, but what remains of Kioto is probably more like Old Japan than even Jeddo, where, as we have seen, certain innovations have been made. The town is built on a plain, entirely surrounded by mountains, opening only towards the north and south to give passage to the Kamogawa, a small stream, which the Kiotans have widened by frequent dams and make believe to be a river. The streets are narrow, rectangularly disposed, and like those of Jeddo in appearance, but sad looking and emptier. Everywhere one sees tea-houses, theatres, shows, and the signs of pleasure, but nowhere the indications of work. Only foot-passengers are encountered, few jinrickishas, and no horsemen are seen in the streets. It is a kind of Japanese Paris, whose great world has gone away to Jeddo. But the little world which remains is more picturesque than that of Jeddo. Both men and women are handsomer, and, the latter especially, better dressed, wearing more silk, brighter colours, and having the hair more elaborately ornamented. These brilliant little persons come upon one in the street with all the dazzling effect of a great lady on a Japanese fan.

Kioto is the home of the best ivory-carving, bronze, and lacquer-work in Japan; yet one cannot find examples of either art in the shops. The *chefs d'œuvres* hide themselves in cabinets, and to see them one must pass many patient hours, waiting while the cherished pieces are taken one by one out of their wrappings. The prices asked are amazing, for every rich Japanese is an ardent and discriminating collector, and these Kioto things are especially beautiful. There is a Government silk-weaving establishment in the town, but we found very few looms at work, and none of them were employed upon those elaborate silk brocades which we had hoped to see growing in the native hand-looms. Instead of these, some very ordinary work was being woven on machines which, although primitive in their details, were European in principle, and therefore quite uninteresting to us. This place, like the Insetz Kioku at Tokio, is built on a grand scale, and full of polite officials, but is evidently not paying its working expenses.

At night we strolled through the street devoted to theatres and entertainments, and, for about a shilling, visited a juggler, a conjurer, an exhibition of the magic lantern, and a theatre. The first two shows were remarkable from the fact that the feats and tricks exhibited were exactly the same as those commonly seen at home. The magic lantern, however, surprised us, by showing views of the Victoria Tower, Notre Dame, portraits of animals at the "Zoo," and a number of similar subjects, described by a voluble little Jap showman to a delighted audience; while, at the theatre, we saw repeated the same scenes and clever acting we had witnessed at Yokohama.

November 20.—Drove three hours in jinrickishas to Kameyama, the "Tortoise Mountain," through whose ravines the Oigawa river runs in a series of rapids to join one of the affluents of the Yodogawa. The natives shoot these rapids in large boats, and timber is rafted down by the same speedy route to Osaka. The cañon is narrow, and the hills are of gneiss, rising from a thousand to fifteen hundred feet on either side of the valley, whose steep sides are covered with trees, among which great patches of scarlet maple give extraordinary beauty to the view at this time of the year. Putting our jinrickishas on board one of the big, box-like boats, we pushed out into the stream, four coolies managing the craft, with two short oars on the starboard side, one long oar in the stern, and a bamboo pole in the bow. The water runs very fast in some places, while in others it is sluggish; but the transit became exhilarating now and then, when we ran down a long straight flight of steps, of which, indeed, we wished there were more. On the way we met many boats being laboriously towed up-stream by coolies, and admired the skill with which a practicable path has been exploited beside this wild and boulder-strewn stream, as well as the cleverly arranged bamboo guards which guide the tow-ropes past rocky peaks and prevent their being caught in inaccessible places. We landed at a point where the rapids merge into a wide and quiet stream, cumbered with boats and timber-rafts, and drove back to Kioto, barely catching the four-o'clock train to Hiogo, thanks to the stupidity of our new guide, the "Light of Asia," as we had too good reason to nickname this unenlightened heathen.

November 21.—The Peninsular and Oriental steamer *Malacca* from Yokohama, bound for Hongkong, entered the port of Hiogo at noon, and, tarrying only just long enough to pick us up, at once commenced the passage of the far-famed "Inland Sea." The beauties of this voyage are, I think, overrated. The scenery is exactly like that of the rest of Japan, but enhanced in effect by its lake-like character. On one side of the traveller lies the mainland of Niphon; on the other the coast, first of Shikok, and then of Kiusiu, now nearer together, now further apart, and sometimes approaching each other so closely as to form narrow straits. Conical hills, the corpses of extinct volcanoes, rise on either shore above rounded hill-sides, which are covered with foliage, except where they are terraced and cultivated. The feet of the mountains stand, as is so commonly the case in Japan, on a low shelf-like shore, and almost every indentation in the coast-line is occupied by a brown, toy-like village, the home of fishermen, whose boats are thickly scattered over the glancing water which forms the foreground of these rustic pictures from our decks.

November 22.—We threaded the Straits of Shimonoseki, famous on account of the bombardment of Choshiu's town and batteries in 1864, and entering the open sea, shortly afterwards changed our course to south-west and steered for Nagasaki.

November 23.—Nagasaki is a dead port. It is not so well placed for business as Yokohama or Kobé, and, while these settlements have injured their elder sister, the stagnation of trade has finished her completely. There are only four European merchants left in the place, and enterprise, either in despair, or to console itself, has taken refuge in keeping grog-shops. Everything in the foreign quarter looks decayed and lifeless, while even the native town is dull, dirty, and uninteresting. The harbour scenery is magnificent, forcibly recalling that of Dartmouth, but with a wider stretch of land-locked anchorage, circled by higher and steeper hills than in the case of the pretty little Devonshire town. The *Iron Duke*, the *Champlain*, a French war-steamer, a Russian man-of-war, and the *Sunda* (Peninsular and Oriental) were the chief ships in the harbour, and as we arrived the band of the English iron-clad was playing "God save the Queen." The strain seemed like a memory of home.

Our first care was to visit "Desima," the artificial island, only a few square yards in extent, separated from the native town by a narrow stone bridge, where, after the expulsion of the Portuguese from Japan in 1637, their commercial rivals, the Dutch, were installed and practically imprisoned. Of the lives which the traders of Holland passed in Desima, so well described by Kæmpfer, I shall not pause to speak; but the Dutch and Portuguese cannot be mentioned in connection with Nagasaki without a reference, however imperfect, to the short but bloody page of history which records the rise and fall of Christianity in Japan during the latter half of the sixteenth and first half of the seventeenth centuries. It was here that this terrible little drama was played, and yonder in the harbour stands the wooded island of Papenberg, the scene of merry pic-nics to-day, but the place from whose sheer cliffs four thousand Christian natives were hurled into the sea after Japan had decreed the uprooting of the cross within her borders.

In 1542 a Portuguese ship, bound for Macao, already a Portuguese settlement, was blown out of her course and anchored with difficulty in the port of Bungo, in the island of Kiusiu. This was the first European vessel that ever touched the shores of Japan, but she was kindly received, and the occurrence led to the establishment of a trade between the Daimio of Bungo and Macao. Seven years later, a young Japanese fugitive sailed on one of the Portuguese traders to Goa, where he became converted to Christianity, returning shortly after to his home, accompanied by some Jesuit fathers, among whom was the celebrated Francis Xavier. They were welcomed with open arms, and Xavier's devoted labours, backed by the pompous ceremonial of the Roman Church, which delighted the impressionable Japanese, brought immense numbers of natives under the standard of the cross within a few years. These converts, in their enthusiasm for the new religion, actually sent an embassy to the Pope in 1585, to assure him of their entire submission to Rome. An enormous ecclesiastical establishment sprang up in Japan, numbering hundreds of churches and hundreds of thousands of converts, while it has been said that the reigning emperor himself leant towards the doctrines preached by the Jesuit fathers.

But, sheltered in the first instance by a feudal lord, one of a coalition of clan-leaders who were struggling against the concentration of power in the hands of the Shogunate, then administered by Taiko Sama, the ablest man and greatest figure in Japanese history, Christianity became at length a political bond between certain rebellious feudatories, and a synonym with treason. The Portuguese clergy too became haughty with increasing success, mimicking the pomp of Rome and claiming precedence over the native aristocracy, besides introducing the spirit of the Inquisition, a thing wholly repugnant to Japanese ideas of toleration. Christianity, in fine, seemed already threatening to become an *imperium in imperio* in Japan, when the State determined on its eradication. In 1587 the Jesuits were ordered to quit the country, and the Buddhist clergy, seeing their own wishes seconded by the power of the Shogunate, threw all the weight of their influence with a superstitious people into the scale against the new faith. Persecutions, deportations, and massacres followed, and for the first third of the seventeenth century the history of Christianity in Japan is a long record of bloodshed. Deprived of their leaders, menaced with torture and death, but still faithful to their creed, the Christians at last took up arms, and made a final stand in the stronghold of Simabara, in 1638.

Meanwhile the Dutch, who landed for the first time in Japan in 1600, had been allowed to establish a small factory on the island of Firando, near Nagasaki. They were careful to make the Government understand that their religion had nothing in common with that of the Jesuit fathers, and if, during the persecutions, one of them were asked by a Japanese if he were a Christian, the answer was, "No, I'm a Dutchman." But they were jealous of the commercial supremacy of the Portuguese and hated their religion, with which, in the person of Spain, they were indeed at deadly strife, and spared no intrigues against their rivals, to the extent, as some say, of being traitors to the Christian faith itself. Be this as it may, it is certain that the Dutch aided the Japanese in subduing the stubborn remnant of Christians, who made their final stand at Simabara, and it was by Dutch guns that the walls of this last stronghold of the cross in Japan were battered to the ground. In the massacre which followed the taking of Simabara no less than forty thousand victims were slain, and Japanese Christianity perished in a sea of blood. It had grown up in a night, matured in half a century, and was utterly rooted out in less than a hundred years after being first planted in the country.

The Dutch gained little from their treachery towards the religion, loyalty to which had ruined their rivals. They were allowed to occupy the little island of Desima, being strictly confined within its limits, and watched by a special police. Once a year they were obliged to express their contempt for the Christian religion, and, it is said, to spit upon the cross; while they were only allowed to import two ship-loads of merchandise per annum. But the Dutchman knew how to transmute his chains into gold, and small as Desima is, it was big enough to hold some large Dutch fortunes in the seventeenth century.

At Nagasaki the *Malacca* took in a supply of Kagoshima coal, which looks like excellent fuel. It came alongside in great junks, and was discharged by means of small straw baskets, passing from hand to hand in a continuous stream, along two lines of natives, among whom were many women and girls. On the other side of the ship, the steam crane was loading cases of dried fish, the machine being cleverly rigged with a snatch-block, so as to make it double-acting, hauling one case from the boat to the deck, while it dropped a second into the hold. It was a characteristic last view of Japan; man *versus* science; the East against the West. Which will win?

Leaving Nagasaki harbour, one sees, for the first time in Japan, mountains rising directly from the sea, instead of from a plain. At the southern corner of the islands, the low terrace which marks an old sea-level and forms the present shore almost universally elsewhere, disappear; and we take leave, not of a country strange in this respect, as in so many others, to all our former experiences, but of bold, familiar-looking sea-cliffs, against whose feet the great Pacific waves are breaking in sheets of foam.

CHAPTER X.

NEW JAPAN.

November 25-27.

THREE days on board ship, with fine weather overhead and a spanking monsoon astern, was just what we wanted to arrange our ideas of the curious land we had left. The chief interest of Japan for Europeans commences with the year 1853, when the American, Commodore Perry, arrived in the country, demanding the establishment of relations with the United States. This mission, which resulted in the opening of Japan after two hundred and twenty-five years of absolute seclusion, was the beginning of a momentous series of events, including the subversion of the traditional form of Government, the abolition of the feudal system, and the establishment of a so-called Europeanized Government upon its ruins. Neither the history of these occurrences nor the present political position of New Japan can be understood without some reference to Old Japan, while there still remains much that is inexplicable in recent events and great uncertainties in regard to the future of the country.

The notion that the Mikado was a spiritual power, while the Shogun—or Tycoon, as we erroneously called him—was a temporal ruler, is long ago exploded. Authentic Japanese history dates from the third century, since when, and probably for ten centuries previously, down to the present day, the Mikado has always been the supreme power, the Son of the Gods, invisible, speaking only from behind a veil, but absolute master of Japan. From the eighth century, he resided at Kioto, surrounded by his court, and, when he called them together, the daimios, or feudal lords of the empire; but his authority was exercised by the " Kwambaku " (Keeper of the Inner Bolts), a kind of Grand Vizier, in whose hands were the army and the treasury, the Mikado himself having already become a mere idol.

Towards the end of the twelfth century these powers were snatched from the family in whose hands they had centred for hundreds of years, by the head of a rival house, who possessed himself of the richest part of Niphon, established a new capital, and, while theoretically commander-in-chief of the Mikado, became the practical master of Japan. This was the first Shogun, named Yoritomo, a vigorous monarch, who administered the power which he had usurped in the interests of the country, and governed it with honour and success for fifty years. Yoritomo's heirs, however, were feeble men, who soon became reduced to a dependence, like that of the Mikado, on powerful ministers, occupied with family aggrandizements and feudal quarrels; and, for nearly four centuries after the death of the first Shogun, the country was covered with blood and ruins by the struggles of the clans. Japan became a prey to military supremacy; every bond between man and man, except that of lord and vassal, was snapped; religion and the arts almost perished; and, though the Shogunate still existed, anarchy reigned.

Then a great man, named Taiko Sama, originally a groom, arose and was followed by great heirs. The Shogunate again became the controlling power in the state; and, by the opening of the seventeenth century, Yeasu, the successor of Taiko and builder of Jeddo, found himself absolute master of Japan, though nominally the vassal of the half-mysterious emperor. At this time the dual Government was in its apogee, the Mikado's divinity and supremacy were fully acknowledged, foreign commerce began to develop, the arts reached their culminating point, and the country was wisely administered by a powerful monarch. The immediate successors of Yeasu were also vigorous men, who continued his politic rule, and nothing of much moment occurred during their reigns except the Christian persecutions already alluded to, the final expulsion of the Portuguese, and the absolute closing of Japan to foreigners.

But even a strong central power could not vitally alter the character of a feudalism, the outcome of four hundred years of clan fighting, or destroy plotting on one side, which came to be met by surveillance and control on the other. The feudatories were played off one against the other, but every man was watched. The daimios were forbidden to see one another without leave, and forced to live at Jeddo during half of every year, their wives and children being left there as hostages when they visited their estates. Although disaffection was always latent, the clans, being without cohesion, were powerless during strong administrations; but there was no stable equilibrium in the situation, and the feuds of families might become dangerous at any moment under a weak ruler.

Such was the condition of Old Japan when Commodore Perry arrived in 1853, asking for a treaty of friendship with the United States, and prepared, if need be, to enforce his request. Perry's arrival profoundly disturbed and alarmed the whole country, one of its first effects being to unite the clans in a policy of resistance to the admission of the foreigners. The feudatories, indeed, began at once to cast cannon and build forts, loudly demanding of the Shogun the immediate expulsion of the foreigners. Meanwhile Perry, ignorant, like all the rest of the world, of the Mikadonal supremacy, had addressed his demands to Ii Kamon-no-Kami, the regent for a Shogun still in his minority. Ii Kamon-no-Kami was a man of powerful character, who, finding that Perry was not to be put off, and fully convinced of his power to insist on what he demanded, finally gave way, and signed a preliminary convention with the United States, without any reference to the court at Kioto, giving similar privileges to England and Russia later in the same year, equally on his own responsibility.

Four years later, at the close of the China war, Lord Elgin and Baron Gros appeared with a naval force in Jeddo Bay, and demanded an extended and definitive treaty. Convinced of the hopelessness of resistance, aware that reference to Kioto was only a farce, involving delays which might be dangerous, and with recent events in China before his eyes, the regent again gave way, and made the required agreements with the chief European Powers in 1858.

Upon this the anger of the feudatories broke forth, and clans which had nothing in common but disaffection to the Shogunate found themselves firmly united under a banner inscribed with the words, "Honour the Mikado, and death to the barbarians." Powerful as this watchword proved to bring the scattered feudal elements together, it was nevertheless a sham in the mouths of the four great southern clans, Satsuma, Choshiu, Tosa, and Hizen, who now put themselves at the head of the popular movement. The real object of this ambitious coalition was to raise itself to power on the ruins of the Shogunate, which had at length supplied the desired opportunity for effective attack by its disregard of the two strongest prejudices of the military caste, viz. veneration for the Mikado's divine power, and hatred of the foreigner. It must be remembered that the aristocracy and military caste have always formed the public opinion of Japan, the people being, as we have already seen, a mere inert mass, without any interest or influence in political affairs.

It was in the midst of a perfect tempest of excitement against the foreigner, and when the Mikado, at the instance of the coalition, was sending urgent orders to the "Bakufu," or Shogunal Government, for the expulsion of the "barbarians," that settlers began to establish themselves in Yokohama, where the first godown was opened in July, 1859. Then began a series of cowardly and murderous attacks upon Europeans by samurai and "ronins," or outlaws, belonging to one or other of the disaffected clans. Ii Kamon-no-Kami himself was one of the first victims, and such were now the relations between the Bakufu and its vassal clans, that the regent's successor was powerless either to check the evil or to punish the assassins. The foreign ministers made reclamation after reclamation, but without result, and, pressed on both sides, the position of the Shogun became daily more critical. At length the daimios openly refused to pay their contributions to the treasury, or live at Jeddo as they had been accustomed to do, but withdrew to Kioto, which city became a hotbed of intrigues against the Shogun.

While such was the attitude of the southern clans, the northern feudatories, and especially the Aidzu clan, remained faithful to the Shogunal interests, and at this time it happened that the capital and person of the Mikado, always in charge of one or other of the daimios, was defended by Aidzu. But the Mikado was a talisman whose possession was necessary to the success of the allied clans, for his edicts had the weight of divine authority, though he himself was a powerless mouthpiece in the hands of his guardians for the time being. An attack upon Kioto was accordingly made by Choshiu, with a view to securing the Mikado's person, but he was beaten by Aidzu, who, together with the Shogun, remained masters of the situation for the moment, and dragged from the Son of the Gods an order to punish Choshiu's attempt.

Two events now occurred which, for the first time, gave the Japanese incontestable proof of European power, and had great weight in the decision of important issues a few years later. Unable to obtain redress at the hands of the Bakufu for the murder of a Mr. Richardson, cut down, without provocation, and in broad daylight, by the retainers of Satsuma, the English bombarded Kagoshima, belonging to this prince, in 1863; while, in 1864, a combined squadron destroyed the batteries of Shimonoseki, whence Choshiu had fired upon foreign trading vessels entering the straits.

The defeat of Choshiu's attempt on Kioto had not disheartened the coalition of southern clans, but it now became evident that their military preparations, although ostensibly directed against the barbarians, were really aimed at the Shogun. The civil war, so long impending, between north and south, the partisans of the Shogun and Mikado respectively, at length broke out, and ended, after some years of conflict, in the overthrow of the former and death of the Shogun in 1866. Stotsbashi, the last of these rulers, unwillingly took up the reins, no longer of power, but declared himself ready to lay them down as soon as the daimios in council had fixed the bases of a new constitution. For this purpose he convened the princes of the empire at Kioto, when the four clans, now supreme from a military point of view, and prepared with a programme for the division of the spoils, proposed the abolition of the Shogunate and a return to the primitive constitution, or single rule of the Mikado, such as it was before the creation of the dual power by Yoritomo. Stotsbashi was forced to resign, but Aidzu, who was still in charge of the palace at Kioto, would not abandon the cause of the Shogunate without a struggle, and prepared for resistance. His troops were, however, surprised and replaced by those of the allied clans, himself and the Shogun retiring hastily to Osaka, and, in January, 1868, the Mikado, then a boy of twelve years, issued notices declaring the re-establishment of his sovereignty throughout the empire. The resistance of the northern clan was soon crushed. Aidzu marched on Kioto, but was defeated in a bloody battle at Fujimi, about five miles from the capital, while the deposed Shogun, whom he had persuaded to share his policy, was pursued to Jeddo, and forced into retirement. Such, after a duration of seven centuries, was the end of the Shogunate.

The foreign ministers, who were settled at Jeddo, observed a strict neutrality during the civil war, but a murderous attack on the British legation caused the retirement of all, except the American diplomats, from the capital to Yokohama. The settlement itself lived in constant fear of attack, until, upon the native governor having declared himself powerless to defend the Europeans, a number of French and English troops were quartered at the Bluffs as a matter of precaution, though happily their services were never required. The triumph of the four clans, however, was no sooner achieved, than the men who had proclaimed "Death to the barbarians" hastened to assure the foreigners of their friendship and peaceable intentions. The assassinations suddenly ceased. The representatives of the Powers were invited to present their credentials to the Mikado, and, for the first time in history, Europeans were admitted to an audience with the Son of the Gods. Japanese ambassadors were accredited to the more powerful foreign states, and, to the astonishment of everybody, Japan abandoned quite suddenly her old exclusive attitude, and presented herself for admittance into the family of civilized nations.

The hatred, or, more accurately perhaps, the fear, of foreigners was, however, none the less a reality in Japan; and if its new rulers were ready to ratify treaties which they had recently denounced, the explanation must be sought in the lessons which Satsuma and Choshiu had learned from the bombardment of Kagoshima and Shimonoseki. When, the restoration of the Mikado being effected, the samurai asked to be led against Yokohama, their instructed leaders said, "Wait; there is something to do first. We must borrow the arms, methods, and discipline of the barbarians before we can hope to expel them. Remember China." We deceive ourselves if we suppose that the rulers of Japan love us any more now than they did then. They have always dreaded lest foreign intercourse might result in foreign domination, and now bide their time—safe-guarding as best they can the independence and integrity of the country, and looking forward to becoming the equals of European states in the powers of offence and defence. As for the people, they know and care nothing about politics, but remain, what they have always been towards Europeans, polite, tolerant, and indifferent.

Scarcely was the revolution accomplished than the four clans begged the Mikado to take their territories and soldiers. It was apparently an act of suicide; but, while the whole world wondered, the request was granted, and the fall of the Shogunate was almost immediately followed by the destruction of the feudal system. The daimios were dispossessed and indemnified by pensions, which represented only a tenth part of their former incomes, while the Government charged itself with the support of the feudal soldiery who had hitherto been dependent on the lords. The samurai, as we have seen, were compensated, very inadequately, for the loss of their rice by pension-bonds, while, in place of a number of separate feudal forces, an imperial army was organized on European models. The great princes, from whom these astounding proposals came, were already masters of the empire, and obeyed or disregarded their own edicts as they pleased; but the smaller men were helpless and could not resist. The disestablished and disendowed daimios were once more obliged to live at Jeddo, and their fiefs were converted into provinces, of which they became simply revocable and nonhereditary governors, subject to the Imperial Council. Thus, within ten years, the coalition had destroyed the Shogunate and abolished the feudal system, and it now only remained for them to rule.

The new constitution consisted of the youthful Emperor and an Imperial Council, the mandatories of the four clans, who, with empty promises of representative institutions, took up the reins of power as the mere proxies of the coalition. But these men soon found that the throne of the Shogun was no bed of roses. They were obliged to satisfy not only the *parvenus* of the coalized clans and old functionaries of the Shogunate, whose reactionary influence they feared; but many followers of the dispossessed daimios, who, while they claimed a share of power, looked, in accordance with their ingrained feudal instincts, to their own lords for orders. Iwakura, Sanjo, Kido, Okuma, and Itagaki, the able leaders of the movement, apart, every minister in the Government represented the claims of his own clan, and the old aristocratic rule was replaced, not by a controlling central will or powerful public opinion, but by a factious and sometimes distracted oligarchy. The coalition was fettered from the outset by its coadjutors, men who could not be dispensed with, and whose discontent it was dangerous to brave. The situation was dominated by cabals. At one moment, Satsuma, the greatest of the princes and a cabinet minister, was in full rebellion, and, at another, some almost equally great men defied the edicts of the Government, whose energy was wasted in adjusting difficulties and making concessions. Public business in such an assembly could never be a steady, forward movement towards a definite goal, but was characterized by uncertainty and vacillation. They decided only to repent, began but did not finish, schemed but did not execute. It was a state of things having all the disadvantages of despotism without its power of following a definite line of action.

Such is the Government which signalized its accession to power by plunging into the path of European civilization with an ardour that astonished the world. This step meant, and still means, spending much money. The pensions of the feudal soldiery, wretched as they are, cost Japan one-fourth of its whole national income. The new naval and military expenditure forms one-fifth of the annual budget, and it is impossible to say how much money is laid out in the ostensible Europeanization of the country. But, headlong as the reform has been, its superficiality strikes the most unobservant traveller. There are two costly railways, which, however, do not tap the wealthy districts, and are comparatively valueless in the absence of roads. Timber cannot be felled, metals and minerals cannot be mined, petroleum wells cannot be sunk, rice even becomes a drug sometimes, for want of roads; while hothouse manufactories make a show of fostering the industries of the West on a soil which is unprepared for their reception. Only in naval and military reforms is any solid character to be discovered; the remaining Government enterprises are for the most part expensive playthings, which dazzle and deceive Europe without benefiting Japan. Meanwhile, the country which has started such a costly establishment has very little money, and the stock of that is rapidly diminishing. Japan parted with her gold "kobangs," ignorant of their value, many years ago, at ruinous prices, to the Dutch. There is nothing to indicate the existence of private hoards at the present day, and the Government, while claiming to have a reserve of ten millions sterling, is shrewdly suspected of empty coffers. On the other hand, there is more than twenty millions of paper money in circulation, an amount which is being daily increased, notwithstanding the depreciation of its value. The balance of trade is against the country to the extent in nearly a million pounds annually, and the exports of treasure have exceeded the imports by five millions during the last four years.

While such is the state of the national exchequer, the people begin to complain of their burdens. The agriculturists ask why the taxation should fall almost exclusively on land. All classes are clamouring for the abolition of the samurai pensions, and the Government is inundated with petitions pointing out the uselessness of this class, and begging for its immediate disendowment. Japan, indeed, constantly approaches a financial crisis, which must be met sooner or later, either by a new foreign loan, which, other sources of revenue being hypothecated, would demand material guarantees; the renunciation of an unprofitable external commerce, and a return to the old exclusive system; or the opening of the country to foreign enterprise. With regard to the first of these remedies, a foreign loan, involving a breach of national integrity and danger to the national independence, will be resisted to the last by the Government. The second is impossible, not only on account of the attitude which Europe would certainly take towards any proposals to close the country, but because her views would probably be backed by native objections. For, extravagances apart, Japan has spent some modest sums in effectively educating a number of her young men in the arts and sciences of Europe, thereby introducing a leaven whose influence might be found very powerful in deciding such a question, while the traders and artisans are, as we have already seen, decided gainers by the presence of the foreigner. There remains the question, whether the oligarchy which now rules Japan, incoherent in structure, weak in action, and afraid of European domination, will ever willingly consent to the complete opening of the country. This is the only means by which its resources can be developed or its present expenditure met, and towards this end the chief forces of the situation are working. A public opinion is arising even among the inert and docile masses of Japan. Already it makes itself heard in the popular outcry against the unfair incidence of taxation, and in the petitions against the burdensome samurai pensions. Time, self-interest, and the spread of European education, all favour its growth, which a native press will foster in spite of the muzzle. Feudality has committed *hara kiri*. Will the public voice of Japan, speaking through representative institutions, hereafter decree the death of class rule, and this strange, cultured, and interesting country enter, in fact as well as in word, on the path of modern progress? It is a question which no man can answer.

CHAPTER XI.

HONGKONG—CANTON.

November 28-30.

November 28.—After seven months of absence from England, we were once more on British soil. Hongkong, seized by the English in 1841, is a second Gibraltar, the most advanced of a line of outposts which, commencing with the Rock, extends through Malta, Aden, Ceylon, Penang, and Singapore, to Hongkong, dominating the south of Asia, and making the power of England felt in the extreme East.

The harbour of Hongkong is magnificent. The island itself is so disposed with regard to the mainland as to give the roadstead the appearance of a land-locked lake, surrounded by steep hills, bare and rugged, but tinted at sunrise and sunset with magical colours of rose and crimson. Victoria itself might be a Mediterranean town, so picturesquely do its embowered white houses cling to the hills which rise abruptly from the sea; but the place on near approach has an intensely English air. The town is full of handsome houses, which climb to the cool summit of the Peak, eighteen hundred feet high, becoming widely scattered at the higher elevations, where, however, there are many charming retreats from the heats of summer. A narrow strip of level land borders the sea, and is covered with fine offices and godowns, having wide Continental piazzas. The streets are well paved and well kept, furnished with capital English shops, shaded by trees, and full of sedan-chairs, carried on the shoulders of coolies by means of long bamboo poles. Here and there are handsome club-houses, which would not discredit Pall-Mall; while the hillside rising above the town has been terraced and transformed into beautiful sub-tropical gardens, where the military band plays, and all the world strolls in the afternoon. The street crowd is a very motley one; Chinese, English, French, Germans, and Parsees elbow one another, while here and there is a Sikh policeman or a Portuguese from Macao. Everybody is intent on his own business, and moves briskly, as if time were precious. The native quarter is like Chinatown, San Francisco, but dirtier and more odoriferous, and both its streets and people repel one after the cleanly and polished Japanese. European society is entirely English in character, being formal and exclusive; while the luxury of the wealthy classes far exceeds that of persons similarly situated at home. Balls, races, regattas, and *fêtes* of all kinds help to lighten the *ennui* of life, and the toilette is a cult commanding the enthusiastic devotion of the ladies.

The commercial supremacy of Shanghai allots a secondary part to Hongkong in regard to the Chinese trade; but its importance, though chiefly that of a naval and military station, is nevertheless considerable as a port. Here, however, as elsewhere, the days of immense profits are gone, never to return. A few great houses, the "merchant princes" of the East, once monopolised the China trade, and, before the native wants were accurately known, often made lucky hits which brought in enormous gains. There were then no banks or lenders, and everything was thrown into the hands of large capitalists. How these men lived, and how they entertained in the old days, all the world knows; but open houses are no longer kept in China, and the princely way of life is changed. Native requirements have been gauged. Money can be borrowed. German and Chinese traders have entered the lists, and, with the growth of competition, has come a corresponding diminution of individual gains, although the total returns are larger than ever. The Europeans kick against this state of things, and, while new comers and old firms alike bewail the good old times, there are strong spirits who would like to drive Manchester and Bradford goods farther up the country at the point of the bayonet. Commercial discontent is indeed a dangerous element in the relations of Europe and China.

No Englishman can visit Hongkong without experiencing a feeling of pride in his native country. The flag which floats above our antipodal Gibraltar is within signalling distance of home through a series of similar British stations; and gives, not only security to our exiled compatriots, but protection, justice, and prosperity to the native races who gather beneath its folds.

November 29.—We left Hongkong in one of the great river boats, built on American lines, which run up the shallow Pearl river to Canton daily. This is the first time we have ever sailed with loaded rifles in the saloon, and the bulk of our fellow-passengers secured below and guarded by an armed sentry. One of these steamers was attacked some years ago by a band of pirates, who, coming on board as passengers, rose upon and massacred all the Europeans, and made themselves masters of the vessel, since which time, the second-class Chinese have been stowed below, locked down, and guarded, while arms are put within reach of the whites.

There is nothing striking about the approach to Canton, except the immense extent of the low, brown-roofed town, from which rises one large building, the French cathedral, and a number of high square towers scattered among the houses. The last are pawn-shops, a sure sign of prosperity in a Chinese town, where articles of value are not so much pledged, as deposited for safety against theft and fire. Nor, as it seemed to us, without reason, for, at the moment of our arrival, a great conflagration was raging in Canton, and streets of flimsy houses were being burnt down almost as fast as a man could walk. The river is lined with little boats, each the home of a family, where one sees the mother, baby on back, giving an eye to another child or two, tethered by a piece of string to the gunwale, while she is cooking or otherwise attending to her domestic duties. A crowd of these boats, steered by women, surrounds the steamer on her arrival, holding on to her sides as best they can, while her paddles are still at full speed. The boatmen jump on board, snatching at baggage right and left, and hurrying into their skiffs, followed by distracted owners, who disembark at the imminent risk of drowning, amid jostling boats and the wild cries of the helmswomen.

We landed at Shamien, a small island, ceded to the British after the destruction of the old Canton factory in 1841, where all the foreign merchants reside. The well-kept quay is planted with banian trees, and the little colony, numbering less than fifty, live in charming houses, surrounded by gardens, and approached by good roads. Kind friends received us here, and, after a most agreeable tiffin, we began our exploration of the city, each in a sedan chair, and in charge of a Chinese guide. Canton is a labyrinth of passages—one cannot call them streets—about eight feet wide, bordered by high houses, and covered in above by screens, "glazed" with thin laminæ of oyster-shell, which admit light, but exclude the sun's fierce rays. The shops are very high, and open to the street, and beside each hangs a long vertical plank, lacquered, and gilded with some chosen device, such as "Great and Good," "Peace and Honour," by which, instead of his own name, the proprietor is exclusively known in all his business relations.

Within, is a little altar, dedicated to the god of wealth, and before it burns a fragrant joss-stick. The well-dressed shopkeeper is a picture of official decorum, and, with his two or three serious-looking clerks, bows with solemn politeness as customers enter. One street is devoted to silks, another to jade ornaments, a third to coffins, a fourth to butchers, and so on. The narrow alleys are paved with granite slabs, foul with slime, and choked with a flood of unclean men, through whom the chair-carriers make their way unceremoniously enough. All idea of locality is soon lost in these labyrinths, closely walled in as they are by high and sombre houses, and the ear is distracted by the strange raucous cries of street-sellers, which strike discordantly through the general drone of sound that rises from the crowd.

Returning from this scene to Shamien, across a bridge guarded by an iron gate, was like entering heaven after leaving pandemonium. On one side of the canal were the wide quays, leafy avenues, and well-appointed houses of the concession, the last already lighted for the decorous dinner; while, on the other, rolled a turbid stream of Chinamen, whose cold, unfriendly eyes we were glad to escape, and whose sinister murmur sounded like a perpetual " beware ! " addressed to the confident and careless ears of the settlement.

November 30.—Our chairs carry us rapidly from one sight to another. We visit the shops of the merchants who deal exclusively with Europeans, where, thanks to the introduction of our hosts, the finest silk embroideries, ivory carvings, porcelains, and a thousand other things are shown us by shopkeepers having the manners of diplomats. We see the delicate processes of lacquering in progress; a pair of great elephant's tusks under the graver, which has already been busy upon them for more than a year, and exquisite decorations in featherwork growing under skilful and pliant fingers. Then we are carried to a silk-weaver's, where magnificent brocades are produced, in a miserable little shop which one enters with disgust, by looms of the most primitive construction. These have no Jacquard cards, such as we found in use in Japan, but, in their place, a boy, who, by means of strings tied in a set order to the warp of the fabric, pulls up in sequence the threads proper for each passage of the shuttle. Hard by, is a glass-house, where we find our modern system of blowing an elongated bubble instead of spinning a flat plate centrifugally, in full operation; and finally we visit a street which is full of lapidaries' shops, where they are cutting armlets and earrings from hard green jade with rude wheels.

There are any number of temples and pagodas in Canton, notable for nothing but their filthy ruinous condition, and entire want of architectural interest. The most famous of these is the " Temple of the Five Hundred Gods," gilded statues of Buddhist sages and apostles, remarkable for the expression of the faces, but otherwise conventional and uninstructive figures. In one of the pagodas hangs the Bell of Canton, concerning which a popular superstition declared that the city would be lost when this bell should sound. A fracture now indicates the spot where a cannon-shot struck it by accident during our attack in 1842, and from that moment the defence of the city was considered hopeless.

The "Examination Hall" is a very curious place. The mandarins, or Chinese Government officials, are all appointed after competitive examinations, which are held once in every three years, and, if the country remains stationary under a system from which we expect advance, it is because the test of merit is mere scholasticism. The hall is a huge building containing several thousand cells, each only a few feet square, where sit the candidates, and at one end is an open space for the examiners. Our guide spoke English imperfectly, and before I had mastered his explanation, I took the place to be a yard for holding cattle shows. The famous water-clock of Canton is a dismal arrangement of four wooden tubs, standing one above the other on a dwarf staircase, each dripping slowly into the one below it, the last being furnished with a float, whose rise is measured on a graduated scale, and read in units of time. It is a device unworthy even of a barbarous country.

There is a Tartar Canton as well as a Chinese Canton. In the former, live the ruling race, who do not trade; their houses are scattered along wide, deserted streets, without shops, and hidden by blind walls, behind which no European ever penetrates. The latter is the home of commerce, while the suburbs are occupied by various industries, housed in the wretched way already noted in connection with silk-weaving. Both towns are surrounded by half-ruinous walls, armed with a few rusty old carronades, more like scrap-iron than artillery. One high temple on the walls gives the traveller a good general view of the city, exhibiting a confused medley of wooden and bamboo roofs, dominated by the mass of the French cathedral, the square towers of pawn-shops, and occasional pagodas, from whose crumbling eaves spring shrubs and waving grasses. Beyond the city, the level and cultivated valley of the Pearl river spreads widely, hemmed in by the "White Cloud" Mountains, and the whole landscape is drowned in pearly mist.

In one of the streets we met the *cortége* of a mandarin, on his way to administer justice. He was a fat man, with a pale yellow face, expressionless as a bronze, and occupied a pompous chair, shaded by umbrella-bearers. Before and behind him, clattered a barbaric military rout, and woe to the poor coolie who did not make way quickly as the great man threaded the crowded footways at a rapid walk! We did not follow him to the court, but turned aside to see the notorious prisons of Canton. Outside the walls lay half a dozen men, or rather living skeletons, fettered in such a way that change of attitude was impossible. Their looks were those of tortured animals—we could scarcely believe them men; and in view of an abyss of human degradation, hitherto utterly inconceivable, our pulses quickened and our cheeks burned with almost unbearable shame and indignation. Yet the crowd of natives took no notice of this spectacle "exposed to public derision." The boys squatted under the trees of the courtyard, gambling with all their souls for "sapéques;" and the restless, anxious life of the city went by, without a glance, either of pity or disgust, at the terrible exhibition. Next, at the end of long, obscure and filthy passages, a heavy gate admitted us to a court, reeking with the sickening odour of the foul humanity— humanity!—which lay, sat, or crouched, in such positions as its fetters permitted, behind a grating of strong wooden bars. Moving their manacled limbs we knew not how, a crowd of fierce grinning creatures threw themselves towards the grill, with hands outstretched for alms. Instinctively we recoiled, as if from a physical danger, in presence of these horrible, unhumanized men. Were these things ever men, with mothers, perhaps wives and children? It was difficult to believe it; so deformed and so degraded were they that even sweet pity was for a moment lost in fear, as we watched these worse than wild beasts in their filthy lair. Justice in China has but one weapon, viz. cruelty. The court is a torture-room, the prison is a hell, and the execution-ground a field of inhuman carnage. Captain Cooper, one of our fellow-guests at Shamien, told us that, having once occasion to watch a case of piracy in court, he saw a witness (not a prisoner) bastinadoed until his testimony was made to tally with the judge's ideas of what it ought to be, and worse tortures are always at hand waiting the magistrate's orders.

The execution-ground is a long, narrow alley, where about thirty criminals a week are decapitated. A line of condemned men files before the judge, by whose side stands the executioner, who, with a single stroke of a sword, takes one head after the other, the whole thing occupying only a few minutes. Such a scene was described to us by a European eye-witness, who had seen seven men thus beheaded. For ourselves, we could not find courage to face a similar tragedy. We had supped full of horrors at the prisons, and were glad when evening found us once more seated at the bright Shamien dinner-table, where we tried to forget that, within a few yards of us, nearly a million of our fellow-men were living under conditions which would make existence intolerable for us, and dying, when semi-starvation has driven them to crime, by legalized torture. We left Canton without regret, watching from the deck of the *Powan* steamer a beautiful sunset folding its crimson wings over the seething city, already dim and silenced by distance; and hardly able to realize, when the low brown roofs had slid into obscurity, that such a human ant-heap existed anywhere on the banks of the still and peaceful-looking river.

The Chinaman is a serious man of affairs, gifted, like the Jew, for commerce, and, like him, determined to make money. His commercial morality is high enough to keep him from cheating when cheating hurts his interests, or may endanger future transactions, and he is industrious, exact, and punctual. But no kindly smiles light up his set, yellow face; there is no welcome in his eyes as the foreigner passes, no *bonhomie* towards his compatriots. The Muses are apparently quite neglected in China; the oldest temples in Canton exhibit no traces of architectural power, and such art as now flourishes is minute and slavishly imitative. Its professors are little better than coolies, who pass their lives lacquering, embroidering silk, or carving ivory, imprisoned in the narrow shops of densely crowded streets, without a possibility of contact with nature, and reproducing set patterns for a remuneration of twenty-five cents a day. Of music we heard none, while the "literary classes," as they are called, know how to turn ingenious couplets or write sophistical essays, but are ignorant of all useful or exact knowledge. The appearance of the Chinese is unprepossessing, the few women one sees are repulsively ugly, and the people are without the Japanese cleanliness, whether in street, house, or person.

Although for so long a period in contact with Western civilization, the Chinese still refuse to make use of its material advantages. But if they will have nothing to do with the railway and telegraph, it is not because they do not appreciate the value of these inventions. Their adoption of our ideas, in all that relates to naval and military works, sufficiently proves how competent they are to appraise the value of practical science, but, while they trade with the foreigner, they resent his presence, and would rather make communication more difficult than easier. They understand our civilization well enough, but they will adopt it only when they choose to do so, and meanwhile every Chinaman lives in hope of the day arriving when the last foreigner shall be cleared from the soil of his country.

It is a pity that a people with many excellent, if few amiable qualities, should stagnate under an alien, tyrannous and corrupt rule. The administration is founded on falsehood; the public funds are diverted to official pockets; justice is bought and sold; the miserable condition of the people is disregarded, and the country is at the mercy of rapacious and venal mandarins. But China may even yet strike a blow for national freedom; and the day which gives this country a powerful and enlightened Government will introduce to the Western world one of the most dangerous commercial competitors she has ever yet encountered.

CHAPTER XII.

THE STRAITS SETTLEMENTS.

December 1–10.

December 1–6.—The Pacific and Oriental steamer *Teheran* received us on our return from Canton, and, on the afternoon of the 1st, we saw the coast of China, painted in splendid sunset hues, fading in the distance. We had enjoyed an evening fire in Hongkong, but were glad to be under the punkah before night fell. From the warm waters of the China Sea rise masses of vapour, which condense in the north-east monsoon, forming a pall of grey cloud overhead, or distilling in a thick "Scotch mist." The air is hot and "muggy," everything is clammy to the touch, and everybody searches his wardrobe for lighter clothes. It is a foretaste of the tropics.

December 7.—And this is tropical Singapore? A little island about one-third larger than the Isle of Wight, of low rounded hills, with narrow valleys, and a surface which presents the aspect of one continuous forest. The ship was scarcely at anchor when she was surrounded by a fleet of small, dug-out canoes, each carrying two or three brown Malay boys, naked except for their waist-cloths, who shouted, "All right, sah, have a dive! have a dive!" until we threw overboard some small silver coin, when they turned quickly out of their crazy craft, and struggled for its possession under water. The wharf was crowded with "Klings," or Tamils, immigrants from the Madras coast, who far outnumber the Malays, and run them hard as competitors in every occupation. These are some of the finest fellows I have ever seen, tall, well-made, and handsome, their smooth dark skins set off by a bright cotton garment wound around the waist, and exposing sometimes only the lower leg, sometimes the whole thigh. It was a pleasure to look at their comely bodies after those of the ungainly Chinese. One of them came on board, offering change from a bag of dollars on his shoulder. It was really startling to see this fine, fat, white-haired, and white-whiskered man of business, with a face like a Lombard street banker's, but—without any clothes to speak of.

Singapore is three miles from the harbour, and we walked across the wharf to a "gharry" (one-horse cab) between rows of brilliant parrots, baskets of pine-apples, mangustans, green cocoa-nuts, and bananas, all exposed for sale. The wayside is bordered with palms and tropical trees, but brilliant flowers, saving the lovely crimson hybiscus, are not numerous. Here, for the first time, we saw the cocoa-nut palm and the still more striking "traveller's palm," a graceful vegetable fan, some twenty or thirty feet high. The native cottages are raised on piles, a "survival" from times when the Malays lived exclusively afloat, and built over the water.

In the settlement we found, as usual, a kind welcome following on the presentation of our introduction, and excellent company at the club, where we took tiffin. Singapore is something more than a port at which steamers touch for coal on the way to China. It has a population of nearly a hundred and fifty thousand souls, an export trade of four millions, and imports of equal value. The former are so various that trade fluctuates but little, while the latter are large, because Singapore has become the centre whence Bankok and Saigon, together with all the smaller ports on the coast, are supplied. The most striking feature of the settlement is the numerical and commercial predominance of the Chinese, who are far more prosperous under British rule than in their own corruptly governed country. There are a hundred thousand of them in the town, and, to quote our host, one of the leading merchants, a member of the Colonial Council, and, above all, a cautious Scotchman, "the prosperity of the Straits Settlements, and especially of Singapore, is based on the Chinaman." They are the cultivators who grow tobacco in Sumatra and pepper in Penang, the miners who dig tin in Banca, and the tradesmen, *par excellence*, of the Straits. The whole of the coasting trade is in their hands, and they own land and houses as largely as they do ships. Contrary to what is said of them in America, and too often repeated by Englishmen, they settle permanently in their adopted country, become freeholders, and educate their sons to follow in their footsteps. Many of these men are very wealthy, and live in luxurious style, earning the respect of all unprejudiced Europeans by the good sense with which they dispense their riches. Next to the Chinese in numbers, are the Tamils, who ply every trade, from that of boatman to huckster. These picturesque fellows squat in the streets, selling pine-apples or betel, or keep dirty little shops, where cheap hard and soft wares are sold at ridiculously low prices. Their lips and teeth are stained with betel, and they like to lie in easy attitudes in the shade, being satisfied with little, and destitute of the Chinese commercial spirit. As for the native Malays, they are a short, dark race, without much enterprise or energy and without arts. They make good coachmen and personal servants, but seem to be altogether swamped by the Chinese and Tamils.

After tiffin, we strolled through the native town and markets, where we found Chinese in all the best shops. The town is European in appearance, with white stone houses and green jalousies, reminding us of Italy. On the market stalls we found a fauna and flora entirely new to our experience. Strange and brilliant fishes; ve.etables whose names we do not know, together with mangustans, cocoa-nuts, pumelos, sugar-cane, and durian— the prickly fruit which Mr. Wallace cannot praise too highly, but which few European noses can tolerate.

The foreign merchants live out of town in fine houses, surrounded by large and well-kept gardens. Sometimes one sees a house that might have been transported from Wimbledon Common, but with a lawn shaded by cocoa-palms, up one of whose tall smooth stems, perhaps, a native servant is climbing, knife in hand, to cut green nuts for the curry which forms part of every dinner in the East. The English will certainly carry their athletics to the warmer of the two next worlds, for here are cricket and tennis in full blast at three o'clock in the afternoon, under an almost vertical sun! Thanks to the daily drenching rain, Singapore has excellent turf, and this is how our energetic countrymen turn it to account.

The botanical gardens are a great feature in the settlement. They are laid out in landscape style, with undulating grounds of brilliant turf and well-arranged groups of trees. It seemed strange to see large bushes of stephanotis and alamanda, covered respectively with their fragrant and yellow blossoms; while vincas, dracænas, and caladiums thrive in the open more perfectly than they do under glass with us.

We dined with our friends in one of those spacious and charming houses wherein these exiled merchants so well know how to bring together comfort, luxury, and agreeable society. In the East all the world is young, and married men are the exception; but the bachelors certainly manage their houses well, and, if some graces are absent, entertainment lacks neither order nor refinement. The table was a *parterre* of what we should call "rare exotics," common flowers here; evening costume consisted of a becoming suit of white jean; the servants were Chinese, silent and perfect as usual; and the dishes, especially the curries, delicious. Overhead swung the great punkahs. Now and then a pretty lizard made a rapid run along the wall, hunting insects which we could not see; or a great moth circled slowly around the wax lights. The evening sea-breeze filled the room with over-sweet odours, robbed from the garden without, and the talk was of colonial interests, politics, and gossip. It was tropical home life, full of new colour and charm for us, but colourless enough to these exiles, who, throughout the East never cease to suffer from *ennui* and homesickness.

December 8-9.—Once more we were afloat, and upon a sea which has been made classical by Mr. Wallace's researches on the distribution of animal life. It was Mr. Earl who first pointed out, in a paper read before the Geographical Society in 1845, that "a shallow sea connects the islands of Sumatra, Java, and Borneo with the Asiatic continent, with which their natural productions generally agree; while a shallow sea also connects New Guinea and some of the adjacent islands to Australia, all being characterized by the presence of marsupials." Following up this clue, Mr. Wallace, a few years later, drew his famous "line" among the islands of the Malay Archipelago, dividing them so that, in regard to their zoology, those on one side of the frontier belong to Asia, and those on the other to Australia.

"Wallace's line" coincides with a sea of great depth, which cuts diagonally north-east and south-west across the archipelago, and has so well defined a boundary that it passes in one instance between two islands, Bali and Lombok, only fifteen miles apart, of which the first, situated in the shallow sea, possesses an Asian fauna; while the animals of the latter, rooted in a profound ocean, are purely Australian in their affinities. The wide expanse of sea which divides Java, Sumatra, and Borneo from each other, and from Malacca and Siam, is so shallow that ships can anchor in any part of it, and it is supposed that the continent of Asia extended over the whole of this area at a very recent geological period. The islands east of Java and Borneo, on the other hand, were probably never connected with India, but formed part of a former Australian or Pacific continent. It is indeed remarkable thus to find islands in the same archipelago, constructed on the same pattern, subjected to the same climate, and washed by the same oceans, yet exhibiting the greatest possible contrast in their animal productions. "Nowhere," to quote Mr. Wallace, "does the ancient doctrine—that differences of similarities in the various forms of life that inhabit different countries are due to corresponding physical differences or similarities in the countries themselves—meet with so direct and palpable a contradiction. Borneo and New Guinea, as alike physically as two distinct countries can be, are zoologically as wide as the poles asunder; while Australia, with its dry winds, open plains, stony deserts, and temperate climate, yet produces birds and quadrupeds which are closely related to those inhabiting the hot, damp, luxuriant forests which everywhere clothe the mountains of New Guinea."

A similar line separates the races of the archipelago into Malays and Papuans, who are radically different, physically, mentally, and morally; but this boundary lies somewhat east of the zoological frontier—a circumstance which, taking into consideration the power that man possesses of traversing the sea, "appears very significant of the same causes having influenced the distribution of mankind that have determined the range of other animal forms. . . . It is certainly a wonderful and unexpected fact that an accurate knowledge of the distribution of birds and insects should enable us to map out lands and continents which disappeared beneath the ocean long before the earliest traditions of the human race. Wherever the geologist can explore the earth's surface, he can read much of its past history, and can determine approximately its latest movements above and below sea-level; but wherever oceans and seas now extend, he can do nothing but speculate on the very limited data afforded by the depths of the

z

waters. Here the naturalist steps in, and enables him to fill up this great gap in the past history of the earth."*

December 10.—We reached Penang at daybreak, and, as the ship was notified to leave again at noon, hastened ashore after a hurried breakfast. Penang, or the "Areca Palm Island," is smaller than the Isle of Wight, and consists of a mass of granite, with peaks rising to elevations of three thousand feet, the whole bordered by an alluvial flat, only a few feet above sea-level, and covered for the most part with virgin forest. We took possession of it in 1786, the British Government of India having long desired a naval station on the eastern side of the Bay of Bengal. It was then an uninhabited island, belonging to Queda, a tributary of Siam, and a romantic story says that Mr. Francis Light, who first brought the station to the notice of the East India Company, married the daughter of the King of Queda, and received with her as a dowry the island of Penang, which he sold to the British. As matter of fact, however, the Rajah of Queda did not give his desert island to any one, but sold it to this country for a quit-rent of ten thousand Spanish dollars per annum, Francis Light being the agent in the transaction and the first Governor of the settlement.

A splendid crew of Tamils took us off the ship in a queer boat, having painted eyes at the bow and ending in two horn-like projections astern. The Tamils and the Chinese together, appear to have crowded out the Malays, of whom one sees few in the town, though some of their boats lay around the steamer. Here we discharged a deck cargo of some sixty or seventy Chinese coolies on their way to the tobacco plantations of Sumatra. The "coolie traffic" is now at an end. When a planter wants men he contracts with a "coolie broker" in Hongkong or Macao, who gets the required number of labourers together, puts them on board a passenger steamer, and pays their fare to the Straits. Upon their arrival, the planter advances from thirty to forty dollars per man, which pays the passage money, broker's commission, and a small remittance to relatives in China, leaving about eight dollars in the

* "The Malay Archipelago," by A. R. Wallace.

coolie's hands. The latter signs an agreement to work for one year, advances in kind being made him, and a dwelling found. He clears land and plants tobacco, which the planter takes off his hands at a fixed price, and, at the end of the year, if the advances are not worked out, another contract is made, the man being free to go as soon as he is out of debt, or at the end of three years if still in debt. In the latter case he is of little value to his employer, but generally speaking Chinese coolies free themselves in the first year, after which industrious men can save a hundred dollars per annum. For the careful cultivation which tobacco requires, Chinamen are preferable to the Tamils, who grow coarser crops well, and are excellent managers of horses and bullocks, about which the yellow man knows but little. The planters are careful of the men's health, insisting on cleanliness and sanitation, notwithstanding which they lose a good many coolies, the sun and newly cleared jungle being the chief sources of mortality, though loose living carries off not a few.

The vegetation of Penang is more strikingly tropical than that of Singapore. There are real " Palm groves " here, and the drier atmosphere fosters plants which cannot stand the perpetual rains of the latter place. The harbour is full of shipping, all owned by the Chinese. Tin and pepper are the chief exports, but the trade of this port is on a much smaller scale than that of Singapore.

We cannot help admiring as we proceed the conquests of British commerce, and the splendid spirit of our race, which is daunted neither by climate, distance, political and natural difficulties, nor absence from the things men prize the most. At all the important posts on the way to the far East stand these fragments of England; free ports, administered in the interests of free trade, and with great incidental advantage to native and immigrant races, who, while they prosper under our flag, are working, without knowing it, for the aggrandizement of Britain.

CHAPTER XIII.

CEYLON.

December 11-24.

December 11-13.—We have been on board the *Teheran* for nearly a fortnight, and although society in a Peninsular and Oriental ship, being more exclusively British, is always stiffer and less agreeable than that of a Messageries steamer, the days as usual afloat, seem too short. There is a sweet tranquility and ease about life on board ship in the absence of bad weather, which suit tropical heat and physical languor very well. Our cabin is a snug private room, where everything is always ready to hand. There is neither packing nor unpacking. Our little library is nicely arranged on an empty berth, and we can join the world, or retire to sleep, read, or write when we like. On deck are long chairs, whose arms support our languid legs; and if the society, being English, is very dignified and a little dull, we have been fortunate enough to find a few congenial spirits with whom to discuss questions of interest or talk nonsense at will. Of course it is hot, moist air at 80° in the tropics being more exhausting than a dry heat of 90° in Western America. The morning tub is a momentary heaven, but a printed edict restricts the enjoyment of this paradise to ten minutes, and there is always a queue of impatient men waiting outside the door of the bath-room. The sea is as smooth as a mirror and as blue as a dye-vat; if she were not a steamer, the *Teheran* would be like a "painted ship upon a painted ocean;" yet we see no strange water creatures, of which we supposed the tropical sea would be as full as the tanks of the Brighton Aquarium are of sea-anemones. There are plenty of "bonitos," however, flying away from the bows, and we try to understand their " mode of motion." They rise from the sea and launch into the air, at a very low angle, the final strokes of the tail leaving a series of undulations, like the last ripples of a successful "dick, duck, drake," on the smooth surface of the water. Their longest flights seem about two hundred yards in length, and are sometimes straight, sometimes zigzag and very swift. Notwithstanding the bird-like motion of flying-fish, it is very unlikely that organs which are effective for propulsion in water can be used to much purpose in air, and we conclude that they probably leap rather than fly, leaving the sea with astonishing velocity, and presenting very little surface to aerial resistance. When in mid-ocean we passed through several large patches of floating organisms, which gave the water an ochreous red appearance. They were, doubtless, "salpæ," the small associated molluscs which form the whale-food " of other latitudes; but the quarter-master, who promised to get us a sample in a bucket, proved faithless, and we lost the opportunity of a microscopic inspection.

December 14–15.—Ceylon was sighted at noon, and a few hours later the pilot boarded us from one of those queer boats of which every one has seen models—a simple wooden tube, hollowed from a palm, and steadied by a floating spar lashed to the ends of two long out-riggers. We asked in dismay how we were going ashore with our baggage in a craft where there is only just room for a man to stow his legs between the gunwales; but our anxiety was premature, as there were plenty of big boats waiting for passengers. Galle harbour is a semicircle, half enclosing a small anchorage, full of coral rocks, and imperfectly protected from the southern swell, which rolls in with great force when the monsoon is strong. The crescent-shaped shore is covered to the very margin of the sea with cocoa-nut palms; the blue water is alive with outriggers, and the shallows are carpeted with the brilliant tints of living corals.

We stepped ashore into blazing heat, and were followed to the doors of the Oriental Hotel by a crowd of loafers, peddlers, and mendicants. The hotel piazza was occupied by merchants of precious stones, silver jewellery, inlaid boxes, and ivory carvings, chiefly rubbish; and debilitated loungers looked languidly at the display, while a motley throng of snake-charmers, jugglers, blind and other beggars, filled the road. The most striking element of the crowd is the Cinghalese himself, whose white wraps, effeminate looks, and long black hair confined by a crescent-shaped tortoiseshell comb, make him look exactly like a woman. Native costume consists of a cotton sheet wrapped round the waist, with one end thrown gracefully over the shoulder, but civilization has changed the upper half of the Cinghalese man very much for the worse. When one shouts "Boy!" in the hotel, it is ludicrous to be answered by a grave, white-whiskered old gentleman, with a grey chignon and great comb, petticoated as to his nether end, but otherwise clad in a black cloth jacket, white waistcoat, and spotless shirt-front, like a Paris *garçon*. Women retain the native costume, a white wrap for petticoat, and a short white jacket which falls from the shoulders almost to the waist, exposing a narrow band of dark skin, looking like a brown silk sash. The men are far better looking than the women, but the children, and especially the boys, are superb—clean limbed, with skin like satin and faces like cherubs, having large, lustrous, and intensely black eyes, and a smile such as Greuze painted; they look like lovely girls, and wear very little to spoil their beauty. The crowd is composed of many races. The Tamils are here in force, ousting the indolent Cinghalese, as they do the apathetic Malays, from all the hard-working employments, and are notable for their erect carriage, fine forms, handsome faces, and fondness for brilliant colours. Then there are Afghans, the travelling money-lenders of Ceylon, tall, Jewish-looking, and handsomely dressed, carrying their hooked noses high among races whom they evidently despise. And here is the "Moorman," big, sleek, and well-to-do, a Mahometan by religion, and the trader, *par excellence*, of the island. The folds of his ample robes are full of precious stones, for any of which, if he asks fifty pounds, he will take fifty shillings, and make cent. per cent. on the transaction.

The town of Galle is entered through an old brick archway, still carrying the arms and monogram of the Dutch East India Company, "Vereenigte Oost Indische Co.," and the date, 1669; while to the right and left of this not very imposing relic of mercantile supremacy some queer old fortifications skirt the shore. Behind these "defences" straggle a few poor streets, whose houses are European in aspect, very small and dirty, and inhabited by the lower classes, who seem to make up the chief population of Galle. The town, indeed, is only a point where ships touch; there are not more than a hundred Europeans in the place, and trade centres at Colombo, for which place we started by stage on

December 16.—The road, seventy-two miles in length, follows the coast all the way, being sometimes nearer and sometimes farther from the sea. The way is lined with cocoa palms and bananas, with here and there a breadfruit tree, conspicuous by its large, deeply notched leaves and hanging fruit. The cocoa-nut thrives best close to the sea, and sometimes actually overhangs the water, whence the fringe of tropical foliage which is such a striking feature of Ceylon. The villages are small and scattered, with low, smoke-begrimed houses, or rather huts, built of palm ribs smeared with mud, and with roofs of palm leaves. Shops alternate with dwellings, their open fronts displaying peppers, betel, and dried fish. Inside, squats the shopkeeper, while his wife is cooking in a grimy earthen pot over a tiny fire. The people lie about on the thresholds or within the houses, and are evidently neither industrious nor clean, while the pretty children run quite naked from house to house, or hide behind their mothers' skirts as we pass. There is no cultivation along the road, which is bordered by palms and rank undergrowth, the natives depending entirely on the cocoa-nut. Every man who lounges about one of the wayside mud huts owns perhaps twenty or thirty of the trees around it, and these he protects from thieves by wrapping the trunks with dry palm branches, whose rustling will warn him of night intruders. The milk of the green nuts is his drink, their flesh is his food, the palm flowers bleed "toddy" for him, the midribs of the leaves form his house, and from the leaves themselves he makes every household vessel except the earthen pot. The fibre furnishes material for his only industry, the making of coir rope, at which we see the women working, their wrists covered with silver bangles, and their ears and great toes adorned with silver rings.

The road is alive with foot-passengers and vehicles, the latter drawn by the pretty little humped oxen (*Bos indicus*), which are trained to trot between the shafts of light spring carts. The bullocks' hides are scored with ornamental designs, sketched with a branding-iron, and one meets some spanking turn-outs, both in single and double harness. The heavy traffic is carried on large bullock carts, drawn by teams of much finer animals, the driver sitting on the pole between his beasts, and guiding them partly by rope reins passed through the nostrils, and partly by signal-blows of a stick. All the children and many of the men we meet are beggars; the former throw a flower or bunch of sweet-smelling grass into the coach, saying, "That my present," and wait for acknowledgments in coin, while adult peddlars of sticks, green nutmegs, cocoa-nuts, precious stones, and cinnamon bark, worry the traveller at every step. Now and then the road skirts the shore, a stretch of white coral sand, strewn with big beach stones, also of coral, which the villagers collect and store for building purposes. Great waves of blue-green water break on the coast even in the calmest weather, and the high-tide mark is lined with cocoa palms, whose crowns hang so far seaward that nuts sometimes drop into the water. The country traversed is gneiss, overlaid by a deep soil of red clay, a kind of laterite, locally called ".cabook," derived apparently from the decomposition of the underlying rock, and thick in the lowlands, where it has been brought down by rain, but thinner on the uplands. It is hard and tenacious enough to be dug out in blocks, which are dried and then used as bricks for building.

From Kalutara, forty-two miles from Galle, there is a railway to Colombo, the line skirting the coast like the road, and passing through similar scenery. Colombo is a great square white town, the head-quarters of trade, and centre of a large European society. Its harbour is more exposed than that of Galle, and is in course of being protected by a pier, when it will become the rendezvous of all the steamers, as it is already of the ships of the Messageries Maritimes. The "Pettah," or native town, is extensive, but dirty and uninteresting, with wooden houses, dark, crowded, and unsavoury. The costumes are brighter than at Galle, thanks to the prevalence of Tamils, who are here so numerous that the native Cinghalese are lost sight of altogether.

December 17.—Four-fifths of Ceylon consists of flat land bordering the ocean, and called the "maritime provinces." The remaining fifth of the surface is occupied by the "hill-country," a complicated system of mountain ranges, whose highest peaks rise to heights of seven and eight thousand feet, and upon whose slopes lie the coffee plantations. Among these hills, a hundred and twenty miles from Colombo, and fifty miles from Kandy, lies Nuwara-Eliya, one of the most beautiful stations in Ceylon, six thousand two hundred feet above sea-level, situated in the heart of a coffee and cinchona district, and within reach of Pederotallagalla, the highest peak in the island.

We left Colombo for Nuwara-Eliya by the Kandy Railroad, which traverses nearly ninety miles of our route; and passing rapidly through a level country, densely covered with palms, and cleared here and there for rice, soon began to scale the hills by a series of sharp inclines. Palms now gave way to jungle, which clothes the mountains to their summits, except where the forest is broken by "patenas," open parklike expanses of grassy country, sparsely sprinkled with large rhododendrons. It is generally believed that the whole surface of the hill country was once covered with grass, and that the jungle is gradually encroaching on the patenas; but the soil of the latter seems perfectly well adapted to the growth of trees, and cannot, in fact, be distinguished from that of the forest. It is more likely that the jungle once covered all the country, and patenas are formed when, from some cause, the land will no longer carry trees.

The railway ends at Gampola, whence we staged to Rambodda, the road rising all the way. At an elevation of about two thousand five hundred feet the jungle is, for the first time, broken by coffee plantations. White bungalows and great coffee stores began to dot the hill-sides, and we were soon in the heart of the chief coffee-growing district of the island. The road is a fine piece of engineering, winding along hill-sides and skirting ravines, with a wide well-made tract of macadam, from which excellent by-ways diverge to the various coffee estates. We constantly met, or passed, trains of bullock-carts, either taking rice up to, or bringing coffee down from the plantations, and always in charge of Tamil drivers. Rambodda is about three thousand five hundred feet above the sea, and from this place to Nuwara-Eliya the road rises nearly three thousand feet in fourteen miles; so we were now shifted into a light trap, and our bags packed on the heads of coolies. We got new views of a broken and wooded mountain country with every fresh zigzag of the ascent, and found it very cold before we reached the top. As we rose, the flora changed noticeably from that of the plain, blackberry, bracken, and other familiar European plants making their appearance at the higher elevations. Presently, coffee plantations began to give way to cinchona clearings, and a little tea occurred after coffee had been left behind. The summit of the hill was enveloped in a cold mist, and we were glad to see a wood fire burning on the hearth upon our arrival at the hotel. The hotel garden was bright with gladioli and geraniums, and its pretty grounds were planted with pines and cedars which thrive in our own climate, while the hedges were draped with the "datura," a beautiful flower, like a long white lily, called the "devil's trumpet" in Ceylon.

December 18.—Nuwara-Eliya stands on a wide, undulating plain of patena, covered with short turf, sprinkled with rhododendrons, and surrounded by hills, whose sides are either newly planted with cinchona trees, or in course of clearing for their cultivation. The grassy meadow; the little stream; the wide, white road; and cattle grazing here and there, gave the scene such a thoroughly English air that it was difficult to believe we had left bananas and cocoa palms behind us only a few hours ago. At seven o'clock we started to make the ascent of Pederotallagalla, eight thousand three hundred feet above sea-level, and the highest peak in Ceylon. Leaving the hotel, we found the country covered with hoar-frost, and the air was keen. The trail led through jungle, composed almost exclusively of "kina," a kind of small live oak, like a conifer in appearance, springing from a dense undergrowth, quite impenetrable without an axe. Our first acquaintance with a tropical forest was a disenchantment. The trees were insignificant in size, and the foliage monotonous in colour. There were no flowers, animals, or sounds of birds and insects. We disturbed one jungle-cock on the way, but that was all the game we saw. We are told that elephants roam the patenas around Nuwara-Eliya, and frequent the jungle for the sake of the bamboo grass. They know perfectly well where this grows, and make regular rounds of the country, eating it down in place after place successively, and returning over the same ground when the grass has grown again. Elk and cheetah are sometimes found in the forest, where the cobra, the whip-snake, and brown snake harbour, together with the harmless rat-snake, which grows to a length of nine feet. The "wanderoo" monkey lives among the tree-trops; but we were not fortunate enough to see one, neither did we observe an insect of any kind. The trees were draped with orchids, none of which had brilliant flowers. Blackberry, trefoil, dandelion, daisies, buttercups, violets, barberry, and briar grow in the neighbourhood of Nuwara-Eliya, and we found several of these familiar plants on the summit of Pederotallagalla, silently suggesting the dark question, "How did *we* come here, across those torrid plains below?" The view from Ceylon's highest peak is of high ridges, sloping suddenly down to lower grounds of tumbled, wooded hills with patches of open patena here and there. No streams are seen, and everything is tinted with a monotonous green.

December 19-20.—The coffee raised in Ceylon is chiefly "Arab," which flourishes best at elevations of from three to five thousand feet. It grows in bushes, which are usually topped about four feet from the ground, for the sake of convenience in picking. The fruit, when ripe, is cherry-like in appearance, and, after being gathered, is soaked for a time in water, and then "pulped," or stripped of its fleshy envelope. The berries, which are covered with a closely adherent membrane, called the "parchment," are dried in the sun upon asphalt floors, or "barbecues," and passed through a machine, which shells off the parchment, leaving the coffee ready for market. Jungle land, fit for coffee-growing, used to be sold by the Government at prices averaging £5 per acre. Clearing costs £2, and planting £15 per acre. The annual cost of cultivation, after the first two years, is £10 per acre, and the yield of coffee varies from five to eight hundredweight per acre, while its price fluctuates from £3 to £5 per hundredweight. It will be seen that a planter, settled on fertile soil, raising good crops, and realizing high prices, must make large profits, and many fine fortunes have indeed been realised in Ceylon. But, at the present moment, the coffee plant is suffering fearfully from the attack of a fungus (*Hemileia vastatrix*), and the yield of coffee, in the districts most affected, has been reduced by two-thirds. Although the life history of the pest has been made out by experts, no effectual remedy for its ravages has yet been suggested. It seems probable, indeed, that the true cause of the mischief lies in slovenly cultivation. For forty years, the unterraced hill-sides of Ceylon have been losing soil in the rainy seasons, while, during the same period, there has been practically no manuring of the land. Coffee, in fact, has been allowed to wear itself out in Ceylon.

Alarmed at this serious state of things, planters are looking about them for a second string to their bow, and at the present moment every one is planting cinchona. This tree flourishes at elevations where coffee dies out, and immense areas of jungle are now being cleared at heights of from four to six thousand feet. The cinchona seeds are sown in "nurseries," and, at a few months old, the seedlings are planted out, making a fine growth in five years, and yielding bark in eight years. There is scarcely a cinchona tree of this age in the island yet, but if all the plants already in the ground should prove successful, there will probably be a startling drop in the price of quinine a few years hence.

The fear of *Hemileia* has also led to the introduction of Liberian coffee, an African species which grows on the low grounds. A great deal is hoped from the new comer, but very little is definitely known about it at present. The plant has hitherto escaped attack by the leaf disease, but its produce is said to be of inferior quality, and only saleable when mixed with other coffee. India-rubber and cocoa have also been planted, the former experimentally, the latter on a larger and paying scale, but it will be many years before Ceylon can establish a successful rival to coffee.

December 21-22.—Kandy, the capital, was our next objective, to reach which we retraced our steps from Nuwara-Eliya to Gampola, whence a few miles of railway brought us to our destination. On the way we visited the Government botanical gardens at Peradeniya, where we were very kindly received by Dr. Trimen, the director. The object of this establishment is to cultivate a variety of tropical plants, those of commercial value receiving most attention, and to furnish planters with useful information concerning them. Here we saw specimens of nutmeg, cinnamon, vanilla, cinchona, cocoa, cloves, cardamoms, and all the varieties of coffee, besides a splendid collection of palms, and many interesting plants of minor commercial value. One of the most striking features of the gardens was a group of immense bamboos, a hundred and twenty feet high, and from nine to ten and a half inches in diameter. These great grasses were only three months old, and their rate of growth, which sometimes attains a speed of half an inch an hour, can actually be watched. The white ants build curious covered runs up the palm trunks, little tunnels, which look exactly like the stems of creepers, and give the ants perfect protection from the attacks of birds on their journeys from the ground to the foliage. We ought to have been tormented with the Ceylon "land-leech" at Peradeniya, but the weather was too dry; on damp days the creatures are a perfect pest, listening for footsteps, throwing themselves forward on the approach of a passer-by, and fastening themselves in numbers around his ankles, or even crawling all over his body.

"Lady Horton's Walk" is a fine road, running quite around one of the hills overlooking Kandy, constructed by a late governor of the island, and called after his wife. Viewed from this eyrie, the town lies embosomed in steep, forest-clad mountains. A large lake, circled by a wide road, fills a portion of the hollow in which Kandy stands, and upon this sheet of water the chief European houses are built; while the native town stretches away behind them. The roofs are almost buried in foliage, but here and there are open spaces of lawn, surrounded by trees and palms. It is a well-ordered, well-finished English town in the midst of tropical surroundings.

It was evening when we visited the famous temple where Buddha's tooth is enshrined. This sacred relic, long preserved in India, but transferred to Ceylon when that country was in a disturbed condition, is only shown on special occasions. It is, really, a great lump of ivory, but so idolatrous has the once pure religion of Buddha become under the corrupting influence of superstition, that the "tooth" is worshipped like a god. A service was in progress as we entered the building, which was dimly lighted by oil lamps, filled with the clamour of tom-toms and bag-pipes, and pervaded by an overpowering odour of flowers. From time to time a native came in; prayed for a few moments before the shrine; took a bloom from a dish full of fragrant flowers, and left a trifling offering behind. Presently some shaven and yellow-robed priests arrived, whom we followed to the inner temple, where, surrounded by gems, gold, and tinsel, the tooth lies under seven golden covers. Thence we were conducted to the library, containing the Buddhist scriptures written in Cinghalese, on palm leaves. Each sacred book is a bundle of narrow sheets, held between carved plates of gold or ivory, and tied by silk cords. As the leaves are liable to perish from the attacks of insects, a number of young priests are always engaged in transcribing new copies; exquisitely traced with a finely pointed style on the membranous palm. Leaving the temple, with its wild music and powerful odours, we came out through obscure aisles upon a wide lawn, bordered by magnificent palms, into the splendid tropical night, lighted by glowing stars, while the clear, dark air was spangled with slowly moving fire-flies. It was altogether one of the most beautiful and characteristic scenes we had witnessed in the tropics.

December 23-24.—Colombo seemed almost red hot after the delicious coolness of the hills, and even the pier, against which great waves were dashing under the influence of the monsoon, was a warm promenade. This breakwater, which is built of large concrete blocks, will cost the colony a great deal of money, while, unlike road-making, it is not a reproductive undertaking. It will bring all the ocean steamers, now touching at Galle, to Colombo, and thus facilitate the operations of the merchants. On the other hand, it is questionable whether Galle harbour could not be improved, at a small expense, by blowing up the worst rocks, when the railway might be extended, with advantage to the intervening country, to the southern port, which is less open to the monsoon than Colombo, and in a more direct line between England and the far East.

We dined with the German Consul at Colombo, who, on the strength of a chance introduction, received us with a courtesy we can never forget, and, with his charming wife, gave us a most agreeable evening. It was pleasant to sit once more, after so much travelling, at a refined European dinner-table, and listen to well-instructed talk about Ceylon, while the punkah swung overhead, and, through the open windows of the dining-room, we could see the tiny fire-flies sailing about in the obscure verandah. Mr. and Mrs. Freudenberg were good enough to ask us to spend Christmas Eve, the greatest German festival of the year, with them, but the Peninsular and Oriental steamer *Poonah* was inexorable, and we were obliged to bake all that day in a stage-coach, retracing the road to Galle which I have already described. By sunset we were on board our new ship, looking, probably for the last time, at the crescent of cocoa palms lining the shore of Galle harbour, and longing for the screw to turn and create a breath of air in the hot, still, and steaming atmosphere.

Ceylon, as already mentioned, is divided into the "hill country," occupying a position somewhat south of its centre, and the "maritime provinces," which form four-fifths of the surface, and everywhere border the ocean with wide level plains, for the most part unoccupied by, and little known to Europeans. It produces coffee, tea, spices, cocoa-nuts, pearls, and gems. The native arts are cotton and silk weaving, rope-making, and goldsmith's work but the last has little or no merit.

The Portuguese were the first of European nations to establish regular intercourse with Ceylon; and they made themselves masters of the maritime provinces early in the sixteenth century, retaining possession of them for a hundred and fifty years. True to their national policy, they pushed religion and business together, but, finally, behaved with such inhuman cruelty in the course of their proselytising efforts, that the Kandians called the Dutch to their aid, and, after a struggle lasting nearly a quarter of a century, the Portuguese were expelled. This happened in 1656, when the Dutch occupied the maritime provinces, the King of Kandy being supreme in the hill country. During the war with the French, the British took possession of Trincomalee, which was, however, retaken, the sea-coast remaining in the hands of the Dutch till 1796, when we wrested it from them, obtaining formal possession of the country by the Treaty of Amiens. In 1803 we conquered the King of Kandy, but were soon afterwards driven out of the hill country; and it was not till 1815, when the tyrannies of the king had brought about his deposition by his chiefs, that England, on the invitation of the latter, took possession of the capital.

British rule has been of immense advantage to Ceylon. It has given the natives justice, security, and trade, while their proprietary rights have been respected; only jungle lands without owners having been annexed, and a share in the local administration of justice being reserved to the Cinghalese. The country has been covered with excellent roads, and a considerable mileage of paying railroad constructed. During the Dutch occupation, coffee was not grown, partly because the Dutch were not masters of the hill country, partly because they did not wish to create a rival to Java; but, upon its introduction by the British about forty years ago, coffee soon became the most important product of the island. Jungle lands were rapidly cleared to a height of five thousand feet; main roads were pushed into the hill country at Government expense, planters' roads connected with these, and Tamil labour introduced on a large scale, with the result that the coffee trade reached a yearly value of five millions sterling, being half of the whole imports and exports of the colony. In the early days, jungle sold at £1 an acre, but as the colony grew prosperous, it was eagerly sought at prices which, a few years ago, reached £15, and, in special cases, even £30 an acre. The money produced by land sales was wisely spent by the Government in roads and works of improvement, including irrigation, which had been so neglected by the apathetic native cultivators that the island depended almost entirely upon importation for the rice which planters required for their coolies.

Thus, for many years, coffee-planting and Ceylon flourished together, until the annual product reached a million hundredweight of berries. Meanwhile the planters were seldom able to work their estates without the aid of borrowed money, which was furnished on easy terms by the banks and merchants of Colombo; plenty of money being always obtainable in England for advances on such excellent landed security. Prosperity and the abundance of capital stimulated a spirit of speculation among the planters, a sanguine but not commercially able class, who bid against one another for uncleared land, until prices rose, as we have already seen, to unnatural heights, and the acreage under cultivation was increased by nearly seventy-five per cent. Suddenly, the leaf disease appeared, and, within six years, reduced the total yield of coffee by nearly fifty per cent., in spite of the greater area of the plantations, stopping at the same time the hitherto ready advances of capitalists. Commercially speaking, Ceylon is in a bad way at present. If there were a market for estates, probably three-fourths of all the plantations in the island would be advertised for sale; but, as matters stand, mortgagee and cultivator can only hope for better times, and plant Liberian coffee and cinchona in the mean time. Little benefit, however, is to be expected from the former plant, which appears to have already degenerated in the soil of Ceylon. Its yield per acre is small as compared with that of *Arabica;* the berries are of inferior quality, and the tree will only grow in the unhealthy low grounds. Cinchona-planting, on the other hand, promises well, but is still in the experimental stage, and many years must elapse before the full results of trials now in progress can be known. Forty years of careless cultivation have produced a crisis in the affairs of the colony, which is at present acute, and promises to be long-continued. The difficulty has, however, been faced, not by despondency, but by courageous efforts to introduce new industries, and British energy will probably prove too much for *Hemileia vastatrix* in the long run.

CHAPTER XIV.

MADRAS—CALCUTTA.

December 25—January 4, 1881.

CHRISTMAS DAY! and we lie on deck, torpid with the heat, while our relatives at home are sitting round the fire, cracking nuts, and drinking claret, with the snow covering everything outside. The *Poonah's* passengers are on their way out; and as they have been together for four weeks, while we have newly joined the ship, we feel rather out in the cold, spite of the "festive season." But the season is not festive on board our steamer. Not one of these people, who have known each other for a month, has the courage to suggest some common festivity. There are lots of children, but no one proposes a Christmas game even for them. We have had no Christmas Church service, and the bough of mistletoe, which some frolicsome steward has hung from the awning, might be a life-belt for all the notice we take of it. Never have I spent so dull a Christmas Day. Never have I thought my countrymen so stiff and unsocial.

We have now seen the last of settlement life in the East, and, shall learn in India how England rules, rather than how she influences a native population. It is time, while the palms of Ceylon are fading on the horizon, to arrange our ideas of the remarkable series of commercial outposts which we have passed since leaving Japan.

The Portuguese; then the Dutch; and lastly the English. It seems to have been the rule throughout the East. The first came with commerce in one hand and religion in the other, caring less for business than for the supremacy of the Church, and advocating her interests with the sword. The second forgot religion for the sake of trade, but was fond of large profits, and exploited new countries in his own interests, without caring much for those of the natives. The Englishman is in the East, first and foremost to trade; next, to make native races accept Western ideas of civilization, at least as far as is needful for the conduct of business. He builds roads, introduces autonomy into the settlement town, administers justice, enforces order, and erects churches, the last, apparently, for the sake of his beloved "respectability," and not at all because he is anxious to proselytize. Rich societies, indeed, send him out missionaries, whom he distrusts, not because they are ministers of religion, but from the fear that they may embroil his nation with native power or prejudice, and thus put hindrances in the way of trade. His relations with the flag are admirable. The power of England is always regarded as something to fall back upon in case of emergency, never as a governing agency. He himself provides for the maintenance of order and the administration of justice, while the minister, or

Consul, supports rather than overrules his authority. French settlements, on the other hand, are not autonomous, and expect to be governed rather than upheld by their officials; while the Germans always operate under foreign flags, and that so well, that they are everywhere our most dangerous commercial competitors. It seems probable, however, that a German Hongkong or Ceylon would have its energies seriously crippled by bureaucratism.

Whether England has bought her commanding position in the East too dearly is a great question. We talk with pride of a national trade of two thousand millions sterling per annum; but America does the same amount of business without having spent a dollar on conquest, and Germany turns over thirteen hundred millions a year for which she has paid practically nothing. If we regard the increase of trade in the last ten years, a period during which we have spent large sums on "little wars" waged on behalf of commerce, while America and Germany have laid out nothing for similar ends, we find that England has added three hundred millions to her returns, but Germany has increased hers by only thirty millions less, and America by two hundred millions more than ourselves. To count the cost of England's commercial position is impossible. We know that the bill is inconceivably big, but other nations, who do not care to pay as dearly as we do for trade, are doing well enough to make it doubtful whether the vast sums we have spent on commercial wars is money well invested.

December 27.—European Madras lies spread along an extensive bund, backed by a level and uninviting country. The curved arms of two unfinished piers received the *Poonah* on our arrival, and these, in their present state, hardly break the violence of the great waves which, driven by the monsoon, fall in heavy surf upon the exposed shore. The beech is lined with large buildings—custom-house, godowns, and merchants' hongs, while, at some distance southward of the town, is Government House, half hidden in a mass of green foliage. The ship's anchor was hardly down before she was surrounded by surf-boats, big, flat-bottomed craft, made of planks, without ribs or framing, and sewn together with fibres. Ten Tamils, naked but for their waistcloths, form the crew of each boat, and an eleventh man steers. Their oars are long poles terminating in large wooden disks, and the rowlocks are wooden pins to which the oar is tied by a fibre rope. No sooner was a boat alongside than its headman clambered up the ship's side and began touting for passengers. "Master want boat?" "How much?" "Seven rupee, go ashore, come back." "Seven iniquities! We shan't go ashore at all unless you'll take us there and back for four rupees." "All right, master. Take ticket!" Therewith he shoved a bit of tin stamped with the number of his boat into our hands, and disappeared to make bargains with other passengers. How well those ten naked and muscular black fellows looked as they pulled for the shore! They rowed the stroke out till their bodies were horizontal, recovered quickly, and kept well together. We rode easily over the big swells, and as we approached the broken water the men shouted and pulled like demons; but we got through without a wetting, and were carried ashore each by two strong fellows, who demanded a rupee for services not included in our original contract.

Madras has a delapidated, almost ruinous appearance. The best buildings are out of repair; even the churches are spotted with dark mossy stains, and the plaster is peeling from the walls. Second-class houses are falling to pieces, and the mortar has disappeared from the joints of brick walls. Private bungalows are usually surrounded by large gardens, but these are rarely well kept. A house is often approached by pretentious entrance-gates, standing alone and unsupported by any wall or fence. The residences are low, spreading over considerable areas, and placed very far apart, so that visiting is almost out of the question if people do not keep horses. The native town, which hides behind the European bund, contains several hundred thousand inhabitants. Its streets are narrow, ill-kept, and dirty, bordered on either side by mean houses, built of mud, and displaying no trace of ornament or beauty. The people are all Tamils, and the bazaar, a large open space surrounded by poor shops and stalls, is crowded with these people, buying fruit, rice, and a thousand and one small European articles. I am always wondering how many matches are made in the world; it is the one product of civilised life which every country has learned to appreciate. Of course the fellow who had sold us our tin tickets declared they were not good for the return journey, and asked a fancy price to take us back to the steamer. A few flourishes with a walking-stick, and the thunder of some good German oaths, however, soon changed his tone, and shortly afterwards we were once more on board. We lay in the roads all night, and I went on deck at five o'clock a.m.,

December 28, to see the Southern Cross, this being our last chance of a peep at the famous constellation. It is far less beautiful than the Great Bear, or Orion, and not more striking than Cygnus, which it slightly resembles. The heavens look strange in these low latitudes. The Bear was upside down, and almost unrecognisable in this position; Orion stood right overhead; Sirius was high above the horizon, and below it hung other stars which were entire strangers to us.

December 29.—Although the sun is very hot, the air is already much cooler than when we were nearer the line; the sea is perfectly calm, and we are again surprised at the absence of life from these tropical waters. We begin to get a little more friendly with our fellow-passengers. The captain is a pleasant, musical man, who brings people together in the evening around the piano, under the lighted deck awning, where we form little groups and listen to the singing. We are strong in young civil servants, who appear to pass their spare time in discussing the chances of promotion, or, in other words, the health of the officials above them. All these men are socially very agreeable, but cramped in their ideas and interests. They possess in an eminent degree that refinement which we missed so much in the States; yet we are constantly forgetting that America lacks cultivation in our admiration of the greater adaptability and force of character which distinguish the Yankee. The friends of English lads, without capital, are tempted by the £300 or £400 a year with which their sons can make a start in life, by passing the Indian Civil Service examinations. Ten years later, when these boys are men, and perhaps married, they find themselves with an income of about £800 a year, with impaired health and energies, a wife to keep and family to educate in England, the sense of self-reliance weakened, and with no outlook but continuing to tread the official mill in anticipation of a pension. In compensation, they have the satisfaction of belonging to a service which gives them a good "position," but the commercial men, whom they envy for their success, but cannot emulate in enterprise, are far better off and perhaps the more valuable national servants of the two classes.

December 30—*January* 4, 1881.—Since we left Madras, my *vis-à-vis* at table had been a well-looking, well-dressed, and well-informed man, whom, from his appearance and conversation, we took to be the head of some commercial Calcutta firm. This morning he was missing, both at breakfast and tiffin, and in the course of the afternoon I recognised him on the bridge of the steamer, in the smartest of uniforms, and in charge of the ship. Our supposed merchant was the Hooghly pilot. Calcutta lies at the head of a great delta called the Sunderbund, hundreds of square miles in extent, through which the Ganges seeks the sea by a vast network of rivers. The Hooghly is one of these streams, having a channel flowing through low banks of alluvium, and obstructed by numerous shoals. The shoals shift so rapidly that their positions require to be surveyed from day to day, and their latest changes of place telegraphed to the head-quarters of the pilot service. The tide up and stream down the Hooghly run so fast that if a ship touches ground she is lost, and there are a hundred and twenty miles of this ticklish navigation between the open ocean and Calcutta. The very difficulties of the situation have created the most perfectly organized system of pilotage in the world, and to understand the perils of the Hooghly was to know why our pilot is as well paid as a Peninsular and Oriental captain, and looks such a tremendous swell on the bridge.

Some time before reaching Calcutta, the river narrows considerably, looking rather like the Thames at Putney, but being three times as wide, with low banks of mud, overgrown with palms, and sprinkled with occasional villages. After seven hours of slow and cautious steaming, we saw a forest of masts rising before us, and, a little later, were boarded by the harbour-master, who came off from shore in a boat propelled in a very curious way. Three natives sat on each gunwale, facing *across* the craft, and rowed from this position with very long, disc-ended oars. It looked like a game of "pull baker, pull devil!" but the stroke on each side, being delivered in a direction slightly oblique to the course, resulted in a forward movement. Approaching the city, we passed the palace of the King of Oudh, an immense mass of buildings without any architectural pretensions, on the left bank of the river. Here the dispossessed monarch lives, surrounded by his concubines, retainers, and menageries, we paying him a lakh a month in compensation for the loss of his former territory. Then came jute-mills, ship-building yards, and engineering works, the fine botanical gardens, still called the "Company's Gardens," and, opposite these, Garden Reach, once a favourite suburb, whose splendid bungalows have been invaded by works and wharves, and are now deserted by the fashionable world. A jungle of masts lines the left bank of the stream for the last three miles of the journey. The ships are for the most part of the finest class; it does not pay to send small ships into a harbour where such heavy pilotage dues have to be paid. A hundred thousand tons of shipping often lies in the port at one time, and almost every vessel is English. The general aspect of the river is thoroughly industrial in character, reminding us of the Thames again and again.

Calcutta is so European in appearance that, on stepping ashore, we could have thought ourselves once more at home, but for the heat, the natives, and the tropical vegetation. The left bank of the Hooghly is bordered by a wide quay, called the Strand, beyond which is the "Meidan," a vast expanse of grass, crossed by many wide roads, and dotted with statues of public men. At one end of this open space stands Government House, at the other, great barracks, and the intervening space is bordered by shops, offices, and warehouses. About a quarter of a mile below the city stands the citadel, built by Clive soon after the battle of Plassey, and near it are remains of the famous ditch, dug in 1742, to protect the English factory from Mahratta attacks. The servants of the East India Company in Calcutta were too busy making money in 1756 to think of properly entrenching themselves in the settlement, and when on the 17th of June in that year, the young Mahratta tyrant Suraj-ood-Dowlah, sat down with fifty thousand troops around the wealthy factory, the garrison—a hundred and seventy-four in number, not ten of whom had ever seen a shot fired—after a gallant defence, was obliged to surrender. Then followed the tragedy of the Black Hole, which has made the name of Suraj-ood-Dowlah infamous. A hundred and forty-six European prisoners were thrust into a chamber, not twenty feet square, with only a single window, and locked up for the night, in one of the hottest months of the year. When the door of their prison was opened next morning, only twenty-three ghastly forms were dragged out alive. It is the one incident connected with Calcutta which no Englishman can fail to be reminded of as soon as he lands on the banks of the Hooghly.

The streets, squares, private residences, and public offices of Calcutta are more imposing than those of most European cities, and the bungalows, which extend to considerable distances in the neighbouring country, are many of them little palaces. The fashionable world of Calcutta is to be seen every evening for a couple of hours before dinner, driving on the Strand, which is crowded with carriages like Hyde Park in the season. On the one hand is the river with its forest of tall masts, on the other the palms and lawns of the beautiful Eden Gardens, and overhead, at this time of the year, a sky flushed to the zenith with the crimsons of sunset. At six o'clock, the band plays and the world of well-dressed men and women leave their carriages and promenade while listening to the music. But for its frame of tropical foliage, the scene would be entirely European in character. It is not the East, it is London transported to the East. At seven o'clock every one goes home to dinner and the river-side is deserted.

North of Calcutta lies the native bazaar, a vast extent of narrow streets, and squalid-looking houses of tumble-down brickwork. Each house is a shop, where the native trader squats, with his hookah beside him, surrounded by piles of bright cottons or miscellaneous European wares. To a stranger's eye the whole bazaar looks as if it might be bought up, shops, stocks, and good-will, for a song. Certainly no outsider could ever suppose himself standing upon the foundations whereon rest the great mills and stately warehouses of Manchester. But such is the fact. These dingy shops, only a few feet square, supply the most populous districts of India with all their foreign requirements, and send British textiles across the Himalayas, and as far as Afghanistan; while, among the natives who squat within, hams on heels, are solid men, whose bills at forty days are taken by the European merchant for sums which vary from £100 to £10,000, according to the circumstances of his customer. The streets of the bazaar are full of importunate touters, who run alongside every passing gharry, offering all sorts of trifles for sale, and the same thing occurs, in a modified degree, in the chief street of the European quarter.

Once more, to our utter astonishment, we found the ubiquitous Chinaman, settled this time in a Calcutta Chinatown, and the carpenter and shoemaker *par excellence* of this great city. Elsewhere, we have seen the Chinese competing with white races at lower rates of pay, but a Chinese artisan in India demands twice as much wages as a native, and is thankfully welcomed by employers at that price. One knows not where this child of industry will not appear. Certainly it would be a great improvement if the foreign community of Calcutta could replace their lazy, caste-ridden Hindoo domestics with one-tenth their number of capable Chinese servants.

The "mild Hindoo" makes an unfavourable first impression

on a stranger. His Aryan type of face is agreeable enough, especially after long sojourning among Mongolian races; but he is evidently a born loafer, happiest when squatting idly on his haunches, and overpaid by the scanty wages he commands. Take, in illustration, the unnecessary swarm of native servants in private houses. Scarcely had we arrived in our hotel before two white-robed and turbaned fellows presented themselves at the bedroom door for hire. Each sahib must, of course, have a man —a cumbrous arrangement, for which we were by no means prepared, until we found that, without a body-servant, we could not get a bath, or have a bed made, and might even starve amid plenty at the *table d'hôte.'* The scene at dinner in the Great Eastern Hotel is something perfectly ludicrous to a new-comer. There are more waiters than diners; but none of them belong to the house, every guest having one, sometimes two, gorgeously clothed private attendants, who stand with folded arms, each behind his master's chair, watching his every mouthful, and elbowing through a noisy crowd of rival flunkies for every new dish which the sahib demands.

The dress of the common people varies a good deal both in material and colour. In its most characteristic form it may be described as consisting of a cotton sheet worn over the head, with one end wrapped around the body and the other thrown over the left shoulder. The women's "sarong" is simply a strip of cotton, which they have the art of draping very gracefully about their slender figures. There is, however, no limit to the splendour of well-to-do natives. Calcutta was *en fête* on New Year's Day, and we had an opportunity, both on the racecourse and at a fancy fair held in the Zoological Gardens, of seeing far more brilliant crowds than we had ever yet beheld in the East. The grand stand was crowded with fat, rich natives (a wealthy native is always fat), gorgeous in violet velvet, scarlet silk, and gold embroidery, while the wide space within the course, where the people congregate, was a moving mass of white and red. More than ten thousand natives were present at the fancy fair, and the kaleidoscopic crowd was dressed in robes of violet, scarlet, green, and gold. All the hues of the rainbow, and all the tinsel of the East glittered before our bewildered eyes, mixed, in endless colour groupings, with the white garments of the people.

The crows are one of the most striking minor features of Calcutta. Fed to a great extent by the leavings of European meals, which the natives will not touch and the climate would spoil, these birds haunt the city in immense numbers. Hindoo consideration for animal life makes them so tame that one can tempt a crow into one's bedroom with a bit of bread. They roost at night, so thickly crowded among the trees of the Eden Gardens, that the boughs are bent, nearly to breaking, by their weight, while their even-song, when assembling for rest, almost drowns the music of the band playing on the Strand.

Private life is very luxurious, and private houses are very splendid in Calcutta. We dined at one "chummery," or establishment of associated bachelors—a common form of housekeeping here—and were entertained in a palace, fed with dainty dishes, refreshed by fine wines, and waited upon by obsequious slaves, our hosts being simply a knot of young men engaged in commerce, who gave us a most agreeable evening, and an exalted idea of the energy and intelligence which distinguish our merchant compatriots in the East.

CHAPTER XV.

IN THE HIMALAYAS.

January 4-8.

THERE is no station in the Himalaya Mountains more accessible from Calcutta than Darjeeling. Kinchinjanga, once believed to be the highest mountain in the world, is in full view, and Everest, now known to be its superior in altitude by a thousand feet, is also within sight from this point. The district is interesting as a centre of the tea cultivation, and Darjeeling itself can be almost reached by rail and tramroad. These considerations determined our wavering choice of the spot for making acquaintance with the snowy range of India; and four days after our arrival in the Hooghly, we started for the north.

Leaving Calcutta by the Eastern Bengal Railway, we reached the banks of the Ganges in five hours, traversing a flat country, covered for the most part with rice-stubble, and diversified, but not ornamented, by mean mud villages, widely scattered palms, and stunted trees. The holy river, a swift muddy stream, about two miles wide, running between high banks of alluvium, was crossed in a steamer; and, on its farther side, we took the Northern Bengal Railway, about sunset. This is a "famine railway" of metre gauge, built in a great hurry five years ago, in anticipation of a scarcity in Northern Bengal, which happily did not occur. It compares most unfavourably with the American narrow-gauge railroads, which are for the most part mountain lines, having steep gradients and sharp curves, but whose trains, equipped with powerful engines, and capacious carriages, run at a speed of twenty miles an hour. The Northern Bengal, on the other hand, traverses a perfectly level country, but its engines and carriages are toy-like, and the shaking at a speed of only sixteen miles an hour is terrible. I once travelled at the rate of forty miles an hour on the Denver and Rio Grande Railroad, an American metre line, but it would be impossible to attempt such a thing on the Northern Bengal. "It's awfully snaky work at twenty-five miles an hour," said a young engineer, who knew a great deal about Indian railways. We passed a wretched night in our "sleeping-car," a comfortless, dirty carriage, with only a narrow bench for a bed, no bedding; a cupboard, without soap or towels, for a lavatory, and no attendant;—this in a country where men are worth threepence a day. Sleep, except by snatches, was out of the question, on account of the shaking; and we reached Silligouri, the end of the line, just as the sun was rising, dirty and broken-backed, having compassed a hundred and ninety-six miles in twelve hours, at the reckless speed of sixteen miles and a third per hour.

At the present moment the Indian Government is distracted by the question of rival gauges. It has already constructed many miles of metre-gauge line, which is cheaper to build, and better suited to general Indian requirements than the five feet six inch gauge of the trunk lines. But some of these railways have failed to do what was expected of them, and the authorities are now said to be in favour of a return to the broad-gauge policy, which in my opinion would be a serious blunder. The metre gauge is a magnificent success in the States, under much more difficult conditions than exist in India generally; and I fully believe it is only Indian locomotives and rolling stock which are at fault. These are much too small, and, as the question is a most important one for the country, nothing ought to be decided in the matter without the Government being fully informed of all that has been achieved by metre lines in the western states of America.

January 5.—We rose very slightly in traversing the two hundred miles accomplished during the night, and are now in the " Terai," a plain of malarious land out of which the Himalayas rise quite suddenly. The Terai has the reputation of being the most deadly part of India; it is densely covered with vegetation, and it is supposed that portions of the streams flowing from the hills sink in its soil, and, percolating through the deep vegetable mould which covers it, produce miasmatic exhalations, which cover the country like a fog to the depth of several feet. It was at one time dangerous for a European to sleep for a single night on low ground anywhere in the Terai, but much of the country has recently been cleared for tea-planting, to the great improvement of its sanitary condition. This work has been done, under white direction, of course, by the natives, or "metchis," who are said to suffer no ill effects from the malaria, but become ill on leaving a district which is deadly to Europeans. As the sun rose it revealed the near spurs of the Himalayas outlined on the pure morning sky, while a neighbouring military camp came also into view, and a number of tame elephants carrying great loads of timber for works in process of erection. A steam tramway, occupying one side of an excellent road, runs from Silligouri to within eighteen miles of Darjeeling, and in the course of a few months—in the States it would be days—the line will be finished. The Himalayas are too steep to be directly scaled, and the road now skirts great ravines, now zigzags upwards. At one point, where the ascent is very sharp, the tramway actually passes under a certain bridge, makes a wide circle, rising all the time, and finally crosses over the same bridge it went under only a few minutes before. It is like travelling up the spirals of a great corkscrew.

The tropical forests which cover the flanks of the Himalayas are no less disappointing than those of Ceylon. The jungle consists of small spindly trees, crowded together, with a dense undergrowth of bamboo and tall grasses in the lower grounds, while, about a thousand feet above the level of the Terai, all the trees are tied up, as if with ropes, by great climbers, whose foliage hides that of the branches from which they hang. The stems of these lianas seldom cling to the tree-trunks, but rise from the earth into the boughs just as a stay from the bulwark rises to the mast of a ship. It is evident that the epiphytes cannot have grown like this originally. Each has probably climbed the trunk of its host in the first instance, and one of its many air-roots, having reached the soil, has become the main support of the creeper. If, after this had occurred, the first liana stem decayed, the air-root would look like an original stem. The jungle at this elevation is rich in orchids, whose flowers are for the most part inconspicuous, and, wherever an open space occurs, it is occupied by great tree-ferns. The character of the vegetation changes with the elevation, but not in a marked manner. Palms, banians, fig, orange, and peach trees, prevail up to a thousand feet. At four thousand feet the palms die out, and oak, chestnut, maple, and hydrangea appear. At eight-thousand feet laurels and limes are seen, and we are told that oaks and chestnuts disappear at ten thousand feet, giving place to fir, holly, rhododendron, and pear, while raspberries, primroses, violets, and anemones flourish at the same elevation.

Thirty miles from Silligouri we reached Kursiong, the present end of the steam tramway, about four thousand five hundred feet above sea-level, where we took a "tonga," or small two-wheeled trap, drawn by a pair of swift Thibetan ponies, in which we drove the remaining distance of eighteen miles to Darjeeling, the whole journey of three hundred and sixty miles from Calcutta having occupied twenty-eight hours.

January 6.—Darjeeling is situated on a spur of the Himalayas, and is seven thousand feet above sea-level. The district was originally obtained by the British from the Rajah of Sikkim, for the purpose of erecting a military sanatorium. A glance at the map of India shows that Sikkim, British and independent, projects like a tongue beyond our general northern frontier, dividing Nepal on the west from Bhotan on the east, and stretching northward to the summit of the Himalayas. The southern half of this tract once belonged to the Rajah of Nepal, from whom it was taken by the East India Company in 1817. In the same year we ceded it to the Rajah of Sikkim; but in 1828, the surveyors who were engaged on the boundary line between Nepal and Sikkim reported so favourably on the district around Darjeeling for a sanatory station, that in 1835, the Company took it back from the rajah, paying him three thousand rupees a year for it, a rent which was ultimately withdrawn on account of the unlawful detention of Drs. Hooker and Campbell many years later. British Sikkim includes all the land south of the Ranjit, east of the Balasun and west of the Mahadana rivers, while independent Sikkim stretches northwards to the snows of the range, on the other side of which lies the elevated plateau of Thibet, inhabited by Tartar races, and ruled by China. With such a geographical position it is not surprising that a conspicuous mixture of races should form the most striking feature of Darjeeling in the eyes of new-comers. There are nearly a hundred thousand people in the district, of whom four hundred are Europeans, and the rest either Lepchas (the aboriginal hillmen), Bhoteas (immigrants from Bhotan), Nepalese, or Thibetans. Both Lepchas and Bhoteas have distinctly Mongolian faces, wear pigtails, and are debased Buddhists by religion. The Nepalese, who form a third part of the population of British Sikkim, are a short, agile race, with nothing of the Mongol in their features, yet altogether different from the plainsmen in appearance. They are Hindoos by religion, good agriculturists and artisans, and largely employed as coolies in the tea plantations, or, called Ghoorkas, after the ruling race and dynasty of Nepal, become some of the best soldiers in the native army of India. The Thibetans only appear in Darjeeling once a year, when they bring yaks (oxen) and ponies for the teaplanters, and fine woollen cloth for the native bazaar. They come across the Himalayan passes from Lassa, and are three months on the road; stay two or three months trafficking, and then return. These people are thorough Mongols in appearance, Buddhists by religion, and, though nominally ruled by China, subjects of the Dalai Lama. They are here now, and, between them and the numerous Bhoteas, Darjeeling seems full of Chinese faces, almost every one we meet having high cheek-bones, a yellow skin, and oblique eyes. We slept in Hindostan, and have waked in Mongolia.

Degraded as Buddhism appears in Japan and Ceylon, it has been reserved for the Indian races to sink it to the lowest depths of idolatry and superstition. Near our hotel is the Bhotean Buddhist temple, a mean wooden building, decorated with gaudy colours, and containing three gilt figures of Buddha, together with drums, cymbals, conchs, and copper horns used in the ritual. At the entrance are several " praying-wheels," including one two feet in diameter and six feet high, and about twenty small ones. These all stand on vertical axels, and are full of prayers printed on long slips of paper. A hideous old woman turns the big cylinder with a crank, and a projecting stick, striking a bell once in every revolution, announces that ten million prayers, the number which the wheel contains, have been offered up. The wheels are like large canisters, painted red, and adorned with gilt characters. Private persons use small praying-cylinders furnished with a handle, and whirled around by the aid of a weight attached to the cylinder by a chain. When a great function is going on, the Lamas, or priests, wear hideous masks, and blow conchs and long copper horns; but the whole service is quite meaningless, and prayer consists only in endless exclamations of the Buddhistic formula, "Om mani padme om!" (the jewel of the lotus leaf), to multiply the repetitions of which mystic adjuration is the object of the praying-wheel.

It is difficult to say which is the dirtiest race among those enumerated above, but I think the palm must be given to the Bhoteas. These fellows are great porters, and very useful for all sorts of heavy outdoor work, provided it is not regular. Put a case of beer, weighing three hundred pounds, on a Bhotea's back, and he will carry it cheerfully anywhere up or down these hills, but give him a hoe or a shovel, and he soon quits. The women are as good carriers as the men. They say that a lady, who was moving house in Darjeeling a few years ago, was astonished to meet her grand piano, going up the hill to the new bungalow, on the back of a Bhotean woman. Nepalese, Bhoteas, Lepchas, and Thibetans wear each distinctive dresses, and even a new-comer soon learns to distinguish between the races, whether by their clothes or faces. Their houses, however, are very much alike, being mere shelters made of mats, run up in a few hours and struck like a tent; the dwellings of nomads who had ceased to be nomadic.

We meet the Bhotean women on every hill-side path, always spinning as they walk. The wheel is a stick about the size of a pencil, with a wooden disc at one end. The wool is carried in a hank on the right wrist, and the machine is set whirling by a swift movement of the hands. It hangs supported by the thread in process of forming, which, when sufficiently twisted, is wound bobbin-wise round the stick. This is a very pretty and skilful operation, which looks as if the spinner were playing at cup and ball the wrong way about.

The native bazaar at Darjeeling is a large square, surrounded by shops, where, mingled with rice, beans, sweetmeats, and betel, one sees Reading biscuits, canned fruit, Day and Martin's blacking, yellow soap, glass beads, dip candles, braces, penny ink-bottles, pocket-combs, mixed pickles, tin-tacks, pocket-mirrors, nails, peg tops, square-iron, marmalade, oil-cans, jams, memorandum-books, and a thousand other things. The ground is covered with heaps of various grains, and here the mixed races I have endeavoured to describe meet and bargain, with cowries and bits of flat copper for money. There is no Indian element in the scene. It is the market-place of Tartars on the march.

January 7.—Darjeeling is almost always in the clouds, and the snowy peaks of the Himalaya are rarely visible at this time of the year, except for an hour after sunrise, and then very capriciously. We were fortunate enough to get one good view of the range during our stay, on the only day when the mists had risen for three weeks previously. Seen from Darjeeling, Sikkim presents the appearance of a number of high, consecutive, parallel ridges, running east and west. These are all densely wooded, and their outlines are broken here and there by gaps, which indicate the points where rivers, flowing from the snows of the watershed, break through on their southward course to the distant Ganges. Behind the ridges, and overtopping them, is a beautiful range of snowy peaks, among which Kinchinjanga, the loftiest mountain in the world—Everest only excepted—rears its pointed summit to a height of twenty-eight thousand feet. From Kinchinjanga, an immense spur, called the Singalila range, stretches south to the plains of India, separating Sikkim from Nepal on the west; while a similar but smaller ridge, called the Chola range, running southward from a peak named Dankia, fifty miles east of Kinchinjanga, divides Sikkim from Bhotan.

We reached the "Observatory" this morning shortly after sunrise, and found about one-fourth of our southern horizon clear of clouds. The view in this direction consisted of numerous spurs, similar to that upon which we stood, partly jungle-covered, partly cleared and planted with tea. White, thread-like roads wound around the steep hill-sides, and numerous white bungalows, looking like toy houses, were scattered here and there among the plantations. Darjeeling itself, a widely spread group of more or less handsome dwellings, lay at our feet; and the lieutenant-governor's summer residence, crowning a hill near our position, formed a prominent feature in the foreground. Northwards, however, everything was covered with mist, which filled the valleys below our feet with an unbroken sheet of vapour, and rolled slowly in great cumuli along the flanks of the wooded ranges. Behind these billowy masses, and extending, as it seemed, a considerable distance towards the zenith, lay a thick horizontal layer of stratus, above which was the blue. We stood, for a long time, looking at the topmost cloud-beds, hoping they would lift, but they did not. Suddenly, however, a tiny white peak peeped *above* their level surface, at a height where we should have looked only for a star; and, while we could scarcely believe our eyes, the summit of Kinchinjanga was slowly unveiled before us. During the following hour and a half, thirty degrees of the northern horizon cleared, bit by bit, in the same way, bringing into view some forty miles of snowy summits, of whose great elevation, however, we could form no idea, because everything below them was hidden. But, presently, the mists cleared from the valleys, and we saw both the peaks and the low grounds at the same moment, all the intervening space being still covered with clouds. Then, for the first time, the stupendous character of the scenery revealed itself, and we realized, with some emotion, the sublimity of the Himalayas.

Tea and cinchona are largely grown around Darjeeling; the former spreading widely over the whole surface of British Sikkim, while the latter, which was introduced in 1862, by Dr. Anderson, of the Botanic Gardens at Calcutta, on Government account, already occupies more than two thousand acres, planted with over three million trees. Cinchona flourishes at the same elevations as in Ceylon, but its cultivation has passed out of the experimental stage in India, the Government gardens already supplying great quantities of a cheap and excellent febrifuge both to the army and the public.

Tea flourishes in India from the plains of the Terai up to elevations of five thousand feet, but the best qualities are grown at heights of from two to three thousand feet. The plant matures in three years, and continues yielding until it is about thirty years old. The trees are pruned in the "cold weather," and, a month afterwards, they "flush," or put forth leaves, and, these being picked, "flushes" succeed each other at intervals of a few weeks throughout the rainy season. The leaves, after picking, are allowed to wither, and, when they will roll without breaking, are compressed into balls and slightly fermented. The balls are next opened out, the leaves dried in the sun, and finally "fired," by shaking in iron trays over burning charcoal. When quite crisp, they are run through sieves of six different meshes, yielding as many different qualities of tea, to which the Chinese names of Peko, Souchong, Congou, etc., are given.

We hear constant complaints that tea-planting does not pay in India, and "dear labour" is always cited as the cause of this by the planters. But, in Darjeeling, there are plenty of Nepalese labourers, whose wages are only 2s. 8d. per week; although, in Assam and Cachar, the largest tea-growing districts of India, there is no native labour, and the planter has to depend on immigrants from Bengal. The cost of moving these men, making due allowance for losses by death and desertion, is ninety-seven rupees each. The coolie engages for three years, receiving five rupees wages per month during that time, which brings his value to 3s. 8d. per week. At the end of three years he gets a trifling bonus on re-engaging, and thenceforth costs only five rupees a month, or 2s. 3d. per week. These prices justify neither the planters' outcry nor the charges which are so constantly made against Government of overcare for the immigrant's condition. The true reason why India competes at a disadvantage with China has really nothing whatever to do with this cheap-labour cry. In the latter country, tea is grown around the hut of every peasant. He picks his few pounds of leaves, as do tens of thousands of others like him, and takes them to the village curer and sorter, who sells direct to the European merchants in Shanghai, Whampoa, and other ports. From the garden to the wharf there is a minimum of expenses, while the merchants' profits are of course regulated by the market.

In India, on the other hand, great companies, with boards of directors, sitting very often in London, own large estates in the foot-hills of the Himalayas. The local superintendent, in each case, is an important and highly paid official, with an expensive European staff, and a number of native "sirdars," or foremen. The company has its agent in Calcutta, who, in addition to receiving consignments of tea, and charging brokerage, supplies everything required on the estate, down to the nails, sheet-lead, and hoop-iron of the tea-chests, on all of which articles he gets a good commission.

In a race between the thrifty Chinese peasant proprietor, who works for a bare subsistence, and the great company, with its well-paid directors and many expenses, there is no question which will win. If tea-growing does not pay in India, it is not because Nepalese and Bengali coolies are living in luxury on half a crown a week. To hear planters talk on the burning question of coolie importation, one would think that the Indian Government is bent on destroying tea-culture in India, by a sentimental immigration policy, dictated by Exeter Hall, which makes labour inordinately dear; but, like a good many other people with grievances, these gentlemen shun figures in their philippics, and find it easier to rail at humane provisions for the proper treatment of labour, than to make themselves acquainted with the true economical reasons of their failure to compete with China.

January 8.—Darjeeling, as we left it, was wrapped in a fog so thick that we could hardly see twenty yards before us. It was very cold, and we were glad of heavy wraps for a long time after we began the descent of the Himalayan flanks. Presently, however, we emerged into sunshine, and saw the plains of India below us stewing in tropical heat. In the course of a few hours we slipped by insensible degrees from a chilly to a hot climate, and, arrived at Silligouri, prepared ourselves for another awful night in the "sleeping-carriages" of the Northern Bengal Railway.

CHAPTER XVI.

BENARES.

January 10–13.

ALTHOUGH the East Indian Railway is the chief line in India, its sleeping-carriages, like those of the Northern Bengal, give the traveller only a bench to sleep on, lavatories without soap or towels, and no carriage attendants. Anglo-Indians carry their own bedding, and so many other comforts, that a man getting into a night train looks as if he were changing house and travelling with his furniture. This is all very well for people who move about with a bed-maker, a soap-bearer, a tooth-brush tender, and a human towel-horse; but travellers like ourselves are obliged to camp out as best they can on Indian railways. We begin to loathe the swarms of servants with whom Europeans surround themselves in India. When the fellow whose business it is has lighted his master's pipe, or another has brushed his clothes, each squats on his haunches and sleeps till he is wanted for similar services. Caste prejudices prevent Hindoo's from waiting at table, so that, in addition to the little army of Hindoo servants required for the most modest establishment, a Mahometan or two must be kept for the dining-room. A man, indeed, can neither eat, drink, sleep, ride, nor drive without first putting in motion a ridiculously elaborate machinery of service. The English are to blame for fostering a system which the native abuses in the interests of his natural indolence. In Bombay, we are told, domestic service has been brought very nearly into accordance with European practice, and it seems undignified on the part of the English in Bengal to continue the extravagances of a practice which arose in the old, ostentatious days of the Company's rule.

Leaving Calcutta, the East Indian Railway follows the Hooghly for about a hundred miles, and then strikes north-west to the Ganges, pursuing the course of this river as far as Cawnpore. There it turns west, and, in another hundred miles, reaches the left bank of the Jumna, which stream it follows to Delhi, the terminus of the line. About half-way between Calcutta and Delhi is Benares, lying on the left bank of the Ganges, and reached by a bridge of boats, which will soon be superseded by a railway bridge, now in course of construction. The country traversed is without any marked features, the Ganges valley being an apparently level plain of fine detritus, whose enormous extent and thickness recall to our minds the Bluff formation of the Mississippi. The piers of the new bridge at Benares are sunk a hundred feet into this alluvium, and there is still an unknown depth of it below. Engineers in India do not attempt to get down to the bed rock for their foundations; they only go deep enough to avoid the scour of the river. The plain is well cultivated, wheat at this time of year being the predominant crop, while clumps of trees and palms give a slight relief to what would otherwise be a monotonous scene. Wood is so scarce, or ants so destructive, that the telegraph posts are made of stone, and the line is fenced with cactus, a capital frontier for all kinds of animals. We were struck with the number and beauty of the Indian birds, especially after birdless Japan. The crows are no less numerous in the country than in Calcutta, and live on the most familiar terms with both man and beast. It is curious to see them perched upon the quiet oxen, or antediluvian-looking buffaloes, waiting for such treasures as may be found in their droppings. Lovely little green parrots, with long tail feathers, flew from tree to tree, flashing in the sunlight, while many other brilliant birds, whose names we do not know, are common, and, all alike, are tame.

Benares is the "Holy City" of India, the most formally religious country in the world. Every circumstance in the life of a Hindoo, from his birth to his death, is closely connected with religious observances, and the most insignificant as well as the most important acts cannot be performed without being accompanied by religious rites. Indian theology is professedly founded on the Vedas, of which there are four, the oldest, or "Rig-Veda," containing a collection of hymns and invocations, which formulate—if such a word may be used in the case of matters too chaotic for formulation—the religion of the primitive Hindoos. Originally, Vedism was pure nature-worship—the firmament, fire, sun, moon, the air, and the earth being the objects most frequently addressed, although a few doubtful references to monotheism may be detected here and there among the hymns. Vedism seems to have been accompanied from very early times by what may be called old Buddhism, forming a kind of intellectual protest against mere nature-worship, which could not altogether satisfy the best minds even of the primitive Aryan peoples. This belief was in an Almighty Creator, who, having made the world, withdrew Himself from His work, only keeping the knowledge and worship of Himself alive among men by the teachings of successive Buddhs, or prophets, of whom Sakya-Muni, the Buddha of all succeeding time, is said to be the twenty-fifth and last. Early Buddhism and Vedism, or Brahmanism, were always at war; their contests being essentially of the same character as those of superstition and reason in all ages; but the appearance of Sakya gave such an impulse to intellectuality as opposed to idolatry in religion, that, for a time, India deposed her Vedic deities and accepted those pure but sad doctrines of Buddha, which have already been set forth in connection with the theologies of Japan. The practice of Sakya's teaching was, however, too difficult; and his "eightfold path" of self-renunciation too hard to tread, so that, within a few centuries of its introduction, Buddhism became Pharisaic in character, monastic in practice, and ritualistic in worship, falling finally to the mere adoration of relics and idols. Whether or not

Buddhism in India was destroyed, as some think, by actual Brahmanical persecution, is an open question; only the obscure and [doubtful evidence of certain temple sculptures seeming to indicate that the religion of Sakya died a bloody death at the hands of its rivals, the Brahmans. Be this as it may, we know that, since the tenth century of our era, Buddhism has been replaced in India by Puranism, a religion based on an immense extension and perversion of the early Vedas, and invented by the Brahman, to suit the idolatrous tastes of the masses. Brahma, Vishnu, and Mahadeva, or Siva, are the triad of this theology, taking the lead in a chaotic polytheism, which makes a god of every animate and inanimate object, and connects religious rites with the most trfling as well as most important acts of life. Of the Hindoo trinity, Brahma, the supreme deity, is no longer worshipped, but only devoutly contemplated. Vishnu, or rather Rama, is Krishna, a deified hero of the national epic "Ramayana," while Siva, worshipped by the great mass of the people, represents the reproductive powers of nature, and is symbolized by the "Lingam," or Phallus. Siva's devotees are divided into sects, the Saivas and Saktas, of whom the latter adore only the Sakti, or female counterpart of the phallic symbol. To enumerate the lesser gods of the Hindoos is impossible, for everything is a god, and for the most debased and trivial object of worship a hidden meaning is claimed. Transmigration is the creed of all the sects, as it was that of the Indian Buddhists, and the chief aim of Hindoo worship is to obtain a deliverance from future existences—an object which is supposed to be effected by a reunion of the purified souls of men with the primitive spirit pervading all nature.

Benares stretches for some miles along the north bank of the Ganges, exhibiting, as seen from the river, an immense number of temples of Hindoo architecture; the tall and slender minarets of Aurungzebe's Mosque, a monument of Mahometan supremacy planted in the very heart of Brahmanism; and a number of great buildings, the houses of rich, religious rajahs, who visit the holy city as a matter of piety, and sometimes dedicate their mansions to the use of pilgrims. The river-bank is a terrace from which wide flights of steps descend to the water, where the Hindoos prepare themselves for worship by ablutions. These "bathing ghats" are occupied by a brilliantly coloured crowd, and the river itself is thickly fringed with red and white figures, while its banks are sprinkled with men and women either going to or returning from the stream. A nearer view shows that the bathers observe a prescribed ritual in their ablutions, the mouth, eyes, nose, and ears being first washed, and then the limbs in a certain order; some prayers are repeated, kneeling on the ghat; and the "lotah," a vessel of brass, is filled with Ganges water, to be carried away for home use. Thus prepared, and taking the utmost care to avoid anything which might defile him on the way, the devotee passes to the temple. Women have ghats of their own, which are scarcely separated from those used by the men. They purify with the same ceremonies, retaining their dress in the water, and changing it for clean robes on leaving the bath. It is surprising how skilfully they substitute a dry skirt and sarong, or overwrap, for their wet things without any exposure of themselves.

Among the many holy places in Benares, visitors are usually shown the Temple of Nepal, the Golden and Monkey Temples, and the Mosque of Aurungzebe, together with the pit—one cannot call it a temple—where snake-worship, introduced by Tartars six centuries before Christ, but never eradicated among this superstitious people, is carried on. Hindoo temples are characterized by an architecture which has nothing in common with that of Europe. The arch was unknown in India before the Mahometan conquest, and the native builder capped his closely grouped columns with spreading brackets, on which he placed bearers or architraves, and covered in by doming over the space between any four columns with gradually diminishing horizontal courses of flat stones. These domes are sometimes low, sometimes spire-like, but always decorated, as indeed is every portion of the building, with carvings whose originality, variety, and beauty have perhaps never been excelled. Mosques, on the other hand, are distinguished by the Saracenic arch, tall minarets, and a more sparing use of ornament. We shall see by-and-by, at Agra and Delhi, the matchless buildings which resulted from the union of Saracenic with Indian art; works which were justly the pride of their creators, the Mogul emperors, as they are still the glory of India and the wonder of the world.

A European must set aside all his preconceived ideas of worship on entering a Hindoo temple. We visited one which was full of great monkeys, who lolled in corners, or scampered at large about the shrine; the priests being apparently mere keepers of a zoological house, and the god an idol-monkey, to whom worshippers offered a few grains of rice or a libation of Ganges water. The Golden Temple was crowded with people, some making offerings, some praying at the shrine, while others were kneeling before low stands carrying volumes of printed prayers, which were recited in a sort of chant. Holy cows were numerous, and the mixture of their sanctified droppings, Ganges water, rice grains, and crushed flowers which befouled the floor, suggested to our minds that a broom and a bottle of Condy's fluid would be a welcome gift to the god.

Our temple visits impressed us strongly with the intensely idolatrous character of the Hindoos, and especially with the prominence of phallic worship in their cult. Not only are the temples of Siva sown broadcast with the Lingam and Sakti, but the same symbols are found in every stone-cutter's shop in Benares. It is probable that the worship of Siva is as conventional in character as these are in form, and that when a man halts for a moment at a wayside shrine, pours a few drops of Ganges water from his lotah over the stone, and gives a pice to the priest, he does nothing more than satisfy the religious instinct which is part of every Hindoo's nature. But it must not be forgotten that it is only since India has come under British rule that the worship of Siva has ceased to be accompanied by obscene rites, and if these are no longer observed, it is due, not to Brahman purity, but English repression.

The streets of Benares exhibit considerable artistic feeling on the part of the native builders. They are narrow and tortuous, but the houses, which are two and three storied, are clean and white. The open ground floors are occupied, as usual throughout the East, by shops, each of which is flanked by stone or wooden columns, carved in the Hindoo style, and connected above, either by a decorated Saracenic arch or carved architrave. Little verandahs of stone, pierced with geometrical or flowing figures, and carried upon carved stone brackets, relieve the house fronts, and, here and there, the crooked streets give suddenly on wide open spaces, where the business of the bazaar goes briskly forward, and brightly coloured groups of people are buying and selling. At almost every street corner is a small shrine, where men and women pause for a moment in passing, to throw yellow flowers or pour water from the lotah upon the symbol, leaving a few small coins with the priest, who squats lazily within the little alcove.

Benares is famous for its chased brass-work, and certain streets are wholly devoted to this manufacture. The brass is beaten up out of sheet metal into trays and vases; brazed by one man, turned in the lathe by another, and chased by a third, each art craftsman having his own shop, where only one of the three operations is carried on. The tools employed are very few, and of the simplest character. A hammer and anvil, and a little charcoal fire, urged by the breath, in an earthen pot, is all the first man wants. The lathe of the second is only a mandril wound around with a strap, which a boy pulls, giving some half a dozen turns, first in one and then in the opposite direction The third, with a few small hammers and chisels, outlines the design and finishes the work at one and the same operation, the decorations growing up on the metal under his skilful fingers without previous sketching.

Native merchants of importance do not display their wares in shops, and their houses are almost as difficult of access as a fortress. Wishing to buy some of the gold brocade for which Benares is famous, we called on one of the chief dealers in silks, who is also a banker. After passing through many passages and guarded doors, we reached a room buried deep in the house, where the merchant sat in state, surrounded by his book-keepers, and servants. Even here, no goods were to be seen, but the brocades were fetched, one at a time, from a neighbouring apartment by assistants. Meanwhile, the great man remained motionless and impassive, not deigning to speak except when the most costly things were shown, but ordering everything to be brought for our inspection, with the manner of a prince. When my companion had made a purchase, the money was taken by a cashier, and only in greeting us and saying farewell did the merchant's manner pass from dignity to cordiality; then he was as polite as a Japanese. The natives of India are very fond of privacy. Their houses, like those of Pompeii, show blank walls to the world, while the family life goes on within and unseen. They hate to be overlooked, or to have their business known, and it is this instinct, as much as security, which makes the trader withdraw his operations from the public eye.

In an incidental way we had already seen the famous Eastern conjurer several times. He ate swords and charmed snakes in Ceylon; swallowed stones and reproduced them from his stomach in Madras; and showed a variety of feeble tricks in Calcutta; but we were anxious to see some of the wonderful feats of Indian magic about which one hears so much, and sent for a great man. He was no better than all the others. He played thimble-rig, showed string puzzles, breathed fire, and finally exhibited the often-described mango trick; planting a seed in the ground, and inducing its magical growth to a tree. We have seen this wonder half a dozen times in India, and nothing can be more clumsy than its performance. One can actually watch the magician manipulate the mango branch, concealed in the bag with which he covers the seed while the growth is supposed to be taking place. Third-rate Euroapen conjurers are far superior to any

Indian magicians we have met with, and I am disposed to think that the travellers' stories about these men are written by people who know nothing about legerdemain.

The "burning ghat" of Benares lies by the river-side, and a funeral procession is a common sight in the streets. First comes a band of people, wailing, led by a man who swings an earthen pot filled with live coals. The kinsmen follow, with heads newly shaved, and their garments flying loose, crying, "Rama! Rama!" After them, the bier, a stretcher of woven bamboo, on which lies the corpse, sprinkled with red and yellow dust. A great wood pile receives the body, fire is applied, and when the whole has burnt to ashes these are scattered on the surface of the holy river. Returning from the burning ghat, we met a picturesque array. Some half-dozen elephants, a couple of camels, and a little body-guard of native soldiers, all glorious in tinsel and bright colours, were drawn up in the street, waiting for a rajah, who was bathing in the Ganges preparatory to visiting the shrine. Presently the great man returned, purified and gorgeously attired. The howdah of a kneeling elephant received him; the drivers said a few words in a low tone to their beasts, and the barbaro-religious procession got under way for the temple, where, a libation having been poured, and a few yellow flowers thrown over the Lingam, the pious work of the day would be completed.

Our last view of Benares was like our first. In the foreground was the yellow Ganges, and on the bank a picturesque crowd of bathers, behind whom rose, with broken and beautiful outlines, the white walls of great religious buildings, massive, like the centuries through which the Hindoo theology has endured, and as profusely fanciful in their decorations as the strange polytheism which still binds the mind of India with the fetters of degraded superstitions.

CHAPTER XVII.

LUCKNOW—CAWNPORE.

January 14-15.

ONCE more, our time being precious, we ventured into an Indian sleeping-carriage, leaving Benares by the Oudh and Rohilcund Railway, another metre-gauge line, which carried us, rather more comfortably than usual, to Lucknow, a distance of two hundred miles, in twelve hours, or at the rate of nearly seventeen miles an hour. Oudh, of which Lucknow is the capital, was annexed by the British in 1856. The country forms part of the alluvial valley of the Ganges, on one of whose tributaries, the Gumti, Lucknow is built. The northern part of Oudh is covered with forest, cleared here and there, and supporting a scanty population, who live by pasturing cattle. For the rest, the soil on the left bank of the Gumti is arid and sandy, while that lying between the Gumti and the Ganges is a fertile delta irrigated by wells. The province contains eleven million people, of whom ten millions are Hindoos.

About the middle of the last century, a Persian mercantile adventurer, named Saadat Ali Khan, went to seek his fortune at the Mogul court of Delhi, and, being a man of ability, he obtained the administration of Oudh, then part of the Imperial dominions. His son succeeded him, but though, in the growing weakness of the decaying Mogul empire, Saadat's office may appear to have become hereditary, Saftar Jung, his successor, was in no sense an independent ruler. In the course of time, however, a provincial governor succeeded in becoming a feudatory prince, with virtual independence, and at his death, in 1798, a struggle for the succession occurred, which ended in the British seating a half-brother of the late ruler's on the throne, under the title of Saadat Ali II. This man ceded nearly half of Oudh to the English in 1801, since which time the kings, having no real ruling to do, took to dancing girls, cock-fighting, drinking, and building stucco palaces for their women. Saadat Ali's immediate successors went deeper and deeper into the mire, so that our Resident at the court of Lucknow hardly ever saw the monarch, who was plunged in the lowest vices. In 1837 there was another struggle for the succession, when England again interfered, a step which terminated in a treaty providing for the partial introduction of British civil administration. Two more kings followed, during whose reigns the condition of the country went from bad to worse, until England, after much hesitation, annexed the country in 1856, transferring the king to Calcutta, where his great palace on the banks of the Hooghly is one of the first objects to strike the eye of the traveller arriving at the capital of Bengal.

Such are the circumstances, and such were the men under whom the "City of Palaces" arose, and it is not therefore surprising to find that among all the vast buildings reared by the kings of Oudh, there is scarcely one which commands respect or admiration. The city stands on a great plain, on the right bank of the Gumti river, extending over thirteen square miles, and having a population of two hundred and sixty thousand people six-tenths of whom are Hindoos. The European portion of the town is characterized by broad roads, beautiful houses and grounds, and abundant turf and trees; while the shops are unusually handsome. The native bazaar is picturesque, but its houses are inferior to those of Benares. An arched gateway opens upon a long, narrow, and crowded thoroughfare, lined upon either side by small shops for the sale of gold and silver brocade, silver chasing and inlaying, and precious stones, besides the usual miscellaneous goods. The shops exhibit little artistic taste in construction, although they are all flanked by carved wood columns, which support Saracenic arches.

As for the court suburb, the best that can be said of it is that it is vast and sumptuous, while the worst is happily embodied in the phrase, "Lucknow is a city of stucco nightmares." Its seraglios and palaces, which cover several square miles of ground, are built of brick and stucco, and were designed by ill-educated Europeans, who gave the last touches of ostentatious vulgarity to a debased Saracenic style. Bad as it is, this dash of European art among Oriental buildings makes Lucknow unlike any other Indian town, and it must be confessed that the very number and size of its palaces give an air of magnificence to the city, which only disappears when the buildings themselves are examined in detail. To describe these palaces would be a thankless task, their only interest for us resides in the fact that some of them formed serious obstacles to the advance of the troops whom Havelock, Outram, and Campbell led to the relief of the dauntless garrison which held the Lucknow Residency so tenaciously against terrible odds during the dreadful days of 1857.

When Lord Canning landed in Calcutta in 1856, India appeared to be profoundly tranquil. The annexation of Oudh had been peaceably effected, and the deposed king was residing near Calcutta. The chief commissionership of Oudh had, however, unfortunately, been given to a man who, instead of endeavouring to reconcile the chiefs and people to a foreign rule, interfered unwisely with the tenures of estates belonging to the native aristocracy, and in so doing sowed the seeds of disaffection among classes which he should have tried to conciliate. The bulk of the sepoy army was recruited from Oudh, and all the soldiers of this country lost certain privileges, which gave them importance in their native villages, when the province was annexed. Delhi, too, the old Mahometan capital of India, had been allowed to retain its king and a mock court, although the former had been authoritatively informed that the royal title would lapse on the death of its existing owner. The king's favourite wife was, however, bent on the succession of her son, and not only did her influence cause Delhi to become hostile to the Government, but Southern India, and even Persia were excited to enmity against the British by her intrigues. Further, a man named Nana Sahib, who lived near Cawnpore, and was the adopted son of a rajah to whom the British Government paid a large annuity, had the impudence to demand a continuance of this payment after the rajah's death. On this being refused, he vowed vengeance against the dominant race, and, at a later stage of events, became one of the foremost leaders of the Mutiny.

It is doubtful whether the smouldering disaffection in Oudh and Delhi would have culminated in the revolt of the whole native army but for an unexpected incident. The Enfield rifle had lately been introduced, and its cartridges were greased for the lubrication of the barrel. While the touch of beef in any shape defiles a Hindoo, and causes the loss of caste, the Mahometan has a pious horror of pork. An alarm was raised among the sepoys at Dumdum, a school of musketry near Calcutta, that Government had caused the new cartridges to be smeared with ingredients which would defile both Hindoo and Mahometan. A sudden excitement arose and spread like wildfire among the sepoys of both creeds, and, in the course of a few days, almost every regiment in India was infected with alarm and passion.

Such was the state of things in April, 1857, a month which passed without disturbance, only because, as afterwards transpired, a general conspiracy had been organized for the simultaneous revolt of every regiment at every station in Hindostan on the last Sunday of May, at the hour of church service, when all Europeans, without regard to age or sex, were to be massacred. An unexpected transaction, however, at Meerut, near Delhi, led to a premature outbreak. The 3rd Native Cavalry at that station refused to touch the new cartridges, and were put in irons by the captain commanding. On the following Sunday, the 10th of May, the troops broke out, liberated the prisoners, massacred all the Europeans in the station, and started for Delhi. There, they were joined by the 38th Regiment, on duty in the city; the Europeans were overpowered and shot, and sovereignty offered to the king by the mutineers. The news of the outbreak and establishment of a Mogul throne was at once telegraphed to Calcutta, but, in consequence of the Persian war, Lord Canning had no troops at hand, and sent to Madras, Bombay, and Ceylon for every available white regiment, while a steamer was despatched to intercept Lord Elgin, then on his way to China with troops.

At this time, the Punjaub was administered by Sir John Lawrence, with a large body of able civil servants under him, and these men lost no time in disarming the native regiments at Lahore, Umritsur, Peshawur, and elsewhere. A regiment at Jhelum succeeded in escaping with their arms, and some regiments at Sealkote followed their example, but they were cut to pieces on their way to Delhi by John Nicholson, afterwards one of the greatest heroes of the Mutiny. These measures were so skilfully conceived and boldly executed, that they gave security for a time to the Punjaub; but, meanwhile, there was scarcely a regiment, from Allahabad to the Sutlej, which was not in revolt; Delhi became the seat of a revolutionary government, and its capture became every day more urgent and more difficult.

In Oudh, as we have seen, the aristocracy were disaffected to English rule, and the people followed the suit of their natural leaders. Sir Henry Lawrence was the Resident at Lucknow, where he soon found himself surrounded by the disloyal retainers of the old native court, and numerous sympathizers with the revolted sepoys. There were at this time nine native regiments in the town, and only seven hundred Europeans. One of the regiments revolted, but, on being attacked by Lawrence, the sepoys threw down their arms and fled. Three weeks later, on the 30th of May, five other regiments broke out, murdered their officers, and fired the cantonments, and, by the middle of June, every regiment in Oudh had mutinied. Lawrence was shut up in the Residency by the end of June, with a garrison of nine hundred Europeans and eight hundred natives, and the siege began. The house, a mansion built by one of the kings of Oudh, stood in its own grounds, surrounded by a low mud wall, closely girdled by the native town. It is now a mere ruin, pitted all over with shot-marks, but the mud wall no longer exists; the native quarter has been cleared away, and the grounds have been converted into an ornamental garden, the position of every battery erected by the defence being marked by dwarf columns carrying inscribed slabs. All this has been done with unostentatious good taste; but the Residency and grounds, while they properly remain a memento of a great national peril gallantly met, now give but little notion of the space wherein hundreds of persons, combatant and non-combatant, women and children, were cooped up and rained upon with shot and shell for fifteen weeks, in the middle of an Indian summer. The mutineers occupied the houses of the native town, while the besieged threw up detached works at more or less advanced points around the house. One of these, named the Cawnpore Battery, was so desperate a post that it was always held by volunteers, no officer being placed in permanent charge of it. Near it, was a work defended by sixty-five boys from the "Martinière," a foundation school in Lucknow, while other batteries are known as Duprat's, Anderson's, and the Redan. Sir Henry Lawrence was killed by a shell only a few days after the siege began, and, before the garrison was first relieved by Havelock, in September, it had lost four hundred men, eleven ladies, and fifty children; while, between that time and the final relief by Sir Colin Campbell, a hundred and twenty of the original garrison, and four hundred of the men whom Havelock threw into the place, had died. Of the relief itself I shall speak as the story of the Mutiny progresses.

Cawnpore was another station in the north-west, garrisoned by three native regiments, who revolted on the 5th of June, dismissing their officers, plundering the treasury, and marching off to Delhi. General Wheeler, who was in command, had only two hundred European soldiers on the spot, and, fearing an outbreak, had already entrenched himself in the open plain. Into this little work the whole European population was crowded, and here, for three weeks, the feeble garrison, with their sick and dying all round, without hospital stores, and short of both ammunition and food, were sapped, bombarded, and starved. By the third week, a hundred of them were dead, and the rest nearly starving. The attack was conducted by Nana Sahib himself, who had fomented the spirit of revolt among the Cawnpore troops. On the 26th of June, the Nana offered to treat, promising the protection of his escort to the garrison. The terms were accepted; boats were provided for the conveyance of the survivors to Allahabad, and, on the morning of the 27th of June, they moved down to the river. No sooner were the boats in mid-stream, than they were deliberately fired upon by the Nana's order. Grape and musketry opened on the defenceless whites from both sides of the river, and, of those who got to shore alive, the women and children were taken to the Nana's house, while the men were shot in the water, only four of the latter escaping.

The perilous condition of the garrisons of Lucknow and Cawnpore formed the chief cause of anxiety at Calcutta. The Punjaub had been saved by the masterly movements of Sir John Lawrence and his officers. At Benares, the commissioner and his associates succeeded in warding off the danger until a small reinforcement arrived under Colonel Neill, who then moved on to relieve the important fort of Allahabad, which was besieged by the mutineers, who had possession of Allahabad itself. In this he succeeded, re-establishing order in the city, and making a terrific example of the revolted sepoys. Meanwhile, Colonel Havelock had returned to Calcutta from the Persian expedition, and formed a movable column, from reinforcements which now began to arrive in driblets, to proceed upwards from the lower provinces to the scenes of the revolt. Reaching Allahabad on the 30th of June, he was met by the news of the surrender of Cawnpore. In his anxiety to relieve this town, Neill had despatched a small force only a few days before Havelock's arrival, and upon this little band the Nana had turned immediately after the surrender of Wheeler. Havelock hastened after the handful of white soldiers, overtook it at Futtehpore, at which place he commenced his victorious career. The enemy, nearly four times his number, was completely routed, and the Nana's brother, who was in the field, hastened back to Cawnpore, with the alarming news that the British were in full march on the town.

The Nana at once massacred all the women and children, survivors of the scene on the river, and threw them, dead and dying, into a well; after which he marched against Havelock, but, being decisively beaten, fled across the Ganges into Oudh. Next morning, when our troops marched into Cawnpore, the sight of the well told them the story; after that there was no more quarter given to sepoys.

Colonel Neill was now left in charge of Cawnpore, while the victorious Havelock pushed on to Lucknow. Whereas, in Hindostan generally, the people were neutral, and many of the native aristocracy remained loyal to the British, both the landed class and people of Oudh were hostile, and the whole country in revolt; a large army of sepoys, strong in the sympathy of the country, was ready to dispute every inch of ground, while Havelock's force did not exceed fourteen hundred men. On the 25th of July, however, he worsted the enemy, twelve thousand strong, and, on the 4th of August, defeated twenty thousand mutineers at Busserut. Then the cholera broke out in his camp. Neill was again threatened in Cawnpore, and Havelock was at length obliged to suspend operations and wait for reinforcements. While waiting, he again fought the enemy on the 16th of August, and then, after ten successful engagements, lay unwillingly on his oars for aid from Calcutta.

On the 16th of September, Outram reached him with fourteen hundred men, raising his force to two thousand five hundred, and, gracefully leaving the command in the hands of Havelock, who was his junior officer, accompanied him as a volunteer. On the morning of the 25th of September, the two succeeded in forcing their way into the Residency at Lucknow, after a whole day's desperate fighting, in the course of which the little force lost over four hundred and fifty men, and Neill was unfortunately killed. Even after the garrison was thus relieved, they were too weak to escort the women and children to Cawnpore, still less to recover the city, now occupied by a large rebel army abundantly furnished with military stores. Further reinforcements, however, reached

Calcutta in November, and marched, under Sir Colin Campbell, up to Cawnpore. Thence, this general started on the 9th of November, with five thousand men, and forced his way into the Residency, after three days of continuous and heavy fighting. A skilful retreat to Cawnpore was effected by part of the garrison, in charge of the women and children; but the gallant Havelock, worn out with his labours, died of diarrhœa. Outram was left with a sufficient force in charge of the Alum Bagh, one of the "stucco nightmares," on the outskirts of the town, to keep open communications with Cawnpore, and Sir Colin Campbell returned to the latter place, just in time to save the general in charge from a disaster. The Gwalior contingent had mutinied in October, and marched to attack Cawnpore, but were met by Campbell before they reached the town, and completely overthrown.

To turn to Delhi, which had become the head-quarters of the revolutionary movement. This city was invested by our troops by the end of May, the small besieging force taking up a commanding position on "the ridge," a chain of low hills, whence the town is overlooked from a distance of a mile. The impossibility of taking a vast place like Delhi with the weak force under the command of General Barnard, was self-evident, and, during fourteen weeks from the commencement of the siege, the besiegers were really themselves besieged. More than thirty attacks were made on Barnard's lines, but Lord Canning stuck to the position through all difficulties, wisely seeing that, as Delhi had become the rallying-point of the mutineers, the retirement of the army from before it would stimulate the spirit of revolt.

Meanwhile, Sir John Lawrence was raising Sikh regiments in the north-west, and, on the 14th of August, Nicholson arrived at Delhi with a force that brought the numbers of the attack up to seven thousand men. On the 3rd of September the siege train arrived, and then, for a month, fifty guns poured shot and shell into the town. On the 14th, an assault was delivered, and Delhi recovered, though at the price of Nicholson's life, and a loss of three thousand five hundred men. It took six days' fighting before the whole town was in our hands, but on the 20th resistance ceased. The king fled, but was captured by Major Hodson, at Humayoun's tomb, a few miles outside the city, and the same officer, in pursuit of the king's sons, found them surrounded by so great a crowd of armed and unarmed men that, fearing a rescue, he shot them in the road, and with them perished the last heirs to the throne of the Great Moguls.

The outbreak had already been crushed in Central India, and by the end of December, 1857, the Company's authority was re-established everywhere but in Oudh. Early in 1858, Sir Colin Campbell found himself at the head of a force of nearly twenty thousand men, with which he advanced to the capture of Lucknow. Outram, left as we have seen at the Alum Bagh, had been twice attacked by a force six times his number, but had held his own, and now, after ten days' incessant fighting, the city was completely recovered. The Mutiny was practically at an end, although, here and there, bands of rebels continued to resist. Nana Sahib escaped the closest pursuit, but died in the jungles of Nepal, in 1859. All the other leaders were either killed, captured, or executed. The Sepoy Rebellion was the death-warrant of the East India Company, and, on the 1st of November, 1858, the Queen was proclaimed Sovereign of India. Such, in brief, is the story of the Great Indian Mutiny, a national disaster which was retrieved by the efforts of a few heroic men, many of them civilians by profession, but who became brilliant soldiers because they were capable of rising to the height of a great occasion, and burned with the same desire which finds expression on one of the noblest among many noble tombs at Lucknow: "Here lies the body of Henry Lawrence, who tried to do his duty."

Cawnpore is a town of nearly a hundred and twenty thousand inhabitants, lying in the midst of a flat alluvial plain on the banks of the Ganges. There is no sign left of Wheeler's entrenchment, which was only a low mud wall thrown up in the very midst of the plain, and open to attack from all sides. Wheeler has been much blamed for choosing such an indefensible position, especially as there was an old building by the river-side, which would have sheltered his front, while his rear would have been protected from attack by the stream. A little north of the site of the entrenchment stands the memorial church, a fine Romanesque building, within which are many monumental tablets, recording dreadful deaths with a simplicity that is at once touching and terrible. The "Well" is about a mile from Wheeler's entrenchment. On the 15th of July the news of Havelock's victorious advance reached the Nana. Of the prisoners who had escaped from the boats, four were men, and they were taken out and shot. The women and children were confined in a small room, and fired upon from the windows, and, when all were either dead or wounded, the bodies were thrown into the well. This infamous spot is now enclosed by a marble structure, and the exact site of the well is marked by an angel figure, while a large and tasteful garden surrounds the sad memorial of England's darkest Indian tragedy.

Cawnpore is the greatest market town in India. All the produce of the north-west finds its way to the bazaar, which is of enormous size and crowded with merchandise, especially grain and cotton. The last is extensively grown in the neighbourhood of the city, and is now being profitably manufactured into twist and cloth at mills which have been established by Europeans within the last few years. The increase of manufactures in India is a matter of the highest national importance. Hitherto, the natives have subsisted entirely on agriculture, and, so great is the pressure of population on the acreage, that the cultivators in many parts are always only a little way removed from hunger, while a dry season inevitably produces scarcity, and sometimes famine. The statesman of our time is never allowed to forget this permanent danger to India. In the days of the Company, as in those of the Mogul emperors, famine was looked upon as an irresistible foe, whose course could not be checked, although, as often happened, whole districts were depopulated by dearth, and the soil returned to jungle for want of tillers. England no longer folds its hands in the presence of such calamities, but every Indian statesman feels that his reponsibilities are sensibly lessened by the growth of industries which, by employing labour, diminish the pressure of the population on the soil.

CHAPTER XVIII.

AGRA.

January 16-18.

AGRA lies on the west bank of the Jumna river, which makes a great horse-shoe bend immediately below the city. The population is a hundred and fifty thousand souls, of whom one-third are Mussulmans. The walls include eleven square miles, only half of which area is inhabited; the remainder consists of ruins, ravines, and dusty patches of desert. Agra was the creation of Akbar, the Great Mogul, who established his metropolis and palace here in 1566. Before his day, Delhi had always been the Mahometan capital of India, but this city ceased to attract any attention from Akbar's successors for eighty years, when his grandson, Shah Juhan, built modern Delhi, which then, again, became the capital of the conquerors. These towns, and the splendid architecture which dstinguishes them among all other cities of the world, are so identified with Mogul rule that, in view of descriptions to follow, it will be convenient to introduce a short but necessary sketch of this brilliant dynasty, which raised India to the greatest prosperity she ever attained under native rule, and the art of building, in particular, to a height of excellence which has never been equalled elsewhere.

In 1526, certain disaffected Hindoo princes persuaded Baber, the sixth in descent from Timour the Tartar, to undertake the invasion of India. Baber was a Mogul, or member of that nomad Tartar tribe whose incursions had harried India ever since the end of the thirteenth century. Hindostan was in an anarchic condition, and the kingdom of Delhi had become restricted to a very small territory when Baber attacked and captured the city in 1526. He only reigned four years, but during that time he extended his conquests until he became master of all Northern India. He was succeeded by his son, Humayoun, in 1530, who soon lost the kingdom to a revolted soldier of fortune, named Shere Khan. Sixteen years later, the weakness of this man's successor gave Humayoun an opportunity of recovering his throne; but he did not long enjoy the crown, being accidentally killed by a fall only six months afterwards. Humayoun's son, Akbar, who succeeded him at the early age of thirteen, was destined to become the greatest of all the Mahometan rulers of India. He was contemporary with Queen Elizabeth, his reign having begun two years before and ending two years after hers. He never fought a battle which he did not win, or besiege a town which he did not take, but he preferred administration to war, and the glory of his reign depends less on his conquests than the admirable institutions by which they were consolidated. Akbar was entirely free from Mahometan bigotry or religious bias. He treated Hindoos and Mussulmans alike; married a Hindoo princess; made Hindoos his counsellors, and developed Indian nationality to the utmost of his power. Under him there arose a new creed and a new architecture, of which, while the former has decayed, the works of the latter remain, the boast of India and the wonder of the world. Akbar died in 1605, and was succeeded by his son Jehangir, who, though an able man, was a sot. In 1627, Shah Juhan, son of Jehangir, ascended the throne, and proved the most magnificent of all the Moguls. His reign embraced the most prosperous period of native rule in India; the country and finances were well administered by him, and, though he spent immense sums in gratifying his love of splendour, especially in architecture, he left large amounts in the national treasury. He was succeeded, in 1658, by his son Aurungzebe, a bigoted Mussulman, and the last of the line worthy of notice.

During these reigns, the empire was extended over nearly all India, and the numerous towns, palaces, and mosques which were erected by the Moguls testify to their enterprise and magnificence. Mogul rule existed, but did not flourish, throughout the eighteenth century, but, in 1803, the British possessed themselves of Delhi. They did not, however, destroy the Mogul dynasty, but, as we have already seen, allowed a mimic royalty to disport itself in the city until 1857, when the king, who had identified himself with the cause of the Mutiny, was exiled to Burmah, and his sons were slain.

The chief buildings in Agra are the Fort and Palace ; the Taj Mahal, or Tomb of Shah Juhan's wife, and Akbar's Tomb at Sikandra, four miles from the city. Our first visit was to Sikandra, the road to which has been called the "Appian Way" of India, being bordered by tombs, originally ambitious structures, but now in partial or complete decay. If Benares breathes the spirit of Hindooism, Agra and its neighbourhood bespeak Mahometan supremacy in every building that meets the eye. The bizarre spires and colonnades of the native artist, profusely decorated with pantheistic carvings, are seen no more, but their places are taken by the scalloped arches, swelling domes, and aspiring minarets characteristic of Saracenic architecture.

Akbar's Tomb was raised by his son in 1613, in the midst of a large garden enclosed by high quadrangular walls, whose sides are pierced by massive gateways of red sandstone. From each gate a causeway leads to a central platform, about four hundred feet square, on which the mausoleum stands, the intermediate spaces of garden being filled with handsome trees. The tomb itself is three hundred feet square, and rises in five terraces, pyramidally arranged to about a hundred feet in height. Around each of these terraces runs an arched gallery, surmounted by rows of kiosques. The topmost story, which is of white marble, is an open court about seventy feet square, surrounded by narrow vaulted cloisters, whose sides are formed of pierced marble screens, while, in the centre of the court, stands a sarcophagus of white marble, exquisitely sculptured. This is only a duplicate of the stone under which the dust of Akbar lies, in a lofty vaulted hall, occupying the centre of the pile and lighted only by a few small openings. The main gateway of the garden is a massive red sandstone structure, covered externally with inlaid Arabic inscriptions, geometrical figures, and floral arabesques. Within, it is a lofty vaulted chamber decorated with coloured arabesques, which are seen to great advantage by the light of sunbeams straying through pierced stone screens. On either side of this room are mortuary chambers, containing the remains of Akbar's sisters, who repose under marble sarcophagi of exquisite design and execution.

Already Sikandra had given us very exalted ideas of Mogul architecture, and it was with high expectations that we next turned to the Fort of Akbar. This is the central object in Agra; its walls are seventy feet high, and about a mile and a half in circuit, surrounded by a deep moat filled from the river Jumna. Within these commanding walls is the Palace of the Great Mogul, comprising halls of public and private audience, the king's private apartments, the zenana, or women's quarter, the famous Moti Musjid, or Pearl Mosque, and other less important buildings.

"The Pearl Mosque," says Bayard Taylor, "is in truth the pearl of all mosques of small dimensions, but absolutely perfect in style and proportion. It is lifted on a lofty sandstone platform, and, from without, nothing can be seen but its three domes of white marble and gilded spires. These domes crown a corridor, open towards a court, and divided into three aisles by a triple row of exquisitely proportioned Saracenic arches. The Moti Musjid can be compared to no other building I have ever seen. To my eye it is absolutely perfect. While its architecture is the purest Saracenic, it has all the simplicity of Doric art. It is a sanctuary so pure and stainless, revealing so exalted a spirit of worship, that I felt humbled as a Christian to think that our noble religion has never inspired its architects to surpass this temple to God and the Prophet." This enthusiastic praise is not thrown away on the Moti Musjid, but it does not characterize the building, which is pure and stainless indeed, but much too dainty to evoke any of the religious emotion which is felt in the aisles of a Gothic church. It is a bridal chamber rather than a fane, but over-refined and architecturally feeble; delicate as a shell, and beautiful as a woman is beautiful.

The greater part of Akbar's original work at Agra was cleared away by Shah Juhan, to make way for suites of magnificent chambers, decorated with carving, painting, and inlays of precious stones. These apartments overhang the river from the height of the walls, and are connected by projecting belvederes, from which the emperor could watch his yachts or the water sports. The most beautiful of them all is the hall of private audience (Dewan-i-Khas), a marble colonnade of Saracenic arches supported on twin columns, whose graceful bases, capitals, and shafts are inlaid with onyx, heliotrope, agate, and carnelian, disposed in floral designs. This lovely room opens upon a square courtyard, whose noble simplicity throws the exquisite, if feminine, beauty of the Dewan-i-Khas into the highest relief. The hall of public audience is a much larger colonnade of red sandstone, with massive columns and fine Saracenic arches. Within, stands a throne, and the hall opens on a vast courtyard. Here the emperor administered justice, or sat, surrounded by his nobles, to watch the fights of animals or view his elephants and horses. There are no great saloons or galleries, throughout the palaces of the Mogul emperors. These monarchs, the decendants of nomads, carried the life of the camp into their most luxurious capitals. There was a central pavilion, the Dewan-i-Am, for the display of the king and the public administration of justice, and a smaller pavilion in which he consulted his peers and council. But his private life was passed in the zenana, and great suites of reception-rooms, such as are found in European palaces, would have had no use.

Among the original works of Agra Fort which Shah Juhan did not replace with marble structures is a palace built by Akbar for his son Jehangir. It is entirely of sandstone, and Hindoo both in construction and ornament, but as I shall have to examine the distinguishing characteristics of Hindoo and Mahometan architecture when describing Futtehpore-Sikri, a town of Akbar's, which we have yet to visit, the Jehangir Palace is best spoken of here simply as one of the Great Mogul's happiest efforts to develop the constructive capacities of Hindoo architecture.

On a bend of the Jumna, about a mile below the Fort, lies the Taj Mahal, the glory of India, and the tomb of Shah Juhan's favourite wife, the "Exalted One of the Palace." This mausoleum was begun in 1630 and finished in 1648. During these eighteen years it employed twenty thousand men, and cost the prodigious sum of two millions sterling. The labour was forced, and so poorly paid in rations of rice that the poet describes the Agra peasants as crying—

> "Have mercy, God, on our distress;
> For we too die with the princess!"

"The Taj," to quote Bayard Taylor again, "like the Tomb of Akbar, stands in a large garden, enclosed by a lofty wall of red sandstone, with arched galleries around the interior, and entered by a suberb gateway of sandstone, inlaid with ornaments and inscriptions from the Koran in white marble. Entering, an avenue of cypresses appears before you. Along its centre sparkles a row of fountains, each throwing up a single jet. On both sides palms, banians, and feathery bamboos mingle their foliage. Down such a vista, and over such a foreground rises the Taj." We tried hard to be enthusiastic about the "wonder of India," and failed. We visited it in full daylight; when painted with the rosy light of sunset, and in bright moonlight,—but always to come to the same conclusion. An ethereal beauty characterizes the Taj; but this must be ascribed chiefly to its exquisite material and delicate colour. Marble retains its virginal whiteness in the pure air of India, and contrasts exquisitely with the clear blue of the sky; but the building would lose more than half its attraction if formed of a coarser stone. Architecturally, it has no charm. It is a great cubical mass, with truncated corners, and walls deeply excavated by cavernous arches which lead nowhere. These recesses give the only relief to the structure, which has not even a moulding to break its monotonous flatness. Instead, there are flat bands, bordered with black marble, and inlaid with Arabic inscriptions, but there are no structural lines which carry the delighted eye from one point to another of the pile, and no constructive arrangements of any sort in the Taj. Still it charms. To quote Bayard Taylor once more : " So light it seems, so like a fabric of mist and moonbeams, with its great dome soaring up like a silvery bubble, that even after you have touched it and climbed to its summit, you may almost doubt its reality." This is extravagant praise, but it describes the effect which the Taj produces on the mind when its beautifully textured white marble is lighted either by the full moon or the faint rose tints of the setting sun.

In describing the Palace of Akbar, I have already mentioned the use of marble inlaid with precious stones. This art resembles Florentine work of the sixteenth century, and became characteristic of Mogul architecture after the death of Akbar, appearing first at Sikandra, where the inlaid figures are purely geometrical. Twenty years later, the inlay of Akbar's time gave way to a mixed style, imperfect flowing figures being added to the purely geometrical ornament of an earlier date, but, by the time the Taj was built, Indian *pietra dura* work had reached its highest development, and beautiful floral forms had replaced the stiffer and cruder designs of former times. The sarcophagi of Shah Juhan and his wife, which lie within the Taj Mahal, are enclosed by a quadrangular screen of pierced marble, or jali-work, exquisitely executed; a piece of lace in stone. The pilasters which support these jali screens are thickly covered with floral inlays of precious stones, and the interior walls of the Taj are similarly decorated, but the jewels are used simply and without ostentation, as befitted the taste of a builder like Shah Juhan, whose errors were all on the side of over-refinement.

The Taj abuts on the Jumna by a magnificent terrace walk, whence the view, especially at sunset, is extremely beautiful. The spectator is placed almost at the crown of a great bend in the river, which sweeps away on either hand, and is lost in the misty distances of the plain. On his right, overhanging the stream and about a mile away, rise the battlemented walls of Akbar's Fort, crowned with the white pavilions and domes which Shah Juhan added to the frowning pile. Beyond this splendid monument of Mogul art, is seen the handsome railway bridge which now spans the Jumna, the work of that modern civilizer, the English engineer, and as beautiful, in its way as Akbar's towers. On the left, among the ruins of domes and minarets, and just beyond the farthest kiosque of the garden enclosure, is the burning ghat, where a flicker of light tells us that the body of a Hindoo is crumbling into ashes, to be thrown into the water and float to the holy river by-and-by. The opposite bank is lined with the remains of palaces, once belonging to the omrahs, or nobles of Akbar's court, who were bound to appear at the palace daily, and lived in close attendance on the monarch. Some massive foundations here look as if there had once been a bridge across the Jumna, but that is not likely. Tradition says they are the first courses of a palace, so ambitiously designed that Shah Juhan forbade its completion, saying, "If the building is very good it may eclipse the Taj; if not, the effect of my work will be spoiled."

The river is full of shoals, where great turtles lie basking, or slide lazily into the water and paddle to new quarters with only their noses above water. As the sun sets, the smooth surface of the river glows with rosy light, while, here and there, the wakes of slowly moving boats relieve the sheet of warm colouring with long triangles of purple. Now the night falls; the Jumna suddenly darkens, and we turn to see, by the enchanted light of a full moon the swelling domes and tall minarets of the Taj, "clothed in white samite, mystic, wonderful."

In pursuance of his policy of conciliation, and with a view to the amalgamation of Hindoo and Mahometan, Akbar married a

Hindoo Princess. She bore him twin boys, who died in infancy, at a moment when the emperor, returning from a campaign on which his wife had accompanied him, halted at the foot of a rocky ridge, where now stand the ruins of the town of Futtehpore-Sikri. Here lived a "faquir," or holy man, Sulim-Chisti, who persuaded the royal couple that a son would be born to them if they took up their abode at this spot. Sulim's prophecy proved correct, and to commemorate the birth of an heir to his throne, Akbar, in 1570, founded the palace of Futtehpore-Sikri, where the court afterwards resided, but only for a few years. Akbar's headquarters at this time were fixed at Agra, which city he had begun to build in 1566, and it was soon found that the transfer of the capital to Futtehpore was a mistake, the water proving scarce and alkaline, while the position of Agra, on a great river, made its situation far more suitable for a metropolitan palace.

Futtehpore is twenty-five miles from Agra, and the road between the two places traverses a badly irrigated and poorly cultivated country, having few villages, and those inhabited chiefly, as it appeared to us, by beggars. Just before reaching the old city, ridges of red sandstone rise gently out of the plain, terminating in abrupt clifts; and upon the summit of one of these ridges Akbar's various palaces and mosques are grouped. The city walls are seven miles in circumference, and enclose the two villages of Futtehpore and Sikri. Many of the Mogul emperor's buildings are in ruins, others partially so, while some still remain intact, and Government is engaged in extensive works of restoration and preservation here as well as at Agra and Delhi. The chief objects of interest are the great Entrance Gates, the Mosque, the Tomb of Sulim-Chisti, the House of Birbul, and the Five-Storied Pavilion. All these buildings display the finest characteristics of the Mogul school of architecture, but, before entering the beautiful city, I must try briefly to show what Hindoo architecture originally was; how it was influenced by the Mahometan conquest in the first instance; afterwards by the Moguls; and, finally, trace the decay of the eclectic style which arose from the fusion of Hindoo and Mahometan ideas of constructive art under Akbar's fostering influence.

Hindoo architecture is characterized by the absence of the arch, the dislike of flat surfaces, and the lavish use of carved surface ornamentation. Failing the arch, the Hindoos domed in their buildings by gradually diminishing horizontal courses of masonry. They abhorred all flat surfaces, and the carvings in high relief, whether of men, animals, or gods, with which their structures are covered, are unequalled in the world for profuse and various invention.

From the end of the twelfth to the arrival of the Moguls in the early part of the sixteenth century, India was under the rule of the Afghans, or Pathans, who brought with them from Central Asia the Mahometan mosque, with its Saracenic arches, bulbous domes, tall minarets, and unrelieved surfaces. Scarcely, however, had the foreign invader settled in the country, than a new school of architecture arose from the adaptation of Pathan ideas to the habits of Hindoo artisans; and this school, which is still prevalent, although in a debased form, throughout Upper India, passed through three distinct phases before the advent of the Moguls. The first Pathan period is characterized by the use of a sham arch, without true *voussoirs* or keystones, which the native workman did not know how to make, and by the lavish use of ornament. In regard to the last, the Hindoo sculptor, however, was no longer "fancy free." In place of his gods, whom the Mussulman hated, he traced texts from the Koran, in conventionalized Arabic characters, and his deeply cut inventive groups of animate things were replaced by inscriptions dictated by the conquerors, and produced in comparatively flat relief. But if the Hindoo sculptor danced in fetters, he danced gracefully, and added the loveliest of adornments to the grand general outlines of his master for more than a hundred years. At the end of this time, the style in question gave way to that of the second Pathan period, when there came into vogue a gloomy fortress-like building, which, though totally without ornament of any kind, had a masculine beauty of its own, somewhat like that of mediæval Norman strongholds. Hindóo influence disappeared entirely, while the use of the true arch, with *voussoirs* and keystone, became universal. The second period endured for two centuries, and is strikingly illustrated by many of the tombs in the neighbourhood of Delhi. It was followed by a third Pathan period, which had only lasted for fifteen years before the rise of the Mogul school, of which it was clearly the progenitor. The third Pathan period is characterized by bolder arches, a great extension of constructive ideas, and a return to the use of Hindoo ornament, which is no longer lavishly or slavishly employed, as was the case in the first Pathan period. It would now seem as if the Mahometan architect, while relying on his own enlarged ideas of construction, confided such portions of his work as required enrichment to the Hindoo, leaving the character of the decoration to the discretion of his collaborateur. There are very few examples of the third Pathan period in India, and of these, the Kila Kona Mosque at Delhi is the best. Although in partial ruin, the building is a magnificent work, which proclaims aloud the fact that the true terms of a great alliance in art had at length been concluded. In the first Pathan period the Hindoo was a slave; in the second, he was discarded altogether; but in the third, he became the partner of the Afghan architect, who furnished the grand outlines, directing where, not how, they should be decorated by the refined and imaginative Hindoo sculptor. It remained for the Tartar Akbar to inaugurate a fourth, or Mogul, school of Hindostani architecture, characterized by the employment of Hindoo treatment, which had hitherto been capricious, accidental, and fluctuating, on a declared system of eclecticism and amalgamation.

Futtehpore-Sikri belongs to a time when these principles were most fully accepted, and its palaces, though in partial ruin, exhibit magnificent examples of purely Hindoo construction, elevated by Mahometan boldness and adorned by enrichments, wherein the Indian imagination is at once chastened and stimulated to the highest conceivable efforts. As it is impossible to picture any portal more stately than the great Entrance Gate of Futtehpore, so there is nothing in the world to surpass in delicacy the lacelike marble tracery which surrounds the tomb of Sulim-Chisti, the faquir. The bijou palace known as Birbul's House is architecturally faultless, while its whole surface is covered with low reliefs of such indescribable beauty and variety that one stands entranced before this building, as if in the presence of an inspired work of antique Greek art. Akbar's Mosque at Futtehpore is perhaps the finest in India, and there is not a palace, an audience chamber, or a tomb within these precincts that does not challenge our wonder and admiration. To describe Futtehpore-Sikri is as impossible as to give an account of the Venus of Milo or the Apollo Belvedere, but, as in the galleries of the Louvre or Vatican which hold these glorious inspirations, so within these walls, we feel ourselves in the presence of works designed by the very genius of art. And it must be remembered that the artificers of Akbar's city used modest means to produce their effects. Futtehpore is no dream realized in white marble, like the Taj or Moti Musjid, but is built almost entirely of red sandstone, and has not a single meretricious beauty.

After Akbar's death, it remained for his grandson, Shah Juhan, to give the world the Taj Mahal and the palaces of Agra and Delhi. Of these, the two first have already been described, and it is generally considered that they form the culminating point of the eclectic, or Mogul, school. For my own part I cannot agree with this view of the case. The Hindoo carvings, which give so much beauty to the robust outlines of Akbar's work, were set aside entirely by Shah Juhan, who substituted for them the use of marble and precious stones, a form of decoration which not even his refined taste could always keep on the right side of the line separating ostentation from dignity, while his softer contours, flatter surfaces, tamer outlines, and effeminate curves are disguised, but not concealed, by the beauty of the material in which he worked. The Pearl Mosque and hall of private audience at

Agra are his happiest efforts—instinctively one avoids calling them great efforts—but their purity and beauty recall the calm of the cloister, or white robes of a nun, and have none of the masculine grace and vigour which inform Akbar's work. The Mogul school of architecture, indeed, arose, and culminated, under Akbar, for though the way had been prepared for it by the third Pathan period, it was he who gave it force and direction. With the Taj and marble palaces of Agra, a decadence began, which Aurungzebe, Shah Juhan's son and successor, and a bigoted Mussulman, did his best to complete by sweeping the last vestige of Hindoo influence from Indo-Saracenic art. But it was one thing for the pious emperor to purge the mosques of the Prophet of every line and curve that could symbolize idolatry, and quite another thing to divorce from art the native genius which had given birth to the *chefs d'œuvres* of the Mogul school. The Hindoo architect was suppressed, but it was not native art that suffered. Mosques and tombs were built by orthodox mediocrities, and Mussulman taste fell rapidly from bad to worse, until, reaching the level of the Lucknow "nightmares," it became incapable of further degradation. Meanwhile the Hindoo still preserves the constructive lessons he first learnt in the sixteenth century, while he has lost nothing of his exquisite hereditary taste. He builds beautiful houses for such native rajahs as are wise enough to resist the Europeanization of their homes, and, I doubt not, could again produce, under another Akbar, buildings as beautiful as those which justly rank among the wonders of the world.

CHAPTER XIX.

DELHI.*

January 19-21.

DELHI, as we have seen, was the Mahometan capital of India until Akbar carried the court to Agra, where it remained for nearly eighty years, when the arch-builder, Shah Juhan, wishing to eternize his own memory, as he had already done that of his wife, ordered the construction of a new city north of the metropolis of Baber and Humayoun. This he called, after himself, Juhanabad the town of Juhan, but it is better known to us as Delhi, the most interesting, as Agra is the most beautiful, city in India. For here within the space of a few miles, are collected not one, but many Delhis, a series of cities superposed, as it were, one on the other, whose ruins, like the stratified rocks of the earth, are full of fossils, historical, ethnographical, and architectural, which, in the absence of any Hindoo history prior to the Mahometan conquest, supply the place of written records, as organic remains reveal the past history of life on the earth.

The original Delhi was built about eleven miles from modern Delhi, by Rajah Dilli, about the time Roman invasion of Britain. During a period of eight hundred years, it was only occasionally inhabited by the native princes of India, but Anang Pal I. rebuilt it in A.D. 736; it was fortified by his successors in 1052, and ruins of this work, called the Fort of Lalkot, still remain. The kings having made the city their residence, its suburbs began to extend, but remained without defences until they were surrounded by walls, in 1180, by Rajah Pithora, the last of the Hindoo kings, of whose fort the ground still shows the traces. Throughout the

---

* For their sketches of Indian architecture and archæology, this and the preceding chapter, are much indebted to the works and researches of Ferguson, Cunningham, and Keene.

tenth and early part of the eleventh centuries, Delhi suffered repeatedly from predatory incursions of the Afghans settled at Ghuzni, in Afghanistan; but upon the death of Mahmoud of Ghuzni, in 1030, his kingdom became so distracted by internal troubles that Delhi had respite from foreign invasion for nearly a hundred and fifty years. During the latter part of this time Hindostan was divided into two hostile camps, whose rival rulers, the King of Delhi and the King of Canouj, were engaged in deadly strife. Simultaneously, a powerful Afghan government arose under Mahomet Ghori, who invaded India in 1176. Within a few years, the conqueror overran the Punjaub, and, in 1193, captured Delhi, which became his capital. Twelve years later, he had totally demolished the Hindoo power, and Northern India came permanently under Mahometan rule. Mahomet Ghori left Delhi and his Indian conquests in charge of an able slave, named Khootub-ood-Deen, who raised the famous Khootub Minar, or Column, to commemorate the capture of the city, and ultimately became King of Delhi, which city continued to extend, under him and his successors, until a second fortified town, called Siri, an offshoot of the capital, arose in 1304.

The Mahometans, in their turn, were invaded by the Moguls, a Tartar tribe settled in Central Asia, who first attacked Delhi in 1298. The Moguls had no object except plunder; but from this date down to the early part of the sixteenth century, when, as we have already seen, they conquered India, their predatory incursions never ceased. In 1321 another fortified city was built by Mahomet Toghluck, and called, after himself, Toghluckabad, and, four years later, his son and successor joined Siri to Delhi by walls, which protected the suburbs while connecting the two towns, more than a mile apart. In 1354 a king named Firoze Shah, with a passion for architecture, built a new and magnificent city, named Firozabad, and made it the capital. Forty-four years later, Firozabad was sacked by the Moguls under Timour, and never recovered its prosperity. In 1540-45 Shere Shah extended Delhi from the site now occupied by Humayoun's tomb to the point where the southern gate of the present city stands, and at that time the town occupied nearly twice the space of modern Delhi. A few years later, Agra was chosen as the head-quarters of the Mogul sovereigns, who deserted the old capital until 1635, when Shah Juhan commenced to build Juhanabad, the Delhi of to-day. Modern Delhi itself has passed through great vicissitudes. It was plundered by the Persians in 1739 and 1756, when the city was given over to general massacre, and Shah Juhan's treasures in gold, silver, and precious stones carried off. It was taken by the Mahrattas twice, in 1758 and 1759, and further plundered. Pillaged again by free lances from Rohilcund in 1788. Taken by the British in 1803. Defended by them, under Colonel Ochterlony, against Holkar in 1804, and stormed by us in 1857, when the Sepoy Mutiny was crushed. At the present day it is a flourishing city of two hundred thousand inhabitants, and our greatest military centre in India.

The famous buildings of modern Delhi are the Fort, with its enclosed mosque and palaces, the Jumma Musjid, and some mosques and temples in the town. The Fort was begun in 1638, and took twenty years in building. It is entered by the Cashmere and Lahore Gates, of which the latter is as massive and dignified as any work of Akbar's time. This leads directly to the hall of private audience (Dewan-i-Khas), conceived in the same spirit as the building which served for a similar purpose at Agra, and of which it is clearly a development. Of all Shah Juhan's marble palaces this is perhaps the finest. The hall of public audience (Dewan-i-Am) is a great colonnade of the same character as the public hall at Agra, supported by sandstone pillars, and open on three sides, with the throne, a debased example of realistic *pietra dura* work, occupying the fourth side. The Pearl Mosque is a small, beautifully finished building of white marble, but too restless and pronounced in style to bear comparison with the purer gem of Akbar's city. Within the palace of Delhi once stood the famous "peacock throne," so called from the figures of two peacocks placed behind the royal seat, their expanded tails inlaid with sapphires, emeralds, pearls, and other jewels, so as to represent life. These glittering birds were covered by a golden canopy, supported on either side by an umbrella—the Oriental symbol of sovereignty—of velvet embroidered with pearls, and having handles of solid gold thickly studded with diamonds. It is said that this piece of work cost six millions sterling, and it was carried off by the Persian Nadir Shah, who sacked Delhi in 1739.

The Jumma Musjid (Friday Mosque) is one of the finest buildings in the East, but, like all the rest of Shah Juhan's work, it shows signs of a coming decadence in its flat *façade* and false arches, which compare very unfavourably with similar work at Futtehpore-Sikri. From the summits of its tall minarets, however, there is a comprehensive view of Delhi, which presents to the eye a vast collection of white, flat-topped houses, interspersed with trees. Several wide streets converge on the Jumma Musjid, which stands in a large open space. Here and there, the minarets of other mosques break the monotony of the house-tops, while, in the distance, are seen the great domes of kingly tombs, beyond which the Khootub Column rises like a tall factory chimney. Towards the river, the country is a dead flat, but in the opposite direction, the ground rises gently to the "Ridge," a low range of limestone rock, about a mile distant, and the spot where the British commenced the siege of Delhi, with a mere handful of men, in 1857.

In one corner of the great courtyard of the Friday Mosque we found a white-bearded Mussulman in charge of a casket containing some very sacred relics of the Prophet: a Koran twelve hundred and eighty-four years old, and another a hundred and sixty-four years its senior; a (red) hair of Mahomet himself, and the impress of his foot in a slab of marble. The Korans are probably genuine, and the hair may be so, but the footprint is a manifest swindle. All were "brought to India by Timour, five hundred and fifty years ago," said the grey-beard—a pious action which probably compensated, in the opinion of the Tartar general, for his five days' sack and massacre of Delhi.

The Chadni Chowk is the main street of Delhi. It is a wide

thoroughfare, bordered by native shops, which are a good deal Europeanized, and neither clean nor interesting. Down the centre of the roadway runs a channel of water, now, unfortunately, enclosed, and bordered with trees. In the days before the Mutiny, when the King of Delhi, Bahadoor Shah, still kept up his mimic court, the Chadni Chowk was brilliant with richly dressed natives, riding caparisoned horses, lounging in their howdahs, or carried in palanquins. Those days are gone, but the street is still picturesque with its parti-coloured crowds, busy shops, and rows of green peepul trees.

We drove one day to the Ridge, where a handsome column has been erected to the memory of the great John Nicholson, whose fame is second to that of no other hero of the Mutiny. This is the spot where the first British batteries were erected, and where the so-called besiegers were attacked more than thirty times before they were strong enough to take the offensive. Even after the arrival of Nicholson, with troops from the Punjaub, the British force numbered only seven thousand men, while Delhi was defended by more than sixty thousand sepoys. The city was stormed on the 4th of September, and an entrance effected through the Cashmere Gate, which was blown in after a splendid display of personal courage. The cessation of our fire was the arranged signal for Lieutenant Horne to move forward with four soldiers, carrying powder-bags. Behind him came Lieutenant Salkeld with a port-fire, and four other soldiers, also carrying bags. Horne laid his petards, and jumped, with his men, unhurt into the ditch beneath the walls; but the enemy, divining the bold intention of the movement, opened a deadly fire on Salkeld's party, who were not more than ten yards distant. Salkeld, however, laid his bags, but fell, shot through the arm and the leg, before he could apply the match. He handed this to Sergeant Burgess, bidding him light the fuse, but the man was shot dead in the attempt. Sergeant Carmichael then picked up the port-fire and lighted the fuse, but fell immediately, mortally wounded. Seeing him drop, Sergeant Smith rushed forward, but finding the slow-match burning, threw himself into the ditch. In another moment the gate was destroyed, the storming party entered, and made good their footing in the city. Salkeld died of his wounds, but all the survivors of the gallant little party received the Victoria Cross.

Returning to Delhi, we met a marriage procession in the Chadni Chowk. It is part of the religion of every Hindoo to marry, and mere children are married, although they do not live together until they have come to the age of puberty. Marriages are celebrated with absurd extravagance, and the poorer Hindoos often ruin themselves in making a display such as public opinion demands on these occasions. The procession in question was fully ten minutes filing past us, and was nearly half a mile long. First, came pipers and drummers, making the most horrible music. Led horses followed, tricked out in all manner of finery, some of them carrying silver anklets around their legs. Next, a long string of carriages, and then the bridegroom, a lad of seventeen, handsomely dressed, riding a pony, his face almost hidden by a tinsel fringe, and surrounded by a crowd of friends and relatives. Lastly, more musicians and led horses. The happy man was on his way to the bride's home, which must be decorated within and without. The wedding feast must be lavish. Nautch-girls must be hired to entertain the guests, who include every connection and acquaintance of both families. Everybody makes a harvest out of the unfortunate father, and many a shopkeeper and ryot gets hopelessly into the hands of the money-lender on these occasions.

Among much that is European in the native town, certain arts and trades flourish which are specially characteristic of India. Here is a fellow selling sweetmeats wrapped in silver-foil. His customers are all grown men, who all believe that eating silver will make them strong! This idea is so widely spread that it keeps quite a number of silver-beaters at work in Delhi. There, is another man, twisting thread from two strands of tinsel. He uses a couple of small spinning wheels, like those we saw in the hands of the hill-women at Darjeeling; sets them revolving, each in an opposite direction, by quick movements of the hands, and allows the issuing threads to twine together. It is very simple, but more like legerdemain than spinning. Here are women sitting half naked in the open shops, turning the upper millstone, just as they did when it was said, "Two women shall be grinding at the mill." There, is a miniature painter, the special artist of Delhi, who paints the architectural *chefs d'œuvres* of Shah Juhan and Akbar, or the beauties of their courts, with wonderful delicacy on ivory.

The Jumma Musjid is crowded with worshippers on Friday, the Mussulman sabbath. The people arrive by twos and threes, entering unshod, and immediately seeking the tank, which occupies the centre of every Mahometan mosque. Here they wash hands, face, and feet in a prescribed order, and then kneel, either within the colonnade of the mosque itself, or in the open courtyard, prostrating themselves and repeating texts from the Koran. From one of the towers of the Musjid, we giaours looked down on the scene. The mosque was crowded with men; no women, except a few very old crones, being present. All the worshippers were well dressed in white, red, green, or yellow robes. Some, who wore green turbans, had made the holy pilgrimage; others, in saffron robes, had visited less distant shrines, while undistinguished devotees had put on their best clothes as we do on Sundays in England. Seen from our eyrie, the brilliant crowd, whether moving confusedly about or bowing to the ground as one man, was a charming picture, losing nothing by its framework of white roofs and houses embowered in foliage, above which the minarets of distant mosques reared their slender shafts, while a tender blue sky, peopled with wheeling crows and kites, canopied the scene.

A drive of eleven miles across a dead level of irrigated land brought us to the site of Old Delhi, purposing a visit to the Khootub Column, the Forts of Lalkot and Raj Pithora, and some early Mahometan tombs. The way, like that from Agra to Futtehpore, is lined with mausoleums. It was the Mussulman custom for a man to build his own sepulchre at some distance from the city and use it, during his lifetime, either as a place of retirement from the heat of the town or for the entertainment of his friends, but after his burial the building was festive no more. The Tomb of Saftar Jung, whose name has already occurred in connection with the history of Oudh, is a good example of the degradation which befell Mogul architecture only a century after the building of the Taj. Plaster takes the place of stone, size replaces symmetry, the *façade* is flat, pierced with sham arches, and is destitute of the beautiful native sculpture.

At length we reached the site of ancient Delhi, the scene of India's oldest authentic records. Here a city first arose about B.C. 76, and passed through the vicissitudes already described. Here are the ruins of Fort Lalkot, Pithora's Fort, Khootub's Column and Mosque, and the tomb of his successor, Altumsh. The column is perhaps the most wonderful triumphal shaft in the world. It is not complete, yet it rises two hundred and forty feet, tapering from a base of forty-seven feet to nine feet diameter at the top. It is built in five stories, each of which terminates in a balcony supported by graceful brackets, thickly clustered and beautifully carved. The style is that of the first Pathan period, and the minar was commenced soon after the conquest of India by Mahomet Ghori. Its history is written in the inscribed bands that surround it, and for boldness of outlines and grace of execution it is not surpassed by any later Indo-Saracenic work. We climbed to the top, and looked over the ruins of Fort Lalkot and Raj Pithora's defences. Of the former there remain some fragments of massive walls, flanked with enormous bastions, and three gateways can still be made out, each of which appears to have been defended by a portcullis. The works of the last Hindoo king are marked only by an obscure line of earth mounds. Khootub's Mosque was the first Mahometan place of worship ever built in India, and was erected immediately after the Afghan settlement. The ruins exhibit a strange medley of native and Mahometan work. The columns are pure Hindoo, dating, according to Cunningham, from the tenth century, and appear to have been taken by the conqueror from the temples of Old Delhi.

They are covered with the profuse and imaginative carvings common to native work, but where idolatrous figures appeared upon them too prominently, these have been broken off by Mahometan zeal. The west wall of the mosque is pierced with enormous arches, or rather arch-shaped openings in horizontally coursed masonry, such as characterize the early days of the first Pathan period, before the native mason had learned how to shape *voussoirs*. The surface is covered with carved bands of Arabic character, enrichments which are eloquent of repressed Hindoo art. A southern gateway was added to the mosque, in 1300, by Allah-ood-Deen, displaying the first Pathan style in its greatest perfection, and plainly marking the moment of contact between Afghan and Hindoo art. In the courtyard stands an iron pillar, the oldest relic of the vanished Hindoo city of Delhi. Its history, scratched on its face in Sanscrit, connects it with a monarch who appears to have reigned three centuries before the Christian era. The column is of wrought iron, and proves that the Hindoos were acquainted with the art of working large masses of malleable iron at a very early period.

Our homeward route took us past Humayoun's tomb, begun by his widow in 1560, and finished by Akbar after sixteen years' work. That is the way the Great Moguls were buried! Not far from this mausoleum is the Kila Kona Mosque, a beautiful example of the third Pathan period, to which reference has already been made in sketching the rise and fall of Indo-Saracenic architecture. Presently, we came to another of the vanished Delhis, Firozabad, formerly a town of a hundred and fifty thousand souls, but now a collection of ruins. And how did this once splendid city fall into decay? By a process with which India, and Delhi in particular, has been only too familiar—the inrush of the invader, who, whether Afghan, Tartar, or Persian, swooped down for centuries on these devoted plains whenever he was strong enough to plunder.

It was about the end of the fourteenth century that the terrible Timour fell, first upon Central Asia, and then upon India. Having crossed the Indus, he "advanced to Bhurtnere, which was surrendered by the inhabitants on terms, but by one of those mistakes which seemed always to occur in his capitulations, they were put to the sword, and the town burnt to the ground. Villages and towns were abandoned as he advanced, but on his arrival at Delhi he found himself encumbered with captives, and according to the statements of prisoners, which were doubtless exaggerated, he caused a hundred thousand men to be massacred in cold blood. A battle was fought under the walls of the capital between the veterans of Timour and the effeminate soldiers of the empire. The emperor, Mahomet Toghluck, was defeated, and fled to Guzerat, and Timour entered the city, and caused himself to be proclaimed emperor. Disputes, as might have been expected, arose between the citizens and his ferocious soldiery, and the whole of the Mogul army was let loose on the devoted city. The inhabitants sold their lives dearly, but their valour was quenched in blood. The scenes of horror defy description; entire streets were choked up with the dying and the dead. For five days Timour remained a tranquil spectator of the plunder and conflagration of the city, while he celebrated his victory by a magnificent feast. This whirlwind of desolation lasted six months, and Timour recrossed the Indus in March, 1399." * Such is one of many Indian tragedies—a bloody series, which opened before history began, only to close, if it has closed, with the dreadful scenes of the great Mutiny.

But if the story of Delhi is chiefly one of bloodshed and plunder, only broken by the prosperity of Mogul rule; yet in the very midst of Firozabad, where we have seen Timour's devils—as we might, if we please, see those of Afghanistan and Persia—let loose, there stands a stone pillar, known as Asoka's "lat," which tells of far different, if far distant, days in India. Asoka was a Buddhist King of Hindostan, who reigned three centuries before Christ, a true disciple of Sakya, whose pure and unselfish philosophy was as yet uncorrupted by superstition. Governing on the principles of his faith, he caused to be set up in various parts of

* Marshman's "History of India."

his dominions stone pillars, inscribed with certain edicts, which, there is every reason to believe, formed the basis of society in India under his rule. These decreed the protection of life and property, the extension of cultivation, the establishment of public worship, the ordination of a clergy, the administration of justice, the practice of religious toleration, the abandonment of frivolous pursuits on the part of the king, the condemnation of vain festivities, the love of righteousness, and the duty of charity. Such were Asoka's famous edicts, still legible to the Pali scholar on the column which Firoze Shah thought it worth while to bring with infinite pains from the foot of the Himalayas to Firozabad. We read the words through a distance of more than two thousand years, red, for the most part, with bloodshed, or black with oppression, and then we talk of progress! The Briton is master in Delhi now, and has ruled India for more than a century; but at what time during that period could the Christian master of Hindostan have raised such another pillar as Asoka's, and truly declared that its decrees embodied his principles of government?

CHAPTER XX.

JEYPORE—BOMBAY.

January 22-29.

January 22.—We left Delhi for Jeypore by the new Rajpootana State line, opened only three weeks ago, travelling again by night, for on the 29th our steamer leaves Bombay, and every day is precious in this country of strange interests. Rocked by a gentle speed of fifteen miles an hour, we slept well, and, on waking, found ourselves no longer in the alluvial plains of which we had begun to think all India consisted, but traversing a bare, sandy plateau, with ridges of hills on either side of us. Surely we were still in a Pullman car, crossing the great American desert which lies between the Rocky Mountains and the Sierra Nevada ! India must have been a dream. Such were our first thoughts; our second, that we were skirting the Indian desert, that wide, sandy region in the north-west, from whose central town, Bekaneer, all the best camels in India come.

On the rise of Mahrattas, in the early part of the eighteenth century, the Rajah Jeysing was placed in charge of their possessions in the province of Jhansi, and, in 1728, founded Jeypore, which still remains independent. The city stands on a plain, surrounded on all sides, except the south, by limestone hills, the soil being sterile, and the cultivation meagre. Jeypore was laid out on a regular plan, and has considerable architectural pretension. The streets are straight and wide, and the houses are built in the Indo-Saracenic style; covered with stucco painted bright pink and adorned with rude frescoes. The rajah's palace is a huge ambitious building, with a good deal of the "stucco nightmare" about it, standing in the centre of the town. Internally, it affords, like the houses of almost all the great natives, a melancholy instance of commonplace splendour. Its rooms are filled with vulgar European furniture, and decorated with cheap European prints and pictures. Its courts and passages are crowded with a brilliantly dressed swarm of servants, who do little besides looking picturesque, and the gardens are laid out ostentatiously, but without taste.

How shall I describe the appearance of the streets? The people are Rajpoots, the finest men and women we have seen in India. Every one is well dressed, in colours as bright and various as those of a kaleidoscope. A brisk, well-to-do air pervades the place, such as we have not seen in any other native town. Camels are as common as horses in England, and magnificent ox-teams are harnessed to the country carts, with their solid wooden wheels and tinsel canopies. The open market-place, where lie heaps of various grains, is crowded with gaily-dressed men, some a-foot, some on camels, and here comes, as we stand admiring the grouping, a four-in-hand barouche, full of gorgeous native swells. The team tears along the road at a gallop, and behind the carriage clatters a small troop of native lancers. There, are half a dozen "faquirs," or holy men, naked and smeared with ashes from head to foot, begging food from door to door, and respected by all the world for their piety.

Who has not seen India has already walked through Jeypore if he have read the lines which I cannot forbear quoting from Mr. Edwin Arnold's charming poem, the "Light of Asia." Who has seen India knows that no more perfect description is possible than that which Mr. Arnold gives of native city streets.

> " Forth fared they by the common way a-foot,
> Mingling with all the Sâkya citizens,
> Seeing the glad and sad things of the town :
> The painted streets alive with hum of noon,
> The traders cross-legged mid their spice and grain,
> The buyers with their money in the cloth,
> The war of words to cheapen this or that,
> The shout to clear the road, the huge stone wheels,
> The strong slow oxen and their rustling loads,
> The singing bearers with the palanquins,
> The broad-necked hamals sweating in the sun,
> The housewives bearing water from the well
> With balanced chatties and athwart their hips
> The black-eyed babies ; the fly-swarmed sweetmeat shops,
> The weaver at his loom, the cotton-bow
> Twanging ; the millstones grinding meal, the dogs
> Prowling for orts, the skilful armourer
> With tongs and hammer linking shirts of mail,
> The blacksmith with a mattock and a spear
> Reddening together in his coals, the school
> Where round their gooroo, in a grave half-moon,
> The Sâkya children sang the Mantras through,
> And learned the greater and the lesser gods ;
> The dyers stretching waistcloths in the sun,
> Wet from the vats—orange and rose and green ;
> The soldiers clanking past with swords and shields,
> The camel-drivers rocking on the humps,
> The Brahman proud, the martial Kshatriya,
> The humble toiling Sudra ; here a throng
> Gathered to watch some chattering snake-charmer

> Wind round his wrist the living jewellery
> Of asp and nâg, or charm the hooded death
> To angry dance with drone of pipe and gourd;
> There a long line of drums and horns, which went,
> With steeds gay painted and silk canopies,
> To bring the young bride home; and here a wife,
> Stealing with cakes and garlands to the god,
> To pray her husband's safe return from trade
> Or beg a boy next birth; hard by the booths
> Where the swart potters beat the noisy brass
> For lamps and lotas; thence by temple walls
> And gateways, to the river and the bridge
> Under the city walls."

Such is a Hindoo town, and such, exactly, is Jeypore, though the rajah has added some features which are entirely European. He has established a college, where an excellent English education is given; a school of art, and workshops where marble-carving, brass-chasing, filigree work, gold-inlaying, enamelling, electro-plating, watchmaking, turnery, carpentry, and engine-building are taught.

The Jeypore enamels are famous for the beautiful colours, transparency, and hardness of their paste, but they are full of mechanical imperfections. Indian art always wants finish. The brass-workers of Benares cover with exquisite chasing vases and plaques which are untrue in shape and roughly brazed at the joints. In the beautiful inlays of Guzerat, thread-gold is laid on iron with perfect taste, but the shields and swords thus decorated have no fine finish. Ahmedabad work—brass-chasing thrown up by a background of black lac—is excellently designed, but never quite cleanly cut; while Indian jewellery is rough, no matter how valuable its stones or their settings. The *pietra dura*, jali-work, and carved soapstone of Agra, together with the miniature-painting of Delhi, are exceptions to this rule, being all as perfect in mechanical execution as in beauty and delicacy of design; but the stone-workers of India have always been among her best craftsmen, probably because of their training under the great builders, Akbar and Shah Juhan, while ivory-painting is not a native art.

January 23.—About four miles from Jeypore lies the palace and city of Amber, the ancient capital of Rajpootana, deserted by the court on the founding of Jeypore, and now in partial ruin. The palace stands high on a hill-side, which forms part of a wide rocky basin, open to the plain only in one direction. Towards this gap the town slopes from the foot of the palace walls, and some of its temples and flat-roofed houses pass through the opening into the level country beyond.

The palace of Amber is built in the Indo-Saracenic style, and is a fine pile, although it cannot compare with the works of Akbar or Shah Juhan. The hall of public audience is purely Hindoo in character, and of the beauty of this chamber, it is said, such a report came to the ears of the Mogul emperor that, unable to endure an architectural rival, he sent a military force to teach his general respect. The rajah, however, being forewarned, covered his carved columns and architraves with plaster, entertained the messengers in halls of Puritanic simplicity, and sent them back satisfied to their master.

January 24.—We left Jeypore for Bombay by the new Rajpootana State Railway, and were soon traversing a still more desert-like region than that which we had crossed on approaching the rajah's city. Cultivation and irrigation almost disappeared, the surface of the ground was covered with an alkaline efflorescence, while herds of black-buck cropped the scanty grass within gunshot of the passing train. From the alluvial flats, of which the country consists, bare hills rise steeply on either hand, and the scenery forcibly reminded us of the great American desert. The hills are of crystalline limestone, full of white and grey marbles, with which the permanent way is frequently ballasted. The line is neatly bordered by a cactus hedge. Many of the larger bridges are not yet completed, and we occasionally cross the dry bed of a river on a temporary embankment, whence we can see the bridge works proceeding, either a little higher up, or lower down the stream. These suggest unpleasant thoughts of the race against time, which is so often an element in Indian engineering. The bridge-builder knows that within a month, or perhaps a week, a torrent will sweep away the embankment which now carries the train, and the Government is insisting that the line, once open, must be kept open, while the unhappy engineer is perhaps waiting for such trifles as bolts and nuts, or the cholera breaks out in his camp, and he cannot keep his men from flying. Anyway, he is between the devil and the deep sea.

In the afternoon we halted for refreshment at Ajmere, the prettiest town we have seen in India. It stands on the highest part of the plateau, whose northern slope we have climbed by very gentle inclines, and is probably more than two thousand feet above sea-level. The air was bright and cool, and the hills which close around the town were lighted, as we left it, with sunset tints that recalled the colouring of Virginia City when Mount Davidson glows rosy red across valleys filled with illuminated dust haze. The night soon fell, and, laying ourselves along the hard benches of our Indian Pullman, we slept.

January 25.—When we awoke we were still in America, traversing old lake-beds; but about nine o'clock the character of the country changed. Fields of wheat, in ear, began to diversify the sandy wastes; bullock-wells became numerous, and we saw, for the first time, the hide bucket commonly used for irrigation replaced by an endless chain of earthen pots. Presently a few trees appeared, but trees with gnarled branches and scanty foliage. Great monkeys swung about in these, or dropped to the ground and bounded away before the train in a series of tremendous leaps. As the line fell, by easy inclines, to lower levels, the soils improved, irrigation increased, crops of cotton and castor-oil plant mingled with the wheat, great storks wandered in the fields, and long-legged wading birds fished in every pond and tank. Finally, the hills were left behind us, and we entered on a flat and fertile country before sunset. Once more, and for the last time, we sought the luxurious couches of an Indian sleeping-car, and on

January 26 reached Bombay, having compassed the six hundred and ninety-seven miles which separate this city from Jeypore in forty-five hours, at the alarming speed of fifteen and a half miles per hour. We had been travel-stained in America, notably after staging out of the Yosemite Valley, when our nearest relations could not have recognized our begrimed faces; but we were never so deeply buried in alluvial soil as on this occasion. The Rajpootana State line, with its marble ballast, was not so bad, but the Bombay and Baroda Railway appears to be laid in dust and ashes throughout its entire length.

Bombay was ceded by the Moguls to the Portuguese in 1530, and formed part of the dower of the Infanta of Portugal on her marriage with Charles II. The king, who lost money annually by the island, transferred it to the East India Company in 1668, for a yearly rental of £10; and the town is therefore the oldest of the East India Company's settlements in Hindostan, while the terms on which it was acquired first invested the Company with the political power which it only exercised elsewhere in India after the battle of Plassey had brought the country under British rule.

Until of late years, Bombay, although the chief seaport of Western India, and a town of seven hundred thousand inhabitants, was considered a very subordinate place in comparison with Calcutta and Madras. The railways and cotton cultivation have, however, changed all that, and Bombay looks a busier town than Calcutta. It is built on a cluster of islands, connected with one another and with the mainland by causeways, but much of it is low and flooded during the rainy season. The harbour, a vast anchorage protected by mountainous islands, is one of the finest in the world. There are not many Europeans in Bombay, and the bulk of its trade is in the hands of the Parsees, who are both numerous and wealthy. There is no distinction between the European and native quarters as in other Indian cities, but English, Parsee, and Hindoo shops and offices stand side by side, even within the precincts of the "Fort," where are the Government offices, law courts, post office, banks, and municipal buildings. The architecture of the city is quite unique, Hindoo ornamentation being adapted to European construction in a very curious and pleasing way. On the harbour side, and towards the north, lies the native town, properly so called, the real centre of the trade of Bombay. The houses of this populous and prosperous quarter are far superior to those of native Calcutta, and the streets are crowded by foot-passengers and bullock-waggons. The artisans and shopkeepers are more like those of the West, and business is carried on with Western activity rather than Eastern apathy.

The Parsees form one of the most conspicuous features of Bombay. These people are Persians by birth and Zoroastrians by religion, and were settled for centuries in Western India before they began to rise to importance under the favourable conditions which British rule established in Hindostan for the development of trade. At the present moment they are the chief owners of property and leading merchants in the island, an active, intelligent race, taller, handsomer, and paler than the Hindoos, with whom, however, they share, as philology proves, a common Aryan origin. The Parsees wear an Asiatic costume, but assimilate more nearly than any other Eastern people to the customs of Europeans, speaking, and causing their children to be taught, English, while adhering rigidly to their religious customs and observances. Every morning and evening they seek the shore, and prostrate themselves in adoration before the sun. For them, as for the Persians, Ormuzd is the beneficent creator of man and source of all his happiness, while Ahriman is the author of evil, and between these two there is everlasting war.

The famous "Towers of Silence," the Parsee burial-ground, are situated a few miles from Bombay, on high ground, which overlooks the harbour and town. Here, within a large garden, are a number of round towers each about twenty feet high, the interior of which is built up solidly with masonry to within five feet of the top, within the exception of a well, about fifteen feet in diameter, which occupies the centre. The bodies of the dead are deposited between the well and the parapet of the tower, a space which is divided into three rings, one for the remains of adult males, a second for women, and the third, or innermost ring, for children. The trees in the garden are tenanted by hundreds of vultures, who dispose of a body in a very few minutes, and the bones are from time to time thrown into the central well. When this is full another tower is built, and thus do the Zoroastrians prevent that defilement of mother earth, which their religious code forbids.

January 27–28.—The Caves of Elephanta, on the island of that name, about an hour's sail from Bombay, are examples of the rock-cut temples of which the early Brahmans and Buddhists have left so many, especially in Southern India. Elephanta is Brahmanical, and is supposed to date from the tenth century, although, in the absence of any Hindoo history earlier than the Mahometan invasion, the age of all these works is uncertain.

The sun was hot, but a pleasant breeze was blowing, as we threaded our way through the scattered shipping in the harbour. After passing several table-topped islands, we landed by a rude pier at Elephanta, and climbed a steep hill to the entrance of the caves. They are excavated in a dark-green trap rock, and consist of three chambers, whose roofs are supported by stout, barrel-shaped, fluted columns. The walls are covered with carvings of Siva in his male and female aspects, while the main entrance is faced by a colossal triple bust, representing the heads of the Hindoo triad, Brahma, Vishnu, and Mahadeva. In the middle of each chamber is a quadrangular shrine, supported externally by bold and beautiful carvings of Siva, and each enclosing a gigantic Lingam. Phallic worship, pure and simple, was evidently the distinctive feature of Brahmanism at the time when these caves were made. The Vedic hymns, on which *old* Brahmanism rests, are free from Phallism, but it seems probable that the pure philosophy of Buddha, which, as we have seen, conquered Brahmanism and dominated India for a time, was ultimately vanquished by a cult distinguished chiefly by obscene rites which survive in a modified form among the Saivas to the present day. Elephanta is somewhat disappointing. The excavations are not extensive, and the work is far inferior to that of the rock-cut temples of Southern India. It was the one mistake of our trip to go from Madras to Calcutta by sea, for we thereby lost an opportunity, only to be found in the Deccan, of learning from these, his best and uninfluenced works, what the Hindoo sculptor and architect was before he wore the graceful chains of the Mahometan conqueror.

A spanking breeze swept us quickly back from Elephanta to Bombay, where we arrived at the hour when all "the world" takes its evening drive on the Apollo Bunder. The fashionable crowd was for the most part Parsee, and the Parsee ladies, who, unlike most Orientals, are not confined to the privacy of the house, were especially brilliant, both in their equipages and toilettes. They have fair, handsome faces, and their dress consists of graceful wraps of brightly coloured silks, which fall from the crown of the head to the ground, while the forehead is covered, almost to the eyebrows, with a white linen band. Their husbands Europeanize themselves as to coats and trousers, but retain their tall stiff hats of oil-cloth. A military band discoursed excellent music, and as night fell the gay parti-coloured crowd, the glancing lights, the tranquil sea, the spangled sky, and dimly outlined island hills, formed a picture by which we shall always pleasantly remember Bombay.

CHAPTER XXI.

ENGLAND AND INDIA.

TWENTY-FOUR years ago England undertook to govern two hundred millions of Asiatics on European principles, and if, in accordance with those principles, we admit that only those Governments are good which exist for the interests of the governed, the question to be asked of British rule in India is not, "What has it done for England?" but "What has it done for the Indian people?" Perhaps no man has ever spoken with more authority and liberality on the problem of England's work in India than Dr. Hunter, the statistician of Hindostan, to whose arguments, if not to his very words, it seems to me the duty of every patriotic Englishman to give all the currency he can. For, from the moment when the Queen's sovereignty was proclaimed throughout India, the responsibility for the good government of the country passed into the hands of Parliament, and therefore into those of the British electoral body, who owe to Indian affairs a share of the attention which they give to home politics.

England has been supreme in India for more than a century, and during this period many remarkable changes, which are wholly due to her acts or influence, have taken place in the country. Thousands of square miles of jungle, once inhabited only by wild beasts, have been converted into fertile land. Malarious swamps have been drained, and are now, in some instances, covered with healthy cities. The remote interior of the country has been joined to the sea-board by railways. Great rivers, once effectually separating provinces, have been spanned. Hundreds of miles of canals have been made, and enormous areas of land have been irrigated. And, apart from these physical changes, others, of even greater importance, have occurred. The native states of India, formerly always at war with each other, are now trading peacefully together. The bloody raids of Afghans, Persians, and Tartars, who, for seven hundred years before the coming of the British, broke through the north-western frontiers of India and ravaged the unhappy plainsmen at will, have been stopped. Piracy has been crushed. Predatory castes, who made a profession of pillage, have been put down. Justice has taken the place of oppression. Instead of a swarming soldiery, there is a police; instead of more idolatrous temples, there are schools.

But England has developed the commercial capacities of Hindostan no less remarkably than she has pacified the country. She has created great trading cities such as never existed in ancient

India, whose capitals were merely the camps of her monarchs, and dependent for their prosperity on the presence of the court. Calcutta has a population nearly double that of any British town except London, and Bombay is one and a half times larger than Liverpool or Glasgow; yet the former was only a cluster of mud huts when our countrymen first settled on the Hooghly, and Charles II. was glad, as we have already seen, to let the latter to the East India Company for a rent of £10 per annum. When the English first became the rulers of India her yearly exports were not worth more than a million sterling, but they rose to a value of eleven millions in 1830, while, in 1880, India sold the world no less than sixty-six millions of her own produce. Besides the enormous extention of cultivation which these figures indicate, India has been benefited by the introduction of manufactures and the opening of mines. Twenty-seven years ago there was not a cotton-mill in the country, now there are more than a million and a half of spindles. Jute-mills have been established; paper-mills are rising, and now we hear of large shoe factories being started at Cawnpore. Coal has been discovered in several provinces, and the mines employ many thousands of hands.

If we turn next to the moral aspect of British rule in India, we find that, although Christianity has made little progress, from causes which will not be here discussed, education has been taken out of the hands of an ignorant and bigoted priesthood, and two millions of native children are now receiving public instruction, which, while it fits them for the battle of life, frees them also from the superstitious terrors that once held the Indian intellect in bondage, and made progress impossible. Another remarkable result of our influence has been a great revival of letters. Five thousand native books were published in India in 1878, and the vernacular journals now number more than two hundred and fifty, while their readers must be reckoned by millions. Even the family life of the Hindoo is touched by the modern intellectual movement. The zenana itself begins to hear and echo liberal ideas, and there are signs that woman may yet hope to arise from her degradation in India. Finally, the first throbs of a new political life may be detected in the establishment of autonomous municipalities on the ruins of the old village guilds, which had utterly disappeared under the oppression of the Mussulman.

Such is a brief sketch of the work which has already been accomplished by the British in India. It is an agreeable picture, from which one turns with less pleasure to the consideration of what yet remains to be done. The masses of India are, perhaps, the poorest people in the world, a large proportion of the population having outgrown the food-producing power of the country. The very merits of our rule have helped to bring about this state of things, which has become so alarming of late years that many excellent people almost begin to despair of the Government being able either to cope with the increasing poverty of the people, or pay its own way. From the earliest times, India has had an undeserved reputation for wealth. She has certainly been, and still is, the greatest accumulator of the precious metals known to commerce, while the splendour of her native courts and the magnificence of her rich natives have aided in building up the tradition in question. But the condition of the masses is the true test of a country's wealth or poverty, and, judged by this standard, India is, and always has been, an exceedingly poor country. Its people are, almost without exception, small husbandmen, without accumulated capital, living from hand to mouth, and completely at the mercy of a treacherous climate. In the days before our advent, invasion, internal war, famine, and pestilence effectually prevented any increase of population, and kept the pressure of the people on the soil within bearable limits. At the time when India passed into our hands there was land enough for every one who wanted it; not more than a third of Bengal was cultivated, and the difficulty of the landowners was to find tenants. But one of the first effects of English supremacy was to remove many of the old checks on the increase of population, and so effectually was this done in Bengal that the same area which fed twenty-one millions in 1780 has to support sixty-three millions in 1880. The average population in British districts has now become three times as dense as that of the native states, and is greater than that of England, France, or Ireland, by twenty, twenty-five, and fifty per cent. respectively, while in certain districts of Northern India the people are three or four times as thick as in England. Two-thirds of all the farms of Bengal are between two and three acres in size, and, allowing four persons to each peasant family, twenty-four millions of human beings are struggling for existence on the produce of fifteen million acres of land. Such a pressure exists nowhere else in the world. In Ireland there are only a hundred and sixty-nine persons to the square mile; in France a hundred and eighty; in England, cities excepted, two hundred; but in Bengal the people number more than seven hundred per square mile. The result of this vast increase in the population has, of course, been to drive the cultivator on to poorer and poorer lands, for which he is, nevertheless, obliged to pay exorbitant rents because of the competition for farms. This again has led to an undue clearing of jungle-lands, entailing a serious increase in the risk of drought, while, in the absence of wood, the dung which should go back to the land is used for fuel. The village pasture-grounds even are brought under the plough, and the cattle degenerate for want of sufficient food.

Meanwhile, although agriculture retrogrades, rents continue to advance, the ryot growing always poorer and the landlord richer. When the "permanent settlement" of Bengal was made in 1793, tenants were scarce and land was plentiful, and we created a body of landowners without making provision against an enhancement of rents which no one at that time could possibly have foreseen. Before the middle of the present century, however, rents had risen to such a height that the landlords' powers were curtailed by the Rent Act of 1859; but the increase of the people and the natural operation of economical laws have proved stronger than legislation, and land still continues to increase in value. While such has been the result of the Cornwallis settlement of Bengal, the greater part of Madras has always remained in the hands of the Government, besides whom, there are only a few other large landowners in the presidency. Population has increased by about one-half during the last twenty-five years, but the extension of cultivation has more than kept pace with the increase of numbers, two-thirds more land being tilled. Meanwhile the Government, recognizing that this expansion resulted from the reclamation of inferior lands, have only increased their rents by one-fourth, so that the average rates of rent per acre have been reduced nearly one-fourth, with the effect that if the Madrassee ryot is poor it is because he is eaten up by rapacious money-lenders, and not by grasping landlords. For, apart from the question of rent, the early marriages which are a religious duty among the Hindoos, and the ruinous expenditure which the celebration of these marriages entail, too often keep the southern peasants in the hands of money-lenders, who find, under our rule, a substantial security for usurious advances in the valuable tenant right which that rule assures to the cultivator. Thus, whether in the north or the south, peasant life in India is a constant struggle for a bare subsistence, a struggle which would end in starvation in the first dry season but for British aid and relief. Happily, this condition of things does not exist throughout all India, but the description applies to large and increasing areas in the most fertile part of the country, where population has outgrown the food-producing powers of the land. India, as a whole, produces more food than she consumes, and reckoning on the very moderate scale of native wants, could support five or six millions more people than she does if the production were equally distributed. But the people are not adequately fed, even in localities where the pressure of population on the soil is light; while in districts like Bengal, where it is heaviest, one-fifth of the ryots are insufficiently nourished, and several millions are always hungry.

Over-population in India is the direct result of British rule; but, serious as are the difficulties which we have made for ourselves by the removal of the old checks on the increase of the people, the new state of things, being a result of civilization, must be met by the resources of civilization. Industrial life, of which something has been said above, is already sensibly lightening the pressure of the population on the soil in certain districts, and the first care of every Indian statesman should be to promote manufacturing and mining enterprises to the utmost of his power. Migration from the overcrowded centres should be strenuously encouraged. The cry of the tea-planters of Assam and Cachar is for labour, and the Government should take care that no vexatious restrictions shall interfere with its easy transfer. The great native princes and landowners could render invaluable assistance to their poorer countrymen by exploiting, to their own profit as well as for the benefit of the people, hill country, now jungle clad, which would pay well for being brought under the plough. A fourth way of relieving the difficulty is by increasing the produce of the soil by irrigation and manuring. Irrigation, whether on a large or small scale, is a State affair, for the people have no capital, and a Government already pressed for funds must move circumspectly in a matter of such magnitude. With regard to fertilizers, it is sad to see the potential wealth so carefully hoarded in China and Japan, wastefully squandered in India, where all the dung is dried for fuel, and the sewage of great cities allowed to run into the rivers. But over and above all these remedies, the one thing needed in Bengal, the most densely populated and fertile region of India, is an equitable land law. A Commission of Inquiry, appointed in 1879, has already reported on this important subject, and the principles which they lay down for the guidance of legislation are drastic enough to shock Conservative ears, even now that the Irish Land Bill has passed. After declaring that the undue competition for land in Bengal will, if unchecked, reduce the whole agricultural population to misery and degradation, they say, " The land of a country belongs to the people of the country ; and while the vested rights should be treated with all possible tenderness, no mode of appropriation and cultivation should be permanently allowed by the ruler which involves the wretchedness of the great majority of the community, if the alteration or amendment of the law relating to land can by itself, or in conjunction with other measures, obviate or remedy the misfortune."

The prime difficulty of British rule in India arises from the poverty of the people. Men who have scarcely enough to live on cannot bear taxation, and the question is how to maintain a government of European efficiency from an Asiatic source of revenue. England pays forty shillings a head to the imperial exchequer, to say nothing of local burdens, more easily than India pays three and eightpence per head without local burdens. It is quite true that we do not take as much from the Indian people of to-day as the Mogul emperors extorted from a much less numerous population; but the struggle for existence was not then so severe among the masses, while the Mogul Government was financially flourishing, because it gave the country very much less than we try to do Our trouble lies in the fact that what we take scarcely pays for the cost of our administration, the problem being, how to give India peace, security, prosperity, justice, and education, without overburdening its destitute people. We must keep up a large army if India is to be secured from the foreign invasions and internal disturbances of the last and preceding centuries. We must make roads, railroads, and canals if she is to be commercially prosperous; there must be a magistracy and police if justice is to be done, and schools if her children are to be taught. All these things cost money, and some of them must, in the nature of things, cost more money every year. Meanwhile, finance ministers may either economise expenditure or increase taxation, and as a matter of fact they have done both. But neither process is exhausted. Nearly two-thirds of the average annual income of India is derived from the land, while the traders, a large and wealthy class, contribute scarcely anything to the national exchequer. This portion of the community can afford, better than any other, to pay for the advantages of the rule under which it flourishes, and must ultimately be reached by some form of direct taxation. On the other hand, our military expenditure is too extravagant in certain particulars. The scale of extra pay, especially to the higher officers, is much too liberal, and there is no longer any need, since the introduction of railway communication, for keeping up a separate head-quarters in each presidency. A multitude of posts in the various branches of the civil service are filled by expensive imported labour, although there is now an ample supply of competent and trustworthy native labour available at a very cheap rate. As India can only afford to pay at the most moderate rate for the advantages of civilization, it is England's duty to cheapen the blessings of her rule down to the very lowest point that is compatible with efficiency. Even when this has been accomplished, the English have further sacrifices to make in the interests of good government in India. The time is not far distant when representation of some kind will have to accompany taxation, and the Indian people be allowed a share in the management of their own affairs. This involves parting to a certain extent with our control of the country, but the step will be forced upon us by the very character of our rule. For we are governing India, not as conquerors, but in the interests of the Indian people. We are trying an experiment new to the history of the world, and every step we take on the path we have chosen for the administration of Hindostan leads us nearer to the establishment of representative institutions. The legislative councils of the imperial and local governments have already a native element in their composition, which, although not yet elected, is nominated with a view to its being representative in character. Certain municipal councils and local district boards are now elective bodies, and the native press begins to ask that some of the chief of these should have the right to send members to the Legislative Councils. Lastly, every native boy whom we educate in our schools will learn, without our designing to teach the doctrine, that manhood will bring him not only the duty of considering, but the right to a voice in, the management of his country's affairs.

Such is the present position of England in India. We may look back with pride to what has been accomplished. We may justify our presence in the country, and satisfy the national conscience by the consideration that we are determined to rule India, not in our own interests, but in those of her poor and swarming populations; and we may hope that, difficult as is the work yet remaining to be done, the same energy and devotion which has already accomplished so much will carry our great experiment to a successful issue.

CHAPTER XXII.

HOMEWARD BOUND—FROM BOMBAY, THROUGH EGYPT, TO ENGLAND.

January 29—*March* 8.

AT last we have found a Peninsular and Oriental steamer which bears comparison with the American Pacific mail-boats for comfort and cleanliness. The *Sumatra* is not a large vessel, but she is fairly fast, while her discipline is excellent, her table and service good, and her cabins spotless. This is because Captain Briscoe is an officer who overlooks everything on board his ship, and keeps everybody up to his duty. A card in the state-rooms of all Peninsular and Oriental steamers informs passengers that the commander makes a daily inspection of the ship, but this is really done on board the *Sumatra*, and with such good results that if ever we wander Eastward again we shall think ourselves lucky if we sail with Captain Briscoe.

February 1.—The vessel being in north latitude 14° and east longitude 53°, or a little to the north-west of the island of Socotra, we were fortunate enough to witness the phenomenon of the "Milky Sea," rarely seen except in this part of the world. The whole ocean, from the ship to the visible horizon, looked exactly as if it were covered with snow, making it easy for us to imagine that we were locked up in the arctic regions. The snowy surface evidently reflected the light of the sky, for Venus, being very bright, threw a distinguishable line of radiance across it, while the phosphorescent crests of waves were now and then seen breaking above the layer of shining matter which overlaid the water. A current is always encountered north of Socotra, which, on the day in question, set the ship fourteen miles to the northward of her course. This stream was crowded with large jelly-fish, visible, not only during the day, but also at night, when, being themselves non-luminous, they appeared as whirling black discs in the general phosphorescence of the ship's wake. The ship's officers fully believed that the Socotran current brings with it, besides jelly-fish, enormous quantities of decayed and phosphorescent matter, to whose presence they attribute the appearance of the Milky Sea.

The fact, however, that the seeming snow reflects light and is broken through by small waves disposes of this explanation, and we soon convinced ourselves that the phenomenon is really due to a thin layer of mist lying on the water, exactly resembling one of those local fogs which every one has seen, and which give to a valley, or even a slight depression in the surface of the country, the appearance of being snowed up. It occurs when the sea is several degrees colder than the atmosphere, and the latter heavily loaded with aqueous vapour. Under these circumstances a layer of air immediately in contact with the water is chilled below the dew-point, and becomes misty, while that above remains transparent, and the upper surface of such a fog, which is probably only a few inches thick, is seen by the reflected light of the sky. In the Arabian Sea there is usually a difference of only one or two degrees between the temperatures of the air and the water, but the former is always almost saturated with aqueous vapour. The first of these conditions prevailed throughout the voyage, except on the night in question, when I found from the engineer's log that while the sea was only 70°, the atmosphere was 79° Fahrenheit. I conclude therefore that the same ocean current which carried the jelly-fish brought this lower temperature with it, and by chilling the moist air in its immediate neighbourhood, the night being perfectly calm, caused a local fog, which gave rise to the curious appearance of a Milky Sea.

February 4.—We reached Aden to-day, and the ship was at once surrounded by canoes full of Somali men—black fellows, with African faces and long woolly hair, like a mop of corkscrew curls. These fellows have fine eyes, laughing faces, and beautiful teeth. They shout, "Have a dive! have a dive!" like the Malay boys at Singapore, and struggle in the water for small coins. A crew of these Africans, who seem animation itself compared with the listless Hindoo, rowed us ashore. They laughed, chatted, and shook their dyed ringlets as if life was a joke which they thoroughly enjoyed, and they rowed well into the bargain. As we neared the shore, two of them jumped overboard, and swam home by a short cut, holding their clothes at arm's length above the water, all the rest of the body being immersed.

The scenery at Aden is very remarkable. The rocks consist of many superposed volcanic overflows, which are as fresh in appearance as if poured out yesterday. The beds of lava are generally horizontal, but have weathered into the most needle-shaped hills I have ever seen, some of the sharpest peaks being carved out of perfectly level strata. Yet there is now no rainfall where every mountain profile bespeaks, in terms far more emphatic than usual, the influence of denudation by water. The volcanics are variously and brightly coloured, but quite bare of vegetation; the sea from which they spring is brilliantly green; the air is indescribably transparent, and the outlines of distant objects are startingly distinct. The native town is a collection of low, white, flat-topped houses, containing altogether some twenty thousand people—Arabs Greeks, Jews, Africans, and a dozen other races besides. Along the road, we met strings of camels; donkeys, carrying dignified-looking Arabs dressed in wide robes and large turbans, or loaded with skins of distilled water, going inland, where no drinkable water is found. Women were also seen balancing chatties on their heads; and, by all that is wonderful, here is John Chinaman again! Our captain gave us only a short leave of absence, and we returned from an excursion, which we would willingly have lengthened, just as the sun was setting behind a group of sharp rocky pinnacles, whose outlines were strikingly like the spires of a Gothic cathedral. All the west glowed with amber tints; the sea was a superb green, and the coast, lighted by the sun's level rays, was distinctly seen in its minutest details. The sloping yards and cordage of the native craft in the harbour were ruled in fine black lines on a glowing background of sea and sky, against which the hull and rigging of the distant *Sumatra* stood out with marvellous distinctness.

Next morning we entered the Red Sea, on whose African coast there are no places of importance between Bab-el-Mandeb and Suez. On the Arabian side are Mocha, Hodeda, and Lohaya, all long since beaten in the struggle for existence by our port of Aden, and Jedda, forty-six miles from Mecca, the point where all the Mahometan pilgrimages converge. The approach to Suez harbour is very beautiful. On the left are the Ataka Mountains, which rise from the Arabian desert like a misty mass of melted gems. On the right, a boundless plain of pale golden-coloured sand stretches to the horizon, while the sea is a light torquoise blue. The colouring is so delicate that nothing seems to have defined outlines; one scarcely knows whether the landscape is a reality or a dream.

Before the canal was made Suez was a miserable village of fifteen hundred inhabitants; now it is a wretched town of fourteen thousand souls. The stimulus given by the opening of the canal was transient, and both trade and population are declining. The place lies on low sandbanks, which are wide shoals at low tide and nearly surrounded with water on the flood. Upon the quay, stand the English hotel, an iron railway shed, and a few warehouses, while the streets are narrow and dirty, the houses are mud huts, scarcely relieved by a miserable lath and plaster mosque here and there. The bazaar is neither clean nor interesting, but it is full of donkey-boys and active, lively children, who shout and play with an energy to which we are now little accustomed.

The railway from Suez to Cairo traverses the desert in company with the canal as far as Ismailia, and then turns due west together with the fresh-water canal, the ancient conduit which was reopened to supply the wants of the workmen in the desert during the construction of M. de Lesseps' work. After a while the line crosses the eastern boundary of the Nile Delta, and runs thence over fertile country to Cairo. The city stands at the apex of the Delta, bounded on one side by the Arabian and on the other by the Libyan desert, which approach it so closely that they can be seen, one on either hand, from high points of view in the city. The desert portion of the railway route is dusty and monotonous. The soil, which consist of sand and pebbles, is evidently an old sea-floor; it is quite bare of vegetation and covered here and there with patches of alkaline efflorescence. The fertile track is reached at Zagazig, a town of forty thousand inhabitants, the centre of the Egyptian cotton trade, and containing many large cotton-mills, the property for the most part of Europeans.

The overflow of the Nile does not take place directly, as is commonly supposed, neither is Egypt now converted into a vast lake during the inundation, as was formerly the case; but the water is conducted into a network of canals, and distributed as required. For this purpose the whole of the cultivated land of Egypt is divided into wide basins into which the Nile is introduced by sluices, and where it is kept at a certain height until the soil is saturated and the required quantity of mud is deposited. After the flood has subsided, the water in the basins may either be discharged into the river or into other basins at a lower level, and the whole system is under the control of a special staff of engineers.

Leaving Zagazig, the country is a fertile plain furrowed by ditches from which water is raised and thrown on the fields either by means of small water-wheels driving an endless chain of earthen pots, or by the "shaduf," a balanced pole with a vessel hung from one end. Cotton is one of the chief crops, but beans and wheat are largely grown. The only trees are date palms, having a tall, rough stem, from the top of which springs a tuft of stiff, ungraceful fronds. Buffaloes and oxen are numerous, and camels graze in all the fields. Long-eared goats and sheep with parti-coloured brown and white wool are frequently passed, and the face of the country swarms with peasants at work. Blue cotton is the universal wear, and the women cover their faces from the eyes downwards with a black veil, which hangs from a brass tube occupying the centre of the forehead. The villages are collections of flat-topped, one-storied huts of hardened mud, roofed with cotton stalks, and apparently bare of all comforts within. Fertile as the country appears, it fails to impress the traveller like similiar plains in Japan; the cultivation being less careful, and the people evidently less industrious. The landscape is without beauty, and the costumes of the peasantry are ungraceful in shape and monotonous in colour.

Cairo is the largest city in Africa, and the second city in the Turkish empire. It is the residence of the Khedive, and contains about four hundred thousand people, of whom twenty thousand are Europeans. Among the latter Italians predominate largely, and after them come the Greeks, then the French, lastly Germans and English. The Oriental population consists of Egypto-Arabians, Copts, Turks, and Jews. The town is a labyrinth of narrow, tortuous streets, often ruinous and always filthy, traversed by modern boulevards, the work of some Egpytian Haussmann, which are pretentious but by no means beautiful. The city rests on the Nile, a muddy, cheerless stream, with high and ugly banks, and is dominated by the Mokattam Hills, half-way up whose flanks stand the Citadel and Alabaster Mosque of Mahomet Ali, the founder of the present Egyptian dynasty. Most of the streets are unpaved and inaccessible to carriages. Some are so narrow that two donkey-riders can hardly pass each other, while the projecting balconies of the houses nearly touch one another. These lanes are crowded with a very various if not brilliant crowd: donkeys and their riders, camels with their packs, carriages of all kinds where carriages are possible, turbaned men and veiled women, dogs, water-carriers, peddlers, money-changers, beggars, and shoe-blacks. The dresses are as various as their wearers. Ladies are seen in the |streets wrapped in wide black silk mantles, which give them the appearance of great bats. The Arab women wear black veils, but the Turkish ladies, who sometimes shop in an open carriage, cover their faces coquettishly with white gauze wraps. European coats and trousers are common among men, but the fez is universal as a head-dress. Both sexes darken their eyes and stain their nails; the women wear silver earrings, armlets, and anklets, and the poorer classes tattoo their chins and look exactly as if they wore beards.

The Bazaars are the great attraction to foreigners in Cairo. They occupy a whole quarter with narrow streets, which are lined with open shops, wherein the shopkeepers sit cross-legged, surrounded by their wares. These come from every part of the world, but consist for the most part of ornamental rubbish. Certain streets are devoted to certain trades, and the shop is also the manufactory. Shoes are made, books bound, stones cut, bracelets shaped, and smith's work hammered in little dens five feet wide and seven feet deep, where four or five men sit together at work. The tools are primitive and the work is poor. Carpenters have no benches, vices, rules, or bradawls, but use the floor, their toes, a piece of string, and a nail instead. At night, when the shops are closed, the proprietor, or one of his men, puts up his bed in the street, rolls himself in a blanket, and sleeps.

We soon tired of chaffering with the glib, extortionate shopkeepers, and took donkeys for Old Cairo. The original city is buried in rubbish-heaps, where hundreds of pariah dogs live, each in his own hole, and whence they issue to prowl all day and half the night about the city. Every dog has his own beat, upon which any other dog intrudes at his peril. These creatures have no masters; they look as much like wolves as dogs; and a couple of them usually attach themselves to a new-comer, and follow him everywhere, whining in the most abject way for food. The strong desert wind, blowing across the rubbish-heaps, raised clouds of dust, through which we could hardly see our donkeys' heads, and in this agreeable region one seeks the chief architectural lions of the city.

Between the thirteenth and fifteenth centuries, the east side of Cairo became embellished with a number of splendid mausoleums, now known as the Tombs of the Khalifs and Mamelukes. Their history is obscure, the names of the builders are wanting, and no inscriptions have been preserved, but the ruins are beautiful examples of early Arabian art. Many of the tombs are of vast, extent, having mosques attached, which were once richly endowed but their revenues have long since been confiscated by needy governments, and the tombs are now going to decay. Each of them consists, like similar buildings in India, of a cubical mass of masonry surmounted by a dome, sometimes plain, sometimes beautifully arabesqued and flanked with minarets, occasionally of great height, and always exquisitely proportioned and ornamented. When these delicate spires lift their heads by scores in a sky of the tenderest blue, and glow with the rosy tints of an Egyptian sunset, one forgets the dogs and dust of to-day in the effort to realize the splendour of Mameluke rule five hundred years ago. Cairo itself is full of mosques, among which that of Sultan Hasan, built in the fourteenth century, is the finest existing monument of Arabian architecture. It is partly ruinous, simple, but strikingly artistic in design, and there is probably nothing in Europe finer than its great gateways, pointed horse-shoe arches, and beautifully proportioned minaret, the highest in the world. The leading features of Pathan art, which blossomed into such splendid flower under the Moguls in India, characterize all the Arabian mosques of Cairo. There are the same principles of construction, the same domes and arches, flat surfaces, arabesque decoration, geometrical inlays, pierced stone screens, and carved Arabic characters as Akbar and Shah Juhan used; but the style has more affinities with Akbar's robust work than with the over-refinement of his grandson.

The University of Cairo is the most important seat of learning in Mahometan territory. It was established during the tenth century in the large Mosque of El-Azhar, and is the stronghold of Muslim fanaticism. It educates a very large number of students, who remain from three to six years within the mosque. They pay no fees, and the professors have no salaries, but pick up a small income by private teaching and *douceurs* from the wealthier students. We found the spacious building crowded with men and boys squatting cross-legged on the floor. Each teacher sits on a mat, surrounded by his class, either listening to his explanations or reading aloud. The noise was enough to drown the voice of a Stentor, but no intellectual efforts are interfered with by clamour in the University of Cairo. Study consists in learning by heart, and the subjects taught are religion, jurisprudence, logic, and poetry. There is no independent thought among either teachers or taught, and no new knowledge is acquired or imparted. The professors know nothing of natural philosophy ; and mathematical science, once well understood by the Arabs, is dead. It is a melancholy sight to watch the great crowd of students swinging their bodies rhythmically backwards and forwards as a mechanical aid to getting passages of the Koran by heart.

Islamism has many sects, and of these are the various orders of dervishes. Some of these fanatics, the Rifaiyeh, put nails in their eyes, or chew live charcoal and broken glass ; others, called Saadiyeh, lie on the ground on the Prophet's birthday, and let their sheik ride over them. The Kadiriyeh spend all their time fishing ; while the Mevlewis, or well-known dancing dervishes, hold a "zikr," or service, every Friday, which any one may witness. In their mosque is a ring about twenty feet in diameter, enclosed by a railing, where we found twenty men, dressed in long cloth gowns and tall conical hats, walking round and bowing to their sheik preparatory to dancing. Presently they stopped, the sheik mumbled a prayer, and when that was finished the Mevlewis stripped for action, appearing in white vests and long white petticoats weighted at bottom with lead. Then they spun round, with outstretched arms and closed eyes, at a speed of forty revolutions per minute, their skirts flying out as if they were going to "make cheeses." Meanwhile the sheik walked slowly among the dancers, eyeing each performer critically. After a few minutes they stopped, took another walk round, and then another spin. The zikr lasted an hour, but the men were in good training, and didn't turn a hair.

We crossed the Nile by a fine iron swing-bridge, the work of European engineers, in order to visit the Khedive's palace of Gezireh. The bridge was open upon our arrival, and we waited for perhaps an hour while Nile boats were passing through. Meanwhile an immense and motley crowd, comprising hundreds of camels loaded with fodder, donkeys, carriages, and foot-passengers, assembled on either bank, waiting for the bridge to close, and displaying a scene of as much variety as a native Indian town. Gezireh was a disappointment; the interior of the palace cannot be seen because of the harem, and the exterior, like the palaces of Lucknow, is a "stucco nightmare." But it is only one of many vice-regal follies. The late Khedive was a great man for European "improvements," and all the world knows how lavishly he spent money which he borrowed from Europe on the introduction of Western industries into Egypt. Being curious to see whether the country had really benefited by these manufactories, we visited the vice-regal paper-mill and printing-office, and should have inspected the Khedive's great sugar-mills if they were not shut up. The paper-mill is a large concern, expensively fitted, with not very modern machinery, and costing, as we were told, about £120,000. When at work, it turned out two tons of paper and burned twelve tons of coal a day. For such a production a mill ought not to cost more than £30,000, and every ton of coal ought to produce half a ton of paper! Of course the place is idle, and the once fine shops, wherein everything is now going to ruin, are a most depressing sight. The printing-office was running, but exhibited a scene of incompetent management and slovenly work, which was even more miserable to see than the paper-mill. On the

Nile, near the latter establishment, we saw a fleet of steamers, of which the Khedive had more than a hundred, lying useless and decaying. On our way to the Schoubra Palace, another "stucco nightmare," we saw the skeleton of an old steam-plough, half buried in the soil, one of many supplied from England, and every set worth £1000, all of which are now wrecks. In the Schoubra Palace itself were iron pleasure-boats and a number of other expensive toys, unused and rotting; and in the midst of Cairo is an opera-house, nearly as fine as that of Covent Garden, built and run with vice-regal funds. I do not know how much it cost, but we were credibly informed that the place paid a loss of £200 a night when it was open. Such was "improvement" in Egypt.

Egypt, geographically speaking, and apart from the extensive, but half-savage and wholly profitless provinces of the south, consists of a mere strip of land bordering the Nile and of its Delta. The country has an area two-thirds as great as that of Russia, but is really no larger than Belgium, if its tax-paying part only is taken into consideration. Its population is less by three-fifths now than it was in the days of Herodotus, and its people are miserably poor. The great bulk of them are cultivators, but none are owners of the soil. The land, with few exceptions, belongs either to the Government, or to the Khedive personally, the fellahs being life tenants, but with saleable rights of tenure. The land-tax is fixed at twenty per cent. of the produce, but the mudir, or local governor, can squeeze the farmer pretty much as much as he likes. The farm implements are very primitive, the plough being nothing more than a big hoe, while the dwellings are miserable, windowless huts of mud, thatched with cotton stalks, and furnished only with skeep-skins, baskets, a kettle, and some pots and pans. The food of the people is maize and beans; only the "rich" cultivators eat wheaten bread. They grow wheat, barley, beans, maize, sugar-cane, cotton and indigo; but wheat forms fifty per cent. of the whole cropping. The fellahs are industrious and active by nature, but become apathetic and despairing as they grow older, from the hopelessness of their lot and the oppression of the tax-gatherer. In spite of the efforts which the Government has made during recent years to rule in the interests of the peasantry, Egypt is a backward country. Her spendthrift rulers have tried to Europeanize the state by the importation of foreign ideas at ruinous prices. Meanwhile, her youth continues to be educated on the idea-less system I have already described. Her traders are foreign adventurers, and her people are an oppressed and despairing race. Of national growth there is no visible sign. The former vigour of Mahometan rule is dead, and the lineal descendants of a nation whose prehistoric eminence is the wonder of the modern world are the mere slaves of a power which has lost the art of governing. Radical, indeed, must be the change in Egyptian nationality before any *renaissance* of its ancient glory is possible for this race.

Such was the feeling with which we turned from modern Egypt to the works of ancient Egypt, about which the traveller cannot be wholly silent, although it is impossible for him to say anything new. It was a glorious morning when we left Cairo to visit the Pyramids of Ghizeh, the oldest and most important of the kingly tombs which line the edge of the Libyan desert for twenty-five miles in the neighbourhood of Cairo. The group consists of the Great or Cheops' Pyramid, the Second or Cephren's Pyramid, the Third or Menkera's Pyramid, and a number of smaller structures. A party of Bedouins received us at the base of the Great Pyramid, and the sheik told off two men to assist each of us in the ascent. All the pyramids were once smoothly faced with stone, but this has long since been carried away and used for building purposes, so that no vestige of the original surface remains except on the apex of Cephren's pile. The courses of masonry which have thus been exposed form rough steps, each of which is about three and a half feet high, and the ascent, even with the aid of the Arabs, is extremely fatiguing. These glib rascals are very amusing. They speak half a dozen words in half a dozen languages, and, as they pull you upstairs, chant rhythmically—

"Thāt's ĭt !
Hārd wŏrk !
Twō frăncs !
Būckshĕesh !
Ēvry dăy !"

To my German companion they chorussed in German, and on both of us they lavished any amount of blarney in the hope of getting a bucksheesh in addition to the sheik's fee. In twenty minutes we reached the top, whence the view is peculiar, but not beautiful. Facing northwards, the Nile lies on the right, eight miles away, belted on both sides by a strip of fertile land, which is flanked on the east by the Mokattam Hills, flat-topped, bare, and yellowish white in colour. On the left, stretch the sands of the desert, glaring in the sun, their smooth surface broken here and there by low cliffy exposures of the underlying rocks. Halfway up the Mokattam range stands the citadel, behind which rise the slender minarets of Mahomet Ali's Mosque, and beneath this lies the city, tinted, like the hills and desert, with pale gold or violet-rose by the morning or evening sunbeams. The descent nearly finished our aching legs, but the Bedouins, wild for bucksheesh, dragged us, fagged and perspiring, through the narrow interior passages of the pyramid, which are hot, steep, and slippery. Here we saw the "Great Hall," the "Queen's" and "King's Chambers," and admired their massive and beautifully finished masonry by the light of magnesium wire. This was the hardest day's work we had done during the whole trip. The tramp to the top of Pike's Peak, which is nearly as high as Mont Blanc, is a trifle compared with "such a getting upstairs" as this.

The Egyptian pyramids vary immensely in dimensions, though they are all finished structures, and Lepsius has suggested, in explanation of this curious fact, that each king began to build his own tomb when he ascended the throne, commencing it on such a scale that, if his reign proved short, it might be quickly completed by his successor, and enlarging it by outer coatings as time went on. Cheops' Pyramid, to which Cephren's is little inferior in mass, is large enough to bury St. Peter's, or even Strasbourg Cathedral, while the spires of the Cologne dome itself, the highest building in Europe, would only peep thirty feet above the top of this pyramid, which could swallow up all the rest of the building.

Near the Ghizeh group, stand the Sphinx, several small pyramids and tombs, and a temple, all more or less completely buried in sand. The figure of the Sphinx is too well known for description. It is hewn out of the limestone rock, and only the head is now visible, but the whole figure was once excavated to its base, which is fifty feet below the present level of the desert. The tombs are "mastabas," or rock-cut chambers, containing sarcophagi of granite, and illustrating a method of burial which appears to have taken the place of pyramid-building after the Primæval Monarchy, or Old Empire, had given way to the rule of the Shepherd-Kings. The temple is of unknown antiquity, but a statue of Cephren, the builder of the Second Pyramid, was found within it, and it may therefore well be that this is a relic, and, if so, the only one, surviving from the Old Empire, of which Cephren was one of the early kings. The Sphinx is even older than the First Pyramid, an inscription of Cheops' having been found on it, stating that he, in making excavations, found the "Temple of Isis in the vicinity of the Temple of the Sphinx;" so that, five or six thousand years ago, the builders of the pyramids themselves were unearthing the buried works of a remote and unknown past.

All that we know about Egyptian chronology is based on the interpretation of those hieroglyphics, or figure-writings, which were a puzzle to the world until the discovery of the "Rosetta Stone," now in the British Museum. About the end of the last century, a French officer discovered this slab, which bears a trilingual inscription, written in hieroglyphics, in demotic, or con ventionalized hieroglyphic characters, and in Greek. This discovery resulted in the first decipherment of a few hieroglyphics by Dr. Young in 1814, and their complete elucidation by Champollion in 1821. Previously to this, Egyptologists were acquainted with the lists of Manetho, an Egyptian priest who was employed by Ptolemy II. (B.C. 284) to translate the ancient historical works preserved in the Egyptian temples. This priest wrote a history, which was lost, and prepared a list of Egyptian kings and dynasties, which has been transmitted to us by Josephus, the Jewish historian. Manetho's dates are so astoundingly ancient that, while they stood alone, no one believed in them, but hieroglyphics were found, confirming them so completely, that they are now fully accepted. We may therefore take it as proved that Menes, the first recorded King of Egypt, really lived and reigned five thousand years before Christ. The Primæval Monarchy, of which Menes was the father, lasted for nearly three thousand years, and was succeeded by the rule of the Hyksos, or Shepherd-Kings, Semitic invaders who conquered the armies of the Pharaohs about two thousand two hundred years before Christ, and gave way, five hundred years later, before the "Deliverers," native leaders who established the "New Empire" in B.C. 1700. The New Empire, after lasting nearly twelve hundred years, succumbed to Persian domination, to be succeeded by the period of the Ptolemies, whom Alexander the Great, having defeated Darius and been hailed as the deliverer of Egypt, established on the throne in B.C. 320. The Ptolemies' rule lasted nearly three hundred years, after which Rome administered Egypt for nearly five hundred years. When the Roman power was parted into the empires of the East and the West, the Byzantines became the rulers of Egypt, to be succeeded by its present masters the Mahometans, who conquered the country in A.D. 638, and have remained its masters ever since.

If we want to know what men thought, and how human life was conducted in the remote periods of the Old and New Empires of Egypt, we must go to the museums of Europe, and especially to the Boulak Museum of Cairo. It is not for a traveller now to re-tell how the history of Egypt and Egyptian arts is written on the sculptured stones which have been preserved through such immense periods of time by the dry sands and rainless climate of the desert. But, since the fact is better illustrated at Boulak than anywhere else, it may be noted as remarkable that the oldest Egyptian sculptures exhibit far greater artistic power than those of a later date. There is a wooden figure in this collection called "Sheik-el-Beled" (The Village Chief), which, although dating from the early part of the Old Empire, and therefore presumably some six thousand years old, possesses the same force, though not the same beauty, as Greek work. A similar quality characterizes in a more or less marked degree, all the earliest work; and it is only when we approach later times that Egyptian sculpture becomes conventional. It has been questioned whether the ascertained chronology of Egypt does not probably carry us back to the time when man first arose from a savage condition, but the sculptor who shaped the Sheik-el-Beled was evidently the child of an immensely long antecedent period of highly organized human life, of which, however, no records remain.

That the ancient Egyptians were great polytheists, we learn from the immense number and variety of gods at Boulak. It appears, however that these idols were for the vulgar. The enlightened few held that matter, though perpetually undergoing modification, was, at bottom, eternal, incapable of increase or decrease, but endowed with intelligence and creative power. The priest of Old Egypt was something like a modern materialist in this view, but he clothed his abstract ideas in allegorical forms for the sake of the masses, and represented the various forces and phenomena of nature by a host of divinities. Both priest and people, however, had a singularly firm belief in the immortality of the soul, and there can be no doubt that the extraordinary efforts which the Egyptians made to secure the body from decay were undertaken in order that it might again become informed by the soul when earthly things had passed away. The pyramids with their inaccessible chambers, the rock-cut tombs, the great sarcophagi and the secure coffins within them, lastly, the mummified body itself—all bear witness to the strength of the desire which the ancient Egyptians cherished to keep the person of a man ready for its re-possession by the spirit, in some new and unknown state of existence. "A house is but for a day, a tomb is for ever;" this was the national sentiment, and, without it, the records of ancient Egypt would have perished as those of many unknown early peoples have certainly done.

The name of Marriette Bey is inseparable from Egyptian exploration. Boulak Museum was his creation, and he gave a life of devotion to his researches. Among the most fruitful of these were his excavations at Sakkara, where, for many years, this distinguished man lived in full desert, and where his primitive home is still at the disposal of visitors to the Pyramid and Necropolis of Sakkara. It was a lovely morning when we started with our donkeys by train for Bedrashen, a village on the left bank of the Nile, about twelve miles south of Cairo. Thence we rode in the first place to the ruins of Memphis, the earliest Egyptian capital, founded by Menes, and extended by every succeeding Pharaoh, until Thebes became the metropolis of the New Empire. The city was not neglected after the transfer, but was a flourishing place when the port of Alexandria arose under the great Macedonian conqueror. It retained some importance during the Roman period, but fell into ruin after the destruction of its temples by Theodosius. Even thus it excited the admiration of visitors in the twelfth century; but, after that date, the ruins rapidly dwindled, as stone after stone was carried across the Nile to build Mahometan tombs and mosques in Cairo. At the present moment nothing but a few fragments of brick and granite remain of a city whose streets were many miles long as late as the twelfth century.

West of this ancient capital was the Necropolis, or burial-ground, which covers four square miles, and contains sepulchral monuments of every kind and age, now covered by sand. Here, the kings and nobles of Egypt were interred for many centuries, and here Marriette unearthed a vast number of interesting relics, together with those works of refined art, executed during the days of the Old Empire, to which I have already referred. All the tombs which he opened, except two, have been closed again, in order to preserve them from the air and relic-hunters. These are the Apis Tombs and the Tomb of Ti, the first a burial-place of the sacred Apis bulls, and the last a sepulchre of a private Egyptian gentleman. The chief god in the Egyptian pantheon was "Ptah," the Greek Hephaistos and the Roman Vulcan, whose symbol was the bull. This animal lived in the temple, and, when he died, his obsequies were celebrated with the utmost magnificence. The body was mummified and deposited in a great granite sarcophagus, a whole series of which enormous coffins are found in the Apis Tombs, lodged in vaulted chambers, which are excavated in the solid rock, and connected together by corridors.

The Tomb of Ti is four thousand five hundred years old. Every wealthy Egyptian planned his own tomb during his lifetime, beginning by sinking a well, where the body of the deceased was finally placed. Around the well were excavated one or more chambers, decorated with inscriptions, giving the dead man's titles, and representing his occupations and possessions by carvings in bas-relief. The walls of Ti's Tomb are completely covered with such sculptures. The designs represent domestic scenes, such as feeding ducks and cranes, preparing meats for cooking, milking cows, carpentering, fishing, reaping, gleaning, etc. These are formal in conception, but they show that the artist knew perfectly how to catch expression and display muscular action.

After lunching on the terrace of Marriette's house, not without respectful thoughts of the man who deemed it no hardship to live alone in the desert during many years for the sake of an idea, we mounted our donkeys, and, riding back through Memphis, crossed the Nile by boat, and then rode about three miles across the desert to Heluan, whence we took the train by another line for

Cairo. A magnificent view of the various groups of pyramids is obtained from this bank of the stream, together with distant glimpses of Cairo's domes and minarets. These, as the sun set, became violet-rose in colour, while the delicate limestones of the Mokattam range were painted in still more refined amethystine tints, and, from the feet of the pyramids, the desert sands stretched away to the horizon a sheet of pale gold.

The day after this, my last trip in the East, I joined the Peninsular and Oriental steamship *Assam* at Suez homeward-bound; and almost immediately afterwards entered the canal. The Isthmus of Suez is about seventy miles wide at its narrowest part. Halfway across, it rises into a bank, called "El Gisr" (The Threshold), about fifty feet above the sea, whence the ground slopes rapidly on either side, finally becoming a nearly level plain about two and a half feet above the Mediterranean and Red Seas respectively. North of the Threshold is Lake Balah, and south of it Lake Timsah and the Bitter Lakes, through both of which the canal passes. The isthmus was once a strait which has silted up, but so long ago that the animals inhabiting the two neighbouring seas are now entirely different one from the other. The Egyptians connected the Nile and the Red Sea as early as the fourteenth century before Christ, but this canal fell into ruin, and Pharaoh Necho commenced another in the seventh century. He left it unfinished at the suggestion of an oracle, and Darius completed it during the Persian domination. The Ptolemies extended the work, and created a direct communication between the Red and Mediterranean Seas in the second and third centuries, but this canal had fallen into ruin before the Roman period, and the trade route between the Red Sea and Rome was overland from Koser, a port on the African shore, to the Nile and thence by Alexandria to the Mediterranean. The Ptolemaic canal was restored by the Mahometan conquerors in the seventh century of our era, but was filled up again later for strategical reasons. In the beginning of this century Napoleon revived the project of canalization, but his engineer, Lépere, found a difference of thirty-three feet between the two seas, an error which continued to have an evil influence upon all succeeding schemes, until M. de Lesseps brought forward his plans, which were adopted by the Viceroy in 1854. The Suez Canal was begun in 1858, and carried on under great difficulties, from want of fresh water, until 1863, when the sweet-water canal, which still supplies the desert towns, Ismailia and Suez, was completed and opened. The canal itself was finished in 1869, and declared open late in that year, amidst festivities which are said to have cost the Khedive—or more properly speaking, the Egyptian bondholders—four millions of pounds sterling. The total cost of the great work was nearly thirteen millions. Two thousand ships per annum pass through the canal, and its net receipts now represent a revenue of more than five per cent. on the capital. The passage is uninteresting. From Suez to the Bitter Lakes the banks are high, and the view limited. The Bitter Lakes are like a small inland sea, with water of a deep bluish green. For the last forty-five kilometres of its length the canal skirts Lake Menzaleh, a vast swampy and brackish extension of the Nile mouths. This is a desolate region of sand banks and shallows, the resort of immense flocks of pelicans, flamingoes, and wildfowl. Here the mirage plays strange tricks, making a flock of pelicans look like sheep, camels, or indeed anything you like to fancy them. The water at Port Said is very muddy, and some difficulty is experienced in keeping the harbour free from silt. North-west winds prevail in the Mediterranean during two-thirds of the year, producing a set which carries the Nile mud into the mouth of the canal, and necessitating constant dredging in order to keep the port free.

Four days after leaving Suez we were in full Mediterranean, a blackish blue sea below us, and overhead a European sky of scattered clouds and diffused light, altogether different in its quality from that of the tropics. Malta, as we passed the island, was shining under a sun worthy of Northern India; but the Rock gave us a rough welcome, and we steamed through the Straits of Gibraltar into "dirty weather" in the Bay. Greyer and greyer grew the skies and chillier the air as we neared Old England until, failing to pick up the pilot during daylight on the evening of our arrival off the Needles light, we lay to all night in a heavy south-wester, at the entrance of the Solent, and I landed next day, at Southampton, half glad to be once more at home, half sorry that the Engineer's Holiday was over.

THE END.

LONDON: PRINTED BY WILLIAM CLOWES AND SONS, LIMITED, STAMFORD STREET AND CHARING CROSS.

www.ingramcontent.com/pod-product-compliance
Lightning Source LLC
Chambersburg PA
CBHW051857300426
44117CB00006B/427